CLASSIC TEENPLOTS

Recent Titles in the
Children's and Young Adult Literature Reference Series
Catherine Barr, Series Editor

Books Kids Will Sit Still For 3
Judy Freeman

Best Books for Children: Preschool Through Grade 6
Catherine Barr and John T. Gillespie

A to Zoo: Subject Access to Children's Picture Books
Carolyn W. Lima and John A. Lima

The Children's and Young Adult Literature Handbook:
A Research and Reference Guide
John T. Gillespie

Fantasy Literature for Children and Young Adults:
A Comprehensive Guide, Fifth Edition
Ruth Nadelman Lynn

The Newbery/Printz Companion: Booktalk and Related Materials
for Award Winners and Honor Books, Third Edition
John T. Gillespie and Corinne J. Naden

CLASSIC TEENPLOTS

A Booktalk Guide to Use with Readers Ages 12–18

JOHN T. GILLESPIE and CORINNE J. NADEN

Children's and Young Adult Literature Reference Series
Catherine Barr, Series Editor

Westport, Connecticut • London

Library of Congress Cataloging-in-Publication Data

Gillespie, John Thomas, 1928-
  Classic teenplots : a booktalk guide to use with readers ages 12–18 / by John T. Gillespie and Corinne J. Naden.
      p. cm. — (Children's and young adult literature reference)
  Includes bibliographical references and indexes.
  ISBN 1-59158-312-8 (alk. paper)
    1. Young adult literature—Stories, plots, etc. 2. Teenagers—Books and reading—United States. 3. Book talks. I. Naden, Corinne J. II. Title. III. Series: Children's and young adult literature reference series.
Z1037.A1G48 2006
011.62'5–dc22   2006017624

British Library Cataloguing in Publication Data is available.

Copyright © 2006 by Libraries Unlimited, Inc.

All rights reserved. No portion of this book may be reproduced, by any process or technique, without the express written consent of the publisher.

Library of Congress Catalog Card Number: 2006017624
ISBN: 1-59158-312-8

Libraries Unlimited, 88 Post Road West, Westport, CT 06881
A Member of the Greenwood Publishing Group, Inc.
www.lu.com

Printed in the United States of America

The paper used in this book complies with the Permanent Paper Standard issued by the National Information Standards Organization (Z39.48–1984).

10 9 8 7 6 5 4 3 2 1

Contents

Preface	ix
A Brief Guide to Booktalking	xiii
1. Teenage Life and Concerns	1
Block, Francesca Lia. *Weetzie Bat*	1
Blume, Judy. *Tiger Eyes*	4
Cleaver, Vera, and Bill Cleaver. *Where the Lilies Bloom*	8
Conrad, Pam. *My Daniel*	11
Cormier, Robert. *The Chocolate War*	15
Deaver, Julie Reece. *Say Goodnight, Gracie*	19
Dorris, Michael. *A Yellow Raft in Blue Water*	22
Fitzhugh, Louise. *Harriet the Spy*	26
Fox, Paula. *The Moonlight Man*	29
Guest, Judith. *Ordinary People*	33
Hinton, S. E. *The Outsiders*	36
Mahy, Margaret. *Memory*	39
Mazer, Norma Fox. *Silver*	43
Peck, Robert Newton. *A Day No Pigs Would Die*	46
Rodgers, Mary. *Freaky Friday*	49
Rylant, Cynthia. *A Fine White Dust*	52
Swarthout, Glendon. *Bless the Beasts and Children*	56
Townsend, Sue. *The Adrian Mole Diaries*	59
Wersba, Barbara. *Just Be Gorgeous*	62
Zindel, Paul. *The Pigman*	65
2. Social Concerns and Problems	71
Baldwin, James. *If Beale Street Could Talk*	71
Barrett, William E. *The Lilies of the Field*	74
Bridgers, Sue Ellen. *Notes for Another Life*	77
Carter, Alden R. *Up Country*	81
Childress, Alice. *A Hero Ain't Nothin' but a Sandwich*	84
Cole, Brock. *The Goats*	87
Garden, Nancy. *Annie on My Mind*	91
Kerr, M. E. *Gentlehands*	94
Koertge, Ron. *The Arizona Kid*	98
L'Engle, Madeleine. *A Ring of Endless Light*	101

Lowry, Lois. *Rabble Starkey*		105
Naylor, Phyllis Reynolds. *The Keeper*		109
Neufeld, John. *Lisa, Bright and Dark*		113
Peck, Richard. *Remembering the Good Times*		116
Sebestyen, Ouida. *Far from Home*		120
Taylor, Theodore. *The Cay*		123
Walker, Alice. *The Color Purple*		127

3. Science Fiction and Fantasy — 131
    - Alexander, Lloyd. *Westmark* — 131
    - Asimov, Isaac. *Foundation* — 135
    - Brin, David. *The Postman* — 138
    - Brooks, Terry. *Magic Kingdom for Sale—Sold!* — 141
    - Christopher, John. *When the Tripods Came* — 143
    - Clarke, Arthur C. *Rendezvous with Rama* — 147
    - Dickinson, Peter. *Eva* — 150
    - Garner, Alan. *The Owl Service* — 153
    - Hamilton, Virginia. *Sweet Whispers, Brother Rush* — 156
    - Heinlein, Robert A. *Stranger in a Strange Land* — 159
    - Jones, Diana Wynne. *Castle in the Air* — 162
    - McCaffrey, Anne. *Dragonsong* — 165
    - O'Brien, Robert C. *Z for Zachariah* — 168
    - Pascal, Francine. *Hangin' Out with Cici* — 171
    - Sleator, William. *House of Stairs* — 173
    - Tolkien, J. R. R. *The Hobbit* — 176
    - Yolen, Jane. *Dragon's Blood* — 179

4. Historical Fiction and Other Lands — 183
    - Aiken, Joan. *Midnight Is a Place* — 183
    - Avi. *The True Confessions of Charlotte Doyle* — 186
    - Collier, James Lincoln and Christopher Collier. *My Brother Sam Is Dead* — 189
    - Fox, Paula. *One-Eyed Cat* — 192
    - Greene, Bette. *The Summer of My German Soldier* — 194
    - Levitin, Sonia. *The Return* — 197
    - Morrison, Toni. *Beloved* — 200
    - Myers, Walter Dean. *Fallen Angels* — 204
    - Paterson, Katherine. *Lyddie* — 207
    - Portis, Charles. *True Grit* — 210
    - Pullman, Philip. *The Ruby in the Smoke* — 213
    - Speare, Elizabeth. *Calico Captive* — 218
    - Spiegelman, Art. *Maus: A Survivor's Tale—My Father Bleeds History* — 221
    - Taylor, Mildred D. *Let the Circle Be Unbroken* — 223
    - Westall, Robert. *The Machine Gunners* — 227

5.	Adventure and Mystery Stories	231
	Alexander, Lloyd. *The El Dorado Adventure*	231
	Avi. *Wolf Rider*	233
	Bennett, Jay. *The Haunted One*	236
	Clark, Mary Higgins. *Weep No More My Lady*	238
	Cormier, Robert. *After the First Death*	241
	Du Maurier, Daphne. *Rebecca*	245
	Duncan, Lois. *The Twisted Window*	248
	Forsyth, Frederick. *The Day of the Jackal*	253
	Francis, Dick. *Bolt*	256
	Konigsburg, E. L. *Father's Arcane Daughter*	258
	Nixon, Joan Lowery. *The Séance*	261
	Paulsen, Gary. *Hatchet*	264
	Thompson, Julian. *The Grounding of Group 6*	267
	Voigt, Cynthia. *Homecoming*	270
	White, Robb. *Deathwatch*	273
6.	Animal Stories	277
	Bagnold, Enid. *National Velvet*	277
	Burnford, Sheila. *The Incredible Journey*	280
	Eckert, Allan W. *Incident at Hawk's Hill*	282
	North, Sterling. *Rascal*	284
	Rawls, Wilson. *Where the Red Fern Grows*	287
7.	Sport Stories	291
	Brooks, Bruce. *The Moves Make the Man*	291
	Crutcher, Chris. *Stotan!*	294
	Lipsyte, Robert. *The Contender*	297
	Voigt, Cynthia. *The Runner*	299
	Wells, Rosemary. *When No One Was Looking*	302
8.	Important Nonfiction	307
	Bell, Ruth. *Changing Bodies, Changing Lives*	307
	Dahl, Roald. *Going Solo*	309
	Herriot, James. *The Lord God Made Them All*	312
	Myers, Walter Dean. *Now Is Your Time!*	
	The African-American Struggle for Freedom	314
	Pelzer, Dave. *A Child Called "It"*	316

Appendix:	
Selected Web Sites on Children's Literature and Authors	319
Author Index	325
Title Index	333
Subject Index	341

Preface

It seems incredible that about forty years have passed since I began writing with Diana Spirt (then Diana Lembo) a booktalk manual called *Juniorplots*, which was published by R. R. Bowker in 1967. Although there had been a few other books published as aids to booktalkers, this one was unique in the completeness of the plot summaries, the indications of themes and specific passages for booktalking, and the lists of additional recommended titles that shared these themes. Over the years a series of sequels were published: *More Juniorplots* (Bowker, 1977), *Juniorplots 3* (Bowker, 1987), *Juniorplots 4* (Bowker, 1993), and *Seniorplots* (Bowker, 1989). These books are now out of print, but many of the titles discussed in them are still available and still popular with young readers. The purpose of this book is to present, in a revised, updated, and expanded form, the titles from these volumes that still represent the quality and diversity available in young adult literature. In addition to the criteria involving quality, there was a desire to cover a variety of interests and reading levels from, roughly, grades seven through twelve. Where gaps were noted, new titles such as *Maus* and *A Child Called "It"* were added. Newbery Medal and Printz Award winners were omitted because they are treated similarly in *The Newbery/Printz Companion* (Libraries Unlimited, 2006).

Our aim is to supply material that will facilitate the delivery of booktalks, whether formal or informal, by librarians, teachers, and others involved in young adult literature. There are many ways to introduce books to young people (bibliographies, displays, lists of recommended books, for example), but perhaps the most potent is actually talking about the books one wishes to recommend to either individual patrons or groups. "A Brief Guide to Booktalking" has been included to help the novice booktalker.

The 100 books in *Classic Teenplots* have been organized into eight different sections according to subject matter or genre. They are:

Teenage Life and Concerns
Social Concerns and Problems
Science Fiction and Fantasy

Historical Fiction and Other Lands
Adventure and Mystery Stories
Animal Stories
Sport Stories
Important Nonfiction

After bibliographic information and an indication of general grade level suitability, the detailed material on each of the books is divided into seven sections:

Introduction. The author is introduced usually with some basic biographical material, an indication of other works of interest, and background material on the book being highlighted.

Principal Characters. The important characters in the book are listed with brief material to identify each of them.

Plot Summary. The entire plot is retold, including important incidents and characters. In each case, an attempt was made to retain the mood and point of view of the author.

Themes and Subjects. A list is given of both primary and secondary themes and subjects found in the book to facilitate use of the book in various situations.

Booktalk Material. Incidents suitable for retelling or reading aloud are indicated and the pagination is given for each.

Additional Selections. Four books that explore similar or related themes or subjects at the same reading level as the main title are listed with bibliographic material and brief annotations.

About the Author and Book. Sources of information about the author in standard biographical references are listed. Although some Web sites are given, readers are directed to the special appendix, "Selected Web Sites on Children's Literature and Authors."

Following the body of the work, there is an appendix on important Web sites on children's literature and authors and three indexes. Author and title indexes to all of the books mentioned in the text are followed by a subject index to key topics covered in each of the main titles.

The detailed treatment of the main titles is not intended as a substitute for reading the books. Instead, it is to be used by teachers and librarians to refresh their memories about books already read and to suggest new uses for these titles.

This volume is not meant to be a work of literary criticism or a listing of the best books for young adults. It is a representative selection of books that have value in a variety of situations.

The authors would particularly like to thank two people who have been of great help in the preparation of this volume. The first is Barbara Ittner of Libraries Unlimited for her continued support and the second is our indefatigable and wonderful editor, Catherine Barr. It is hoped that this volume, a companion to *Teenplots* (Libraries Unlimited, 2003), will be of help in spreading the word about the joys of reading.

John T. Gillespie
Corinne J. Naden

A Brief Guide to Booktalking

There is basically just one purpose behind booktalking—to stimulate reading and a love of literature through delivering tantalizing, seductive introductions to books. There are, however, often many different secondary purposes; for example, to introduce specific authors, titles, or themes of books to develop a specific aspect of literary appreciation; to further a particular school assignment; to present yourself to students; or to encourage visits to and use of the library.

Booktalks generally fall into two main categories: informal and formal. The informal booktalk consists of the spontaneous introduction to books that goes on every day in the library with single or small groups of students, often in reply to such questions as "Could you suggest some good books for me to read?" The formal booktalk is explored in this brief introduction.

Before preparing a specific booktalk, three types of knowledge are helpful. The first is to know your audience as well as possible. By this is meant such factors as age and grade levels, the range of abilities and interests, and levels of maturation and sophistication. Take a few moments to inquire about the readers' likes and dislikes. The second is a knowledge of books. This comes in time through reading about books, in book reviewing journals and other secondary sources, but more importantly from reading the books themselves. It is wise to begin a card file with brief notes on each book read. Although these need not be as detailed as the coverage of each title in *Teenplots*, certain topics should be covered. Basically these are: a brief plot summary; a list of a few key passages, particularly at the beginning of the book, that would be suitable for retelling or rereading to an audience; a note on the major subjects or themes covered; and related book titles that come to mind. As this file grows, it can be used to refresh one's memory of books and thus save rereading time and also serve as a source to create new booktalks by "mixing and matching" titles to form a variety of interesting new combinations of titles and themes.

The third is a knowledge of and familiarity with the many aids, such as *Teenplots*, available to help in preparing and delivering a booktalk.

Before choosing the books to be presented, a preliminary framework for the booktalk should be established. First, the physical conditions should be studied (place, time, purpose, number of attendees). Second, the length of the talk should be determined. Most booktalk sessions last fifteen to twenty-five minutes, depending on such factors as the number of books to be introduced and the attention span of the audience. An average length is about twenty minutes. In a classroom period of forty to forty-five minutes, this allows time for housekeeping chores (for example, announcements, attendance taking, the booktalk itself, browsing through the books presented and additional titles, checking out books, and so on).

Deciding on the number of titles to be presented comes next. Some booktalkers like to give short one- or two-minute "quickies," whereas others feel more comfortable spending longer periods, perhaps five minutes, on each title, supplying more details of plot or character and perhaps retelling or reading a key self-contained incident. Still others mix both techniques. The conditions of the booktalk and the preference of the booktalker in the end determine the style used. Also, if a large number of books are to be introduced, a bibliography can be prepared and distributed to students to prevent confusion and give them reading guidance for future visits to the library. This bibliography should contain names of authors, titles, and a brief, "catchy" annotation for each.

In preparing the talk, a connecting link or theme should be decided on. This could be as general as "Books I think you would enjoy reading" or "Some titles old and new that are favorites of students your age" to something more specific, such as American Civil War novels or family crises as portrayed in fiction. The more specific topics are often suggested by a classroom teacher and are assignment oriented. Regardless of the nature of the theme or subject, it supplies a structure and connecting link to produce a oneness and unity to the booktalk. It is used to introduce the talk, to act occasionally as a bridge from one book to the next, and to serve as a conclusion to round out the presentation.

Next, choose the books themselves. Although this seems an obvious point, each book should have been read completely. The ultimate outcome or denouement in a book will often determine the material to be presented in introducing the book. Lacking this knowledge, the booktalker might misrepresent the contents or give an inaccurate interpretation. One should believe in the value of each title to be presented—that the book is worthy of being introduced and that it will supply enjoyment and value to the intended audience. The booktalker does not necessarily have to dote on each title, but should choose good books that will enlighten and entertain the audience regardless of the personal preferences of the presenter. Be sure the selection represents the interests and reading levels of the group—some difficult, some average, some easy; some old titles, some new; some fiction, some nonfiction; and so on.

Having chosen the theme and the books to be introduced, the method and content of each book introduction should be determined. There are several ways of introducing books. The most frequently used is a brief description of the plot to a certain climactic moment. Words of caution: Do *not give* away too much of the plot, stick to essential details (for example, avoid introducing subplots or subsidiary characters), and try not to overwork this technique or students will find the cliff-hanger endings ultimately frustrating. The second method is by retelling or reading a specific self-contained incident, or incidents, that give the flavor of the book. This is sometimes the most satisfying for the audience because a "complete" story has been told and yet, one hopes, a desire for more has also been implanted. One must be very cautious about reading from the book and use that technique sparingly, only when the author's style cannot be produced otherwise. Some booktalkers eschew entirely reading from the book and instead memorize the passages because reading from the book interrupts the immediate eye contact with the audience and can lessen or destroy the rapport one has established. Therefore, passages to be read must be chosen very carefully and should be short and fulfill a specific purpose when simple retelling will not suffice. A third method is to introduce a specific interesting character fully and place him or her within the context of the book. This is a suitable technique for booktalking such works as *The Adrian Mole Diaries* or *Lisa, Bright and Dark*. Using the setting or atmosphere of the novel is a fourth method. Science fiction and fantasies, with their often exotic, fascinating locales, frequently lend themselves to such introductions.

Make sure you are honest in interpreting the book. To present, for example, *My Brother Sam Is Dead* as an exciting action-filled war story is both a disservice to the book and a misrepresentation to the audience.

Some people write down their booktalks and memorize them; others simply prepare them mentally. A rehearsal, however, is necessary to test pacing, presentation, timing, and sequencing. Perhaps friends, family, or colleagues can be an initial test audience. Tape recorders or, better yet, video recorders are also helpful in preparation. Although rehearsals are necessary, always try for sincerity, naturalness, and a relaxed atmosphere in the delivery. Because initial nervousness can be expected, be particularly careful to know the beginning of the talk thoroughly. Once one becomes used to the audience and the surroundings, nervousness usually disappears. Introduce the theme or subject of the booktalk quickly, in a way that bridges the gap between the experience and interests of the audience and the contents of the books you wish to introduce. Be sure to mention both the author and the title of the book (often twice—once at the beginning and once at the end of the presentation), show off the book (dust jackets and covers help sell a book and supply a visual reminder), and then display the book (usually by standing it up on the desk). Try to adhere to principles of good public speaking: include the entire audience in your eye contact; don't fidget, rock, play with elastic bands, or create other distractions; speak slowly, with good intonation, and use pauses effectively; and move quickly from one book to the next. After introducing the last book, conclude by returning to the main theme to round out the booktalk. Happy booktalking!

1

Teenage Life and Concerns

Block, Francesca Lia. *Weetzie Bat.* HarperTrophy, 1989. Pap. $7.99, 0-06-440818-3 (Grades 8–12).

Introduction

Francesca Lia Block (1962–) is a true product of southern California, the locale she uses frequently in her writing. She was born and raised in Los Angeles and environs and attended North Hollywood High School. She began writing poetry and short stories while still young. However, with the publication in 1989 of *Weetzie Bat*, her writing career took off and has continued to soar. The novel is a hip, psychedelic story, part magical fairy tale and part funky realism. While most critics welcomed this imaginative depiction of the teenage punk subculture of Shangri-L.A. (a.k.a. Los Angeles), others had serious reservations. Regardless of the reaction, the author has in this (and subsequent novels in the series), taken the young adult novel in a new direction that explores sensual experiences, the teenage psyche, and the meaning of love and family in a unique, life-affirming fashion. Others in this series include *Witch Baby* (HarperCollins, 1990), *Cherokee Bat and the Goat Guys* (HarperCollins, 1991), *Missing Angel Juan* (HarperCollins, 1993), and *Baby Be-Bop* (HarperCollins, 1995). *Weetzie Bat* is enjoyed by both junior and senior high readers.

Principal Characters

Weetzie Bat, a bleach-blond teenager with a flat-top hairdo
Dirk McDonald, the best-looking guy in school, who is gay
Charlie Bat, Weetzie's father
Grandma Fifi, who gives Weetzie a magic lamp
Duck Drake, a lover for Dirk
My Secret Agent Lover Man, a lover for Weetzie

Plot Summary

In this wild, sophisticated fairy tale, the author takes us into a magical world where love conquers all. At the center of the tale is Weetzie Bat, a skinny girl with bleached hair, pink sunglasses, dangling earrings, and strawberry lipstick. Under all that, she is really almost beautiful.

Weetzie is still in high school in Los Angeles, which she calls Shangri-L.A. She hates high school because no one there even realizes what life is all about. She feels that no one cares, until she meets Dirk McDonald, the best-looking boy at school. He invites her to go to a Jayne Mansfield film festival. They go to lots of shows at night and in the daytime they go to matinees on Hollywood Boulevard. In their psychedelic fantasy world, they like to spend time "duck hunting" together—that is, looking for boyfriends: one for Weetzie and another for Dirk, who is gay. They also go to the cottage of Dirk's Grandma Fifi, where he has lived since his parents died. They feel safe and warm there.

Weetzie's father, Charlie Bat, visits from New York City, and Weetzie hopes in vain for a reconciliation between him and her mother, Brandy-Lynn. She once visited him in New York, where he went to write plays, but she couldn't live there because the subways jangled her nerves.

One day, Weetzie receives a magic lamp from Grandma Fifi that contains a genie able to grant three wishes. She polishes the lamp and out jumps the genie. Weetzie's wishes all come true: a lover named Duck Drake for Dirk, one called My Secret Agent Lover Man for herself, and a house (inherited from Grandma Fifi) where they can all live together peacefully. After Weetzie makes her wishes, she learns that Grandma Fifi has died.

My Secret Agent Lover Man is Weetzie's height. He wears a slouchy hat and dresses in a trench coat. Weetzie's circle of friends also includes a Rastafarian man named Valentine Jah-Love; his Chinese wife, Ping Chong; and their baby, Raphael.

My Secret Agent Lover Man is a more conventional sort than Weetzie. He decides he does not want to have children, so Duck and Dirk volunteer to help Weetzie, who later gives birth to Cherokee Bat. Beautiful and blond, Cherokee Bat is outgoing and loving and the delight of the family group. Duck and Dirk are with her at the hospital and they give the baby their fatherly support.

About the same time, My Secret Agent Lover Man becomes bewitched by Vixanne Wigg, who bears him a child named Witch Baby, who comes to live with Weetzie and company. Witch Baby is the opposite of Cherokee Bat. She has dark hair, curly toes, and purple eyes. She gains attention by being nasty and destructive.

Handsome, charming Charlie Bat dies as a result of drugs. Although he loved his daughter dearly, he never interfered with her chosen lifestyle. Charlie's death, coupled with the news of the death of so many of Duck's gay friends, produces such sadness in Duck that one day he leaves home. Frantically, Dirk searches for him. He walks around the streets of Chinatown in San Francisco. Eventually he finds Duck and convinces him to come home. Weetzie and her family have a joyous reunion.

The night of the reunion the whole family eats linguini and clam sauce. Weetzie looks around at her adored group. She knows they are all afraid. She thinks that love and disease are like electricity, and she will choose to plug into the love current. Weetzie's heart is so full of love that she feels it will hardly fit into her chest.

Themes and Subjects
The author has created a wild magical world where love conquers all. Weetzie and her friends are unusual characters and their view of life is unorthodox, but their world is filled with laughter and love.

Booktalk Material
The character descriptions set the tone of this fantasy novel; see: Weetzie meets Dirk (pp. 4–9); Weetzie meets her dad at the Tick Tock Tea Room (pp. 15–20); the magic lamp (pp. 22–27); Weetzie and My Secret Agent Lover Man (pp. 35–38); Cherokee Bat is born (pp. 51–52); Dirk finds Duck (pp. 84–86).

Additional Selections
A rebellious sixteen-year-old is sent to live with her father in New York in Rachel Cohn's *Gingerbread* (Simon, 2002).

Fifteen-year-old Addy gets help with her personal problems from a ghost that speaks through a parrot in *Angels Turn Their Backs* (Kids Can, 1998) by Margaret Buffie.

Frank, a teenage ghost living in limbo, contacts Eddie through a computer to get help in Lawrence Gordon's *User Friendly* (Karmichael, 1999).

In the humorous novel *Those Darn Dithers* (Holt, 1996) by Sid Hite, the dithering Dithers have a series of adventures involving Porcellina, a dancing pig.

About the Author and Book
Authors and Artists for Young Adults. Gale. Vol. 13, 1991; vol. 34, 2000.
Campbell, Patricia. "People Are Talking About Francesca Lia Block," *Horn Book,* Jan./Feb., 1993, pp. 57–66.
Children's Literature Review. Vol. 33, Gale, 1994.

4 • CLASSIC TEENPLOTS

Contemporary Authors New Revision Series. Vol. 135, Gale, 2005.
Continuum Encyclopedia of Children's Literature. Continuum, 2001.
Drew, Bernard A. *The 100 Most Popular Young Adult Authors.* Libraries Unlimited, 1997.
Gallo, Donald R. *Speaking for Ourselves, Too.* National Council of Teachers of English, 1993.
Gillespie, John T., and Corinne J. Naden. *Characters in Young Adult Literature.* Gale, 1997.
Lives and Works: Young Adult Authors. Vol. 1, Grolier, 1999.
Major Authors and Illustrators for Children and Young Adults (2nd ed.). Vol. 1, Gale, 2002.
St. James Guide to Young Adult Writers (2nd ed.). St. James, 1999.
Seventh Book of Junior Authors and Illustrators. Wilson, 1996.
Something About the Author. Gale. Vol. 80, 1995; vol. 116, 2000; vol. 158, 2005.
Something About the Author Autobiography Series. Vol. 21, Gale, 1996.
Stevens, Jen. *The Undergraduate's Companion to Children's Writers and Their Web Sites.* Libraries Unlimited, 2004.
Twentieth-Century Young Adult Writers (1st ed.). St. James, 1994.
Writers for Young Adults. Vol. 1, Scribner, 1997.
www.francescaliablock.com (personal Web site)
See also listing "Selected Web Sites on Children's Literature and Authors."

Blume, Judy. *Tiger Eyes.* Atheneum, 1982. $16.95, 0-689-85872-8 (Grades 7–10).

Introduction

Judy Sussman Blume (1938–) was born in New Jersey and attended New York University. Her first marriage, to John M. Blume, with whom she had two children, ended in divorce. While still a young housewife and mother, she began taking courses in creative writing. Soon her writing career began to take shape, with a concentration on juvenile literature. Her subsequent phenomenal success as a writer has been rivaled only recently by that of J. K. Rowling, the creator of Harry Potter. Unlike Rowling, Judy Blume writes for a wide variety of age groups, extending from works for the primary grades—*The One in the Middle Is the Green Kangaroo* (Bradbury, 1981), for example—through many books for the middle grades—such as *Then Again, Maybe I Won't* (Bradbury, 1971)—to *Forever* (Bradbury, 1975), the controversial novel for high school readers. *Tiger Eyes* was her first novel written expressly for a junior high audience. It is narrated by fifteen-year-old Davey Wexler, the central character in the novel. The author's courageous honesty in treating subjects once considered taboo has been recognized by such organizations as the American Civil Liberties

Union, which honored her in 1986. This novel is enjoyed by readers in grades seven through ten.

Principal Characters
>Tenth-grader Davey, who mourns the tragic death of her father
>Jason, her seven-year-old brother
>Gwen Wexler, their mother
>Bitsy and Walter Kronick, relatives in New Mexico
>Wolf, a young man Davey meets in the canyon
>Jane Albertson, a new friend of Davey's
>Miriam Olnick, a counselor
>Willie Ortiz, a terminally ill patient

Plot Summary
Even on the day of the funeral, Davey, short for Davis, is in a trancelike state of disbelief over the death of her father, Adam Wexler. He was the manager of a 7-Eleven store in Atlantic City, a job he kept in order to one day pursue his first love, painting. He was mortally shot during a store robbery. He leaves behind a young widow, Gwen, and their two children, Davey and seven-year-old Jason, who because of his youth seems best able to cope with the family loss. Both mother and daughter adored Adam and neither is able to comprehend or accept his senseless death. Davey's anxiety and fearfulness affect her health and even her black schoolmate Lenaya and her boyfriend Hugh are unable to reach her. Davey stays home from school for days at time and at school she has bouts of hyperventilation and nausea. In desperation, Gwen accepts an invitation from Adam's sister, Bitsy, and her husband Walter Kronick to visit them in Los Alamos, New Mexico, where Walter is a physicist. Davey takes with her a brown paper bag she keeps hidden in the closet and a bread knife she puts under her pillow at night.

One day while walking in a canyon near Los Alamos, Davey meets a young man of about twenty. He introduces himself as Wolf; she says her name is Tiger.

When Gwen learns the store in Atlantic City has been vandalized, she decides to stay on in New Mexico. Davey and Jason enroll in school there. Davey becomes friendly with Jane Albertson, who is from a socially prominent family. Jane introduces Davey to her family and later convinces Davey that both should join the Candy Stripers as an outside activity. Davey often meets the mysterious but solicitous Wolf in the canyon. They explore their own private cave. Wolf tells her that his own father is dying. But Davey cannot discuss her father's death with him. In Davey's work with the Candy Stripers, she becomes fond of a terminally ill man named Willie Ortiz. His bravery saddens and inspires her.

One day Mr. Ortiz introduces her to a visitor, his son Martin, who is none other than Wolf. The young man has taken a semester off from his studies at Cal Tech and found a job in town to be with his ailing father. Wolf tells Tiger (Davey) that in the future he will be spending all his free time at the hospital because his father is fading fast.

Gwen now visits a counselor, Miriam Olnick, seeking relief from her growing depression. Gwen begins to date a friend of Walter's, whom Davey does not like. Davey also has frequent clashes with Walter. At one point, she is verbally abusive to him and he slaps her across the face. Walter later apologizes, but Davey is slow to forgive.

Willie Ortiz dies and when Davey returns to the hospital, she is given a note from Wolf promising to come back and see her "when the lizards run." He also sends a small polished stone with a note that says "A tiger eye for my Tiger Eyes."

Although outwardly Davey appears to be making progress—for example, she wins the coveted role of Ado Annie and scores a great success in the school production of *Oklahoma!*—becoming reconciled to her father's death is a slow process. Davey takes her mother's advice and visits the counselor. Slowly, she is able to talk about the most terrifying night of her life when, seemingly immersed in a sea of blood, she cradled her dying father's head in her arms. One day in a final act of acceptance, she takes the brown paper bag that contains her blood-stained clothes from the murder and her many undelivered letters to Wolf and creates a little shrine in their cave in the canyon.

The period of grieving is over, and through catharsis comes a need to rebuild. Gwen gathers her children together and the three return to Atlantic City to begin life again.

Themes and Subjects

The difficulty of accepting the death of a loved one is the main theme of this novel. Also explored are complex family relationships, the place of fear in one's life, problems coping with new situations, and dealing with grief. A subplot involves teenage drinking, and the story contains subtle political and social undertones concerning armaments and racial tensions. All situations are handled without preaching or pat solutions.

Booktalk Material

Of special interest are the introduction of the main characters and the telling of their story before they go to New Mexico. Some specific passages are: the funeral (pp. 1–3); Davey's anxiety and the trip to Los Alamos (pp. 22–28) the first meeting with Wolf (pp. 42–51); the second meeting (pp. 73–75); Davey meets Jane (pp. 84–87); and Mr. Ortiz (pp. 101–03).

Additional Selections

Fifteen-year-old Green, named for her gardening skills, is the only family member to survive a major disaster in Alice Hoffman's *Green Angel* (Scholastic, 2003).

In Lurlene McDaniel's *The Girl Death Left Behind* (Bantam, 1999), a young girl painfully adjusts to the death of her parents and a new life with relatives.

Liam goes through a tangle of denial, anger, shame, and grief when he learns that his father is dying of AIDS in Paula Fox's *The Eagle Kite* (Orchard, 1995).

When her father is murdered, fourteen-year-old Esperanza's happy life is shattered and she and her mother are forced to become migrant workers in Pam Muñoz Ryan's *Esperanza Rising* (Scholastic, 2000).

About the Author and Book
Authors and Artists for Young Adults. Gale. Vol. 3, 1990; vol. 36, 2001.
Children's Books and Their Creators. Houghton, 1995.
Children's Literature Review. Gale. Vol. 2, 1976; vol. 15, 1988; vol. 69, 2001.
Contemporary Authors New Revision Series. Vol. 124, Gale, 2004.
Continuum Encyclopedia of Children's Literature. Continuum, 2001.
Drew, Bernard A. *100 Most Popular Young Adult Authors.* Libraries Unlimited, 1996.
Eighth Book of Junior Authors and Illustrators. Wilson, 2000.
Estes, Glenn E., ed. "American Writers for Children Since 1960: Fiction." In *Dictionary of Literary Biography.* Vol. 52, Gale, 1986.
Favorite Children's Authors and Illustrators. Tradition Books, 2003.
Fourth Book of Children's Authors and Illustrators. Wilson, 1978.
Gallo, Donald R. *Speaking for Ourselves.* National Council of Teachers of English, 1990.
Gillespie, John T., and Corinne J. Naden. *Characters in Young Adult Literature.* Gale, 1997.
Jones, Raymond E. *Characters in Children's Literature.* Libraries Unlimited, 1997.
Lee, Betsey. *Judy Blume's Story.* Dillon, 1989.
Lives and Works: Young Adult Authors. Vol. 1, Grolier, 1999.
McElmeel, Sharron L. *100 Most Popular Children's Authors.* Libraries Unlimited, 1999.
Major Authors and Illustrators for Children and Young Adults (1st ed.). Vol. 1, Gale, 1993.
Major Authors and Illustrators for Children and Young Adults (2nd ed.). Vol. 1, Gale, 2000.
St. James Guide to Children's Writers (5th ed.). St. James, 1999.

St. James Guide to Young Adult Writers (2nd ed.). St. James, 1999.
Something About the Author. Gale. Vol. 2, 1971; vol. 31, 1993; vol. 79, 1995; vol. 142, 2004.
Stevens, Jen. *The Undergraduate's Companion to Children's Writers and Their Web Sites.* Libraries Unlimited, 2004.
See also listing "Selected Web Sites on Children's Literature and Authors."

Cleaver, Vera, and Bill Cleaver. *Where the Lilies Bloom.* Harper-Collins, 1969. $15.95, 0-397-31111-7 (Grades 6–9).

Introduction

The husband-and-wife writing team of Vera (1919–92) and Bill (1920–81) Cleaver lived through much of the time depicted in their novels—the Great Depression and its aftermath. The settings of their novels are usually poor rural areas in the Great Plains, the South, or, as in this novel, Appalachia. The central characters are feisty, indomitable young people (usually female) who manage to overcome poverty, family problems, conflicting values, and painful decisions in order to survive and grow as moral human beings. Their first book, *Ellen Grae* (Lippincott, 1969), for example, is set in the South and involves a bossy, independent eleven-year-old heroine who is faced with the dilemma of betraying a trust or allowing a miscarriage of justice. Their second book was the prize-winning *Where the Lilies Bloom*, a tale of a poor family of rural tenant farmers living in the shadows of the Great Smoky Mountains of North Carolina. Its central character and narrator is the memorable Mary Call Luther, an enterprising and courageous heroine who is determined to keep her orphaned family together regardless of the sacrifices and consequences. Readers in middle school and junior high have loved this novel since it was first published.

Principal Characters

Mary Call Luther, fourteen-year-old heroine and narrator
Roy Luther, her ailing father
Devola, her eighteen-year-old retarded sister
Kiser Pease, thirty-two-year-old landowner who wants to marry Devola
Romey Luther, ten years old
Irma Dean Luther, five years old

Plot Summary

The Luthers are poor tenant farmers in the Great Smoky Mountains of North Carolina. When Roy Luther begins to ail, he makes his daughter,

Mary Call, promise that she will bring in neither doctor nor undertaker and that after his death she will keep the family together without resorting to charity. He also makes her swear never to allow a marriage between her eighteen-year-old retarded sister, Devola, and their crafty landowner, Kiser Pease. The Luther family also includes two younger children, ten-year-old Romey and five-year-old Irma Dean. Their mother died some years before of a fever, and the family now lives in a ramshackle house on the edge of the property owned by Kiser, whom Mary describes as "all cheat and sneak." Apart from grubbing out a bare living, the Luthers supplement their livelihood by gathering wild witch hazel leaves and selling them to Mr. Connell, who owns the local country store some 5 miles away.

Roy suffers a massive stroke, and the children try to nurse him back to health. One day Mary Call and Romey are out gathering herbs to help their father and are caught in a storm. They take shelter in the landowner's house and discover he is suffering from pneumonia and is delirious. Mary Call breaks the fever with medicinal herbs and folk remedies, including covering him with hot onions. She stays with him all night. During that time, she forces Kiser to sign a paper that gives the Luthers ownership of their house and land.

Roy Luther dies. In accordance with his wishes, Mary Call and Romey drag their father's body by wagon up the side of their mountain, Old Joshua, and bury him. Fearing that news of his death will mean foster homes for the children, Mary Call swears them to secrecy and begins an elaborate plan to convince the neighbors that her father is alive and well. They continue to buy razor blades and other supplies for him at the store, and when people call, Roy Luther is always out walking or taking a nap. They begin to isolate themselves completely and when school starts in the fall, they avoid making friends who might want to visit.

The hardest one to discourage is Kiser Pease, who is now courting Devola seriously, bringing such welcome gifts as a pig and a cow. Fed up with the delaying tactics, he demands to see Roy to ask for his daughter's hand. Mary Call has run out of excuses, but an automobile accident sends Kiser to the hospital and grants a reprieve.

Winter brings more trouble to the family. Disaster strikes when Kiser's sister comes to visit him in the hospital. She claims that the Luthers' land is rightfully hers and tells Mary Call the family must vacate within two weeks.

For Mary Call, there is nowhere to turn. Worn out and discouraged, she wonders if life has any meaning but suffering. In desperation, she visits Kiser in the hospital. After revealing her father's death, she offers to marry him herself to save the family, but Kiser claims he loves only Devola.

Mary Call begins to scout the mountain for a dry cave where the family can live until spring. She returns home one night to find Kiser out of the hospital and the family in the kitchen. He has bought the Luther property from his sister, and he offers it to Mary Call as a gift. Once more, he asks permission to marry Devola. Realizing that they really love each other and that perhaps her father was wrong to oppose the marriage, Mary Call consents.

The marriage takes place and Kiser becomes the children's legal guardian. Slowly spring arrives in the valley, and Mary Call, Romey, and Irma Dean are safe and secure in their own home.

Themes and Subjects
The courage, strength, and resourcefulness of Mary Call will inspire all readers. She displays pride and independence despite severe hardship. The authors, who know the region and its people, highlight the social problems of oppressive poverty in the Appalachian hill country. Also included are details about the plants of the region, especially a fascinating introduction to wildcrafting, or gathering wild medicinal plants.

Booktalk Material
The hardcover edition contains drawings of the family by Jim Spanfeller. The paperback edition has several pages of movie stills taken from the film. Among the interesting passages are: Mary Call's promise to her father (pp. 13–15; pp. 15–17, pap.); the hot onion treatment (pp. 27–32; pp. 29–34, pap.); wildcrafting (pp. 54–56; pp. 56–58, pap.); and the burial of Roy Luther (pp. 68–73; pp. 71–76, pap.).

Additional Selections
In *Money Hungry* (Hyperion, 2001) by Sharon G. Flake, Raspberry Hill, thirteen, struggles to find enough money to keep her mother and herself from a life on the streets.

In the Newbery Medal winner *Out of the Dust* (Scholastic, 1997) by Karen Hesse, fourteen-year-old Billie Joe Kelby describes her heartbreaking life of poverty in the Oklahoma Dust Bowl during the 1930s.

An awkward teenager copes with her father's paralysis and the return of the mother who abandoned her years before in Lynn Hall's *Flying Changes* (Harcourt, 1991).

Dirt-poor fourteen-year-old Tess Mathis must confront her past when a scar-faced stranger comes to town in Nancy Springer's *Secret Star* (Putnam, 1997).

About the Author and Book
Authors and Artists for Young People. Vol. 12, Gale, 1994.
Children's Books and Their Creators. Houghton, 1995
Children's Literature Review. Vol. 6, Gale, 1984.
Continuum Encyclopedia of Children's Literature. Continuum, 2001.
Favorite Children's Authors and Illustrators. Tradition Books, 2003.
Fourth Book of Junior Authors and Illustrators. Wilson, 1978.
Gallo, Donald R. *Speaking for Ourselves.* National Council of Teachers of English, 1990.
Gillespie, John T., and Corinne J. Naden. *Characters in Young Adult Literature.* Gale, 1997.
Major Authors and Illustrators for Children and Young Adults (1st ed.). Vol. 2, Gale, 1993.
Major Authors and Illustrators for Children and Young Adults (2nd ed.). Vol. 2, Gale, 2002.
St. James Guide to Young Adult Writers (2nd ed.). St. James, 1999.
Something About the Author. Gale. Vol. 22, 1981; vol. 27, 1982; vol. 76, 1994.
Twentieth-Century Young Adult Writers (1st ed.). St. James, 1994.
Writers for Young Adults. Vol. 1, Scribner, 1997.
See also listing "Selected Web Sites on Children's Literature and Authors."

Conrad, Pam. *My Daniel.* HarperCollins, 1989. $16.89, 0-06-021314-0 (Grades 6–9).

Introduction
Pam Conrad (1947–96) was born and educated in New York City and Long Island but also spent time in Colorado and Texas before returning to her native state. Although her writing career was a tragically short one, she managed to produce an amazing number of books for differing age groups, using different genres and settings. Many of them deal with variations on the theme of loss and its consequences. For example, her first novel for young adults, *Prairie Songs* (Harper, 1985), is set in Nebraska at the turn of the twentieth century and deals with the descent into madness of Emmeline Berryman, a lonely reluctant pioneer who loses her first baby and is unable to face the grueling hardships of her everyday life. In *My Daniel,* also partially set in Nebraska, the author artfully constructs plot shifts between the present, in which a grandmother and her two grand-

children visit a natural history museum, and long ago, when the brother of Julia, now a grandmother, searched for dinosaur bones and encountered an evil fossil collector. Middle school and junior high readers enjoy this novel.

Principal Characters
    Julia Creath Summerwaite, eighty years old and from Nebraska
    Ellie and Stevie, her grandchildren
    Daniel, Julia's long-dead brother
    Howard Crow, a paleontologist
    Oswald Mannity, an evil dinosaur bone prospector
    Hump Hinton, Mannity's confederate

Plot Summary
Eighty-year-old Julia Summerwaite has just stepped off a plane from Nebraska. It is her first trip east. She is visiting her youngest son and her two grandchildren, twelve-year-old Ellie and her younger brother Stevie. Julia makes it clear she has made the trip for only one reason. She wants to go to the Natural History Museum alone with her grandchildren. Her son suspects she wants to see the dinosaur bones.

   A few days later, as requested, Ellie's father drives Grandma Summerwaite and the children to the Natural History Museum, promising to pick them up at the end of the afternoon. Once inside, the threesome slowly head for the fourth floor and the dinosaurs. They stop now and again so that Grandma can rest or Stevie can explore some interesting site. As they proceed, the old lady seems to drift back in time.

   What is history on the Nebraska prairie comes alive for her modern-day grandchildren as she tells them stories of long ago when she was a young girl on the farm. She talks of her brother, their long-dead Uncle Daniel, whom she loved, in her words, "with a white fire."

   At age sixteen, Daniel's passion was fossils. At first, their father was outraged because Daniel spent all his spare time digging in the dirt. But then he heard of paleontologists, men such as Howard Crow who believed that dinosaur bones might be buried in Nebraska. When Daniel heard that Crow would pay a reward for any such discovery, he was determined to find the remains of a dinosaur on their prairie land.

   Julia tells the children about the "dinosaur war" that was going on between Crow and his former employer, Oswald Mannity, who would stop at nothing to win. She was afraid for her brother's safety, but he continued to hunt with his chisel and pick each day. Then one day after a rain, Daniel uncovered huge dark-gray bones.

Daniel and Julia covered up the bones, and Daniel wrote a letter to Crow, dated April 23, 1885, telling him of the discovery. He thought the reward would pay off the mortgage on the farm, so he did not tell his parents, hoping to surprise them. While they waited for Crow, there were scary moments as Mannity sent Hump Hinton, another evil prospector, to search for the bones. Finally, Daniel got a letter from Crow saying he was on the way. Before he arrived, however, Daniel was killed in an electrical storm. Julia told her parents of his discovery. Her father scared off the prospector and they waited for Crow.

At this point in her story, Julia asks her grandchildren if they would like to see what Crow did with the bones Daniel found. They enter a great hall and stand before a dinosaur. The plaque reads: "Brontosaurus, one hundred and forty million years old, sixty-seven feet long, thirty tons. Found near Dannebrog, Nebraska."

Crow had promised that Daniel would be given credit for his discovery. The reward, however, turned out to be only one hundred dollars.

After the story, the children watch in amazement as Julia approaches the base of the dinosaur and begins to climb it. The guard tries to stop her, but Ellie clutches at his sleeves. "It's hers," she explains. "She dug that dinosaur up herself. In Nebraska."

Ellie and Stevie and the guard stand in silence as the old woman slowly climbs toward the head of the dinosaur. Her laughter rings out across the vast room and she sounds like a young girl. "Oh, Daniel," she cries. "We did good, Daniel! We did real good."

The young Julia once again hears Daniel's voice, calling to her over the prairie grasses. She goes to meet him.

Themes and Subjects

In many ways, this is an old-fashioned story of a childhood dream, of family love and devotion, of memories and true adventure. It celebrates the bonds of family ties and praises the human spirit. It paints a warm picture of a long-ago way of life, sprinkled with treachery and deceit but held together by a love and a dream that lasted a lifetime. The old woman's memories come vividly to life as she re-creates the wonder of her brother's discovery for her young grandchildren.

Booktalk Material
Julia Summerwaite's descriptions of life on the prairie during the nineteenth century serve as a fine introduction to this adventurous and loving tale. See: Daniel finds a fossil (pp. 18–20); Daniel succumbs to the magic of dinosaur hunting (pp. 26–29); and Daniel digs a grave and talks about dinosaurs (pp. 37–42).

Additional Selections
Forced to spend summer with a grandmother she has never met, a thirteen-year-old girl discovers hidden abilities in Jenny Davis's *Checking on the Moon* (Orchard, 1991).

Set in the nineteenth century, Pamela S. Hill's *Ghost Horses* (Holiday, 1996) tells how runaway Tabitha, disguised as a boy, joins an expedition in the West digging for dinosaur bones.

Li, a girl who lived four million years ago, and Vinny, the daughter of a modern paleontologist, are the central characters in Peter Dickinson's *A Bone from a Dry Sea* (Dell, 1993).

The lives of eight major scientists involved in dinosaur paleontology are profiled in Susan Clinton's *Reading Between the Bones* (Watts, 1997).

About the Author and Book
Authors and Artists for Young Adults. Vol. 18, Gale, 1996.
Children's Books and Their Creators. Houghton, 1995.
Children's Literature Review. Vol. 18, Gale, 1989.
Contemporary Authors New Revision Series. Vol. 111, Gale, 2003.
Continuum Encyclopedia of Children's Literature. Continuum, 2001.
Gallo, Donald R. *Speaking for Ourselves, Too.* National Council of Teachers of English, 1993.
Gillespie, John T., and Corinne J. Naden. *Characters in Young Adult Literature.* Gale, 1997.
Lives and Works: Young Adult Authors. Vol. 2, Grolier, 1999.
McElmeel, Sharron L. *100 Most Popular Children's Authors.* Libraries Unlimited, 1999.
Major Authors and Illustrators for Children and Young Adults (1st ed.). Vol. 2, Gale, 1993.
Major Authors and Illustrators for Children and Young Adults (2nd ed.). Vol. 2, Gale, 2002.
St. James Guide to Young Adult Writers (2nd ed.). St. James, 1999.
Sixth Book of Junior Authors and Illustrators. Wilson, 1996.
Something About the Author. Gale. Vol. 52, 1988; vol. 80, 1995; vol. 90, 1997; vol. 133, 2002.
Something About the Author Autobiography Series. Vol. 19, Gale, 1995.
Twentieth-Century Young Adult Writers (1st ed.). St. James, 1994.
See also listing "Selected Web Sites on Children's Literature and Authors."

Cormier, Robert. *The Chocolate War.* Knopf, 1974. $19.95, 0-394-82805-4 (Grades 7–10).

Introduction
It is an acknowledged fact that, in his groundbreaking books, Robert Cormier (1925–2000) changed the face of the young adult novel. Not only did he deal with themes and situations never before explored, but he interjected a powerful and pervasive pessimism into his work that often leaves the reader with feelings of bleak despair and the triumph of injustice. During his writing career, he produced about fifteen disturbing novels for young adults beginning with *The Chocolate War* in 1974 and ending with the posthumously published *The Rag and Bone Man* in 2002. Each is a gripping, unsettling exploration of such subjects as corruption, the abuse of power, the dark side of humanity, and the nature of evil. *The Chocolate War* had an interesting genesis. One day the author's son brought home some boxes of chocolates to sell. When the boy was asked if he really wanted to sell the chocolates, he replied that he didn't, and his father returned them to the school without incident. But what if . . . This germ of an idea grew into a novel that created a sensation when it was published. The story of the Vigils and Brother Leon is continued in *Beyond the Chocolate War* (Knopf, 1985). These novels are popular with both junior and senior high school readers.

Principal Characters
Jerry Renault, lonely newcomer at Trinity School
Roland Goubert, called Goober, Jerry's only ally
Mr. Renault, Jerry's father, who is crushed by the death of his wife
Archie Costello, handsome and brutal student who enjoys inflicting pain on others
Carter, president of the secret student association
Brother Leon, headmaster and religious hypocrite
Emile Janza, football tackle and Archie's savage enforcer
Obie, Archie's errand boy

Plot Summary
The power structure at Trinity, a New England parochial day school for boys, involves two elements: Brother Leon and the Vigils. Brother Leon is the Assistant Headmaster, on the surface ingratiating and overly cautious, but underneath a venomous, sinister man who is fiercely ambitious. At

present, because of the Headmaster's prolonged illness, Brother Leon is in charge. If possible, he intends to make this appointment permanent.

The Vigils is the powerful secret society composed of the student elite. Its real power lies with Archie Costello, the Assigner, the officer who conceives and assigns the various hazing tasks that are given to non-members. Archie is intelligent and imaginative, but he is completely heartless and cynical. His ability to make up outrageous assignments is diabolically clever. Archie has as his muscleman or enforcer, Emile Janza, the school bully.

Each year under the direction of Brother Leon, the students sell boxes of chocolates to raise money for the school. This year Brother Leon has overextended himself by buying twice the number of boxes for sale as in the past years, using funds earmarked for other purposes. With 20,000 boxes of chocolates to be sold and only 400 boys in the school, each student will have to sell fifty boxes, a stiff quota. Leon asks Archie for his support in the sale, but both know that he really is asking for the support of the Vigils. Archie plays a cat-and-mouse game with Brother Leon, but he finally agrees to help.

Two freshmen come before the Vigils for assignments. The first is Roland Goubert, nicknamed The Goober, whose assignment is to loosen everything held together by screws in Brother Eugene's classroom. (Brother Eugene later suffers a nervous collapse from this incident.) Before the assignment becomes official, Archie must undergo the black box test. He is handed a box containing six balls, five white and one black. If Archie draws the black ball, he must fulfill the assignment himself. In his three years as Assigner, Archie has been phenomenally lucky. Once again, he draws a white ball.

The other assignee is Jerry Renault, a spunky, well-liked boy, but something of a loner, particularly since his mother's death from cancer a few months before. Jerry lives alone with his father, a dispirited, unassertive man, who, unlike Jerry, accepts unquestioningly whatever life offers.

Everyone knows that Jerry has received his assignment, but no one knows what it is until, on the day the chocolates are distributed, Jerry refuses to accept his quota. Through threats and bribery, Brother Leon learns from a student that Renault's refusal was a Vigil assignment. It will last only ten days and then Jerry will accept his fifty boxes. On the tenth day, however, Jerry's answer is still negative. In his locker is a poster with T. S. Eliot's words on it, "Do I dare disturb the universe?" Somehow, and without thought of the consequences, Jerry has answered that question with a resounding "Yes."

Renault's refusal to sell begins to slow the momentum of the chocolate sales. Several students openly sympathize with Jerry, and sales figures begin to drop. Realizing that his tenure at Trinity depends on the success of the project. Brother Leon becomes desperate. He once more speaks to Archie and demands that the Vigils make Jerry sell the chocolates.

Jerry is summoned to appear before the Vigils to receive his new assignment—accept the chocolates. Again, he refuses. Archie now realizes that it is not just the authority of Brother Leon, but his own authority and that of the Vigils that is being challenged. This calls for sterner measures, organized harassment. Jerry receives anonymous telephone calls throughout the night; his locker is ransacked and school assignments stolen; and finally he is beaten by Emile Janza and a group of neighborhood thugs. In the meantime, the Vigils have taken over the management of the chocolate sales, using threats and other tactics. Once more, the sales figures begin to rise.

Still intent on breaking Jerry's rebellion, Archie promises him the possibility of a fair fight to avenge himself on Janza. He tricks Jerry into coming to the school athletic field. Unknown to Jerry, the students have assembled there to witness a raffle that Archie has organized for the last fifty unsold boxes of chocolates. The rules of the raffle are simple; for each ticket purchased the student not only gets a chance at the chocolates but also has the opportunity of calling a punch for either Janza or Renault.

Until the black box is suddenly presented to Archie, he has forgotten that one of these two assignments could be his. Will his luck continue to hold? He draws once for Janza—a white ball—and once for Renault—another white! The raffle goes on as scheduled. Archie is sure that the crowd is sufficiently anti-Renault, that Jerry will be beaten up, and, at the same time, be the unwitting salesman of his quota of chocolates.

The fight gets out of hand, and, ignoring the rules. Janza begins beating Jerry to a pulp. Brother Leon witnesses the spectacle from a hilltop, but does nothing to stop it. Fortunately, another Brother happens along and intervenes, but Jerry is in very bad shape. As the ambulance approaches to take him to the hospital, he thinks that no matter what the poster says, he should never have tried to disturb the universe. He has lost much more than a chocolate war.

Themes and Subjects

The major theme of *The Chocolate War* is the direct opposite of the usual upbeat young adult book. The message is one of despair and hopelessness—one should not question or oppose the Establishment even when justice and right are on one's side. "One cannot fight City Hall and win." Instead, the comfortable goals of conformity, acquiescence, and personal security are the realistic goals in life. The corrupting influence of power, its misuse, and the premise that the end justifies the means are subthemes. Jerry's ordeal is also another example of an adolescent journey to maturity.

The jacket of the hard-cover edition shows a young boy casting a shadow much larger than himself. Perhaps this could signify that Jerry's sacrifice was not in vain and that his actions might be a positive influence in someone like him in the future.

Booktalk Material
An introduction to the conduct of the school is found in the opening passage when Jerry is being tested on the football field (pp. 1–6). Other vivid scenes are: Archie and Obie talk about Jerry (pp. 13–16); Archie and Brother Leon discuss the chocolates (pp. 22–29); Jerry says no to selling chocolates (pp. 84–85); Jerry's locker is damaged (pp. 192–93); the raffle tickets and the fight (pp. 239–55).

Additional Selections
The Vigils, led by Archie, and Brother Leon, now Headmaster of Trinity, continue their misuse of power in *Beyond the Chocolate War* (Dell, 1985) by Robert Cormier.

In Sharon M. Draper's *The Battle of Jericho* (Simon, 2003), a sixteen-year-old is initially thrilled to be invited to join the Warriors of Distinction at school, but subsequent events are chilling.

A group of youths become tainted with the evil that power brings in William Butler's *The Butterfly Revolution* (Ballantine, 1986), a novel set at High Pines Summer Camp for Boys.

John Knowles's *A Separate Peace* (Scribner, 1960) is an adult novel set in a boys' school on the eve of World War II.

About the Author and Book
Authors and Artists for Young Adults. Gale. Vol. 3, 1990; vol. 19, 1996.
Biography Today: Author Series. Vol. 1, Omnigraphics, 1995.
Campbell, Patricia. "A Loving Farewell to Robert Cormier," *Horn Book*, March/April, 2001, pp. 245–48.
———. *Presenting Robert Cormier*. Twayne, 1985.
Children's Books and Their Creators. Houghton, 1995.
Children's Literature Review. Vol. 55, Gale, 1999.
Contemporary Authors New Revision Series. Vol. 93, Gale, 2001.

Continuum Encyclopedia of Children's Literature. Continuum, 2001.
Drew, Bernard A. *100 Most Popular Young Adult Authors.* Libraries Unlimited, 1996.
Fifth Book of Junior Authors and Illustrators. Wilson, 1983.
Gallo, Donald R. *Speaking for Ourselves.* National Council of Teachers of English, 1990.
Gillespie, John T., and Corinne J. Naden. *Characters in Young Adult Literature.* Gale, 1997.
Lives and Works: Young Adult Authors. Vol. 2, Grolier, 1999.
Major Authors and Illustrators for Children and Young Adults (1st ed.). Vol. 2, Gale, 1993.
Major Authors and Illustrators for Children and Young Adults (2nd ed.). Vol. 2, Gale, 2002.
St. James Guide to Young Adult Writers (2nd ed.). St. James, 1999.
Something About the Author. Gale. Vol. 10, 1976; vol. 45, 1986; vol. 83, 1996; vol. 122, 2001.
Stevens, Jen. *The Undergraduate's Companion to Children's Writers and Their Web Sites.* Libraries Unlimited, 2004.
Twentieth-Century Young Adult Writers (1st ed.). St. James, 1994.
Writers for Young Adults. Vol. 1, Scribner, 1997.
See also listing "Selected Web Sites on Children's Literature and Authors."

Deaver, Julie Reece. *Say Goodnight, Gracie.* HarperTrophy, 1989. Pap. $5.99, 0-06-447007-5 (Grades 7–10).

Introduction

Julie Reece Deaver (1953–) grew up in Glen Ellyn, Illinois. She worked as a teacher's aide in special education and started her writing career in television comedy. *Say Goodnight, Gracie* is her first work for young adults. It is a touching novel about Morgan, a young girl who is painfully adjusting to the death of her dear friend. She is helped through this process by her Aunt Lo, a hospital psychiatrist. These two characters reappear in the author's later *The Night I Disappeared* (Simon Pulse, 2002), in which seventeen-year-old Jamie Tessman becomes terrified and thinks she is losing her mind because of her experiences with a friend from childhood named Webb. Morgan, Jamie's new friend, sees to it that Jamie gets the help she needs by sending her to her aunt. Lo is slowly able to break through Jamie's paralyzing fear and help her unravel some horrifying secrets from her past. Another fine novel by this author is *First Wedding, Once Removed* (Harper, 1990), which is the story of Pokie, who becomes disturbed when her beloved brother becomes engaged. These novels are read by youngsters in grades seven through ten.

Principal Characters

Morgan, a seventeen-year-old girl, and Jimmy, the same age, lifetime buddies
Aunt Lo, hospital psychiatrist
Jimmy's mother
Morgan's father

Plot Summary

Morgan and Jimmy, both seventeen years old, have loved each other forever, not in a romantic sense but as lifetime friends. They don't express how they feel about each other. In fact, when one starts to reveal an emotion, the other is likely to say "Just say goodnight, Gracie"—the line that vaudeville/radio/television star George Burns used to stop the run-on speeches of his wife Gracie.

Tall, lanky Jimmy wants to be a dancer. When he was ten years old, he discovered Fred Astaire. He coaxed Morgan into being his Ginger Rogers, and he has been dancing ever since. When Jimmy drives his MG into Chicago's Loop district three times a week after school to study dance, Morgan goes to an acting workshop.

Jimmy gets an opportunity to audition for a dance part in a touring production of *Oklahoma!* He throws himself so single-mindedly into practice that Morgan is afraid he will be stale at the tryout. She skips school to see his audition.

As soon as Jimmy walks on stage and Morgan hears the first few notes of the musical score, she knows her fears are confirmed. She mentally urges Jimmy to relax and be himself, but he moves around the stage like a scared amateur. He is stiff and wooden, not the wonderfully fluid, talented dancer she knows him to be. Not surprisingly, he doesn't get the part.

Following the audition, Morgan and Jimmy have perhaps their first really serious argument. Morgan is devastated by Jimmy's flare-up. But later her Aunt Lo, a hospital psychiatrist, helps Morgan to understand Jimmy's embarrassment at performing so badly in front of the one person in the world he wanted to impress. They make up verbally, then have a pillow fight.

That fall and winter, Morgan joins Jimmy as an apprentice at a children's theatre. She experiences a small twinge—could it be jealousy?—when Jimmy is kissed onstage. Later, when Morgan gets a chance to perform, she literally falls flat on her face. Jimmy covers up for her. When she tries to thank him, Jimmy says, "I never know what to say when you talk like that."

Morgan replies, "Very simple, Jimmy. Just say goodnight, Gracie."

Shortly after Christmas, they drive into Chicago for their classes. He is wearing the sweater Morgan gave him for Christmas. She forgot her coat, so Jimmy gives her his jacket to wear. Jimmy is late picking her up after class. Her mother arrives and tells her he has been in a car accident. When they get to the hospital, they learn that Jimmy was hit by a drunk driver and has died.

Morgan has a panic attack and is sedated. Later, she tells her father she is handling Jimmy's death well and she throws Jimmy's jacket in the garbage. But when she has another panic attack, she retrieves it. She tries to attend Jimmy's funeral but can't go inside. Her father is late picking her up one day and she becomes terrified that he, too, is dead.

One day, Morgan talks to her father about depression. She learns that Jimmy's mother is getting professional help. Morgan says she doesn't need that; she is coping. Her aunt, however, seems to think that it is Jimmy's mother who is coping. Her father says that depression is a funny thing; the more you lie around, the more depressed you get.

It takes another panic attack and her understanding aunt to make Morgan realize that she has been protecting herself from being hurt by Jimmy's death. Her life will never be the same without him, but she now will start to live again. Morgan knows that the healing has truly begun when she stops on a bridge over the Chicago River, where she and Jimmy once stood, and she tosses his jacket into the wind.

Themes and Subjects

This book deals sensitively with love, friendship, and death. It portrays vivid, real relationships between people: the warmth between Morgan and her parents; the open affection and admiration between Morgan and her aunt; and, above all, the funny, close, and caring love between Morgan and Jimmy. It is an honest, unsentimental look at the stages of grief that humans endure when they suffer the loss of a loved one and a sensitive portrait of grief and healing made more poignant by the youth of those involved.

Booktalk Material

The following passages, illustrating the relationship between Morgan and Jimmy, are a good introduction: the pierced-ears discussion (pp. 6–7); one of their "Goodnight, Gracie" routines (pp. 15–17); Jimmy overpractices for *Oklahoma!* (pp. 33–35); and the make-up pillow fight after the argument (pp. 61–65). Morgan's reactions after Jimmy's death can prompt a discussion of the ways in which individuals deal, or fail to deal, with sorrow and disappointment in their lives; see: Morgan refuses to go inside to Jimmy's funeral (pp. 128–31); Morgan talks to Aunt Lo about wearing Jimmy's jacket to bed (pp. 150–51); Morgan and her father talk about depression (pp. 173–75); and another panic attack (pp. 200–06).

Additional Selections

When college freshman Jesse Harmon's deaf younger brother is killed by a drunk driver, his family is torn apart in Eve Bunting's *A Sudden Silence* (Fawcett, 1990).

Karen Hesse's *Phoenix Rising* (Puffin, 1995) is a tale of life, death, and hope, set on a Vermont sheep farm where Nyle, thirteen, and her grandmother are surrounded by the effects of a nuclear accident.

Biracial teenager Anna must assume adult responsibilities when her mother takes her own life in Jackie French Koller's *A Place to Call Home* (Aladdin, 1997).

In Patricia Calvert's touching novel *The Stone Pony* (NAL, 1983), Jo Beth must adjust to the death of her older sister.

About the Author and Book
Authors and Artists for Young Adults. Vol. 52, Gale, 2003.
Contemporary Authors New Revision Series. Vol. 135, Gale, 2005.
Lives and Works: Young Adult Authors. Vol. 2, Grolier, 1999.
St. James Guide to Young Adult Writers (2nd ed.). St. James, 1999.
Something About the Author. Vol. 68, Gale, 1992.
See also listing "Selected Web Sites on Children's Literature and Authors."

Dorris, Michael. *A Yellow Raft in Blue Water.* Picador, 2003 (1987). Pap. $14, 0-312-42185-0 (Grade 10–Adult).

Introduction
Michael Dorris (1945–97) came from a mixture of Native American, Irish, and French ancestry but considered himself a member of the Modoc tribe. His writing, which spans various time periods, genres, and a range of intended audiences from young children to adults, tends to focus on the past and present Native American experience. Although his life was tragically short, he made a significant contribution to Native American literature specifically and American literature in general. *A Yellow Raft in Blue Water*, his highly original first novel, tells the story of three generations of lonely, complex, Native American women. The first narrator is Rayona, a fifteen-year-old girl of mixed heritage; the second is her mother, Christine; and the last is her grandmother, who is known in the family as Aunt

Ida. Each story complements the others by adding extensions in both plot and time. The locales are the Pacific Northwest (the Seattle area) and a reservation in Montana. Using reverse chronological order, the novel extends over a forty-year period from the 1980s to the closing years of World War II. Some of the language and incidents are sexually explicit but always in keeping with the author's narrative purpose. Though written for adults, this novel also appeals to senior high school readers.

Principal Characters
   Rayona, fifteen-year-old part Native American, part African American
   Christine, her mother
   Aunt Ida, her grandmother
   Father Tom Novak, a priest
   Norman and Evelyn Dial, who take Rayona to live with them
   Ellen De Marco, a white college student

Plot Summary
Rayona's visit to her Native American mother, Christine, in a Seattle hospital is interrupted by the arrival of her black father, Elgin. As long as Rayona can remember, her parents have had a life of separation, numerous affairs, heavy drinking, and short-lived reconciliations. Rayona, who has lived a pillar-to-post existence with her mother, longs for the security and stability of the middle-class families she sees on television.

   Christine is so insulted by her husband's indifference toward her that when he leaves, she grabs her medicine, dons a Candy Striper's uniform, and meets Rayona in the parking lot. They go home in Christine's beat-up Volare. The next day, Christine orders Rayona to pack her belongings—they are moving to the Indian reservation in Montana where Christine's mother, Aunt Ida, lives. Using an expired credit card for gas and food, the two arrive at Aunt Ida's. The old lady shows such hostility toward her daughter that Christine grabs her two plastic bags and hitches a ride from a passing motorist, leaving her daughter behind.

   Rayona is miserable living with Ida, a taciturn, solitary woman who speaks only an Indian language. Rayona, fortunately, understands her. At the reservation school, she is taunted because of her mixed parentage. In desperation, she accepts the help of a do-gooder priest, Father Tom Novak. Together they go to a jamboree in Helena. On the way they stop at a state park where Rayona sees a beautiful yellow raft in the water. She swims to it, as does Father Tom. When he develops a cramp and she helps him, he becomes sexually excited. Afraid she will tell others of his misconduct, he encourages her to plan not to return to the reservation.

Rayona meets Norman Sky Dial and his wife Evelyn, who live in a trailer in the park. She tells them her parents are wealthy and away in Switzerland. They take her in and she is loved by them. She also meets a white lifeguard and college student, Ellen De Marco, who discovers the truth about Rayona. The De Marco family volunteers to help her find her mother.

Rayona is reunited with her mother on a reservation, where she is living with Dayton Nickles, a friend of Christine's brother who was killed in Vietnam.

Christine's story is now told, beginning in the 1960s. She adored her younger brother Lee, but when he became involved in the civil rights movement and was against the Vietnam War, she goaded him into joining up. With Lee gone, she leaves the reservation and goes to Seattle, where she meets Elgin and begins a stormy relationship. Rayona is born on the day Christine learns her brother has been killed.

Over the years of a stormy marriage, Christine learns she has only a few months to live. Desperate to give her daughter a home, she takes her to Aunt Ida and leaves her.

Ida's story begins during the last years of World War II and reveals a deep, dark secret. Her mother, suffering from heart disease, sent for her younger sister, Clara, a vivacious, fun-loving girl, to help run the household on the reservation. Ida worships her aunt. When it is later revealed that Clara is pregnant by Ida's father, Ida—to avoid a scandal—volunteers to accompany Clara to a convent in Denver. There she waits out the pregnancy and brings back the baby, Christine, as her own.

Ida returns to face the shame and censure of the reservation community. When her mother dies and her father wanders off the reservation, Ida takes in as a companion and lover the once-handsome Willard Yellow Dog, now grotesquely scarred from war wounds. She becomes pregnant but tells no one. Willard undergoes facial surgery that restores his good looks. Ida, knowing that he once again will be the catch of the reservation, lets him go and later bears his son, Lee. In isolation, she raises her family and eventually sees each leave her: her daughter for an unfulfilled life in Seattle and her son to die in Vietnam.

Themes and Subjects

This is essentially a novel of character, featuring three indomitable women who will remain in the reader's memory long after the book is finished. It contains many themes, such as the crippling effects of rejection, the tragedy of betrayed love, the need for belonging, and the gutsy fortitude required to endure life's problems. It examines the defenses that people develop to help them survive but that often create barriers to honest relationships. The gritty stubbornness and pride that each of these women has developed both shield and divide them. In these contrasting stories, the unity of time and the multiple shades of truth are explored. Although the novel deals with emotions that transcend race, it also gives an unforgettable portrayal of Native American culture on the decline, a look at past and present life on the reservation, and a glimpse of racial prejudice.

Booktalk Material
An introduction to the three overlapping life stories in the book will interest readers. Some important passages: Christine and Rayona join a video club (pp. 19–22); the trip to Aunt Ida's (pp. 25–30); Rayona joins the God Squad (pp. 41–45); the raft at Bearpaw Lake and the incident with Father Tom (pp. 58–64); and finding a scrap of letter and its consequences (pp. 80–86).

Additional Selections
   Hatter Fox (Ballantine, 1986) by Marilyn Harris is a touching story about a Navajo girl and her many problems.
   In Robert Lipsyte's *The Chief* (Harper, 1991), a young Native American boxer is rescued from drugs, pimps, and hookers by a tough but understanding ex-NYC cop.
   Two plots, one involving the historic death of a young Cheyenne girl, and the other a contemporary love story about two Native Americans, are traced in Marcus Stevens's *Useful Girl* (Algonquin, 2004).
   When his father kills another brave, Thomas Black Bull and his parents are forced into the wilderness, where he vows never to return to the white man's world in Hal Borland's *When the Legends Die* (Dell, 1984).

About the Author and Book
Authors and Artists for Young Adults. Vol. 20, Gale, 1997.
Children's Books and Their Creators. Houghton, 1995.
Children's Literature Review. Vol. 58, Gale, 2000.
Contemporary Authors New Revision Series. Vol. 75, Gale, 1999.
Continuum Encyclopedia of Children's Literature. Continuum, 2001.
Drew, Bernard A. *100 More Popular Young Adult Authors.* Libraries Unlimited, 2002.
Favorite Children's Authors and Illustrators. Vol. 2, Tradition Books, 2003.
Lives and Works: Young Adult Authors. Vol. 3, Grolier, 1999.
St. James Guide to Young Adult Writers. St. James, 1999.
Seventh Book of Junior Authors and Illustrators. Wilson, 1996.

Something About the Author. Gale. Vol. 75, 1994; vol. 94, 1998.
Twentieth-Century Young Adult Writers (1st ed.). St. James, 1994.
See also listing "Selected Web Sites on Children's Literature and Authors."

Fitzhugh, Louise. *Harriet the Spy.* Delacorte, 2000 (1964). $15.95, 0-385-32783-8 (Grades 5–8).

Introduction

Although the writing career of Louise Fitzhugh (1928–74) was unfortunately very short (she died of an aneurysm at age 46), she brought such honesty and originality to her works that she is assured a lasting place in the history of children's literature. Born into a wealthy Tennessee family, her youth was beset by personal problems and she only achieved fulfillment after college when she moved to Greenwich Village and became part of the bohemian life. Candor and sincerity are also trademarks of her writing, particularly her two best novels for middle and junior high readers. One is *Nobody's Family Is Going to Change* (Farrar, 1974), a tough-minded vision of a prosperous middle-class black family in which the children do not want to follow their parents' plans for their future. The second is Fitzhugh's masterpiece, *Harriet the Spy,* a derisive look at society as seen through the eyes of a lonely youngster who spies on her neighbors and classmates and records her impressions. As Zena Sutherland said, this book is "a milestone in children's literature because of the power with which Fitzhugh reveals the emotional anguish of the contemporary American child." Readers in grades five through eight enjoy reading about Harriet.

Principal Characters

Harriet M. Welsch, an irrepressible eleven-year-old
Miss Catherine Golly, her governess
Mrs. Welsch, her mother
Sport and Janie Gibbs, a boy and girl who are Harriet's school friends
Marion Hawthorne, Harriet's nemesis
Dr. Wagner, a psychiatrist

Plot Summary

On this, the last day of summer vacation, eleven-year-old Harriet M. Welsch, who added the initial herself, is spending the day with her beloved governess, Catherine Golly, whom she refers to as Ole Golly. They take the subway to Far Rockaway, which is a long way from Harriet's home on the East Side of Manhattan, not only in distance but in terms of wealth. Ole Golly is trying to show Harriet that not everyone lives as she does, but Harriet is only fascinated by the fact that Ole Golly's mother is a foolish woman. She also notes that Ole Golly treats her foolish mother with great kindness.

Harriet writes her observations in a notebook, which Ole Golly has encouraged her to do. Over the past three years, she has filled fourteen composition books with her observations and has even set up a spy route. She regularly spies on the De Santis, who own the corner grocery store; the Robinsons, who have no children; a cat-loving artist named Harrison Withers; and Mrs. Plumber, who is a wealthy widow.

Harriet is very serious about her spying and always dresses in the proper attire: blue jeans, sweatshirt, and a belt with necessary spy tools.

Back at Gregory School, a small private institution, Harriet resumes her friendships with Sport, whose ambition is to be a ballplayer, and with Janie Gibbs, who wants to be a scientist. Harriet doesn't much like any of her other sixth-grade schoolmates, mostly because they always support Marion Hawthorne against Harriet in class elections.

Marion wins once again, but that blow is nothing compared with Mrs. Welsch's decision that Harriet must go to dancing school. Ole Golly tries to soften the blow by suggesting that dancing is something all spies should know how to do. But this is followed by a much greater crisis when Ole Golly is fired after a misunderstanding with Harriet's mother.

Things go from bad to worse. Harriet misses Ole Golly dreadfully. She is unmoved when she is given the part of an onion in the Christmas pageant. Then she loses her notebook in the park. By the time she finds it, Janie has read it. She makes Sport cry when she reads that Harriet describes him as "like a little old woman." Janie refuses to give Harriet back her notebook. Unnerved, Harriet decides to buy another and start again.

When her classmates write nasty notes to her, Harriet tells her mother she is ill and stays home from school. But a classmate's father tells her mother about the notebook incident. Harriet returns to school and plots revenge on all her classmates, especially when she learns they are planning a Spy Catcher's Club. Before that happens, her mother takes her to see Dr. Wagner, a psychiatrist.

Dr. Wagner suggests to Mrs. Welsch that she write to Ole Golly for help with Harriet. Ole Golly writes Harriet a letter. She tells Harriet to apologize to her friends. She says that sometimes it is better to soften the truth in order to spare people's feelings. Golly also writes that she doesn't miss Harriet because "gone is gone." She tells Harriet to feel that way, too.

Back in school, Harriet is chosen to be the editor of the sixth-grade page in the school newspaper. She attacks the job with great enthusiasm and hard work. In addition, she prints a general apology to her classmates. It works. Janie and Sport are once again her friends.

Themes and Subjects
The author honestly explores a child's growing awareness that people's feelings should be considered when interpreting the truth. The potential hurtfulness of innocent writings about the ways in which people act is crisply depicted.

Booktalk Material
Readers will be interested in the description of Harriet's spy route as well as her relationship with friends Sport and Janie. These passages are of interest: Janie's lab and dancing school (pp. 74–82); the Christmas pageant (pp. 149–55); and the Spy Catcher Club (pp. 205–23).

Additional Selections
Flack, a sixth-grader, doesn't foresee the unusual and often funny situations that will arise when he runs for class president in Carol Gorman's *Dork on the Run* (HarperCollins, 2002).

Because she is always accompanied by the class nerd, Dinah's hopes for popularity are slim in Barbara Park's *Buddies* (Avon, 1986).

Motherless sixth-grader Alicia finds a female role model in her teacher in Phyllis Reynolds Naylor's *The Agony of Alice* (Macmillan, 1985), part of a lengthy series.

The class clown runs for class president and tries to develop election-winning habits in M. M. Ragz's *French Fries Up Your Nose* (Pocket, 1994).

About the Author and Book
Authors and Artists for Young Adults. Vol. 18, Gale, 1996.
Biography Today: Author Series. Vol. 3, Omnigraphics, 1997.
Children's Literature Review. Vol. 72, Gale, 2002.
Contemporary Authors New Revision Series. Vol. 84, Gale, 2000.
Continuum Encyclopedia of Children's Literature. Continuum, 2001.
Estes, Glenn E. "American Writers for Children Since 1960: Fiction." In *Dictionary of Literary Biography.* Vol. 52, Gale, 1986.
Favorite Children's Authors and Illustrators. Vol. 2, Tradition Books, 2003.
Jones, Raymond E. *Characters in Children's Literature.* Gale, 1997.
McElmeel, Sharron L. *100 Most Popular Children's Authors.* Libraries Unlimited, 1999.
Major Authors and Illustrators for Children and Young Adults (1st ed.). Vol. 2, Gale, 1993.

Major Authors and Illustrators for Children and Young Adults (2nd ed.). Vol. 3, Gale, 2002.
St. James Guide to Children's Writers. St. James, 1999.
Something About the Author. Gale. Vol. 1, 1971; vol. 24, 1981; vol. 45, 1986.
Third Book of Junior Authors. Wilson, 1972.
Twentieth-Century Children's Writers (4th ed.). St. James, 1995.
Wolf, Virginia L. *Louise Fitzhugh.* Twayne, 1991.
See also listing "Selected Web Sites on Children's Literature and Authors."

Fox, Paula. *The Moonlight Man.* Aladdin, 2003 (1986). Pap. $4.99, 0-689-85886-8 (Grades 8–12).

Introduction

Born and educated in New York City, Paula Fox (1924–), has lived in a variety of places including southern California and a sugar plantation in Cuba. In 1962 she traveled to Greece and began her writing career with a novel for adults. Her first juvenile work was for very young readers; *Maurice's Room* (Macmillan, 1966) is the story of a young boy who defies parental blandishments and makes his room a collector's paradise and a mother's trauma. Fox's works are characterized by her versatility, dignity, focus on character, and lyrical use of language. Some of the themes she explores are isolation, achieving maturity, and developing emotional independence. Although perhaps best known for her Newbery Medal-winning *The Slave Dancer* (Bradbury, 1973), a brutal narrative of the slave trade as experienced by a young boy, she has written over a dozen noteworthy novels for young adults, including *One-Eyed Cat* (Bradbury, 1984) (p. 192). *The Moonlight Man* explores the complex relationship between a father and daughter as the girl gradually realizes that the father she worships has feet of clay. Junior and senior high school readers enjoy this novel.

Principal Characters

Fifteen-year-old Catherine, who attends boarding school in Montreal
Harry Ames, her irresponsible father
Beatrice, Catherine's mother
Philippe Petit, Catherine's friend who attends college
Madame Soule, Catherine's headmistress
Officer Macbeth, a Royal Canadian mounted policeman

Plot Summary

For three weeks since the end of the school year at the Delraida Boarding and Day School in Montreal, Catherine has been waiting to be picked up by her father, writer Harry Ames. He is best described as debonair, charming, irresponsible, and even undependable. Her father has promised her a seven-week stay with him at his home in Rockport, Maine, while his second wife, Emma, is away in Virginia.

Catherine's mother, Beatrice, and father divorced when she was three years old, and from that time until last year Catherine has been living alone with her mother, an editor in a New York publishing firm. They live in an attractive apartment in Manhattan. Last year, her mother married Carter, an academician, and Catherine attended a boarding school for the first time.

Catherine is now fifteen—well-liked, intelligent, and mature beyond her years. She has made many friends at school and has a special relationship with a nineteen-year-old sophomore at McGill named Philippe Petit, who is spending the summer in a remote Quebec logging camp.

Just as it appears that the headmistress must contact Catherine's mother, who is currently in Europe with Carter, Harry Ames calls from Nova Scotia. After giving her some excuses, he invites Catherine to spend time with him there; he has rented an ocean cottage for a month.

Within two days of her arrival, she discovers a hitherto hidden side to her father's personality. He has a drinking problem. Heeding Catherine's objections, her father seriously limits his drinking. One day they go fishing with the local minister. Her father has no luck and becomes sullen. Another time, Catherine is disappointed when she discovers her father flirting with the wife of his drinking partner.

Through these experiences and their many days alone, Catherine at last becomes acquainted with the enigmatic man who is her father. Once witty, suave, and self-assured, he is now a fifty-year-old hack writer whose charms are running thin as his alcoholism increases. In spite of these failings, Catherine still loves and respects her father. She is still enchanted by his knowledge of literature, foreign countries, and the finer things in life. He thrives on this adulation, but during times of stress in their relationship, he seems to regard her as the personification of his own conscience.

A few days before leaving, Ames befriends a young Royal Canadian mounted policeman, Officer Macbeth, who in his off-hours agrees to take him on a tour of the local bootleggers. Catherine accompanies them and is horrified to notice that at each stop, while she remains in the car, her father is once again drinking uncontrollably. He finally passes out.

With Macbeth's help, she gets him home. But his breathing becomes erratic and Catherine drives to Reverend Ross for help. Together they get Ames to bed. The next morning her father is subdued but haughty and seemingly unrepentant. This angers Catherine so much that she screams, "You're nothing. You're just a drunk, you bastard!" He grabs her and holds her until she says she will forgive him. Their last days are strained at first, but gradually they begin to talk and even laugh together again.

Catherine is met by her mother, newly arrived from Europe. When questioned, Catherine protects her father and does not mention his three-week absence or his drinking bouts. But she wonders inwardly about the future of her relationship with him now that they know one another so well. Particularly distressing were his parting words. His reply to her "See you" was a kiss and "Not if I see you first."

Themes and Subjects
This novel explores father-and-daughter relationships from the perspective of a young girl. The differences between exterior appearances and inner reality are explored. The novel probes the shattering disillusionment and disenchantment of discovering weaknesses in someone previously adored to the point of worship. That this involves a father makes the story doubly poignant, particularly in contrast to the many tender moments that Catherine shares with him. The reluctant recognition and acceptance of the flaws in her father's character are well portrayed. The description of an alcoholic and his subterfuges is truthful and uncompromising. Catherine emerges as a strong, admirable person who, although saddened by these experiences, has matured and grown in independence as a result. The author has also interestingly and often amusingly portrayed small-town life in rural Nova Scotia.

Booktalk Material
An introduction to Catherine's dilemma while she waits for her father and a foreshadowing of events to come should interest readers. Some incidents of importance are: the long-awaited phone call from Harry Ames (pp. 12–16); driving her father's drinking companions home (pp. 21–27); and the morning after (pp. 29–35).

Additional Selections
In *The Warping of Al* (HarperCollins, 1990) by Jessie Close, Al tries to cope with a domineering father and a subservient mother.

Sophie's life spins out of control when her father files for divorce to marry his older daughter's roommate in Caroline B. Cooney's *Tune in Anytime* (Delacorte, 1999).

In *Dirty Laundry: Stories About Family Secrets* (Viking, 1999), edited by Lisa R. Faustine, eleven original stories by young adult writers explore family relationships.

Rain or Shine (University of Nebraska, 1986) by Cyra McFadden is a nonfiction memoir that traces the author's devotion to her father, a celebrated rodeo announcer, and a difficult father-daughter relationship.

About the Author and Book
Authors and Artists for Young Adults. Gale. Vol. 3, 1990; vol. 37, 2001.
Bostrom, Kathleen Long. *Winning Authors: Profiles of the Newbery Medalists*. Libraries Unlimited, 2003.
Children's Books and Their Creators. Houghton, 1995.
Children's Literature Review. Gale. Vol. 1, 1976; vol. 44, 1999; vol. 96, 2004.
Contemporary Authors New Revision Series. Vol. 105, Gale, 2002.
Continuum Encyclopedia of Children's Literature. Continuum, 2001.
Drew, Bernard A. *100 Most Popular Young Adult Authors*. Libraries Unlimited, 1996.
Estes, Glenn E. "American Writers for Children Since 1960: Fiction." In *Dictionary of Literary Biography*. Vol. 52, Gale, 1986.
Favorite Children's Authors and Illustrators. Vol. 2, Tradition Books, 2003.
Fourth Book of Junior Authors and Illustrators. Wilson, 1978.
Fox, Paula *Borrowed Finery: A Memoir*. Holt, 2001.
———. "On Language," *School Library Journal*, March, 1995, pp. 122–26.
Gallo, Donald R. *Speaking for Ourselves*. National Council of Teachers of English, 1990.
Gillespie, John T., and Corinne J. Naden. *Characters in Young Adult Literature*. Gale, 1997.
Jones, Raymond W. *Characters in Children's Literature*. Gale, 1997.
Lives and Works: Young Adult Authors. Vol. 3, Grolier, 1999.
McElmeel, Sharron L. *100 Most Popular Children's Authors*. Libraries Unlimited, 1999.
Major Authors and Illustrators for Children and Young Adults (1st ed.). Vol. 2, Gale, 1993.
Major Authors and Illustrators for Children and Young Adults (2nd ed.). Vol. 3, Gale, 2002.
St. James Guide to Young Adult Writers (2nd ed.). St. James, 1999.
Something About the Author. Gale. Vol. 17, 1979; vol. 60, 1990; vol. 120, 2001.
Stevens, Jen. *The Undergraduate's Companion to Children's Writers and Their Web Sites*. Libraries Unlimited, 2004.
Twentieth-Century Children's Writers (4th ed.). St. James, 1995.
Twentieth-Century Young Adult Writers (1st ed.). St. James, 1994.
Writers for Young Adults. Vol. 1, Scribner, 1977.
See also listing "Selected Web Sites on Children's Literature and Authors."

TEENAGE LIFE AND CONCERNS • 33

Guest, Judith. *Ordinary People.* Penguin, 1982 (1976). Pap. $13, 0-14-006517-2 (Grade 10–Adult).

Introduction
For publishers, the term "over the transom" refers to the arrival, directly from an author, of an unsolicited manuscript. Such an event usually produces nothing more than a rejection slip, but in the case of *Ordinary People* by Judith Guest (1936–) it began a Cinderella story almost unheard of in publishing circles. Published in 1976, the book became a best-seller, was a selection of four major book clubs, and has remained in print ever since.

The story concerns a family of three, seemingly normal people who live comfortably in the upper-middle-class suburban community of Lake Forest, Illinois. They are forty-one-year-old Cal Jarrett, a successful tax attorney, his wife Beth, and their seventeen-year-old son Conrad (Con). All three are beset by guilt and sorrow resulting from two rarely mentioned tragedies in their lives: the accidental death of an older son and Con's suicide attempt six months later. The novel, which is told in brief, abrupt episodes, covers one year and details the shifting relationships and adjustments that these traumatic events ultimately cause in the lives of these "ordinary people." Senior high school readers enjoy this novel.

Principal Characters
    Conrad (Con) Jarrett, a seventeen-year-old who attempted suicide
    Cal Jarrett, Con's father and a successful attorney
    Beth, Con's snobbish mother
    Dr. Berger, local psychiatrist
    Jeannine Pratt, new girl in town

Plot Summary
A month after he returns home from eight months of treatment in a mental institution for attempting suicide, seventeen-year-old Conrad Jarrett wonders if he is really making progress. At school he has always been a perfectionist and straight-A student. But he now lacks motivation and, having lost a year, finds it difficult to relate to his old friends, who are now seniors.

In many ways, Con has an ideal father. Cal is attentive and generous, although often overly solicitous in his attempts to prevent a relapse. He is a self-made man and successful tax attorney. Con's mother, on the other hand, was raised in a well-to-do middle-class environment. Since Conrad's return she has continued her efficient, well-organized life of meticulous housekeeping, golfing, bridge, and other social events as though nothing has happened. Behind her cold matter-of-factness and independence, Con feels an objectivity bordering at times on indifference. Each family member is alone in a private world of sorrow and silence resulting from the death more than a year before of Jordan (nicknamed Buck), the lighthearted, carefree older son. He drowned when the boat in which he and Con were sailing capsized during an unexpected storm on Lake Michigan.

Cal suggests that Conrad begin to see a local psychiatrist, Dr. Berger. Obviously eccentric, Berger impresses Con with his candor, humor, and relaxed attitude. Con begins seeing the doctor twice a week. Berger tries to ease his tension by having him give up his after-school swimming classes. Con does not tell his parents at first, but his mother finds out and accuses her son of being deceitful and causing her embarrassment. Cal defends his son and the parents quarrel. Con's mother expresses resentment over the attention Cal is showing his son at the expense of her own feelings. Many quarrels follow.

At Christmas, Con's father gives him a new car. Con reacts in a dazed way. Beth again accuses Cal of overindulgence.

The Jarrett marriage is floundering, but Con is improving. He becomes sufficiently free from his prison of passivity and guilt that he wins a fistfight with Kevin Stillman. More constructively, he becomes friendly with Jeannine Pratt, a new girl in town. They begin dating and Con feels the responsibility of having someone depend on him.

To help pacify Beth, Cal takes her to Dallas for a weekend to visit with her brother and sister-in-law. Unfortunately their short vacation ends with more recriminations when Beth again accuses Cal of indifference and apathy.

While his parents are away, Conrad stays with his grandparents. Although he is able to weather his grandmother's well-intentioned nagging, on Sunday night he reads about the suicide of Karen Aldrich, one of his close friends at the hospital. He is once again thrust into an emotional crisis and he courageously and unflinchingly relives both his suicide attempt and the death of his brother. In a painful session with Dr. Berger the next day, he confronts and explodes his guilt that somehow he should have saved his brother's life.

By the end of the summer, the Jarretts decide on a trial separation while Beth goes to Europe to sort things out. Conrad, though, has grown in confidence and self-understanding and checks himself out of Dr. Berger's care. Thinking of the many changes the year has brought to his family, he realizes that "it is love, imperfect and unordered, that keeps them apart, even as it holds them somehow together."

Themes and Subjects
The author seems to be saying that in this life there really are no "ordinary people." Conrad's quote about the paradoxical effects on family love is an important theme. Another is that sorrow, although often destructive, can lead to greater self-understanding. The author has beautifully captured the doubts and anxieties of adolescence. Conrad's recovery is convincingly told and the sessions between the boy and his "hip" psychiatrist are revealing and entertaining. They are bound to challenge a teenager's conventional image of a "shrink."

Booktalk Material
An excellent introduction is a discussion of Con's feelings about the constructive and destructive elements in love (p. 245). Other passages of interest are: Con's first visit to Dr. Berger (pp. 35–41); his visits with Karen (pp. 49–54); Beth confronts him about dropping the swimming classes (pp. 100–04); and the quarrel on Christmas Day (pp. 117–19).

Additional Selections
The death of their oldest son destroys Ellie and Tucker's marriage but their younger sons try to bring them back together in Catherine Anderson's *Always in My Heart* (NAL, 2002).

After his beloved grandfather dies, Max is packed off to a boarding school by his divorcing parents in *The Way Home* (DayBue, 2004) by Robert Earle.

Fireflies (Warner, 1999) by David Morrell is a "nonfiction novel" about the death of the author's fifteen-year-old son from bone cancer.

After her twin sister is killed in an accident, Tina, overwhelmed with grief, finds she is becoming more and more like her dead sister in *I Miss You, I Miss You!* (Farrar, 1999) by Peter Pohl and Kinna Gieth.

About the Author and Book
Authors and Artists for Young Adults. Gale. Vol. 7, 1992; vol. 66, 2006.
Contemporary Authors New Revision Series. Vol. 138, Gale, 2005.
See also listing "Selected Web Sites on Children's Literature and Authors."

Hinton, S. E. *The Outsiders.* Viking, 1967. $16.99, 0-670-53257-6 (Grades 6–10).

Introduction
S. E. Hinton (1950–) was born in Tulsa, Oklahoma, and attended the Will Rogers High School. There she realized that the books written for her age group failed, in her estimation, to depict the realities of teenage life—gangs, girls, violence, and the struggle between the "haves" and "have nots." She gave up writing about horses and cowboys and started on more serious work. The result was *The Outsiders*, a novel about three brothers growing up in the shadow of gang culture and street rumbles. When it was first published in 1967, it created a sensation for a number of reasons. It ushered in a new realism in young adult fiction. Never before had anyone written with such bite and passion about the raw and violent world of street gangs. It is also one on the few successful novels written by a teenager. She was fifteen when she started the novel and it was published when she was seventeen. The publisher was convinced that boys would not read a book on the subject by a female and therefore disguised her sex by using only her initials (S. E. stands for Susan Eloise). Although much of the plot is melodramatic and the characters stereotypical, the saga of Ponyboy and his brothers continues to appeal to readers in grades six through ten.

Principal Characters
   Ponyboy Curtis, a member of the Greasers gang
   Darry and Soda, his brothers and only family
   Two-Bit Mathews, Steve Randle, Dally Winston, and Johnny Cade, all
      Greasers

Plot Summary
Fourteen-year-old Ponyboy Curtis, who tells the story, is on his way home when he is attacked by five members of a gang called the Socs (for Socials). His screams for help bring members of his own gang, who drive away the Socs. Ponyboy's gang is the Greasers—the hoods, poor kids from the wrong side of the tracks who have long, well-greased hair and wear jeans and leather jackets. Their rivals and dread enemies, the Socs, are the "haves," who dress well, drive around in expensive cars, and have lots of money.

Ponyboy's only family is two older brothers. His parents were killed in a car accident, and the court allowed the three brothers to stay together "as long as they behaved," a condition they find harder to meet each day. Ponyboy's brothers are very different. Twenty-year-old Darry is quiet, thoughtful, and very intelligent. He has had to give up the prospect of a college education and become a manual laborer to support the family. Ponyboy regards Darry's frequent lectures and his sullenness as signs of dislike and hostility. By contrast, sixteen-year-old Soda is outgoing, always joking, and a great pal to Ponyboy. Soda is a school dropout now working in a garage.

The most memorable night in Ponyboy's life begins innocently enough when he and two Greaser members, Johnny and Dally, meet two Soc girls, Cherry Valance and her friend Marcia, at a drive-in. In spite of initial hostility, Ponyboy has a long talk with Cherry. They discuss their differences and finally agree that, rich or poor, growing up in today's world is a tough business. While taking the girls home, they have a narrow brush with the Socs, but manage to avoid violence. Ponyboy is late getting home, and Darry, who has been worried about him, becomes angry and, in the ensuing argument, strikes him. Now convinced that Darry really dislikes him, Ponyboy runs out into the night. He meets Johnny in a park and while they are talking, the five Socs they met earlier that evening drive up. They grab Ponyboy and shove his head into a fountain, holding him until he passes out. When he comes to, he is lying by the fountain next to Johnny, who is clutching his switchblade. Beside him is the body of a dead Soc, Bob Sheldon. To save Ponyboy, Johnny drove off the gang by murdering their leader.

The boys panic. They seek out Dally, who gives them money and directions to a hideout in an abandoned church in a rural area many miles away but accessible by freight train. After a week in hiding, Dally shows up to check on them. Johnny has decided to give himself up. As they are about to leave, fire breaks out in the church, trapping some schoolchildren who have been playing inside. The boys risk their lives and save the children, but during the rescue all three are injured. Johnny is critically injured when a flaming timber falls on him and breaks his back.

They return home as celebrities. The emotional greeting he receives from Darry convinces Ponyboy that his brother really loves him. But news from the hospital is bad—the doctors give little hope for Johnny's recovery.

The Socs want a fight to avenge their leader's death. The Greasers win the skin rumble—fists, no hardware—but are battered themselves. Dally and Ponyboy rush to the hospital to tell Johnny the news, but while they are with him, he dies.

Dally goes berserk when he hears of Johnny's death and robs a grocery store. The gang tries to help him, but reach him just as he is shot down by police.

The deaths numb both gangs, and there are indications that some members want an end to the senseless violence. Ponyboy is cleared of charges in Bob Sheldon's death and is not sent to a foster home as he feared. The brothers return home stronger and more united as a result of these ordeals.

Themes and Subjects

This novel explores the causes and consequences of gang culture without preaching or moralizing. It examines the effects on youngsters who live surrounded by violence. The author also touches on differences between economic classes and how they influence youngsters growing up. Despite the amount of brutishness and terror in this novel, positive themes including loyalty of friends and the importance of families are also present.

Booktalk Material

A selection from the recording of the Broadway musical *Grease* might set the mood. To introduce the differences between the gangs' points of view, use the passages where Cherry cites the Socs' case well (p. 46) and Ponyboy explains what it means to be a Greaser (p. 140). Ponyboy's narrow escape from the Socs (pp. 12–15) will be of interest as well as the park incident that results in Bob's death (pp. 61–65).

Additional Selections

A homeless boy in the slums of Rio de Janeiro joins a street gang and is drawn into a life of crime in Ineke Holtwijk's *Asphalt Angels* (Front Street, 1999).

In Richard Wright's novella *Rite of Passage* (HarperCollins, 1994), a fifteen-year-old black boy runs away from his Harlem home and joins a gang.

Young Kaninda Bulumba is rescued from his native country only to encounter gang violence in his new home in London in Bernard Ashley's *Little Soldier* (Scholastic, 2002).

Lisa Wolff's *Gangs* (Lucent, 2000) explains why gangs are formed, their activities, and how society and the law deal with them.

About the Author and Book
Authors and Artists for Young Adults. Gale. Vol. 2, 1989; vol. 33, 2000.
Biography Today: Author Series. Vol. 1, Omnigraphics, 1995.
Children's Books and Their Creators. Houghton, 1995.
Children's Literature Review. Vol. 23, Gale, 1991.
Contemporary Authors. Vol. 133, Gale, 2005.
Continuum Encyclopedia of Children's Literature. Continuum, 2001.
Day, Jay. *Presenting S. E. Hinton.* Twayne, 1989.
Drew, Bernard A. *100 Most Popular Young Adult Authors.* Libraries Unlimited, 1996.
Fourth Book of Junior Authors and Illustrators. Wilson, 1978.
Gallo, Donald R. *Speaking for Ourselves.* National Council of Teachers of English, 1990.
Gillespie, John T., and Corinne J. Naden. *Characters in Young Adult Literature.* Gale, 1997.
Lives and Works: Young Adult Authors. Vol. 4, Grolier, 1999.
Major Authors and Illustrators for Children and Young Adults (1st ed.). Vol. 3, Gale, 1993.
Major Authors and Illustrators for Children and Young Adults (2nd ed.). Vol. 4, Gale, 2002.
St. James Guide to Young Adult Writers (2nd ed.). St. James, 1999.
Something About the Author. Gale. Vol. 19, 1980; vol. 58, 1990; vol. 115, 2000; vol. 160, 2005.
Stevens, Jen. *The Undergraduate's Companion to Children's Writers and Their Web Sites.* Libraries Unlimited, 2004.
Twentieth-Century Young Adult Writers (1st ed.). St. James, 1994.
Writers for Young Adults. Vol. 2, Scribner, 1997.
www.sehinton.com (personal Web site)
See also listing "Selected Web Sites on Children's Literature and Authors."

Mahy, Margaret. *Memory.* Dell, 1988. Pap. $6.99, 0-440-20433-X (Grades 8–12).

Introduction
Margaret Mahy (1936–) is probably the most distinguished and best known of contemporary New Zealand writers of books for children and young adults. She is an extremely prolific author, with more than 150 picture books to her credit plus many short story collections and novels, ranging from those for beginning readers to those for young adults. Two of her books for young adults have won Carnegie Medals in Great Britain: *The Haunting* (McElderry, 1982), about an eight-year-old boy and his encounter with a wizard, and *The Changeover* (McElderry, 1984), another novel that deals with witchcraft and the occult. Like her other novels,

40 • CLASSIC TEENPLOTS

Memory is multilayered. It takes place (except for a brief epilogue) over a period of a few days in a city in present-day New Zealand. Except for a few local references, however, the situation and events could easily be transported to contemporary America. This thoughtful novel is best suited for junior and senior high school readers.

Principal Characters
   Jonny Dart, a nineteen-year-old who is troubled by his sister's death
   Bonny Benedicta, his sister's friend
   Sophie, a shabby old lady
   Nev Fowler, a bully

Plot Summary
At nineteen, Jonny Dart believes he is washed up, a has-been. As a child growing up in New Zealand, he showed great talent as a tap dancer. He and his older sister Janine had achieved fame and fortune dancing in a TV commercial for Chickenbits. But five years ago, when Jonny, his sister, and her best friend Bonny Benedicta were walking along the high cliffs, Janine lost her footing and fell to her death. Jonny feels responsible and has been drifting ever since.

Exactly five years after the accident, Jonny goes to a local pub and gets drunk. On impulse, he goes to the Benedicta home to see Bonny, but her mother says she has moved into town. He discovers her address is the Colville downtown area. That brings back more painful memories—Jonny and his family lived there many years before, and he remembers being victimized there by a sadistic bully called Nev Fowler.

Jonny gets into town and falls asleep on a traffic island. When he wakes up he is approached by a shabby old lady in her eighties wearing a strange red hat shaped like a flower pot and pushing a shopping cart. Her name is Sophie, and she invites him home. She lives in what is called Tap House, a filthy place full of untended cats. Despite the shambles, Jonny likes the old lady and realizes she is in an advanced stage of senility.

The next day, the two take money from their savings accounts for food and Jonny begins to clean up the house. He discovers a pile of receipts, all signed with the name of Spike.

The next day, Jonny decides to go home and stops at a local pub for food. There he meets Nev Fowler again. Fearful that such people live in Sophie's neighborhood, he returns to the old lady.

In a package of faded photographs, he finds a picture of a distant cousin of Sophie's named Alva Babbitt. He is wearing the same type of blazer that Jonny wears, which is obviously the reason that Sophie began to talk to him. Sophie thinks he is her cousin, an old flame her family forbade her to marry. He also finds an unopened letter addressed to Bonny Benedicta, who now lives next-door. He finds Bonny and tells her about Sophie, whom Bonny has always regarded as a nuisance. But she suggests he seek help for Sophie from the Aged Citizens' Council.

An official at the council thinks Sophie may have Alzheimer's disease and will eventually have to be institutionalized. But the council will supply visiting nurse and cleaning services in the meantime. When Jonny returns to Sophie's, Spike is there taking money from her. Although Sophie owns the house, Spike has persuaded her that she owes him rent. Jonny throws Spike out and warns him never to return.

That evening, Bonny comes to dinner with Sophie and Jonny. Jonny kisses her impulsively, but Bonny resists his advances. After she leaves, he is on the second-floor balcony when a van stops in front carrying Nev, Spike, and another hood. They taunt Jonny until in desperation he jumps down on them. His shoulder is badly injured, but he is able to fight while Bonny summons the police. Before he is driven to the hospital, he asks Bonny the question that has been tormenting him for five years. She tells him he was in no way responsible for his sister's death. Jonny breaks down, sobbing tears of pain and grief.

Six months pass and Jonny reappears at Sophie's house. After a stay in the hospital coupled with some help from a therapist, he is healthy again and is now anxious to make something of his life. He tells Bonny, who he realizes can be no more than a dear friend, that he has a job in construction and that he plans on caring for Sophie until the inevitable separation. Sophie's reaction after the usual string of "oh dears" is a simple "that's nice."

Themes and Subjects

This novel explores the interrelationship of past and present. Both Jonny and Sophie are prisoners of memory. She is trying to recall the past and he to forget it. In both cases, memory has distorted reality. Sophie, although ill, emerges as a dignified, loving person, and through caring for her, Jonny learns to care about himself. His reorientation and return to health result jointly from his emerging sense of responsibility and his confrontation with the past. The corrosive nature of guilt is explored, as is the nature of friendship.

Booktalk Material
A discussion of memory could serve to introduce this thoughtful novel. Specific passages are: Jonny visits the Benedictas to find Bonny (pp. 5–22); his first meeting with Sophie (pp. 33–36) and his introduction to Tap House (pp. 42–48); the two have tea and Jonny spends the night (pp. 52–58); and the morning after (pp. 61–69).

Additional Selections
Death and the mysticism of the Catholic Church are the themes of the eight stories in David Almond's *Counting Stars* (Delacorte, 2002), which are based on the author's English childhood.

Elaine Marie Alphin's *Simon Says* (Harcourt, 2002) is a thoughtful novel about a brooding sixteen-year-old boy who enters a boarding school for the arts.

Shadow People (Delacorte, 2000) by Joyce McDonald is a tense story of violence created by four angry and frustrated teens.

After he is involved in a deadly accident, Matt struggles with his guilt while spending a summer working for his girlfriend's mother in Nancy Woodruff's *Someone Else's Child* (Simon, 2000).

About the Author and Book
Authors and Artists for Young Adults. Gale. Vol. 8, 1992; vol. 46, 2002.
Children's Books and Their Creators. Houghton, 1995.
Children's Literature Review. Vol. 78, Gale, 2002.
Contemporary Authors New Revision Series. Vol. 77, Gale, 1999.
Continuum Encyclopedia of Children's Literature. Continuum, 2001.
Drew, Bernard A. *100 Most Popular Young Adult Authors.* Libraries Unlimited, 1996.
Favorite Children's Authors and Illustrators. Vol. 4, Tradition Books, 2003.
Fourth Book of Junior Authors and Illustrators. Wilson, 1978.
Gillespie, John T., and Corinne J. Naden. *Characters in Young Adult Literature.* Gale, 1997.
Jones, Raymond E. *Characters in Children's Literature.* Gale, 1997.
Lives and Works: Young Adult Authors. Vol. 5, Grolier, 1999.
Major Authors and Illustrators for Children and Young Adults (1st ed.). Vol. 4, Gale, 1993.
Major Authors and Illustrators for Children and Young Adults (2nd ed.). Vol. 5, Gale, 2002.
Ninth Book of Junior Authors and Illustrators. Wilson, 2004.
St. James Guide to Children's Writers (5th ed.). St. James, 1999.
St. James Guide to Young Adult Writers (2nd ed.). St. James, 1999.
Something About the Author. Gale. Vol. 14, 1978; vol. 69, 1992; vol. 119, 2001.
Twentieth-Century Young Adult Writers (1st ed.). St. James, 1994.
Writers for Young Adults. Vol. 2, Scribner, 1997.
See also listing "Selected Web Sites on Children's Literature and Authors."

Mazer, Norma Fox. *Silver.* HarperTrophy, 1988. Pap. $5.95, 0-380-75026-0 (Grades 6–10).

Introduction
Norma Fox Mazer (1931–), whose husband is the equally famous young adult writer Harry Mazer, has many distinguished novels for teenagers to her credit. In them she explores the problems and pleasures of the period of maturation and self-discovery known as adolescence. In addition to themes relating to growing up, she often delves into complex family relationships. For example, in an earlier novel, *After the Rain* (Morrow, 1987), teenager Rachel feels responsible for caring for Izzy, her terminally ill grandfather. However, Izzy is completely unlovable. He is a tyrannical, demanding, selfish old man. The conflicts that Rachel feels in this situation are realistically portrayed. In *Silver*, Sarabeth, the central character, has only a single parent, her mother, and many of her friends who are children of divorce also face family problems. *Silver* is told from a first-person point of view and takes place over a period of four months. It is suitable for readers in grades six through ten.

Principal Characters
Sarabeth Silver, a teenager who lives in a trailer park with her mother
Janie, Sarabeth's young mother
Cynthia and Billy, their friends in the park
Leo, a chimney sweep
Grant Varrow, a wealthy schoolmate
Mark Emelsky, a young man Sarabeth likes
Patty, a troubled teenager

Plot Summary
Sarabeth and her mother, Janie, who was just sixteen when her daughter was born, live in a trailer park. Sarabeth's father, Ben Silver, was killed in an auto accident only three and a half years after she was born. Janie cleans houses to earn money for food and rent. They are poor but there is great love in the household. Both Sarabeth and her mother have learned to accept their situation and feel grateful that they have each other. Janie has a boyfriend named Leo, who is a chimney sweep by trade. Sarabeth and her mother also have good friends in the trailer park, including Cynthia and her husband Billy.

Shortly before Sarabeth is due to enter junior high school, Janie discovers that the local school district boundaries cut through the trailer park.

When a trailer in the upper part of the park becomes vacant, they move in so Sarabeth can attend the much superior Drumline schools. There, Sarabeth is drawn to classmate Grant Varrow, a beautiful girl of obvious wealth.

Sarabeth attends a school dance and meets a somewhat rabbity-looking boy named Mark Emelsky. He is a vegetarian. He impresses Sarabeth because they share open, friendly attitudes toward people and life.

Sarabeth accidentally learns that her mother has had to borrow money from Cynthia, their friend in the park. To help out, Sarabeth secretly takes a job cleaning a neighbor's trailer. Janie finds out and is so angry that she slaps her daughter. Cynthia brings about a reconciliation.

Mark calls Sarabeth and after the conversation she grabs a pillow and imagines what his kisses would be like. She slowly becomes friends with Grant, who she discovers is also missing a father. Sarabeth begins having lunch with Grant and her friends Asa, Jennifer, and Patty. One day while talking about boys, Sarabeth lets slip that Mark has kissed her, but before she can explain it was really only a pillow, she has suddenly acquired great status with the group and is too embarrassed to tell the truth. Grant insists that she come to a pajama party at Patty's. They all have a splendid time. During the evening, Sarabeth—called Silver by the group—reveals the truth about Mark the Pillow.

At a concert that Patty, Grant, and Sarabeth attend, Patty, who is given to black moods, shows signs of stress. During intermission, she breaks down and confesses to Sarabeth that she is being sexually abused by her uncle and her mother does not believe her. Grant and Sarabeth try to get help, even going to the school library in an abortive attempt to find written advice. When another attack occurs, Patty vows she will not return to her uncle's home, where she lives. Sarabeth takes her to her trailer, tells her mother Patty's story, and begs that Patty be allowed to stay. Patty's mother is called but steadfastly protects her brother until Patty jumps out of a trailer window and breaks her foot. Only then, with her daughter at her feet in agony, is Patty's mother able to accept the truth.

Patty stays with the Silvers until her mother can find a job and a new home. It is not an easy time for any of them: three people in a tiny trailer (not to mention the cat Tobias and his catch of the day), with Patty still suffering bouts of depression and uncertainty. However, after a month, Patty's mother is able to take her daughter to a new home. Prompted by the mutual outrage of all Patty's close friends, Asa tells her father, Judge Goronkian, about the attacks and a criminal charge is brought against Patty's uncle.

After many attempts at building a friendship with Mark, including a date in which there is a real kiss, Sarabeth realizes he is attracted to someone else. Anyway, there are lots of other boys around and, in addition to her mother, she now has some new friends to rely on.

Themes and Subjects
In this novel, a sensitive, outgoing young girl faces economic hardships and difficult social adjustments. In overcoming them, she finds friendship and a degree of maturity. The story shows that wealth and position do not guarantee happiness and security. The power of love and the inner strength it brings are well shown in Sarabeth's relationship with her mother. The effects of divorce and the important role fathers play in the development of young girls are well portrayed. Sexual abuse and its consequences are realistically but sensitively handled. Other important themes are friendship, poverty, snobbery, and boy-girl relationships.

Booktalk Material
An introduction to Sarabeth and her situation on entering junior high school should interest readers. Some important passages are: poverty in the Silver household (pp. 1–5); Sarabeth dreams of a friendship with Grant (pp. 20–27); Sarabeth cleans the neighbor's trailer and her mother's reaction (pp. 67–72); the reconciliation (pp. 75–82); and Patty tells about her Uncle Paul (pp. 161–69).

Additional Selections
Peter, who lives with his mother and verbally abusive stepfather, sets out to find the truth about his dead father in David Patneaude's *Framed in Fire* (Whitman, 1999).

Kelly, fifteen, slowly comes to realize she is not alone as she recovers from the sexual abuse inflicted by her father in Beth Goobie's *Who Owns Kelly Paddik?* (Orca, 2003).

Twelve-year-old Tex, who has a growing interest in sex, is horrified to learn that his stepsister is being sexually abused in Tim Johnston's *Never So Green* (Farrar, 2002).

In Eve Bunting's *Is Anybody There?* (Harper, 1988), Marcus, a latchkey kid, believes someone has been coming into the house while he and his mother are away.

About the Author and Book
Authors and Artists for Young People. Gale. Vol. 5, 1991; vol. 36, 2001.
Children's Books and Their Creators. Houghton, 1995.
Children's Literature Review. Vol. 23, Gale, 1991.

Contemporary Authors New Revision Series. Vol. 129, Gale, 2004.
Continuum Encyclopedia of Children's Literature. Continuum, 2001.
Drew, Bernard A. *100 Most Popular Young Adult Authors.* Libraries Unlimited, 1997.
Fifth Book of Junior Authors and Illustrators. Wilson, 1983.
Holtze, Sally Holmes. *Presenting Norma Fox Mazer.* Twayne, 1987.
Lives and Works: Young Adult Authors. Vol. 5, Grolier, 1999.
Major Authors and Illustrators for Children and Young Adults (1st ed.). Vol. 4, Gale, 1993.
Major Authors and Illustrators for Children and Young Adults (2nd ed.). Vol. 5, Gale, 2002.
Mazer, Norma Fox. "Silent Censorship," *School Library Journal,* Aug., 1996, p. 42.
St. James Guide to Young Adult Writers (2nd ed.). St. James, 1999.
Something About the Author. Gale. Vol. 24, 1981; vol. 67, 1992; vol. 105, 1999.
Something About the Author Autobiography Series. Vol. 1, Gale, 1986.
Twentieth-Century Young Adult Writers (1st ed.). St. James, 1994.
Writers for Young Adults. Vol. 3, Scribner, 1997.
See also listing "Selected Web Sites on Children's Literature and Authors."

Peck, Robert Newton. *A Day No Pigs Would Die.* Knopf, 1972. $25, 0-394-48235-2 (Grade 7–Adult).

Introduction

Robert Newton Peck (1928–) has lived as colorful a life as any of his many literary creations. His many occupations include stints as a lumberjack, soldier, hog butcher, owner of a publishing company, and paper mill worker.

> 'Tis the gift to be simple
> 'Tis the gift to be free
> 'Tis the gift to come down
> Where we ought to be.

These opening lines of the Shaker hymn "Simple Gifts" describe the honest and wholesome values under which Robert Peck was raised. This novel, his first, takes us back to a gentler and less complicated period—the locale is rural Vermont and the time is the late 1920s. The story, as told by Rob, begins when he is a boy of twelve and ends one year later when he suddenly has to assume a man's responsibilities after the death and burial of his saintly father, who was the hog butcher in the area. Although this touching novel was originally written for adults, both junior and senior high school students enjoy it.

TEENAGE LIFE AND CONCERNS • 47

Principal Characters
Rob Peck, a young Shaker boy in New England in the 1920s
Ben Tanner, his neighbor
Rob's father
Aunt Mattie

Plot Summary
One lovely New England spring day, Rob Peck becomes so furious at the teasing he receives because of his plain Shaker clothes that he plays hooky after recess. On his way home he sees Apron, the prime Holstein cow of his neighbor, Ben Tanner, struggling with a difficult labor. Fearful that the calf will choke before being born, Rob ties one end of his trouser to a tree and the other around the calf's head and then beats Apron into motion. It works. The calf is born alive, but suddenly Apron begins choking. Robert reaches into her gullet and yanks out a hard ball of matter. But the cow bites his arm severely and stomps him unconscious.

The ball of matter was a goiter and its removal saved Apron's life, but young Rob must spend a week in bed recovering. In appreciation, Tanner wants to give Rob a piglet, but Rob's father insists that it is not the Shaker way to accept gifts for neighborly acts. Tanner than claims it is only a birthday present for Rob, who joyously accepts the gift—the first thing he has really wanted and owned.

Rob spends most of his spare time with his pet, named Pinky, who lives in a nearby unused cow crib. He takes her into the woods with him and together they explore nature. Rob confides to Pinky things he couldn't to a human friend.

While Pinky is growing to maturity, many events take place that involve the Peck household. One stormy night Rob and his father prevent their neighbor from digging up the body of his illegitimate daughter. Another time Rob witnesses the bloody and brutal matching of a weasel and young terrier in an enclosed barrel. But there are good and humorous times too—Pinky wins a 4H blue ribbon and Aunt Mattie tries to show Rob how to diagram a sentence but decides it would be easier to teach Pinky. And, tragically, Rob learns one night that his father's health is poor and that he will die soon.

After unsuccessful attempts at breeding, Rob realizes that Pinky is barren. The apple crop is bad that fall and the hunting season brings no meat to the Peck table. On a mid-December morning with little food left in the larder, his father turns to Rob and says, "Let's get it done." The boy knows his father's meaning. Although his heart is breaking, Rob helps him in killing and dressing his pet. It is the only time the boy ever saw his father cry.

In late spring, Rob's father dies in his sleep. Rob automatically assumes the responsibilities of heading the household. He arranges for the funeral and digs his father's grave in the orchard. That night, when he is alone after the service, Robert Peck walks to the orchard to say his last farewell to his father.

Themes and Subjects
Besides presenting one of the most tender pictures of family life in all young adult literature, particularly of a close father-son relationship, this book movingly re-creates a way of living governed by simple virtues and truths. The passage from boyhood to manhood is also touchingly portrayed. The reader gets a glimpse into Shaker beliefs and the graphic realities of farm life. Other subjects covered are rural American life in the 1920s and a boy's close attachment to his pet.

Booktalk Material
Episodic in form, the book contains many incidents that are complete in themselves, such as: Rob's first encounter with Apron (pp. 3–8); Mr. Tanner gives Pinky to Rob (pp. 21–23); Rob talks with his father about baseball and elections (pp. 32–37); and Rob diagrams a sentence (pp. 52–60).

Additional Selections
An unloving grandfather is only one of many problems a fourteen-year-old boy encounters when he goes to live on his grandparents' farm in Oregon in Winifred Morris's *Liar* (Walker, 1996).

In Will Weaver's *Striking Out* (Harper, 1993), farm boy Billy Baggs begins a baseball career in spite of his parents' lack of enthusiasm.

A fourteen-year-old discovers a new life when he accepts an invitation from his grandmother to spend time on her northern Minnesota farm in Gary Paulsen's *Alida's Song* (Delacorte, 1999).

The story of the Shakers from their origins in England to their history in the United States is covered in *The Shakers* (Watts, 1997) by Jean K. Williams.

About the Author and Book
Authors and Artists for Young Adults. Gale. Vol. 3, 1990; vol. 43, 2002.
Children's Literature Review. Gale. Vol. 45, 1998; vol. 156, 2005.
Contemporary Authors. Vol. 182, Gale, 2002.
Continuum Encyclopedia of Children's Literature. Continuum, 2001.
Drew, Bernard A. *100 Most Popular Young Adult Authors.* Libraries Unlimited, 1996.

TEENAGE LIFE AND CONCERNS • 49

Fifth Book of Junior Authors and Illustrators. Wilson, 1983.
Gallo, Donald R. *Speaking for Ourselves.* National Council of Teachers of English, 1990.
Gillespie, John T., and Corinne J. Naden. *Characters in Young Adult Literature.* Gale, 1997.
Jones, Raymond E. *Characters in Children's Literature.* Gale, 1997.
Lives and Works: Young Adult Authors. Vol. 6, Grolier, 1999.
McElmeel, Sharron L. *100 Most Popular Children's Authors.* Libraries Unlimited, 1999.
Major Authors and Illustrators for Children and Young Adults (1st ed.). Vol. 5, Gale, 1993.
Major Authors and Illustrators for Children and Young Adults (2nd ed.). Vol. 6, Gale, 2002.
St. James Guide to Young Adult Writers (2nd ed.). St. James, 1999.
Something About the Author. Gale. Vol. 21, 1980; vol. 62, 1990; vol. 108, 2000; vol. 111, 2000.
Something About the Author Autobiography Series. Vol. 1, Gale, 1986.
Stevens, Jen. *The Undergraduate's Companion to Children's Writers and Their Web Sites.* Libraries Unlimited, 2004.
Twentieth-Century Young Adult Writers (1st ed.). St. James, 1994.
Writers for Young Adults. Vol. 3, Scribner, 1997.
www.blahnik.info/rnpeck (personal Web site)
See also listing "Selected Web Sites on Children's Literature and Authors."

Rodgers, Mary. *Freaky Friday.* HarperCollins, 1972. $16.89, 0-06-025049-6 (Grades 6–9).

Introduction

Mary Rodgers, the daughter of composer Richard Rodgers, is a woman of many talents. As well as raising a family (one of her sons is the distinguished Broadway composer Adam Guettel, of *A Light in the Piazza* fame), she has written several books for children and young adults as well as the music for such shows as *Once Upon a Mattress.* The terrifically funny and inventive fantasy *Freaky Friday,* her first novel for older children, was a tremendous success when it was published, and it has been filmed twice by Hollywood. Annabel, the heroine of the novel, has a fourteen-year-old neighbor, Boris, with a severe adenoidal condition. Boris later became the central character in *A Billion for Boris* (Harper, 1974), an uproarious sequel that features a television set capable of delivering tomorrow's news. What one critic said of *A Billion for Boris* applies equally to *Freaky Friday*: "[It] assumes an urban and sophisticated frame of reference on the part of the reader and evokes so much New York City local color that it really is the perfect New York City book." Upper elementary and junior high readers enjoy these books.

Principal Characters
    Annabel Andrews, thirteen, and in rebellion against all authority
    Mrs. Andrews, in constant conflict with her daughter
    Ben, Annabel's six-year-old brother
    Bill Andrews, Annabel's father
    Boris Harris, Annabel's fourteen-year-old neighbor

Plot Summary
One Thursday night, thirteen-year-old, self-willed Annabel Andrews has another of those persistent disagreements with her mother. They focus on four subjects: Annabel's sloppy appearance; the tidiness, or lack of it, of her room; the junk food she eats; and, most of all, her freedom. Her mother doesn't like her to attend kissing parties with friends in Greenwich Village or to walk alone in Central Park. In short, Annabel is in the throes of a teenage rebellion against all authority, against the private school she attends, and against her parents and docile six-year-old brother Ben, who she calls Ape Face. Things would be different if she were in her mother's place!

    Annabel awakens on Friday to find that a transformation has occurred—she has turned into her mother! Welcoming the idea of a day of freedom and retribution, she awakens her "supercool" father (now husband) Bill Andrews, an advertising executive, and begins preparing breakfast. Ape Face appears and greets his mommy as usual. Warily, Annabel peers into her room. Who could that marshmallow-chomping, comic-book-reading ogress be? Certainly not her mother—she loathes marshmallows. Without too many incidents, she gets the kids off to school and Bill to work.

    Her quiet morning is broken by a surprise visit from her neighbor, fourteen-year-old Boris Harris, who has a severe adenoidal condition. Annabel has an unrequited crush on Boris and can't resist, in her mother's guise, making a few complimentary remarks on her own behalf.

    When Boris leaves, she starts the laundry. She overloads the machine with both clothes and detergent, and soon the kitchen is awash with water and soap suds. At this point Mrs. Rose Schmauss, their cleaning lady, arrives. But when Rose begins lecturing her employer about what a pig her daughter is and falsely accuses Annabel of drinking the family gin (Rose is actually the tippler), they argue, and Annabel, in a fit of self-righteous wrath, fires her.

To calm herself, Annabel goes to the store and on her way home meets Ape Face returning from nursery school. She tries to call him Ben and feeds him a lunch of cold macaroni. Ben confides to her that he really loves and admires his sister and wishes she would be kinder to him. In spite of her callous exterior, Annabel is touched by her brother's love.

Mr. Andrews calls to say he is bringing two clients home for dinner, the Framptons. He reminds her that she has an appointment at school to discuss Annabel's record. Annabel asks Boris to babysit Ben.

At school, Annabel learns that her double has played truant. The officials also discuss Annabel's dismal school record. The school psychiatrist suggests the problem may be in the Andrews's home life. Annabel stoutly defends the Andrews and sincerely promises to change Annabel's attitudes and work habits.

Back home, Ben is missing. Boris says a beautiful chick appeared at the door and took him. The Framptons soon arrive. Dismayed and despairing, Annabel rushes to her bedroom and begs for the spell to be broken. Suddenly her mother is sitting beside her and Annabel is the real Annabel again. Her mother has spent the day as her daughter having her hair fixed, buying some snappy clothes, and getting the orthodontist to remove her braces. She returned as the "beautiful chick" Boris saw. Ben is back, the Framptons are appeased, and Annabel has a wonderful time with Boris. She even finds out that his name is really Morris—it's those adenoids again. Although she has learned many valuable lessons from this experience, she never finds out how her mother was able to produce such a "freaky Friday."

Themes and Subjects
Annabel has the rare opportunity of seeing herself as others see her. On the surface, this is a delightful, often hilarious fantasy, but it also makes some valid points about the generation gap and family relationships. Youngsters will identify with both Annabel's rebelliousness and her growing sense of responsibility and compassion.

Booktalk Material
A brief description of the role change between mother and daughter can be used to introduce the book. Other passages for a booktalk are: the transformation (pp. 1–2; also for pap. ed.); breakfast (pp. 11–14); Boris appears (pp. 27–30); and Ben talks about his love for Annabel (pp. 56–59).

Additional Selections

Norbert, the alien who lives in Alan's nose, helps the boy when he goes on a camping trip in the humorous *Noses Are Red* (Tundra, 2002) by Richard Scrimger.

In Phyllis Reynolds Naylor's *Simply Alice* (Simon, 2002), Alice, a ninth-grader, is dealing with family, friendships, and embarrassing situations in the lighthearted continuation of a lengthy series.

Through the help of his dream girl, a puny youngster tries a regime of body development in Karen T. Taha's *Marshmallow Muscles, Banana Brainstorms* (Harcourt, 1988).

A spunky girl who lives with her widowed father is transported back in time via her apartment building's elevator in Edward Ormondroyd's *Time at the Top* (Purple House, 1963).

About the Author and Book

Children's Literature Review. Vol. 20, Gale, 1990.
Contemporary Authors New Revision Series. Vol. 90, Gale, 2000.
Fifth Book of Junior Authors and Illustrators. Wilson, 1983.
Jones, Raymond E. *Characters in Children's Literature.* Gale, 1997.
Major Authors and Illustrators for Children and Young Adults (1st ed.). Vol. 5, Gale, 1993.
Major Authors and Illustrators for Children and Young Adults (2nd ed.). Vol. 7, Gale, 2002.
St. James Guide to Children's Writers (5th ed.). St. James, 1999.
Something About the Author. Gale. Vol. 8, 1976; vol. 130, 2002.
Twentieth-Century Children's Writers (4th ed.). St. James, 1995.
See also listing "Selected Web Sites on Children's Literature and Authors."

Rylant, Cynthia. *A Fine White Dust.* Atheneum, 2000 (1986). $16, 0-689-84087-X (Grades 7–10).

Introduction

Cynthia Rylant (1954–) frequently uses scenes from her childhood in her work. She grew up as part of a large family in Appalachia, where she lived with several other family members in a four-room house without running water. She was eventually able to attend college and for a time worked as a college English teacher and a librarian. In the years that she has been writing books for young people, she has scored amazing successes at various levels. For the primary ages, she has written several prize-winning texts for picture books, including two Caldecott Honor Books and the charming series of Henry and Mudge books. For an older audience, she is best known for the Newbery Medal-winning *Missing May* (Orchard, 1992), a moving novel of love, death, and grieving. *A Fine White Dust*, a Newbery Honor Book for 1987, contains many elements typical of this author's innovative and powerful novels, including a young, sensitive central character who is coping with disillusionment and difficult situations. Although there is no happy ending, there is a resolution and hope in this novel suitable for readers in grades seven through ten.

Principal Characters
    Pete Cassidy, a thirteen-year-old in North Carolina
    Mother and Pop, his parents
    The Man, a preacher
    Rufus, Pete's atheist friend

Plot Summary
Thirteen-year-old Pete Cassidy has a growing interest in attending church, which he does by himself in his small hometown in North Carolina. He can't say exactly why he felt he couldn't stay home on Sunday mornings, but he began to invite himself to church with the neighbors and then started going by himself when he was in the fourth grade. Mother and Pop have never cared about formal religion and don't even like to talk about it, so they were mildly surprised when Pete showed an interest, but did not interfere.

    One day Pete sees a hitchhiker outside town. There is something different about him. A few days later, in the town drugstore, Pete sees the Man again. He knows this is no ordinary stranger; he has light blue eyes and a special kind of look. To Pete, it is like a small explosion. The Man just seems to swallow him up. At first, Pete wonders if he isn't some kind of crazy strangler. In fact, Pete is kind of glad that his best friend, Rufus, a confirmed atheist, comes in at that point and gets him away from the Man's stare.

    At a revival meeting one hot, steamy night, the assistant pastor introduces the revival preacher and—to Pete's astonishment—it turns out to be the Man. The Man puts his hands on Pete's head and asks him if he has been a sinner. Pete admits he has. The Man tells him he has been born again, and Pete faints. When he wakes up he knows he has been "saved." Never in his thirteen years has he felt such happiness. But the next morning, when Pete tells his parents that he has been saved, there is some friction. Pete becomes more critical of his parents' irreligious attitudes. He also tells Rufus that he has been saved and their conversation ends in a falling out between the two old friends. This doesn't matter to Pete, who is certain he is in the right. He will go his own way.

Pretty soon, going "his own way" means running away with the Man, who offers him the opportunity to travel, see the world, spread the word, and save people. The Man says he hates to see Pete's life wasted; if he goes with the preacher, he will help to save so many. Spellbound, Pete is willing to leave his home and go with the Man. He agrees to meet the preacher after a prayer meeting. He leaves a note for his parents and even sees Rufus, telling him that he is leaving after the revival meeting.

Pete goes to the appointed spot, but the Man never shows up. Rufus appears instead and tells Pete to go home. The Man, it seems, has already left town with a girl named Darlene Cook. Apparently he forgot all about Pete Cassidy.

Pete is stunned. He cries like a baby, and it takes some time before he is able to straighten out his emotions. After about three weeks, Darlene comes back to town. She won't explain where she has been. The town speculates that the Man was a devil in disguise or that he cast a spell upon the girl.

Pete decides that he doesn't hate the Man for leaving, figuring the preacher just wanted to find someone to erase his loneliness. In the meantime, Pete has learned to appreciate his life. He has a mother and father who care about him; he has a best friend, too. Rufus may be a hard-nosed atheist, but Pete figures he's a good, honest person and friend. After his experiences with the Man, Pete keeps his religion more to himself. He knows he needs God, but he doesn't need the church quite as much as he once did. Symbolically, at the end of the story he throws out the broken pieces of a ceramic cross that belonged to the Man. To Pete, they're now just pieces of fine white dust.

Themes and Subjects

Pete Cassidy is portrayed as a serious young man with an interest in religion, an interest that leads him to become spellbound by the attentions of the mysterious preacher who comes to town. Through his disappointment, he learns that religion is a private decision. It is part of him and will grow with him. But he also learns that he must allow others to keep their private decisions to themselves, including his own parents and his best friend.

Booktalk Material

Pete's feelings about religion set the tone for the novel (pp. 4–7). Other important passages are: Pete meets the Man (pp. 8–10); Pete is saved (p.

21); he has a row with Rufus (pp. 39–44); Pete agrees to go away with the Man (pp. 55–57); Rufus tells him the Man has left town (pp. 79–82); and the letter to his parents (pp. 83–85).

Additional Selections

In Kathryn Lasky's *Memories of a Bookbait* (Harcourt, 1994), a free-thinking teen rejects the religious beliefs of her parents.

Two teenagers meet and fall in love in spite of conflicting religious backgrounds, one the evangelical mission and the other the TV pulpit, in M. E. Kerr's *What I Really Think of You* (Harper, 1982).

After joining a circus to escape his dreary life, a fourteen-year-old boy learns about the meaning of courage and faith from the evangelist D. L. Moody in Dave Jackson's *Danger on the Flying Trapeze* (Bethany House, 1995).

In John H. Ritter's *Choosing Up Sides* (Putnam, 1998), Jake's father, a preacher, forbids his son to pitch with his left hand because he believes it is an instrument of Satan.

About the Author and Book

Authors and Artists for Young Adults. Gale. Vol. 10, 1993; vol. 45, 2002.
Biography for Beginners. Favorable Impressions, 2005.
Biography Today: Author Series. Vol. 1, Omnigraphics, 1995.
Bostrom, Kathleen Long. *Winning Authors: Profiles of the Newbery Medalists.* Libraries Unlimited, 2003.
Children's Books and Their Creators. Houghton, 1995.
Children's Literature Review. Gale. Vol. 15, 1988; vol. 86, 2003.
Contemporary Authors New Revision Series. Vol. 74, Gale, 1999.
Continuum Encyclopedia of Children's Literature. Continuum, 2001.
Drew, Bernard. A. *100 Most Popular Young Adult Authors.* Libraries Unlimited, 1996.
Favorite Children's Authors and Illustrators. Vol. 5, Tradition Books, 2003
Gallo, Donald R. *Speaking for Ourselves, Too.* National Council of Teachers of English, 1993.
Gillespie, John T., and Corinne J. Naden. *Characters in Young Adult Literature.* Galc, 1997.
Jones, Raymond E. *Characters in Children's Literature.* Gale, 1997.
Lives and Works: Young Adult Authors. Vol. 7, Grolier, 1999.
McElmeel, Sharron L. *100 Most Popular Children's Authors.* Libraries Unlimited, 1999.
Major Authors and Illustrators for Children and Young Adults (1st ed.). Vol. 5, Gale, 1993.
Major Authors and Illustrators for Children and Young Adults (2nd ed.). Vol. 7, Gale, 2002.
Meet the Author: Cynthia Rylant. SRA/McGraw-Hill, videocassette, 1990.
Rylant, Cynthia. *Best Wishes.* R. C. Owen, 1992.

———. *But I'll Be Back Again.* Orchard, 1989.
St. James Guide to Children's Writers (5th ed.). St. James, 1999.
St. James Guide to Young Adult Writers (2nd ed.). St. James, 1999.
Sixth Book of Junior Authors and Illustrators. Wilson, 1989.
Something About the Author. Gale. Vol. 50, 1988; vol. 76, 1994; vol. 112, 2000; vol. 160, 2005.
Something About the Author Autobiographical Series. Vol. 13, Gale, 1992.
Twentieth-Century Children's Writers (4th ed.). St. James, 1995.
Twentieth-Century Young Adult Writers (1st ed.). St. James, 1994.
Ward, Diane. "Cynthia Rylant," *Horn Book,* July/Aug., 1993, pp. 420–23.
Writers for Young Adults. Supp. 1, Scribner, 2000.
www.cynthiarylant.com (personal Web site)
See also listing "Selected Web Sites on Children's Literature and Authors."

Swarthout, Glendon. *Bless the Beasts and Children.* Pocket, 1995 (1970). Pap. $6.99, 0-671-52151-9 (Grade 7–Adult).

Introduction

Glendon Swarthout (1918–92) was born in Pinckney, Michigan. After serving in the army during World War II, he became an English professor at Michigan State and later at Arizona State. He used both Michigan and the American West as locales for many of his novels, several of which were made into successful movies. Among them were *They Came to Cordura* and *The Shootist*, starring John Wayne. His novel about the shenanigans in Fort Lauderdale, Florida, during college spring break, *Where the Boys Are*, was also a popular film. Among his many writing awards were the Western Writers of America Spur Award and the Owen Wister Lifetime Achievement Award. His most acclaimed and distinguished work is *Bless the Beasts and Children*, which also became a well-received film. It is the moving story of a group of unlikely heroes, a collection of misfit adolescents sent to a summer camp in Arizona, who concoct a bizarre plan to save a herd of buffalo. Originally intended for adults, it is enjoyed by both junior and senior high school readers.

Principal Characters

John Cotton, a tough, resilient fifteen-year-old at a camp in Arizona
His five rebellious, obnoxious bunk mates
Wheaties, their camp counselor
A herd of buffalo

Plot Summary

Box Canyon Boys Camp—whose motto is "Send Us a Boy—We'll Send You a Cowboy!"—is located in the Arizona mountains near Prescott. At a handsome price for eight weeks each summer, the camp accepts thirty-six scions of wealthy Easterners. There are six boys and a counselor in each cabin. No formal room assignments are made, but during the first week, by a method known as the "shake down," each boy is to choose the friends with whom he will share a cabin.

Fifteen-year-old John Cotton finds himself bunking with five obnoxious, rebellious misfits—the rejects and unwanteds from other cabins. Cotton realizes he is stuck with a teethgrinder, a headbanger, two bedwetters, one of whom also sucks his thumb, and a nailbiter who overeats. Their lack of ability at organized sports is matched only by their ineptitude in all other camp activities. Their counselor, nicknamed Wheaties because of his "all-American boy" attitude, knows he is stuck with a bunch of goof-balls, whom he calls "dings."

Each week, prizes and Indian tribe names are awarded to the cabins on the basis of points scored in the week's activities. During the first award ceremony, Cotton's cabin is, as expected, lowest, and by camp tradition its residents are dubbed the Bedwetters; their trophy is a chamber pot. At this point, Cotton decides to take charge and become their leader. He is a tough, self-reliant, but compassionate boy who has personal problems of his own, such as his much-married mother, but he rarely speaks of them. Like a drill sergeant, he sets down rules. Slowly the boys begin acting as a team, gradually gaining a little self-respect and independence.

During their last week, the Bedwetters go on an overnight camping trip to the Petrified Forest. On the way back, the boys persuade Wheaties to take a detour to see a herd of buffalo on the state's game preserve. Their visit coincides with the second of a three-day thinning of the herd. Hunters are paid forty dollars each to shoot the captive animals. The boys are sickened and appalled by the slaughter. Back at camp, Goodenow, who is severely maladjusted, upchucks, and that night, Lally 2, infantile and overprotected, tries to run away. The boys sneak out of camp and, after finding him, decide that somehow they must get back to the preserve, some two hours away by car, to free the animals that are to be shot the next day.

The boys take six horses from the corral. Taft steals a rifle and box of ammunition, and Goodenow carries along the buffalo head whose custody the Bedwetters won from the Apaches on a bet. In Prescott, they leave the horses and transfer to a pickup truck, again using Taft's stealing abilities. Against Cotton's better judgment, they stop in Falstaff for hamburgers. They are chased by teenage ruffians, but Taft shoots out one of their tires. One mile from the preserve, the boys run out of gas. To test them, Cotton suggests that they go home, but the others refuse. Cotton is delighted because now they have shown the courage and independence he hoped for. After much difficulty, the buffalo are chased from their pen and wander into a large enclosure from which they must be led in order to escape. With quickness of mind, the boys take one of the preserve's trucks, fill the back with hay, and with the animals following, drive the truck to the end of the compound. There they find the exit blocked by a gate of heavy chains. Cotton takes charge once again. He orders the boys off the truck and drives headlong at the gate, breaking the chains.

Cotton turns the truck around and drives the animals out of the enclosure to safety. But the truck goes out of control and plunges over a steep gorge. When the rangers arrive, they find the remaining five boys red-eyed at their terrible loss, but triumphant in their accomplishment.

Themes and Subjects
The convincing transformation of Bedwetters into heroes through the efforts of an idealistic, courageous young boy is told effectively and, despite the story's tragic ending, with a great amount of humor. Throughout, the author makes a searing indictment of our treatment of natural resources, including wildlife, and paints a scathing picture of the tawdry communities that have destroyed the natural beauty of the West. Anyone who has lived through summer camp will find the details of life at Box Canyon both realistic and full of insight.

Booktalk Material
The author's outcry at the shame of the buffalo slaughter is given on page 110. Other important passages are: the "shake down" into various cabins (pp. 24–26); the awarding of prizes (pp. 32–33); Wheaties is tamed (pp. 48–49); Cotton takes over (pp. 61–63); and stealing the trophies (pp. 134–36).

Additional Selections
Randall R. Platt's *The Cornerstone* (Catbird, 1998) tells how a tough fifteen-year-old charity case changes during his stay at summer camp.

Before Wings (Orca, 2001) by Beth Goobie tells the absorbing story of counselors at a summer camp and of fifteen-year-old Adrien who has mystical experiences.

Prospector Cloyd Atcitty spends a winter in the Colorado mountains to save two grizzly bears in Will Hobb's *Beardance* (Atheneum, 1993).

In *Caribou Crossing* (Winter Wren, 2001), a fast-paced thriller by Kim Heacox, environmentalists are pitted against big oil interests to save a fragile environment.

About the Author and Book
Authors and Artists for Young Adults. Vol. 55, Gale, 2004.
Contemporary Authors New Revision Series. Vol. 47, Gale, 1995.
Fourth Book of Junior Authors and Illustrators. Wilson, 1978.
St. James Guide to Young Adult Writers (2nd ed.). St. James, 1999.
Something About the Author. Vol. 26, Gale, 1982.
Twentieth-Century Young Adult Writers (1st ed.). St. James, 1994.
See also listing "Selected Web Sites on Children's Literature and Authors."

Townsend, Sue. *The Adrian Mole Diaries.* HarperPerennial, 1997 (1986). Pap. $12.95, 0-380-73044-8 (Grade 7–Adult).

Introduction
Sue Townsend (1946–) is an English writer who currently lives in Leicester. Her books about Adrian Mole (which now number six) have sold millions of copies on both sides of the Atlantic. The first two, *The Secret Diary of Adrian Mole, Aged 13¾* and *The Growing Pains of Adrian Mole*, are both included in this omnibus volume. They deal in an uproarious fashion with a boy's journey through darkest adolescence where he has to overcome numerous school and family crises, often with the help of his girlfriend Pandora. The author reputedly based these books of her son's experiences and misadventures at Mary Linwood Comprehensive School in Leicester. Several of the teachers who appear in the books, including Mr. Dick and Miss Fossington-Gore, are supposedly based on staff members who worked at the school in the early 1980s.

It should be mentioned that, in his diaries, Adrian is obsessed with sex, his virginal status, and the length of his penis. Subsequent volumes in the series continue Adrian Mole's journey through nerddom. In the latest, *Adrian Mole and the Weapons of Mass Destruction* (Soho, 2005), he is a solo father in his thirties who works in a secondhand bookshop. These books are enjoyed by adults and mature teenagers.

Principal Characters

Adrian Mole, an irrepressible fourteen-year-old boy in England
Bert, his eighty-nine-year-old, chain-smoking friend
Pandora, a new girl in Adrian's class
Rosie, his new baby sister
Queenie, who marries Bert

Plot Summary

The center of this story, set in England, is Adrian Mole. He is pimply-faced and nearly fourteen years old; above all, he is a worrier. There is almost nothing that Adrian does not worry about. He is overly concerned about nearly every facet of his existence, all of which he confides to his diary, whose entries make up this hilarious book.

Mainly Adrian worries about himself. He has a terrible complexion. It is a fact that certain parts of his body don't seem to keep still. It is also a fact that his voice fails him at embarrassing moments. Another consuming worry is that certainly he must be the only virgin in his class. He worries about his parents; Adrian is an only child and his mother and father are about to break up. His parents are a bit unconventional anyway, so Adrian always worries that he isn't getting the proper nutrition. He worries that Britons don't show the proper respect for the forthcoming marriage of Lady Diana Spencer, and he worries because his eighty-nine-year-old, chain-smoking friend Bert is about to go off to a nursing home.

Adrian also worries about his career. He is convinced that he is turning into an intellectual. However, so far he has remained undiscovered by the world at large. Therefore, he regularly sends off letters and poems to the BBC on brightly colored stationery and, surprisingly, receives some rather interesting replies, which Adrian interprets in his own way.

There is, however, a brighter side to Adrian's existence. There is Pandora, a new girl in his class. Adrian is in love. And even though, as he admits, she is of a "higher social class," it seems that Adrian's feelings of devotion are returned. Adrian soon discovers, however, that being in love with Pandora and having his feelings returned do not change his virgin status.

With his diary entries reflecting both the pretensions of daily life and the confusing world of the adolescent, Adrian lurches through his rocky existence, meeting disaster at every turn, and in between wilting for love of Pandora. His parents do break up—for a time—and Adrian suffers through his mother's affair with "creep Lucas" and his father's dalliance with a "stick insect." But soon after his parents are reunited, Adrian is in for another shock. He is going to be a brother—as though he doesn't have enough problems.

But to Adrian's surprise, "Rosie" quite captivates him, and with the almost constant commotion at his house and between his parents, he often finds himself taking care of the infant. He checks Rosie's pulse frequently to make sure she is breathing properly.

Adrian is also fairly well occupied outside of his home life. His friend Bert, at eighty-nine, gets married to Queenie, who later has a stroke and dies. Bert is in a wheelchair, so Adrian takes care of him (and his dog) a lot (with Bert complaining loudly all the while). The Moles' own dog gives him lots of trouble too. The dog is always knocking something over or is at the vet.

As if all this weren't enough, Adrian Mole must contend with having his tonsils out, rejections of his poems, being picked on by a class bully, a short sojourn with a "gang," which Adrian finds not to his liking, a very rocky romance with Pandora, and a visit from a rather obnoxious American acquaintance. But somehow one gets the feeling that the irrepressible Adrian Mole will carry on for dear old England and the intellectuals out there.

Themes and Subjects
The entries in Adrian Mole's diary are sometimes touching in their naïveté and deeply affecting as the young man pours out his worries and his feelings about a life that does seem rather fraught with crises, imagined and real. The entries also reveal the intimate life of a working-class English family somehow bumbling through. But most of all, they are very funny; from his constant complaints about his family's lack of a proper diet to his rather calm acceptance of his parents' "drinking problems" to his inability—for all his newfound intellectualism—to ascribe the correct motives to the meanderings in opposite directions of his parents and their love/hate relationship. Adrian is a funny, wonderful character and readers of almost any age will enjoy him.

Booktalk Material
A few of Adrian's diary entries will give the comic flavor of this book and point up the "extent" of his worries. See: the dog in trouble (pp. 14–15); Adrian discovers his intellectual nature and writes a poem (pp. 17–18); Adrian visits Bert (pp. 24–25); Adrian breaks out (p. 44); and Adrian faces divorce (pp. 45–46).

Additional Selections

Told in diary form, Catherine Clark's *Truth or Diary* (Harper, 2000) is a breezy narrative that chronicles Courtney's senior year at her Colorado school.

Junior Bradley Gold represents student interests when his school adopts a code of conduct in the comic novel *Behaving Bradley* (Simon, 1998) by Perry Nodelman.

Angus, Thongs, and Full-Frontal Snogging (HarperCollins, 2000) by Louise Rennison is the first volume in the hilarious series told in diary form about the misadventures of Georgia Nicolson, an English schoolgirl.

Told in alternating chapters by Nicole and Brad, the frantic high school social scene comes alive in Todd Strasser's *Girl Gives Birth to Own Prom Date* (Simon, 1996).

About the Book and Author
Authors and Artists for Young Adults. Vol. 28, Gale, 1999.
Contemporary Authors New Revision Series. Vol. 107, Gale, 2002.
St. James Guide to Young Adult Writers (2nd ed.). St. James, 1999.
Something About the Author. Gale. Vol. 55, 1989; vol. 93, 1997.
www.adrianmole.com (Web site)
See also listing "Selected Web Sites on Children's Literature and Authors."

Wersba, Barbara. *Just Be Gorgeous.* HarperCollins, 1988. $14.95, 0-06-026359-8 (Grades 7–12).

Introduction
Before beginning her writing career, Barbara Wersba (1932–) was a profession actress for fifteen years. While recovering from a serious illness on Martha's Vineyard, she decided to give up the theater and become a writer. The result is a series of excellent books for both children and teenagers. She has written two important trilogies for young adults. The first features Rita Formica and begins with *Fat: A Love Story* (Harper, 1987). *Just Be Gorgeous* is the first volume of the second trilogy, about a Manhattan teenager called Heidi Rosenbloom. In it and its first sequel, *Wonderful Me* (Harper, 1989), she is in conflict with a mother and a father who, respectively, want her to be beautiful and talented. In the third installment, *The Farewell Kid* (Harper, 1990), she has graduated from her disliked private school and is in love with Harvey Beaumont III. They make passionate love and find happiness until his mother, an anti-Semite,

intervenes. These books are both humorous and insightful and are suited to mature readers in junior and senior high schools.

Principal Characters

Heidi Rosenbloom, age sixteen, who attends private school in Manhattan

Heidi's mother, who seems to exist only for shopping

Heidi's father, who lives downtown in the Village

Jeffrey, a gay young man whom Heidi meets on the street

Miss Margolis, Heidi's drama teacher

Plot Summary

This is a warm, funny, tender, bittersweet story of two misfits—Heidi and Jeffrey. Heidi Rosenbloom, age sixteen, considers her life and herself a mess. Her parents are divorced. She lives with her mother in Manhattan, attends private school, and has a dumpy shape. Heidi's mother seems to exist only for shopping at Bloomingdale's. She is forever buying Heidi frilly clothes although what Heidi likes to wear is a man's overcoat purchased at a thrift shop. To Heidi, her mother is seeing someone else every time she looks at her.

Heidi's father, who she sees often as he lives downtown in the Village, doesn't regard Heidi as a beauty. He looks on her as an Einstein and expects her to go to Radcliffe. Heidi is sure she hasn't the qualifications for that either.

One day when Heidi is most depressed, her life changes. As she waits in line at a Broadway theater, she watches a young man with bleached-blond hair dancing on the sidewalks for money. On an impulse, she gives him $5. Heidi is so entranced with his dancing that she asks if she can buy him some coffee. She learns that his stage name is Jeffrey. He lives in an abandoned building in Manhattan. He is an orphan. He wants to be a dancer. And oh yes, he is gay.

They become fast friends. Sometimes she goes with him when he tries out for a bit part, which he never gets. She asks Jeffrey to dinner at her apartment. Her mother is delighted that her daughter is finally interested in a boy—until she sees Jeffrey. He arrives with his bleached hair and wearing a woman's fur jacket. Mrs. Rosenbloom tells Heidi not to see him again, an order Heidi ignores.

Despite the fact that Jeffrey talks openly about being gay, Heidi falls in love with him. When her mother begins going to a friend's home in Connecticut and staying overnight on Fridays, Heidi invites Jeffrey so he can have a bath and sleep in a real bed. Jeffrey seems unaware of Heidi's feelings for him, but he tells her that she can do anything if she puts her mind to it.

More than anything, Heidi wants to help Jeffrey get into show business. She enlists the aid of her drama teacher at school, who has had some limited success on Broadway. Miss Margolis goes with Heidi to watch Jeffrey dance on the street. She says he is very good but nothing special. Heidi is crushed by the news and then defiant.

One day Heidi takes a liking to a small stray dog and brings it home. When her mother protests, Heidi tells her that she has to have the dog because she needs someone to love her. Her mother is shocked and hurt. "No one has ever loved a child as much as I love you," she says. Heidi realizes that even though they have trouble communicating, what her mother says is true. Her mother really does love her, and so does her father. For the first time, she feels compassion for her parents.

One day Jeffrey calls with fantastic news. Two friends have decided to try their luck in Hollywood and Jeffrey is going along. Perhaps he can break into television more easily than Broadway.

Heidi is devastated at first as Jeffrey prepares to leave, and then becomes angry at his flippant attitude. Will he just walk out of her life as though they have never known each other? However, as she says goodbye to Jeffrey, he begins to cry. Now Heidi understands. His flippant behavior is his way of breaking away, and she knows he must go because Jeffrey is a dreamer.

Jeffrey never writes, of course, and Heidi realizes she has fallen in love with the wrong person. But it's all right now because she also knows that everything Jeffrey told her she was is true.

Themes and Subjects

This is a love story, in a way, featuring two misfits: an unattractive teenager whose parents both want her to be what she is not and a young gay boy with a single-minded dream. Both are touching and believable and likable, and their friendship warms the heart.

Booktalk Material

Heidi's relationship with her parents and with Jeffrey can open discussions of how the teenage years are often a time of ups and downs and back-and-forth emotions. See: Heidi and her mother argue over her father and "the coat" (pp. 13–16); Heidi meets her father for dinner (pp. 19–26); Heidi meets Jeffrey (pp. 41–49); and Heidi talks about herself to Jeffrey (pp. 61–66).

Additional Selections

Four teenage girls who are spending the summer apart pin their hopes on a pair of jeans that flatters them all in Ann Brashares's *The Sisterhood of the Traveling Pants* (Delacorte, 2001).

A sixteen-year-old heroine named H. F. and her friend Bo, both gay, set off on a trip and learn a lot about life outside their Kentucky homes in Julia Watts's *Finding H. F.* (Allyson, 2001).

Fourteen-year-old Ellen is in love with James, who is involved with Ellen's older brother, in Garret Freymann-Weyr's *My Heartbeat* (Houghton, 2002).

In Jean Ferris's *Eight Seconds* (Harcourt, 2000), set in a rodeo camp, eighteen-year-old Ritchie discovers that his new rodeo friend is gay.

About the Author and Book

Authors and Artists for Young Adults. Gale. Vol. 2, 1989; vol. 30, 1999.
Children's Books and Their Creators. Houghton, 1995.
Children's Literature Review. Vol. 78, Gale, 2002.
Contemporary Authors. Vol. 182, Gale, 2000.
Continuum Encyclopedia of Children's Literature. Continuum, 2001.
Drew, Bernard A. *100 Most Popular Young Adult Authors.* Libraries Unlimited, 1996.
Estes, Glenn E. "American Writers for Children Since 1930: Fiction." In *Dictionary of Literary Biography.* Vol. 52, Gale, 1986.
Gillespie, John T., and Corinne J. Naden. *Characters in Young Adult Literature.* Gale, 1997.
Lives and Works: Young Adult Authors. Vol. 8, Grolier, 1999.
Major Authors and Illustrators for Children and Young Adults (1st ed.). Vol. 6, Gale, 1993.
Major Authors and Illustrators for Children and Young Adults (2nd ed.). Vol. 8, Gale, 2002.
St. James Guide to Young Adult Writers (2nd ed.). St. James, 1999.
Something About the Author. Gale. Vol. 1, 1971; vol. 58, 1990; vol. 103, 1999.
Something About the Author Autobiography Series. Vol. 2, Gale, 1986.
Third Book of Junior Authors. Wilson, 1972.
Twentieth-Century Young Adult Writers (1st ed.). St. James, 1994.
Writers for Young Adults. Vol. 3, Scribner, 1997.
See also listing "Selected West Sites on Children's Literature and Authors."

Zindel, Paul. *The Pigman.* Harper, 1968. $17.89, 0-06-026828-X (Grades 7–10).

Introduction

Paul Zindel (1936–2003) was born on Staten Island, New York, where he and his sister grew up with his single-parent mother, a nurse. His father, a policeman, left the family when Paul was a child. After graduating from Wagner College on Staten Island with a degree in chemistry, he later taught chemistry on the island for ten years at the Tottenville High School. He left to pursue a full-time career writing fiction and plays. His first book for young adults was the groundbreaking *The Pigman*, inspired by students he taught and by Nonna Frankie, the Italian grandfather to the neighborhood. Told from two points of view, it is the story of two teenage misfits—a boy and a girl—and their friendship with a lonely old man, Angelo Pignati, a relationship that produces first happiness and then tragedy. Zindel continued to write about teenage angst in several later novels, and toward the end of his writing career he produced a series of fast-moving adventure stories, such as *Rats* (Hyperion, 1999). *The Pigman* is a moving reading experience for readers of all ages but particularly those in the junior high grades.

Principal Characters
Lorraine Jensen, a high school sophomore
John Conlan, Lorraine's schoolmate and friend
Angelo Pignati, a man whose name they pick from the telephone book
Mrs. Jensen, Lorraine's mother
Mr. and Mrs. Conlan, John's parents
Dennis Kobin and Norton Kelly, who like phone gags
Bobo, the baboon

Plot Summary
High school sophomores Lorraine Jensen and John Conlan are in rebellion against a society they don't understand and families they can't respect. Lorraine's mother tells her that she's not a pretty girl but she doesn't have to walk around stoop-shouldered and hunched. Her father, whom Lorraine refers to as the Bore, put a lock on the home phone. But the teenagers find comfort in their offbeat relationship. One of their amusements is to pick a name from the phone book and try to engage the stranger in a long conversation. They call it a telephone marathon. The idea is just to stick your finger on a number in the directory and then call it up to see how long you can keep the person on the phone.

Lorraine has never been very good at the telephone marathon because she always bursts out laughing. But this time, egged on by schoolmates Dennis and Norton, Lorraine picks "Pignati, Angelo." A jolly-sounding man answers, and so begins their strange friendship. Despite themselves, Lorraine and John get caught up in the life of this cheerful but lonely person, who tells them that his wife is in California. When the teenagers discover his extensive collection of figurine pigs, they nickname him the Pigman and begin to meet regularly at his house. They are confused by their own fascination with him but touched by his innocent sharing of love and his generous, understanding nature.

One day they meet the Pigman at the zoo. He goes there by himself almost every day. He loves animals. He takes them to meet his friend Bobo, a baboon. Sometime later, they discover that the Pigman's wife is actually dead and not in California. They realize he cannot bring himself to acknowledge her death.

Every day after school, John and Lorraine go to visit the Pigman. They have a glass of wine and conversation. He finally admits to them that his wife is dead. They finally tell him they are in high school and not the charity people they pretended to be. Then one day, when they are laughing and having a good time, the Pigman suffers a heart attack. They immediately call for help. He survives and they visit him in the hospital.

While the Pigman is recuperating in the hospital, Lorraine and John use his home as a private place and await his return. They clean up the house the evening before he is due to return home. However, John decides to stage a party that night for their schoolmates. The party gets completely out of hand and John becomes very drunk. The house is damaged and, worse, so is the Pigman's beloved figurine collection. The police take John away.

The old man returns in the midst of the carnage. He does not press charges. Filled with remorse, John and Lorraine call him to explain that they did not mean harm and that the party just got out of hand. They offer to come over to clean up the mess, but he declines. Finally, they get him to agree to meet them once more at the zoo. He arrives and they can see that he is very ill, but he wants to see his friend, Bobo, the baboon. However, when they go to that area, they learn that the animal has died. The Pigman falls to the floor. He, too, is dead.

Lorraine and John are left with feelings of great loss and guilt, aware that with the death of the Pigman, their childhood is also at an end. It is no longer possible to blame others for their actions, only themselves. The Pigman has taught them that. As John said, "We had trespassed too—been where we didn't belong, and we were being punished for it. Mr. Pignati had paid with his life. But when he died, something in us died as well."

Themes and Subjects

The lives of two offbeat, rebellious teenagers are honestly depicted, as is the importance of their relationship with each other. Through their meeting with a lonely, trusting old man, the teenagers experience feelings of love and compassion, which they cannot as yet name. The destruction of the Pigman's home and his beloved figurine collection causes them to look into themselves instead of blaming others for their unhappiness. It is a painful lesson in growing up.

Booktalk Material
The meeting of John and Lorraine sets the tone for the novel (pp. 13–16). Other important passages are: the telephone marathon (pp. 24–30); they meet the Pigman (pp. 38–47); they go to the zoo and meet Bobo (pp. 55–65); the Pigman has a heart attack (pp. 120–22); the party (pp. 144–56); and the last visit to the zoo (pp. 169–73).

Additional Selections
E. R. Frank's *Life Is Funny* (DK, 2002) is a novel of intersecting stories about the hopes, problems, and everyday life of eleven teens growing up in Brooklyn.

Christopher, a fifteen-year-old autistic boy solves the mystery of who murdered his neighbor's dog in Mark Haddon's *The Curious Incident of the Dog in the Night-Time* (Vintage, 2003).

In Joyce McDonald's *Swallowing Stones* (Dell, 1999), two teenagers are brought together by a tragic accident that caused the death of an innocent man.

Sixteen-year-old John falls in love with fellow zine writer Marisol even though he knows she can't love him back in Ellen Wittlinger's *Hard Love* (Simon, 1999).

About the Book and Author
Authors and Artists for Young Adults. Gale. Vol. 2, 1989; vol. 37, 2001.
Biography Today: Author Series. Vol. 1, Omnigraphics, 1995.
Children's Books and Their Creators. Houghton, 1995.
Children's Literature Review. Gale. Vol. 3, 1976; vol. 45, 1998; vol. 85, 2003
Contemporary Authors New Revision Series. Vol. 108, Gale, 2002.
Continuum Encyclopedia of Children's Literature. Continuum, 2001.
Drew, Bernard A. *100 Most Popular Young Adult Authors.* Libraries Unlimited, 1997.
Favorite Children's Authors and Illustrators. Vol. 6, Tradition Books, 2003.
Fifth Book of Junior Authors and Illustrators. Wilson, 1983.
Forman, Jack. *Presenting Paul Zindel.* Twayne, 1988.
Gallo, Donald R. *Speaking for Ourselves.* National Council of Teachers of English, 1990.
Gillespie, John T., and Corinne J. Naden. *Characters in Young Adult Literature.* Gale, 1997.
Lives and Works: Young Adult Authors. Vol. 8, Grolier, 1999.
Major Authors and Illustrators for Children and Young Adults (1st ed.). Vol. 6, Gale, 1993.

Major Authors and Illustrators for Children and Young Adults (2nd ed.). Vol. 8, Gale, 2002.
St. James Guide to Young Adult Writers (2nd ed.). St. James, 1999.
Scales, Pat. "The Pigman and Me," *School Library Journal,* June, 2002, p. 53.
Something About the Author. Gale. Vol. 16, 1979; vol. 58, 1990; vol. 102, 1999; vol. 142, 2004.
Stevens, Jen. *The Undergraduate's Companion to Children's Writers and Their Web Sites.* Libraries Unlimited, 2004.
Third Book of Junior Authors and Illustrators. Wilson, 1972.
Twentieth-Century Young Adult Writers (1st ed.). St. James, 1994.
Writers for Young Adults. Vol. 3, Scribner, 1997.
See also listing "Selected Web Sites on Children's Literature and Authors."

2

Social Concerns and Problems

Baldwin, James. *If Beale Street Could Talk.* Laurel Leaf, 1986 (1975). Pap. $6.99, 0-440-34060-8 (Grade 10–Adult).

Introduction
James Baldwin (1924–87) was born and educated in New York City. After stints as a handyman, dishwasher, waiter, and office boy, he became a full-time writer and lived in Europe, mainly Paris, from 1948 through 1956 before returning to America. He wrote seven ground-breaking novels about the African American experience plus numerous plays and nonfiction works. When he died, American literature lost one of its best contemporary writers, and black people one of their most articulate spokesmen and advocates. Since his first novel, *Go Tell It on the Mountain* (Doubleday, 1953), his voice had been a commanding one. *If Beale Street Could Talk* comes roughly midway in his output. Its title is also that of a famous blues song, and its story is a moving, painful one of black survival in spite of prejudice and injustice. It was originally published in 1974 as an adult novel and is enjoyed by mature readers in senior high schools.

Principal Characters
Fonny, a twenty-two-year-old black man
Tish, nineteen, his girlfriend
Mrs. Rogers, who claims Fonny is a rapist
Officer Bell, a bigoted policeman
Sharon, Tish's mother
Frank, Fonny's father

Plot Summary
Fonny is twenty-two and Tish is nineteen. They are black; he is in jail for a crime he didn't commit, and she has just found out she is pregnant.

So begins James Baldwin's powerful love story of two young people who have made a world for themselves with each other. They may be beaten by the poverty and bigotry and harshness of life in the streets of the city, but they are not beaten down. They have found each other, and it is enough for them . . . or so they desperately hope.

Tish and Fonny have been friends for a long time, and it is only fairly recently that they have realized that they are in love. They are poor, as are their families; both of them work and Fonny struggles at night to wrest beautiful forms from the wood and stone he tries to carve. On the night they discover their true feelings for each other, Fonny takes Tish back to her family's home to tell them of their plans to marry.

Tish's family is happy with the news. Her mother, father, and sister like Fonny, and they realize the depth of the young people's feelings for each other. The reaction is not quite the same in Fonny's household. Although his father, Frank, is genuinely delighted with the coming marriage, Fonny's mother and sisters—whom Tish suspects do not even like Fonny—react as though Tish is beneath their consideration.

Nonetheless, the couple makes plans by first trying to find an affordable loft to rent where they can live and Fonny can sculpt. Almost miraculously, they do find a place. Unfortunately, it is in a neighborhood patrolled by the bigoted policeman Officer Bell. One evening when Fonny defends Tish against the unwanted attentions of a street punk, Bell almost pulls Fonny off to jail. He is stopped by the protests of a witness who defends Fonny and swears that Tish is telling the truth. The officer leaves Fonny alone, but as Fonny later tells Tish, "He's out to get me."

Although the words make Tish uneasy, she cannot believe them. Fonny has never been in trouble with the law, has never been on drugs, has never been arrested.

But Fonny's words seem all too true when he is later picked up on a charge of rape. He has been picked out of a lineup by a young woman who claims the rapist was dark-skinned; dark-skinned Fonny is put into a lineup with three light-skinned men. The woman claims he is the rapist.

So Fonny is now in jail, where he learns he is to be a father. Desperately, Tish assures him that her family and his father are trying to get him out. To that end they hire a white lawyer, who discovers that the woman who accused Fonny has disappeared. The family tries to get together more money, and the lawyer finds out that the woman, Mrs. Rogers, has gone to Puerto Rico.

Tish's family and Fonny's father band together by working extra jobs to try to raise money for Fonny's defense. Tish struggles to keep her job as her time of delivery grows nearer and she struggles to keep Fonny from growing ever more desperate behind bars.

Tish's mother, Sharon, goes to Puerto Rico and locates Mrs. Rogers. Nothing she says will change the woman's mind. When she returns to New York, she learns that Mrs. Rogers has had a miscarriage and is now in an asylum. All hope for her testimony is lost.

Without the main witness, Fonny's trial is postponed. Soon after, Fonny's father, who had been devastated by the postponement, is found dead, sitting in his car with the motor running.

Tish has not been feeling well all day. When her father brings the terrible news about Frank, she opens her mouth, but she can think only of Fonny. She screams and cries, and her time has come.

Themes and Subjects
This love story is harsh and realistic as it deals with two young people who are frightened but brave, vulnerable, and proud as they try to deal with the realities of a life of poverty and discrimination. Their love for each other is particularly haunting as circumstances close in on them, and they cling to each other as a way to ward off their pain and fright. The story is told with great simplicity and dignity. Also compelling is the picture of black family members who share a loving relationship and stand up for one another in times of stress and desperation. Their realness and their caring come through, even as the net around Fonny and Tish grows tighter and their situation more hopeless.

Booktalk Material
The obvious depth of feeling between these two young people is a good introduction to this modern love story. See: Tish first notices Fonny and accidentally hits him in the head (pp. 10–13) their "first date" (pp. 19–29); and the night Fonny asks Tish to marry him (pp. 90–97). Also, the relationship among members of Tish's family can be used to initiate a talk on how family strength can overcome the harshest of obstacles; see Tish's family handles the news of the baby (pp. 33–41) and the family spends the evening together (pp. 47–54).

Additional Selections
A young Caribbean girl challenges her mother's authority and grows to adulthood in Jamaica Kincaid's *Annie John* (Farrar, 1985).

Fourteen-year-old Rainbow has to move in with a foster mother when her real mother deserts her in Alice Childress's *Rainbow Jordan* (Harper, 1982) subtitled *She's Too Brave to Be a Child, Too Scared to Be a Woman*.

There is a conflict in a black community when the pastor's illegitimate son appears in Ernest J. Gaines's *In My Father's House* (Vintage, 1978).

Jeremiah, an African American, and Ellie, who is white, form a relationship and must cope with the reactions of people around them in Jacqueline Woodson's *If You Come Softly* (Putnam, 1998).

About the Book and Author
Authors and Artists for Young Adults. Gale. Vol. 4, 1990; vol. 34, 2000.
Biography Today: Author Series. Vol. 2, Omnigraphics, 1996.
Bloom, Harold. *James Baldwin.* Chelsea, 1986.
Brucoli, Mathew J., and Richard Layman. *Concise Dictionary of American Literary Biography: The New Consciousness, 1941–1968.* Gale, 1987.
Campbell, James. *Talking the Gates: A Life of James Baldwin.* Viking, 1991.
Contemporary Authors. Vol. 124, Gale, 1988.
Contemporary Authors New Revision Series. Vol. 24, Gale, 1988.
Davis, Thadious M., and Trudier Harris. "Afro-American Fiction Writers After 1955." In *Dictionary of Literary Biography.* Vol. 33, Gale, 1984.
Gillespie, John T., and Corinne J. Naden. *Characters in Young Adult Literature.* Gale, 1997.
Helterman, Jeffrey. "American Novelists Since World War II." In *Dictionary of Literary Biography.* Vol. 2, Gale, 1978.
Kenan, Randall. *James Baldwin.* Chelsea, 1994.
King, Malcolm. *Baldwin: Three Interviews.* Wesleyan University, 1985.
Lee, A. Robert. *James Baldwin: Climbing to the Light.* St. Martin's, 1991.
Lives and Works: Young Adult Authors. Vol. 1, Grolier, 1999.
O'Daniel, Thurman B. *James Baldwin: A Critical Evaluation.* Howard University, 1981.
Porter, Horace A. *Stealing the Fire: The Art and Protest of James Baldwin.* Wesleyan University, 1989.
Pratt, Louis H. *James Baldwin.* Twayne, 1978.
Rosset, Lisa. *James Baldwin.* Chelsea, 1989.
St. James Guide to Young Adult Writers (2nd ed.). St. James, 1999.
Something About the Author. Gale. Vol. 9, 1976; vol. 54, 1989.
Standley, Fred L., and Nancy V. Burt. *Critical Essays on James Baldwin.* Hall, 1988.
Sylander, Carolyn Wedin. *James Baldwin.* Ungar, 1980.
Troupe, Quincy. *James Baldwin: The Legacy.* Simon, 1989.
Twentieth-Century Young Adult Writers (1st ed.). St. James, 1994.
Weatherby, W. J. *James Baldwin: Artist on Fire.* Fine, 1989.
See also listing "Selected Web Sites on Children's Literature and Authors."

Barrett, William E. *The Lilies of the Field.* Warner, 1988 (1961). Pap. $5.99, 0-4463-1500-1 (Grade 9–Adult).

Introduction
William E. Barrett (1900–86) was born and educated in New York City. He moved to Denver with his family when he was sixteen. Although he

did not become a full-time freelance writer until 1929, his writing efforts had begun much earlier—his first poem was published at age fifteen. He died at home in Denver in 1986, at age eighty-five. Barrett wrote numerous novels, short stories, and articles. One of his novels, *The Left Hand of God* (1951, o.p.), was translated into ten languages and made into a successful motion picture with Humphrey Bogart. *The Lilies of the Field* was also made into a very successful film in 1963 featuring a young Sidney Poitier. It is a poignant story that is a disarmingly simple commentary on the age-old problem of prejudice. In essence, the book is a contemporary fable that joins two elements: a carefree black GI and a group of German nuns. One reviewer commented, "What joins these unlike forces in a miracle is the vein of basic goodness that Mr. Barrett sees in all men." Though written for an adult audience, it is recommended reading for both junior and senior high school students.

Principal Characters
  Homer Smith, a black ex-soldier
  Mother Maria Marthe, one of five nuns from East Germany
  Mr. Livingstone, a contractor

Plot Summary
The title of this novel comes from Matthew 6:28–29: "And why take ye thought for raiment? Consider the lilies of the field, how they grow; they toil not, neither do they spin: And yet I say unto you, That even Solomon in all his glory was not arrayed like one of these."

Homer Smith, African American and twenty-four years old, has just been released from the Army in Tacoma, Washington. He is traveling through the West in a station wagon seeing the country and enjoying his freedom. When he feels the need or wants money, he works at odd jobs.

One day he stops at a rundown farm that looks as if it could use some help. He asks the woman there for a job and she nods her head. She feeds him a sparse lunch of cheese, bread, and milk and mutters words he cannot understand. But she points to the roof and he understands that she wants him to repair it. Homer repairs the roof and stays for supper, at which time he meets the five women who run the farm. They are all nuns, East German refugees who want to set up a farm for Spanish orphans in the area. They speak very little English.

Homer does not intend to stay and he is irritated by the brisk, commanding manner of the head nun, Mother Maria Marthe. He is especially dismayed the next day when she takes him into the junk-filled foundation of a burned-out house nearby. "You will build a chapel here," she commands. Although he is put off by her demands, and especially by the fact that Mother Maria seems to think God has given Homer to her, he hasn't the heart to leave without doing something. He agrees only to clean the junk out of the foundation. But when he wants to be paid, Mother Maria quotes from the Bible. She begs him to stay and help. Homer, who has never taken on any project of particular responsibility, reluctantly agrees.

The following Sunday, Homer drives the sisters into Piedras, a small nearby town, where they attend mass and he has his first big meal. The sisters eat sparsely. The priest thanks him for his help.

Homer does not have any faith in the chapel project until he meets Mr. Livingstone, a contractor and executor of the nuns' property. Livingstone says the plan to build a chapel won't work. Homer thinks he means it won't work because he is a black man. That changes his mind. Homer resolves to get the chapel built. He gets a job two days a week as a machine operator and spends the rest of the time building the chapel. In the evenings, he gives English lessons—with a southern accent—to the nuns.

Little by little, as the chapel grows, people contribute bricks, even Mr. Livingstone. But Homer gets tired of the hard work and after several weeks leaves for the city, where he spends ten days. At the end of that time, he sees some unwanted bath tubs on a demolition job. He returns to the farm with the bathtubs and two glass windows.

The nuns are happy to see him and say nothing about his disappearance. By now, people have shown up to work on the chapel, which tends to annoy Homer, who now thinks of this as his own project.

At last, the chapel is finished. Before the first mass is celebrated, Homer sits alone quietly in the little church of his creation. Then he packs his station wagon and heads for South Carolina. It is time to go home.

In a few years, the little chapel is a tourist attraction. Called St. Benedict the Moor, it is labeled as a fine example of "primitive" architecture. Mother Maria Marthe comments about the portrait of a dark-skinned man that hangs inside the chapel. It was drawn from memory by Sister Albertine. Mother Maria says the portrait shows a "man of greatness."

Themes and Subjects
Homer's accomplishment of building the chapel demonstrates the benefits of facing a problem realistically. The hero's inner fight to control and channel his emotions should appeal to young people with the same inner tensions. Also running through the story is the theme of religious and racial tolerance.

Booktalk Material
A good introduction to the book using the author's flashback technique is found in Chapter 7 (pp. 89–92). See also the exchange of Bible quotations between Homer and Mother Maria (pp. 32–34).

Additional Selections
An African American man and his sister defy the townspeople who want their property for a turpentine factory in Aaron Roy Even's *Bloodroot* (St. Martin's, 2000).

In apartheid-ridden South Africa, a friendship grows between a black boy and a white boy in *Waiting for the Rain* (Bantam, 1996) by Sheila Gordon.

In Walter Dean Myers's *The Young Landlords* (Penguin, 1979), a group of African American teenagers takes over a slum building in Harlem.

An Italian American Army major wins the love of the residents of the town of Adano when he finds a replacement for the 600-pound bell melted down by the Germans in the World War II novel *A Bell for Adano* (Vintage, 1944) by John Hersey.

About the Author and Book
Contemporary Authors. Vol. 120, Gale, 1987.
Contemporary Authors New Revision Series. Vol. 22, Gale, 1988.
See also listing "Selected Web Sites on Children's Literature and Authors."

Bridgers, Sue Ellen. *Notes for Another Life.* Knopf, 1981. $12.99, 0-394-84889-6 (Grades 7–10).

Introduction
Sue Ellen Bridgers (1942–) was born in the tobacco-farming town of Winterville, North Carolina, a state where she has spent most of her life. *Notes for Another Life* also takes place in a small southern town, a setting also used in the author's two earlier young adult novels. In *Home Before Dark* (Knopf, 1976), the plight of a migrant worker's family and their struggle to establish a permanent home are explored. *All Together Now* (Knopf, 1979) is the story of the summer a young girl spends with her grandparents and of her new friendships, one with a retarded man. In *Notes for Another Life*, her third novel, the author portrays the anguish and heartbreak that mental illness can bring to a family. Though written in the third person, this novel shifts points of view from one character to anoth-

er so successfully that in time the reader not only understands but also sympathizes with each family member. It is an introspective, somewhat slow-moving novel that better readers in grades seven through ten will appreciate.

Principal Characters
    Wren Jackson, thirteen years old
    Kevin Jackson, her sixteen-year-old brother
    Bliss and Bill Jackson, their grandparents, with whom they live
    Tom, their father who is institutionalized for depression
    Karen, their mother, who works in Atlanta
    Jack Kensley, a young pastor
    Jolene, Wren's friend
    Sam Holland, Wren's young admirer

Plot Summary
Thirteen-year-old Wren Jackson and her sixteen-year-old brother Kevin have lived for the past six years with their grandparents, Bliss and Bill Jackson. Their normal family life was shattered when the bouts of depression and withdrawal suffered by their father, Tom, became so severe that he had to be institutionalized, and their mother, Karen, moved to Atlanta to work in a fashionable department store.

However, life for the two youngsters has been far from unpleasant, mainly because Bliss and Bill are caring and devoted grandparents. Wren is successfully completing eighth grade, shows a marked talent for piano playing, and has a good friend in the effervescent, boy-crazy Jolene. Kevin is not setting records in his sophomore class, but he excels at tennis, helps his grandfather in his drugstore, and has a steady girlfriend, Melanie Washburn. Nevertheless, both of them, particularly Kevin, feel keenly the absence of their parents, find the visits to their father painful, and long for the day when their mother will ask them to join her in the city.

During a youth service at their Baptist church, conducted by young pastor Jack Kensley, Wren and Jolene sing solos and fifteen-year-old Sam Holland delivers the sermon. Sam lives with his family on a farm on the outskirts of town, but after meeting Wren he finds excuses to see her at the drugstore. At first, Wren is embarrassed and uncertain about this attention, but gradually she learns to trust and admire this attentive, understanding young man. Sam invites her on an outing, during which Wren meets his family, including his unaffected, affectionate mother, Kathryn, and his father, John, who demonstrates his prowess at finding water with a divining rod.

Karen visits her family. She is a sincere, caring person who is torn between being a good mother and living a life of independence and self-fulfillment. She announces she will soon be accepting a promotion that includes moving to Chicago. For her children, this means even more separation. What Karen does not tell them but later reveals in a letter to Bliss is that she has been begun divorce proceedings against Tom. Bliss has the difficult task of telling the children. Kevin takes it particularly hard. To compound matters, while visiting Tom in the hospital, the boy, mistakenly thinking that his father knows about the divorce, makes a reference to it. Tom is shaken and Kevin feels an additional burden of guilt and remorse.

As summer approaches and Wren begins preparation for eighth-grade graduation, news from the hospital is encouraging. Tom is responding so well to a new drug that he is allowed to return home on an experimental basis. At first he appears normal, but within a short time the signs of withdrawal appear once more and the children's hopes are dashed. Wren is better able to cope with this bad news. Kevin breaks his wrist during a tennis match and loses his girlfriend after a series of prolonged quarrels. Also, Kevin harbors the unspoken fear that he might inherit his father's insanity.

Karen returns home for a visit before moving to Chicago. For Kevin, this is another reminder of rejection in his life. This, plus his father's condition, leads him to take an overdose of Seconal. Bliss finds him in time and gets him to the hospital. Physically, Kevin bounces back quickly, but his psychological recovery is slow. It is only through the help and understanding of pastor Jack Kensley that Kevin is able to articulate and face his fears and problems.

Life gradually returns to normal. Karen is in Chicago, Tom is back in the hospital, Kevin resumes his tennis and his relationship with Melanie, and Wren, now fourteen, looks forward to her first year of high school. At least for the present, the pieces have been picked up.

Themes and Subjects

Without melodrama or sensationalism, the author explores the nature of mental illness and its psychological effects on others. Family relationships and dependencies are strongly portrayed; particularly touching is the closeness of a brother and his younger sister. Conflicts involving family obligations versus self-realization are developed through the characters of Karen and Wren. Other topics are: adolescent friendship, problems of coping with guilt, teenage suicide, the nature of rejection, and the power of love and understanding.

Booktalk Material

Characterization is particularly strong in this novel. An introduction to the three principal women in the book—Wren, Bliss, and Karen—should interest readers. Specific passages are: the church service with Sam Holland (pp. 13–18); Karen thinks about her husband and situation (pp. 23–24); Wren first meets Sam (pp. 24–28); and Kevin tells his father about the divorce (pp. 107–11).

Additional Selections

A young boy finds that his father, who can no longer function mentally, is turning into a frightening, suspicious stranger in Phyllis Reynolds Naylor's *The Keeper* (Atheneum, 1986).

After her boyfriend is killed, Ginny retreats into herself and avoids contact with others in *Falling Through Darkness* (Roaring Brook, 2003) by Carolyn MacCullough.

The driver who survives the drunk-driving accident that killed his friend, a star basketball player, sinks into a deep depression in Sharon M. Draper's *Tears of a Tiger* (Atheneum, 1994).

In Dawn Wilson's *Saint Jude* (Tudor, 2001), Taylor, who is bipolar, makes friends and learns to cope with her condition while an outpatient at St. Jude's Hospital.

About the Author and Book

Authors and Artists for Young Adults. Gale. Vol. 8, 1992; vol. 49, 2003.
Children's Books and Their Creators. Houghton, 1995.
Children's Literature Review. Vol. 18, Gale, 1989.
Contemporary Authors New Revision Series. Vol. 36, Gale, 1992.
Continuum Encyclopedia of Children's Literature. Continuum, 2001.
Drew, Bernard A. *100 Most Popular Young Adult Authors.* Libraries Unlimited, 1996.
Estes, Glenn E. "American Writers for Children Since 1960: Fiction." In *Dictionary of Literary Biography.* Vol. 52, Gale, 1986.
Fifth Book of Junior Authors and Illustrators. Wilson, 1983.
Gallo, Donald R. *Speaking for Ourselves.* National Council of Teachers of English, 1990.
Gillespie, John T., and Corinne J. Naden. *Characters in Young Adult Literature.* Gale, 1997.
Lives and Works: Young Adult Authors. Vol. 1, Grolier, 1999.
Major Authors and Illustrators for Children and Young Adults (1st ed.). Vol. 1, Gale, 1993.
Major Authors and Illustrators for Children and Young Adults (2nd ed.). Vol. 1, Gale, 2002.
St. James Guide to Young Adult Authors (2nd ed.). St. James, 1999.
Something About the Author. Gale. Vol. 22, 1981; vol. 99, 1997; vol. 109, 2000.
Stevens, Jen. *The Undergraduate's Companion to Children's Writers and Their Web Sites.* Libraries Unlimited, 2004.

Twentieth-Century Young Adult Writers (1st ed.). St. James, 1994.
Writers for Young Adults. Vol. 1, Scribner, 1997.
See also listing "Selected Web Sites on Children's Literature and Authors."

Carter, Alden R. *Up Country.* Puffin, 2004 (1989). Pap. $6.99, 0-14-240243-5 (Grades 7–10).

Introduction

Alden Richardson Carter (1947–) was born in Eau Claire, Wisconsin, and educated at the University of Kansas, where he received his undergraduate degree. After a five-year stint in the U.S. Navy, he taught high school English and journalism for four years in Marshfield, Wisconsin, before becoming a full-time writer. As well as a number of excellent young adult novels, Carter has written about twenty nonfiction works, chiefly on wars in American history. In his young adult novels, teenagers achieve growth through facing and overcoming personal problems. For example, in *Growing Season* (Putnam, 1984), Rick, a high school senior, learns to accept responsibility when his parents move from a big city to a Wisconsin dairy farm. In *Up Country,* a somewhat similar situation is presented as sixteen-year-old Carl Staggers is sent to stay with country relatives. In both novels, the main characters learn to adapt and grow toward adulthood through the support of family and friends and their own responsible behavior. These books are read and enjoyed by youngsters in grades seven through ten.

Principal Characters

Carl Staggers, sixteen, who can fix anything electric
His mother, Veronica, who has a drinking problem
Uncle Glen and Aunt June, who live in northern Wisconsin
Signa Amundsen, a schoolmate
Mr. Dowdy, the school principal
Steve, an old friend of Carl's
Mullan, a social worker

Plot Summary

When the Milwaukee police knock on his door, sixteen-year-old Carl Staggers has two reasons to worry. One, on his workbench are half a dozen car stereos stolen by his pal Steve. Two, his mother, thirty-eight-year-old

Veronica, has a drinking problem and a habit of bringing strange men home at night.

This time the problem is Mom, who got involved in a bar fight and hit someone over the head with a bottle. Carl bails her out with his "Plan" money—money that he makes fixing just about anything electric and saves to rescue him from his current life.

When Mom is picked up again, a social worker sends Carl "up country" to Blind River, Wisconsin, to his Uncle Glen and Aunt June. He is to stay with them and attend school there until his mother finishes rehabilitation. Carl is reluctant at first but is slowly drawn into the rural life with his kind aunt and uncle and cousin Bob. But he resists involvement at his new school, including the friendship of Signa Amundsen. He is determined to get back to Milwaukee.

However, weekly phone conversations with his mother make it clear she is not responding to treatment. Carl feels responsible for his mother and he begins to think his Plan will not work out.

Milwaukee police summon Carl back to the city. They are looking for his old buddy Steve. Carl is afraid they will find out about the car stereos, but the police want Steve on a bigger crime. With his mother still in rehabilitation, Carl is given a choice of going to a foster home or returning up country. He goes north again.

Back in the rural environment, he begins to think about what his principal and social worker have told him. He begins to see he has almost been programmed by the alcoholism of his mother. He is a typical child of an alcoholic. He tells himself that it doesn't have to be that way.

Carl checks out every available book in the library on alcoholism and drug abuse. He also confides in Signa about the Plan and his fears for the future. Because of his involvement with the stolen car stereos, which the police soon discover, he believes he will be sent to reform school or back home with his mother. Either way he loses.

Social worker Mullan calls to tell Carl he will not be sent away. Mullan proposes a supervised environment but Carl will have to make restitution for the stereos—about $3,000, which he will have to earn. Mullan asks Carl what he wants to do with his future. Carl replies that he must go back to his mother.

In a Milwaukee courtroom with his mother, Carl receives a warning from the judge: If he follows society's rules, he has a promising future. If he breaks the rules, he will come back before the court to pay for that decision.

Carl returns to his seat beside his mother, but facing a return to his old life, something newly born in him makes him speak up. "I can't do it," he tells the court. "I can't go back to her," he says to the social worker. "I just can't risk everything on her. She might start drinking, and I can't go through that again." The court rules that he be allowed to return up country to his aunt and uncle. When Carl says goodbye to his mother, she tells him she will see him when she gets straightened out. "I'm never coming back," he tells her honestly. "I know, baby, I know," she replies.

Carl goes home to his new family, to school, to Signa, and to a new life up country.

Themes and Subjects
This story presents an interesting picture of how alcohol abuse by a parent can turn a child's life upside down. Carl accepts his mother's alcoholism as though he is somehow responsible for it; because he is unable to stop her from drinking, he feels in some way guilty of encouraging her. Carl is a bright, talented young man; he is aware that what he is doing with the car stereos is wrong, but he rationalizes that his Plan for giving himself a better life outweighs other considerations. It is only when he is able to let down the barriers that prevent other people from reaching him with their caring and their love that he can truly understand right from wrong and see that he can love his mother and still not allow her to ruin his dreams and his chance at life.

Booktalk Material
The contrast between Carl's life in Milwaukee and life in Blind River can serve as an excellent introduction to this study of a boy in turmoil. See: the police knock on the door (pp. 8–10); meeting Mom in the courtroom (pp. 15–20); Mom brings a stranger home for Christmas (pp. 45–49). Also see: Carl arrives in Blind River (pp. 82–87); meeting the principal (pp. 90–93); and Carl takes over the lesson on electricity (pp. 114–16).

Additional Selections
In Nora Martin's *The Eagle's Shadow* (Scholastic, 1997), twelve-year-old Clearie is sent to live with Tlingit relatives in Alaska and comes to accept her mother's desertion.

When the grandmother of fourteen-year-old JP dies, he is left with an impractical mother and a retarded father in *A Face in Every Window* (Harcourt, 1999) by Han Nolan.

Charles Ferry's *A Fresh Start* (Proctor, 1996) explores the problems of troubled teens in a program for young alcoholics.

When her father's gambling brings the family close to financial ruin, First Mate Tate thinks up daring schemes to keep her family afloat in Virginia Masterman-Smith's *First Mate Tate* (Marshall Cavendish, 2000).

About the Author and Book
Authors and Artists for Young Adults. Gale. Vol. 17, 1995; vol. 54, 2004.
Children's Literature Review. Vol. 22, Gale, 1991.
Contemporary Authors New Revision Series. Vol. 114, Gale, 2003.
Gallo, Donald R. *Speaking for Ourselves, Too.* National Council of Teachers of English, 1993.
Gillespie, John T., and Corinne J. Naden. *Characters in Young Adult Literature.* Gale, 1997.
Lives and Works: Young Adult Authors. Vol. 2, Grolier, 1999.
St. James Guide to Young Adult Writers (2nd ed.). St. James, 1999.
Seventh Book of Junior Authors and Illustrators. Wilson, 1996.
Something About the Author. Gale. Vol. 67, 1992; vol. 127, 2003.
Something About the Author Autobiography Series. Vol. 18, Gale, 1994.
Twentieth-Century Young Adult Writers (1st ed.). St. James, 1994.
Writers for Young Adults. Vol. 1, Scribner, 1997.
See also listing "Selected Web Sites on Children's Literature and Authors."

Childress, Alice. *A Hero Ain't Nothin' but a Sandwich.* Putnam, 2000 (1973). Pap. $5.99, 0-698-11854-5 (Grades 7–10).

Introduction
Alice Childress (1920–94) was born in South Carolina but raised in Harlem in New York City. She began her writing career as a playwright (and actress) and had many of her plays performed in off-Broadway theaters. Among her books for juveniles are three highly acclaimed novels for young adults. The first, *Hero,* is the story of Benjie Johnson, a thirteen-year-old heroin user, and his friends, teachers, and family. The central character in the second, *Rainbow Jordan* (Coward, 1981), is in some respects his female counterpart, but her chief problem, apart from finding a home for herself, is how far to go in sexual matters. In the third, *Those Other People* (Putnam, 1989), themes involving racism, suicide, and sexual abuse are explored in a story about a young homosexual boy who witnesses a rape. All three are written from the points of view of several characters, often in strong street language. This technique gives a multifaceted layering effect to these novels and supplies an extra dimension of depth and character development. These novels are read by students in grades seven through ten.

Principal Characters
Benjie Johnson, a thirteen-year-old African American
Rose Johnson Craig, his hard-working mother

Butler Craig, Benjie's more-or-less stepfather
Mrs. Ransom Bell, Benjie's despondent grandmother
Jimmy-Lee Powell, Benjie's friend
Bernard Cohen, a white teacher in an all-black school
Nigeria Greene, a militant black nationalist

Plot Summary
Benjie, a thirteen-year-old African American, is a boy everyone likes. He is friendly and has a wonderful disposition, but something is missing in his life—the sense of really belonging and being somebody. He feels trapped in his tight family circle and feels that Butler Craig has taken his mother's love. His mother, Rose Johnson Craig, is hard-working and devoted. Shortly after Benjie's birth, her husband walked out and she was left to support herself, Benjie, and her aging mother. Four years ago, she fell in love with Butler Craig, who is her common-law husband.

As a youth in Georgia and later in New York, Butler wanted to become a jazz saxophonist, but the need for a steady income forced him to become a janitor in a downtown office building. He is strong, unselfish, and dependable. He genuinely loves Rose, whom he calls "Sweets," and tries hard to be a father to Benjie, but he knows the boy resents his presence in the house.

Also in the house is Mrs. Ransom Bell, Benjie's grandmother. Aging, despondent, and increasingly afraid because she was once robbed and beaten on the street, Mrs. Bell relies more and more on her old-time Baptist religion as a salvation and comfort. The daughter of a Mississippi sharecropper, she has had a tough life and at one time worked as a dancer in a speakeasy. While Rose was still a child, Mrs. Bell's beloved husband died. She still misses him.

School has become a drag for Benjie, and he sees very little hope for his future growing up in Harlem. His environment has destroyed what small seeds of idealism might have grown, and he now feels that "a hero ain't nothin' but a sandwich." He is ready for some form of escape.

Benjie's life on drugs begins with a few joints of pot smoked with friends Jimmy-Lee and Carwell. Under Carwell's influence, Benjie begins to cut class and go to Tiger's place, a comfortable apartment where the kids hang out when Tiger's aunt is working. Tiger runs a little business on the side in candy, hot dogs, and soft drinks, but mostly in pot and heroin. To prove he isn't chicken, Benjie tries his first needle. Soon his trips to Tiger's place become so frequent that Jimmy-Lee is convinced he is hooked and tries desperately to get Benjie to swear off. Benjie says that he can take it or leave it, but eventually he turns to Walter, a pusher, to supplement what he gets from Tiger, and even steals from his grandmother to feed his habit.

Teacher Nigeria Greene alerts another teacher, Bernard Cohen, about Benjie's constant nodding off in class. Benjie is sent to detoxification for a week. At home everyone tries to help him, but one night when he is alone, he steals Butler's suit to get money for a fix. Butler decides to move into a vacant room downstairs to keep peace in the family.

One day Butler catches Benjie in one of the apartments trying to steal a toaster. He chases him to the roof of the building. Benjie tries to run, slips, and nearly falls from the roof. Butler manages to catch him by one arm. Benjie begs Butler to release him and let him die. Instead, Butler drags him to safety and cradles him in his arms.

Benjie now knows that Butler really loves him. To help himself through a terrible case of the shakes, he writes over and over again, "Butler is my father." Benjie learns of his friend Kenny's death from an overdose and goes to the funeral.

This time Butler feels that there are many encouraging signs that Benjie is going to pull through—he is faithful in his trips to the parole office, he is trustworthy with money, and he has resumed his friendship with Jimmy-Lee. But best of all, he has started to call Butler "Dad."

Themes and Subjects

Hero is not just about a family of African Americans and their problems; it deals with themes and experiences that are universal, such as rejection, love, the importance of family ties, poverty, and the problems of growing old. It also depicts the frustration and despair of lives warped by discrimination and need, at the same time showing that people must believe in themselves. Lastly, it is a horrifying picture of the effects of drugs that render a fine boy an enemy in his own home.

Booktalk Material

Many parts of *Hero* are written in street jargon that might be difficult for the booktalker to reproduce, but some passages that could be used are: Benjie introduces himself (pp. 9–10); Butler tells about his youth (pp. 17–19); Grandma tells her story (pp. 31–33); Tiger's place and Benjie's first fix (pp. 67–69).

Additional Selections

Sharon Mathis's *Teacup Full of Roses* (Puffin, 1987) tells about the devastating effects of drugs on an African American family.

After her sister runs away, Caitlin's life comes apart and she descends into drugs and sex in Sarah Dessen's *Dreamland* (Viking, 2000).

Walter Dean Myers's *Scorpions* (HarperCollins, 1988) describes gang warfare, death, and despair in present-day Harlem.

The events leading up to Alex's drug overdose are told first by Alex and then by her friend Donna in Barbara Cole's *Alex the Great* (Rosen, 1989).

About the Author and Book
Authors and Artists for Young Adults. Vol. 8, Gale, 1992.
Biography Today: Author Series. Vol. 1, Omnigraphics, 1995.
Children's Books and Their Creators. Houghton, 1995.
Children's Literature Review. Vol. 14, Gale, 1988.
Contemporary Authors New Revision Series. Vol. 74, Gale, 1999.
Continuum Encyclopedia of Children's Literature. Continuum, 2001.
Drew, Bernard, A. *100 Most Popular Young Adult Authors.* Libraries Unlimited, 1996.
Fifth Book of Junior Authors and Illustrators. Wilson, 1983.
Gallo, Donald R. *Speaking for Ourselves.* National Council of Teachers of English, 1990.
Gillespie, John T., and Corinne J. Naden. *Characters in Young Adult Literature.* Gale, 1997.
Lives and Works: Young Adult Authors. Vol. 2, Grolier, 1999.
Major Authors and Illustrators for Children and Young Adults (1st ed.). Vol. 2, Gale, 1993.
Major Authors and Illustrators for Children and Young Adults (2nd ed.). Vol. 2, Gale, 2002.
St. James Guide to Young Adult Writers (2nd ed.). St. James, 1999.
Something About the Author. Gale. Vol. 7, 1975; vol. 48, 1987; vol. 84, 1996.
Twentieth-Century Young Adult Writers (1st ed.). St. James, 1994.
Writers for Young Adults. Vol. 1, Scribner, 1997.
See also listing "Selected Web Sites on Children's Literature and Authors."

Cole, Brock. *The Goats.* Farrar, 1990 (1987). Pap. $5.95, 0-374-42575-2 (Grades 7–9).

Introduction

Brock Cole (1938–) was born in Michigan and received his education in the Midwest. He earned a Ph.D. from the University of Minnesota in Minneapolis and spent several years as a college teacher of English and philosophy before becoming a full-time writer. When *The Goats*, the author's first novel for young adults, first appeared in 1987, Cole was already known as a writer and illustrator of several successful picture books for children. This novel was a critical success and was followed two years later by *Celine* (Farrar, 1989), the story of a confused high school junior who is trying to distinguish between the phony and the sincere in life. During this quest, she befriends a lonely second-grader named Josh who, because of his parents' separation, feels isolated and unwanted. *The Goats*, which is suitable for a slightly younger audience, is about two thirteen-year-olds—a boy and a girl—who are victims of a cruel practical joke while at a summer camp. The locale is a rural area a few hours outside Chicago. The action takes place over a period of five days. The book is highly recommended for readers in both middle and junior high schools.

Principal Characters
Howie and Laura, two misfit campers
Maddy Golden, Laura's mother
Tiwanda and Calvin, inner-city youngsters
Mrs. Purse, the cleaning lady

Plot Summary
Howie cannot believe what is happening to him. What was to have been an evening cookout on Goat Island with some of his summer camp companions turns into a nightmare. Boys he thought were his friends grab him, strip him, and abandon him, heading back for shore with the canoes. Scared and confused, he discovers a tent platform and inside is a girl named Laura, wrapped in a blanket and sobbing. She, too, has been stripped and left behind. The two realize that they are this year's camp goats—the misfits and outsiders who are so socially immature that they become easy victims of other campers' cruelty.

Determined not to face humiliation, they evade the counselors who come to rescue them. They struggle back to the shore with the help of a log. Breaking into a boarded-up summer cottage, they find some clothes and canned goods. As Howie's parents are in Turkey, they decide to ask Laura's mother, Maddy, to come get them and then head for the municipal beach, where they know there are telephones. Laura is unable to explain coherently to her mother what has happened, but Maddy promises to come two days later during Parents' Weekend. Shortly afterward, Laura's mother is contacted by the camp officials, who say Laura has disappeared. Her mother sets off immediately.

At a gas station, Howie and Laura see school buses and join a group of inner-city children, mostly black. Two of them, Tiwanda and Calvin, offer to help. Howie and Laura get on the bus undetected and soon find themselves at another summer camp. Nicknamed "Bonnie and Clyde" by their new friends, Laura and Howie are accepted into the group. The following morning, Tiwanda gives them five dollars before they leave. Laura makes another call to her mother and leaves a message on her answering machine. Maddy, now at the camp, calls home and gets the message, so she knows Laura and Howie are alive.

They see a family vacating their motel room and Laura has a brilliant idea. Before the vacationers depart, she finds out that they are the Hendricks family. When they leave, Howie and Laura enter the room and retrieve the key. Laura phones the switchboard and pretends to be the daughter, telling the operator that her parents are at the local garage with car trouble and they want to stay an extra night. She and Howie, who is now suffering from a bad cold, move in. The two are exhausted. Laura innocently crawls into bed with Howie to help end his attack of shivers, but unknown to them, they are being spied on by a cleaning lady, Mrs. Purse, who suspects the worst.

That evening the two go to the motel's restaurant and have a good meal, intending to charge it to their bill. At the cash register, Laura is confronted by Mrs. Purse, who escorts her to the motel office for an explanation of the whereabouts of the Hendrickses and of her unseemly behavior that afternoon. Luckily Howie is able to activate a fire alarm and they both escape. They spend the night in an unlocked parked car.

The following day is Saturday, the day of the promised rescue. A major problem is getting to the camp, some ten miles away. On the highway they are picked up by a scruffy man who claims to be a deputy sheriff. But the youngsters are frightened when he pulls off the main highway, stops at a pay phone, and locks them in his Jeepster. Howie notices that there is another set of keys in the car. While driving off, they accidentally run over the foot of a very surprised deputy sheriff, who was only trying to notify his boss that he had located the two missing children.

After abandoning the truck, Laura calls the camp headquarters and learns that her mother is staying at a local motel. When they reach her by phone, Laura tries to explain that she and Howie must not be separated after his parents return from Turkey. Her mother promises and is soon on her way to pick them up. But Howie, fearful he will be returned to camp, runs into the woods. Laura chases after him and reassures him that no one will come between them. Hand in hand, they return to the highway.

Themes and Subjects

This is a novel of both survival and discovery. Two unwanted, unattractive losers not only find ways to live by their own wits and intelligence, but also discover inner resources and self-worth that they did not know they had. The growing respect and love that the two feel for each other is touchingly portrayed. The fact that the author refers to the two principal characters as "the boy" and "the girl" and keeps geographical details to a minimum adds universality to the story. The episode with the inner-city children shows that even among those with few possessions, kindness, understanding, and sharing are possible and that there is a "oneness" shared by all who are abused and forgotten. The emergence of Maddy's deeper feelings concerning her daughter's welfare is an important subtheme. Other ideas explored are the unthinking cruelty that people can inflict upon others, the problems of outsiders, the discovery of the power to love, and the excitement that accompanies accomplishing something worthwhile. On another level, this is a rousing, suspenseful adventure story.

Booktalk Material
An explanation of the title should interest readers. The novel is filled with brief self-contained episodes suitable for booktalks. Some are: abandonment on the island and beginning the trip to shore (pp. 3–16); the stay at the beach cottage (pp. 18–31); stealing clothes at the beach (pp. 41–47); meeting Calvin and Tiwanda (pp. 69–86); and gaining entry to the motel (pp. 113–23).

Additional Selections
Problems with his family and at school are faced by John who is trying to understand himself in *You Don't Know Me* (Frances Foster, 2001) by David Klass.

In alternating chapters, two teenagers describe their decisions to change themselves and their behavior in Todd Strasser's *How I Changed My Life* (Aladdin, 1996).

The story of an unusual friendship between tiny, crafty Kevin and large, slow Max is at the center of Rodman Philbrick's *Freak the Mighty* (Scholastic, 1993).

In Rachel Vail's *Do-Over* (Orchard, 1992) an eighth-grade boy faces many problems including a possible romance and the split-up of his parents.

About the Author and Book
Authors and Artists for Young Adults. Gale. Vol. 15, 1995; vol. 45, 2002.
Children's Books and Their Creators. Houghton, 1995.
Children's Literature Review. Vol. 18, Gale, 1989.
Contemporary Authors New Revision Series. Vol. 115, Gale, 2003.
Continuum Encyclopedia of Children's Literature. Continuum, 2001.
Drew, Bernard A. *100 More Popular Young Adult Writers.* Libraries Unlimited, 2002.
Favorite Children's Authors and Illustrators. Vol. 1, Tradition Books, 2003.
Gallo, Donald R. *Speaking for Ourselves, Too.* National Council of Teachers of English, 1993.

SOCIAL CONCERNS AND PROBLEMS • 91

Gillespie, John T., and Corinne J. Naden. *Characters in Young Adult Literature.* Gale, 1997.
Lives and Works: Young Adult Authors. Vol. 2, Grolier, 1999.
Major Authors and Artists for Children and Young Adults (1st ed.). Vol. 2, Gale, 1993.
Major Authors and Artists for Children and Young Adults (2nd ed.). Vol. 2, Gale, 2002.
St. James Guide to Children's Writers (5th ed.). St. James, 1999.
St. James Guide to Young Adult Writers (2nd ed.). St. James, 1999.
Sixth Book of Junior Authors and Illustrators. Wilson, 1989.
Something About the Author. Gale. Vol. 72, 1995; vol. 136, 2003.
Twentieth-Century Young Adult Writers (1st ed.). St. James, 1994.
Writers for Young Adults. Vol. 1, Scribner, 1997.
See also listing "Selected Web Sites on Children's Literature and Authors."

Garden, Nancy. *Annie on My Mind.* Farrar, 1992 (1982). Pap. $5.95, 0-374-40414-3 (Grades 8–12).

Introduction

Nancy Garden (1938–) was born in Boston and attended Columbia University in New York, where she was awarded a Master of Arts degree in 1962. She then spent several years as an editor for such publishing houses as Houghton Mifflin before becoming a freelance writer of children's books. Her output shows a remarkable range and versatility. In the realm of nonfiction she has written on such exotic subjects as vampires and werewolves. Many of her fiction titles are grounded in the world of fantasy. For example, the Four Crossing books featuring Melissa and friend Jed fighting against an evil hermit, contain elements of both history and mysticism. Her realistic fiction includes *Peace, O River* (Farrar, 1986), the story of two feuding towns, a nuclear waste disposal site, and an engaging heroine caught in the middle. Although the heroine of *Lark in the Morning* (Farrar, 1991) has had a gay relationship before the story opens, this is not the central element in the plot, which deals with the two runaways she discovers hidden near her family's summer house. In *Annie on My Mind*, the main subject is the tender loving sexual relationship between two young women. The story is told with such sensitivity and clarity that this book has became a model of its kind. It is recommended for good readers in grades eight through twelve.

Principal Characters

Liza Winthrop, freshman at MIT
Annie Kenyon, music student
Chad, Liza's brother

Ms. Widmer and Ms. Stevenson, Liza's teachers
Nana, Annie's grandmother

Plot Summary

When the story opens, Liza Winthrop, a freshman at the Massachusetts Institute of Technology, is writing a letter she may never send to Annie Kenyon, who is at school in Berkeley, California. Liza thinks back to their meeting about a year ago in the Metropolitan Museum of Art in New York City. Their attraction to each other was instantaneous and, to Liza, more than a little confusing. A flashback portrays the growing friendship and attraction between the two girls, who come from very different backgrounds. Liza lives in Brooklyn Heights with her parents and brother, Chad; attends the private Foster Academy; and will enter MIT when she graduates. Annie is from a poorer background and attends a public school with security guards. She has a beautiful singing voice and plans to study in California.

After Liza and Annie engage in a more than friendly kiss one day, they realize that their feelings for each other are not what are considered to be the norm. Confused and unsure about "being gay," they restrain their actions, although they are increasingly preoccupied with each other. They see each other every weekend and talk every night. Liza's brother begins to kid her about the person she must be in love with. At Christmas, they present each other with nearly identical rings.

One day Liza and Annie are alone in the home of two Foster Academy teachers, Ms. Widmer and Ms. Stevenson. (Liza is feeding their cats while they are on spring vacation.) From the books in the master bedroom, the girls discover that the older women are also gay. Freed from restraint and alone in the house, they make love in the upstairs bedroom. However, they are "discovered" by one of Liza's classmates and a teacher who were worried when Liza did not show up for a school meeting she had forgotten about.

Liza is forced to tell her parents about how she and Annie were caught, but denies she is a lesbian to protect their feelings. Annie does not tell her parents because, as she says, they would not understand. Ms. Widmer and Ms. Stevenson are fired from the Academy, which makes Liza feel guilty. But Ms. Widmer tells her not to punish herself "for people's ignorant reactions to what we all are." Ms. Stevenson adds, "Don't let ignorance win. Let love."

With confusion and bewilderment on their part and hostility from others, the relationship between the two girls grows strained. They part company in the fall when Annie goes to California and Liza moves to Boston.

Annie sends letters to Liza, but they go unanswered as confusion and guilt continue to cloud Liza's mind and heart.

However, as Christmas vacation nears and Liza tries once again to write to Annie, her mind suddenly is made up. She phones Annie at school. She asks if she is coming home for Christmas. Annie says someone has offered to switch tickets with her so she can go to Boston first for a few days. She has been trying to work up the courage to call Liza. Now, Annie promises to fly to Boston for a few days before they both return to New York. Liza says she will meet her at the airport. She also says that Ms. Widmer was right. The truth has made her free to love Annie.

Themes and Subjects

With directness, sympathy, and understanding, the author tells of the confusion and bewilderment of two young girls as they realize the nature and extent of their feelings for each other. The characters, including the parents and the gay schoolteachers, are portrayed as honest people trying to deal with the situation and their feelings as honestly as possible.

Booktalk Material

The growing relationship between the two girls is the center of this story. See: Liza and Annie meet at the museum (pp. 7–15); the trip to the Cloisters (pp. 50–59); Liza thinks about their increasing closeness (pp. 92–94); they exchange gifts (pp. 111–12); they discover the teachers are gay and they make love for the first time (pp. 157–60).

Additional Selections

Three different viewpoints on being gay are explored in Alex Sanchez's *Rainbow Boys* (Simon, 2001), about three adolescent males and their problems.

Two high school boys fall in love but must hide their relationship from their friends in *Happy Endings Are All Alike* (Allyson, 1999) by Sandra Scoppetone.

In Madeleine L'Engle's *A House Like a Lotus* (Farrar, 1984), seventeen-year-old Polly O'Keefe encounters both lesbianism and a heterosexual romance.

Alex Beekman denies he is gay but, in time, realizes the truth about himself in *Blue Coyote* (Simon, 1997) by Liza Ketchum.

About the Author and Book

Authors and Artists for Young Adults. Gale. Vol. 18, 1996; vol. 55, 2004.
Children's Literature Review. Vol. 51, Gale, 1999.
Contemporary Authors New Revision Series. Vol. 84, Gale, 2000.

Fifth Book of Junior Authors and Illustrators. Wilson, 1983.
Gallo, Donald R. *Speaking for Ourselves, Too.* National Council of Teachers of English, 1993.
Gillespie, John T., and Corinne J. Naden. *Characters in Young Adult Literature.* Gale, 1997.
Lives and Works: Young Adult Authors. Vol. 3, Grolier, 1999.
Major Authors and Illustrators for Children and Young Adults (2nd ed.). Vol. 3, Gale, 2002.
St. James Guide to Young Adult Writers (2nd ed.). St. James, 1999.
Something About the Author. Gale. Vol. 12, 1977; vol. 77, 1994; vol. 114, 2000; vol. 147, 2004.
Something About the Author Autobiography Series. Vol. 8, Gale, 1989.
Twentieth-Century Young Adult Writers (1st ed.). St. James, 1994.
Writers for Young Adults. Supp. 1, Scribner, 2000.
See also listing "Selected Web Sites on Children's Literature and Authors."

Kerr, M. E. *Gentlehands.* HarperTrophy, 1990 (1978). Pap. $5.99, 0-06-447067-9 (Grades 7–10).

Introduction

M. E. Kerr (the pseudonym of Marijane Meaker) (1927–) burst upon the world of juvenile literature with an unconventional novel by the attention-getting title *Dinky Hocker Shoots Smack!* (Harper, 1972). Before youngsters realized the innocence of the title, they had become hooked on M. E. Kerr and have remained loyal fans through a dozen or so subsequent novels. In many of her books, her protagonists face two major problems simultaneously. For example, in *Is That You, Miss Blue?* (Harper, 1976), Flanders must adapt to life in a new prep school while coping with ambivalent feelings toward her separated parents. In *Night Kites* (Harper, 1986), Erick alienates his friends when he beds his best pal's girlfriend while trying to adjust to the news that his beloved brother has AIDS. Similarly, in *Gentlehands,* an average sixteen-year-old boy faces conflicts with his parents over his choice of girlfriend and with his growing suspicions about his grandfather's past. *Gentlehands* is read and enjoyed by students in grades seven through ten.

Principal Characters

Buddy, a sixteen-year-old in a middle-class family
Mr. and Mrs. Boyle, his parents
Streaker, his five-year-old brother
Skye, his wealthy girlfriend

SOCIAL CONCERNS AND PROBLEMS • 95

    Kick Richards, the pot-smoking ex-actor who runs the soda shop
    Frank Trenker, Buddy's grandfather
    Nick DeLucca, an investigative reporter

Plot Summary
Buddy, age sixteen, lives with his mother, his father, who is a sergeant on the local police force, and his young brother, Streaker, in the fashionable summer resort town of Seaville, New York, close to the tip of Long Island. He has a summer job waiting tables at a soda shop run by a pot-smoking ex-actor called Kick Richards. Through him, Buddy meets and becomes enchanted by Skye, the attractive, sophisticated daughter of a wealthy industrialist. Buddy's parents are not enthusiastic about the attachment because of the social differences.

  Inwardly ashamed of his middle-class roots, Buddy takes Skye to visit his grandfather, Frank Trenker, who was born in Germany, migrated to America after World War II, and now lives in Montauk at the end of Long Island. Trenker is a cultivated man who loves opera and knows fine wine. Buddy and Skye find him fascinating.

  Buddy lies to his parents about working overtime in order to spend an afternoon with Skye and her snobby friends at her pool. He meets a houseguest, Nick DeLucca, who is an investigative reporter and, like Buddy, seems out of place in this Waspy environment. Buddy's father finds out and punches Buddy in the face before grounding him for two weeks. But Skye invites Buddy to a picnic at her home and he accepts. After Skye and her friends tell some anti-Semitic jokes, DeLucca reveals that he is a Jew and recites a poem called "Gentlehands," written by his cousin during her last days in Auschwitz. Ashamed and embarrassed, Skye leaves the picnic and asks Buddy to take her to his grandfather. During the evening, Buddy drinks too much wine and passes out. After that, Buddy, who now feels the rift between himself and his parents is irreparable, moves in with his grandfather, whom he now not only respects but loves. Trenker is able to affect a partial reconciliation when he invites his daughter to have dinner with him and Buddy.

  One day Buddy sees DeLucca spying on his grandfather's house. Skye later reveals that the reporter is on the trail of the sadistic concentration camp guard nicknamed Gentlehands who played opera recordings while his victims went to their deaths. DeLucca believes him to be in the area.

  Later that evening, Trenker plays a record for Buddy and Skye from his favorite opera, *Tosca*. The aria is translated as "O gentle hands." Buddy is convinced it is only a coincidence, but evidence mounts against Trenker and the local paper prints a news item headlined "Montauk Man Accused of Being Nazi." Buddy's father, fearful of what will happen, orders his son back home. Buddy continues to believe it is all a mistake even when Skye's brother shows him DeLucca's evidence. When Buddy visits his grandfather, Trenker tells him it is too dangerous for him to come again. He asks Buddy to phone the Stanton Stamp Shop in New York City run by his friend Werner to tell him that "the package from Trenker is on the way." With tears rolling down his cheeks, Buddy says goodbye to his grandfather.

When the story hits the New York papers with further evidence and photographs that also implicate a Dr. Werner Renner, even Buddy must accept the truth. He learns that his grandfather has left Montauk, and he realizes that the "package" was actually Trenker himself. Buddy tells the authorities about the stamp shop. Renner is caught, but Buddy's grandfather escapes.

By the end of the summer, Skye's family is getting ready to leave Seaville; she is about to enter college at Bryn Mawr. Buddy knows that the gap that separates them will only widen and he probably will not see her again. For Buddy it has been a summer of losses but also a summer in which he gained maturity and memories.

Themes and Subjects
In this novel, Buddy grows toward emotional adulthood through the painful lessons of one summer. The novel explores such topics as the difficulties inherent in facing truth; family loyalties; coping with disillusionment; the differences between true and superficial values; and the importance of upholding values even when loved ones may be adversely affected. The need to face consequences for one's decisions is addressed when Buddy makes some unwise choices as well as when he makes the final, fateful decision to reveal his grandfather's whereabouts. Class differences and the difficulties these can produce are well handled, as is the material relating to the Holocaust and anti-Semitism.

Booktalk Material
Without revealing too much about Trenker, the booktalk could introduce Buddy, his home town, and his new friends of the summer and discuss how these relationships cause him problems. Specific passages are: Skye and Buddy visit his grandfather (pp. 18–23); Buddy describes Skye's family to his parents but his father finds out about his lie (pp. 39–43); the picnic, anti-Semitism, and the introduction to "Gentlehands" (pp. 53–56); and Mrs. Boyle visits her father (pp. 72–81).

Additional Selections

Zazoo, a fourteen-year-old girl, and her adoptive grandfather cannot escape memories of war—hers of the Vietnam War and his of World War II in Richard Mosher's *Zazoo* (Clarion, 2001).

The attack on Pearl Harbor in 1941 and its consequences for a Japanese American family are subjects explored by Graham Salisbury in his novel *Blood Red Sun* (pap. Dell, 1995).

In *The Graduation of Jake Moon* (Simon, 2000) by Barbara Park, Jake finds it impossible to cope with his grandfather's gradual disintegration from Alzheimer's.

Katerina, a chronic stutterer, confronts her tyrannical grandfather to help save a rare bird in Tor Seidler's *The Silent Spillbills* (HarperCollins, 1998).

About the Author and Book

Authors and Artists for Young Adults. Gale. Vol. 2, 1989; vol. 23, 1998.
Biography Today: Author Series. Vol. 1, Omnigraphics, 1995.
Children's Books and Their Creators. Houghton, 1995.
Children's Literature Review. Vol. 29, Gale, 1993.
Contemporary Authors New Revision Series. Vol. 63, Gale, 1998.
Continuum Encyclopedia of Children's Literature, Continuum, 2001.
Drew, Bernard A. *100 Most Popular Young Adult Authors.* Libraries Unlimited, 1997.
Fourth Book of Junior Authors and Illustrators. Wilson, 1978.
Gallo. Donald R. *Speaking for Ourselves.* National Council of Teachers of English, 1990.
Gillespie, John T., and Corinne J. Naden. *Characters in Young Adult Literature.* Gale, 1997.
Kerr, M. E. *Blood on the Forehead: What I Know About Writing.* HarperCollins, 1998.
———. *Me, Me, Me, Me, Me.* Harper, 1983.
Lives and Works: Young Adult Authors. Vol. 4, Grolier, 1999.
Major Authors and Illustrators for Children and Young Adults (1st ed.). Vol. 4, Gale, 1993.
Major Authors and Illustrators for Children and Young Adults (2nd ed.). Vol. 6 (under Meaker), Gale, 2002.
Neilson, Alleen Pace. *Presenting M. E. Kerr.* Twayne, 1986.
Roginski, Jim. *Behind the Covers.* Vol. 2, Libraries Unlimited, 1986.
St. James Guide to Young Adult Writers (2nd ed.). St. James, 1999.
Something About the Author. Gale. Vol. 20, 1980; vol. 61, 1990; vol. 91, 1997; vol. 99, 1999; vol. 111, 2000; vol. 160, 2005.
Something About the Author Autobiography Series. Vol. 1, Gale, 1986.
Stevens, Jen. *The Undergraduate's Companion to Children's Writers and Their Web Sites.* Libraries Unlimited, 2004.
Twentieth-Century Young Adult Writers (1st ed.). St. James, 1994.
Writers for Young Adults. Vol. 2, Scribner, 1997.
www.mekerr.com (personal Web site)
See also listing "Selected Web Sites on Children's Literature and Authors."

Koertge, Ron. *The Arizona Kid.* Candlewick, 2005 (1988). $16.99, 0-7636-2542-6 (Grades 8–10).

Introduction

Ron Koertge (1950–) became interested in writing and the power of words at an early age. After receiving degrees in English, he took a teaching position at Pasadena City College in California, where he taught for many years. His first young adult novel was *Where the Kissing Never Stops* (Little, Brown, 1986), in which Walker, a teenager beset by sexual fantasies and yearnings, finally has his first love affair while he is still adjusting to the fact that his mother has become a stripper in a local roadhouse. *The Man in the Moon* (Little, Brown, 1990) is also about a sexually obsessed seventeen-year-old boy who finds love with a compassionate girlfriend. The title comes from the hero's severe case of acne, which makes his face look like a lunar surface. In the novel in between, *The Arizona Kid*, a sixteen-year-old boy experiences his first love affair while staying with a gay uncle in Arizona. All three novels are characterized as irreverent because they deal with sexual situations in frank language. Each is suffused, however, with good humor, believable characters, and a fast-moving plot. They are recommended for mature readers in grades eight and up.

Principal Characters

Billy Kennedy, a sexually obsessed sixteen-year-old boy
Wes, Billy's gay uncle
Lew Coley, stable boy
Abby Dayton, Lew's girlfriend
Cara Mae Whitney, horse exerciser
Jack Ferguson, horse trainer

Plot Summary

Billy Kennedy, sixteen, is a midwesterner and a nice guy with two main worries: he is short and a virgin. Billy spends the summer in Tucson, Arizona, with Uncle Wes, who works at a local racetrack and is gay. Uncle Wes is also a nice guy, and they become good friends. At the racetrack, Billy meets Wes's boss, Jack Ferguson, a respected horse trainer; veteran stable boy Lew Coley; Lew's girlfriend, Abby Dayton; and a blond horse exerciser named Cara Mae Whitney.

One evening, Billy, Lew, Abby, and Cara drive to a butte overlooking Tucson. While Lew and Abby make out in the front seat, Billy and Cara talk. He realizes that much of Cara's bravado serves to hide her own insecurities. The two share stories about their pasts. Billy hopes to become a veterinarian and Cara a horse trainer.

Billy and Cara grow closer and gradually realize that they are in love. With each date they become more intimate. They decide to sleep together. The opportunity comes one weekend when Wes is away. It is a beautiful and fulfilling first-time experience for both.

From Uncle Wes, Billy learns about the alternate sexual lifestyles of homosexuals. He shares Wes's despair and agony over the illness and deaths of friends stricken with AIDS.

August rolls around and Billy realizes sadly that in one month he must leave Arizona. Everyone's attention at the racetrack is focused on the upcoming Labor Day Tucson Derby. A new batch of horses arrives for the races. Lew rashly accepts a five-hundred-dollar bet with Fletcher, a crooked trainer, and his sidekick Grif that The Dark Mirage, the new three-year-old filly sent to Jack for training, will beat their rivals' new acquisition, French Bred. Billy and Lew dig deep into their precious savings to collect the necessary five hundred dollars.

Unfortunately, The Dark Mirage suffers from nerves. At her first workout with Cara in the saddle, the horse bucks and races so violently that Cara faces the embarrassment of being rescued by one of the other riders.

As a last resort, Jack decides to send the horse to a small, quiet training center outside town. The change in surroundings works and while the Dark's performance improves, news comes that French Bred's has not. When the Dark is returned to the stables at the racetrack, Jack is so afraid that Fletcher and Grif might try to harm the horse that he orders a twenty-four-hour watch, with Billy and Lew jointly taking the night shift.

The night before the big race, Lew fails to show up. Billy learns that Lew's father, an eccentric survivalist, has "kidnapped" his son to go on maneuvers. Left on his own, Billy becomes nervous when he hears footsteps approaching. It is Cara, who has come to keep him company. Realizing with sadness that in only two days they will be parting, they once again declare their love. They are interrupted by the arrival of Fletcher and Grif. Courageously, Billy confronts them and manages to scare them off by threatening to report them to the authorities. That night in the stables, Billy and Cara make love once more and promise that although they may be separated, they will always keep in touch.

On the day of the race, Cara and Billy are given the privilege of walking the horse from her stall to the jockey and giving tips on how to handle the horse properly. As expected, The Dark Mirage wins. Lew and Billy collect the five hundred dollars, but this moment of triumph is mixed with sadness as Billy says goodbye to his friends, including Cara.

The next day, Wes takes Billy to the train station. As a parting gesture, Billy gives his uncle his tall-crowned hat, which Wes had given to him. He wants Wes to keep it for him. Wes promises to keep it in Billy's room so it will be there when he returns.

Themes and Subjects
With wit and understanding, the author has created a tender but unsentimental story of two young people coming of age. The necessity of accepting one's physical and emotional makeup is examined. Various types of love are explored and contrasted: for example, the casual physical relationship of Lew and Abby, the tender tentative feelings shared by Billy and Cara, and the homosexual lifestyle of Uncle Wes. All are portrayed honestly and with compassion. The need for tolerance and understanding of others is stressed and Billy's growing love and admiration for his uncle are well depicted. The description of gay life is refreshingly candid without being lurid, and a serious message about AIDS is given. The reader also learns a great deal about behind-the-scenes racetrack life. Courage, the triumph of justice, and coping with parting are other themes that are developed in this novel.

Booktalk Material
A fine introduction to the novel is Billy's arrival in Tucson when he meets Uncle Wes and faints (pp. 1–5). Other interesting passages are: Wes takes Billy to his shop and they discuss AIDS (pp. 17–20); Billy meets Jack and Lew (pp. 24–28); Billy meets Lew's eccentric family (pp. 42–46); he learns a little about Cara and about racetrack betting (pp. 53–59); and Cara and Billy get to know one another (pp. 63–68).

Additional Selections
Charlie and Brandon are close friends but their friendship is shattered when Brandon finds out that Charlie's older brother is gay in A. M. Jenkins's *Breaking Boxes* (Delacorte, 1995).

In Michael Cart's *My Father's Scar* (St. Martin's, 1998), Andy Logan is growing up gay in a straight world with an alcoholic father and a distant mother.

Isabelle Holland's *Man Without a Face* (Lippincott, 1972) tells the story of a teenage boy who engages a disfigured man as his teacher.

A tough delinquent is sent to his uncle's ranch, where he falls in love with a girl who is trying to tame a wild horse in S. E. Hinton's *Taming the Star Runner* (Bantam, 1989).

About the Author and Book
Authors and Artists for Young Adults. Gale. Vol. 12, 1994; vol. 43, 2002.
Children's Books and Their Creators. Houghton, 1995.
Contemporary Authors New Revision Series. Vol. 58, Gale, 1997.
Continuum Encyclopedia of Children's Literature. Continuum, 2001.
Drew, Bernard A. *100 Most Popular Young Adult Authors.* Libraries Unlimited, 1997.
Gallo, Donald R. *Speaking for Ourselves, Too.* National Council of Teachers of English, 1993.
Lives and Works: Young Adult Authors. Vol. 5, Grolier, 1999.
Major Authors and Illustrators for Children and Young Adults (2nd ed.). Vol. 5, Gale, 2002.
St. James Guide to Young Adult Writers (2nd ed.). St. James, 1999.
Seventh Book of Junior Authors and Illustrators. Wilson, 1996.
Something About the Author. Gale. Vol. 52, 1988; vol. 92, 1997; vol. 131, 2002.
Twentieth-Century Young Adult Writers (1st ed.). St. James, 1994.
Writers for Young Adults. Supp. 1, Scribner, 2000.
See also listing "Selected Web Sites on Children's Literature and Authors."

L'Engle, Madeleine. *A Ring of Endless Light.* Farrar, 1980. $20, 0-3743-6299-8 (Grades 7–10).

Introduction

Madeleine L'Engle (1918–) is considered one of the greatest living writers of young adult literature. Among the honors bestowed upon her was the 1963 Newbery Medal for her brilliant science fiction novel *A Wrinkle in Time* (Farrar, 1962). Readers were introduced to the Austin family and the narrator, daughter Vicky, in *Meet the Austins* (Vanguard, 1960). In this novel, Dr. and Mrs. Austin, who are living in a small New England town with their family of four—sons John and Rob, daughters Vicky and Suzy—find that their loving family relationship becomes strained when they care for a troubled orphan girl. In *The Moon by Night* (Farrar, 1963), the Austins, on a cross-country trip, meet the wealthy Mr. and Mrs. Gray and their spoiled son Zachary, to whom Vicky is attracted; and in *The Young Unicorns* (Farrar, 1968), the Austins spend a year in New York City. In an unrelated adventure novel, *The Arm of the Starfish* (Farrar, 1965), a teenager named Adam Eddington is the hero. Adam, Zachary, and the Austins play important roles in *A Ring of Endless Light,* the most mystical, somber, and introspective novel in the series. It is recommended for good readers in grades seven through ten.

Principal Characters
    Vicky Austin, age sixteen
    Her parents and siblings John, Suzy, and Rob
    Grandfather Eaton
    Commander Rodney and his son Leo
    Zachary Gray, a young "bad penny"
    Adam Eddington, an eighteen-year-old college student
    Dr. Jed Nutteley
    Grace and her sick daughter, Binnie

Plot Summary

Vicky Austin, the narrator; her father, Dr. Austin; her mother; older brother John; and younger siblings Suzy and Rob are spending the summer at the New England island home of widowed Grandfather Eaton, a retired pastor. It should be a great summer, but a cloud hangs over the family because Grandfather is dying of leukemia. Vicky cannot accept the inevitability of his death.

After a week on the island, Commander Rodney, the well-liked chief of the Marine Biology Station, has a fatal heart attack after rescuing a young man from drowning. The young man turns out to be Zachary Gray, who has come east to look for Vicky. He tells her the drowning incident was actually a foiled suicide attempt; he says he needs her love and support to give him back the will to live.

Other young men begin to play roles in Vicky's life. One is Leo Rodney, the dead commander's son. She at first regards him as a snob, but his difficult adjustment to his father's death leads her to understand and sympathize with him. The other is Adam Eddington, an eighteen-year-old college student who is working at the station with Dr. Jed Nutteley on communicating with bottle-nosed dolphins. At the station, Vicky meets Basil, a free dolphin who comes regularly at Adam's call to play with him. But Vicky's best times are with her grandfather, who often recites verses to her, such as the Henry Vaughan poem that begins: "I saw Eternity the other night, Like a great ring of pure and endless light."

Vicky's attraction to Adam increases and she becomes more involved in his work. One day Basil brings a female dolphin to play and Vicky names her Norberta. Adam senses that Vicky, in her naïve purity, is miraculously able to communicate with the dolphins. They obey her commands and allow her privileges (denied anyone else) such as riding on their backs. This amazing gift is tested many times, and soon Vicky is receiving thought sensations and dream pictures from the dolphins that convey entirely different concepts of life and time.

The excitement of these discoveries is blunted by a series of tragic events. The baby of pregnant dolphin Ynid dies, Jed Nutteley is struck by a motorcycle and lies unconscious between life and death in the mainland hospital, and Grandfather's condition is steadily deteriorating, so that he often hemorrhages and frequently requires transfusions. On one trip to the mainland with Leo to collect blood for her grandfather, Vicky meets in the hospital's emergency room a pathetic young mother, Grace, and her ailing daughter, Binnie, who suffers from a congenital heart condition that also must be treated with blood transfusions. Vicky feels that except for Adam and his dolphins, she is surrounded by death and dying.

Zachary continues to entertain Vicky in his manic, cavalier manner. He is now taking flying lessons. One day, he, Vicky—he calls her Vicky-O—and his flight instructor, Joe, go for a ride in the Piper Cub. Zachary takes over the controls and in a show of reckless bravura narrowly misses colliding with a passing jet. Back on the ground, Vicky, still in shock from this incident, finds that during her absence Grandfather has had another seizure and is in the hospital. She makes her way to the emergency room. While she is awaiting news of his condition, Grace arrives with a very sick Binnie. She gives the child to Vicky to hold while she seeks help; during Grace's absence, Binnie has convulsions and dies in Vicky's arms. Suddenly the forces of darkness envelop Vicky. She becomes numbed by the accumulated grief and sorrow around her, and even though she learns that Grandfather has weathered his attack and Jed is improving, for several days she appears to wander in a daze. Slowly, through tender support and advice from Grandfather and Adam—and the life-giving gentleness of the dolphins—she is able to accept the present and once again face the future.

Themes and Subjects

This is one of the most profound and shocking of Madeleine L'Engle's novels. On one level it is a novel about dying and various ways of adjusting to death, but more importantly, it explores the meaning of faith and dimensions of human existence. As Grandfather states, "When one tries to avoid death, it's impossible to avoid life." The theme of oneness in nature is explored in the episodes involving animal ESP and nonverbal communication. Wholesome family situations are well depicted, as are various aspects of love and friendship and the necessity of developing and maintaining moral standards to lead a constructive life.

Booktalk Material

A discussion of the dolphin experiments should produce interest. Specific early passages of importance are: Vicky comforts Leo (pp. 31–33); Zachary talks about his life and suicide attempt (pp. 47–53); Zachary and Grandfather discuss cryonics (pp. 42–45); Vicky talks about Zachary and life's problems with Grandfather (pp. 56–64); and Vicky meets the dolphins (pp. 86–101).

Additional Selections

Jenna gains confidence and security when she acts as a chauffeur during a trip from Illinois to Texas in Joan Bauer's *Rules of the Road* (Putnam, 1998).

Zinny, the middle daughter in a large family, suffers extreme depression when her beloved aunt dies in *Chasing Redbird* (HarperCollins, 1997) by Sharon Creech.

Kristen faces many personal problems in Kelly Easton's *The Life History of a Star* (McElderry, 2001), a novel told in diary form about a girl haunted by thoughts of her brother, a Vietnam vet.

Three orphaned brothers confront the loss of their parents in different ways in Jacqueline Woodson's *Miracle Boys* (Putnam, 2000).

About the Author and Book

Authors and Artists for Young Adults. Gale. Vol. 1, 1989; vol. 28, 1999.
Bostrom, Kathleen Long. *Winning Authors: Profiles of the Newbery Medalists.* Libraries Unlimited, 2003.
Children's Books and Their Creators. Houghton, 1995.
Children's Literature Review. Gale. Vol. 1, 1976; vol. 14, 1988; vol. 57, 2000.
Contemporary Authors New Revision Series. Vol. 107, Gale, 2002.
Continuum Encyclopedia of Children's Literature. Continuum, 2001.
Drew, Bernard A. *100 Most Popular Young Adult Authors.* Libraries Unlimited, 1996.
Estes, Glenn E. "American Writers for Children Since 1960: Fiction." In *Dictionary of Literary Biography.* Vol. 54, Gale, 1986.
Favorite Children's Authors and Illustrators. Vol. 4, Tradition Books, 2003.
Gallo, Donald R. *Speaking for Ourselves.* National Council of Teachers of English, 1990.
Gillespie, John T., and Corinne J. Naden. *Characters in Young Adult Literature.* Gale, 1997.
Gonzales, Doreen. *Madeleine L'Engle: Author of "A Wrinkle in Time."* Dillon, 1991.
Herne, Betsy. "A Mind in Motion: A Few Moments with Madeleine L'Engle," *School Library Journal,* June, 1998, pp. 28–33.
Hettinger, Donald R. *Presenting Madeleine L'Engle.* Twayne, 1993.
Jones, Raymond E. *Characters in Children's Literature.* Gale, 1997.
L'Engle, Madeleine. "1998 Margaret Edwards Award Acceptance Speech," *Journal of Youth Services in Libraries,* Fall, 1998, pp. 11–13.

———. *Trailing Clouds of Glory: Spiritual Values in Children's Books.* Westminster, 1985.
———. *Two Part Invention: The Story of a Marriage.* Farrar, 1988.
McElmeel, Sharron L. *100 Most Popular Children's Authors.* Libraries Unlimited, 1999
Major Authors and Illustrators for Children and Young Adults (1st ed.). Vol. 4, Gale, 1993.
Major Authors and Illustrators for Children and Young Adults (2nd ed.). Vol. 5, Gale, 2002.
More Junior Authors. Wilson, 1963.
Ninth Book of Junior Authors and Illustrators. Wilson, 2004.
St. James Guide to Children's Writers (5th ed.). St. James, 1999.
St. James Guide to Young Adult Writers (2nd ed.). St. James, 1999.
Something About the Author. Gale. Vol. 1, 1971; vol. 27, 1982; vol. 75, 1994; vol. 128, 2002
Something About the Author Autobiography Series. Vol. 15, Gale, 1993.
Stevens, Jen. *The Undergraduate's Companion to Children's Writers and Their Web Sites.* Libraries Unlimited, 2004.
Twentieth-Century Children's Writers (4th ed.). St. James, 1995.
Twentieth-Century Young Adult Writers (1st ed.). St. James, 1994.
Writers for Young Adults. Vol. 2, Scribner, 1997.
See also listing "Selected Web Sites on Children's Literature and Authors."

Lowry, Lois. *Rabble Starkey.* Dell, 1987. Pap. $6.95, 0-440-40056-2 (Grades 7–10).

Introduction

One of the highlights of the distinguished literary career of Lois Lowry (1937–) occurred in 1990 when she received the Newbery Medal for *Number the Stars* (Houghton, 1989), a novel based on the Danish underground's efforts to save Jewish families during the Nazi occupation in World War II. Before that, she had written many fine books for the middle grades (several featuring the untamable Anastasia Krupnick) plus many young adult novels such as *A Summer to Die* (Houghton, 1977). *Rabble Starkey* straddles both groups. Although its heroine is a sixth-grader, the concept and interest levels of the novel are such that the book has appeal to readers from sixth through ninth grades. It is a first-person narrative told in candid and often ungrammatical English (e.g., "we was going") by a feisty, intelligent young girl from rural West Virginia. The action takes place over a single school year. During this time Rabble's grammar improves somewhat partly because of her own efforts and partly through the help of her dear friend Veronica (e.g., "we *were* going, Rabble").

Principal Characters
　　Rabble Starkey, twelve years old
　　Sweet-Ho, her mother
　　Veronica Bigelow, Rabble's best friend
　　Gunther Bigelow, Veronica's brother
　　Mrs. Bigelow, Veronica's mother
　　Phil Bigelow, Veronica's father
　　Norman Cox, the local minister's obnoxious son
　　Mrs. Hindler, Rabble's teacher
　　Millie Bellows, the town grouch

Plot Summary

Twelve-year-old Rabble and her loving mother Sweet-Ho (short for Sweet-Hosanna) live in a small apartment above the Bigelows' garage in Highriver, West Virginia. Sweet-Ho is the housekeeper for the Bigelow family, which includes daughter Veronica, also twelve and Rabble's best friend; Mrs. Bigelow, who is sinking into insanity; Gunther, who is four; and kindly Mr. Bigelow, the father.

　　Rabble and Veronica are given an assignment by their sixth-grade teacher, Mrs. Hindler, to construct family trees. Sweet-Ho retells Rabble the story of being fourteen and running off to marry Ginger Starkey, who deserted her when Rabble (whose real name is Parable Ann) arrived.

　　One hot Saturday afternoon, Rabble and Veronica decide to take Gunther to the creek to cool off. They pass the house of old Millie Bellows, the town grouch, who seems immune to any show of kindness or civility. At the creek they are tormented by the bully Norman Cox, who throws rocks at them, one of which injures Gunther. While giving chase, they hear Gunther's frantic screams. Mrs. Bigelow, who has followed them to the stream, has Gunther in her arms. After licking the blood from the wound, she tries to breast-feed him and then enacts a mock baptism scene that half drowns the child before the girls can rescue him and escort a now-passive Mrs. Bigelow home. News of Mrs. Bigelow's breakdown speeds through town. Even crotchety Millie Bellows sends over a Jell-O salad to help. Reluctantly, Mr. Bigelow commits his wife to the local mental hospital. Veronica is so troubled and embarrassed by the situation that at one point she wants to erase her mother's name from her family tree. Mr. Bigelow invites the Starkeys to move into the family house and suddenly Rabble begins to feel part of a real family.

　　Halloween comes and the two girls, in gypsy disguises, dress Gunther as a mini-ballerina and go out trick-or-treating. Millie Bellows is slow to answer her bell and when she does, she is hit in the face by a stone thrown from the shrubbery. Rabble runs after the attacker, and although he escapes he drops a hat that is later identified as belonging to Norman Cox.

Out of pity, the two girls begin visiting and cleaning house for a still-grumpy and ungrateful Millie Bellows. Some of the chores require a boy's strength and Rabble decides to blackmail Norman into helping them by using the threat of revealing him as the stone-thrower.

Mr. Bigelow believes that Sweet-Ho has great untapped potential. Gradually he is able to build her self-confidence sufficiently for her to obtain a high school equivalency diploma and make plans to enroll as a part-time student in the local junior college. He and Veronica are also encouraged by the progress they see when they visit Mrs. Bigelow.

Spring brings many changes. Millie Bellows dies suddenly and a new family, the Elliots, buy her house. Sweet-Ho does so well at college that she becomes impatient to accelerate her studies. The most surprising news comes from the mental hospital. Mrs. Bigelow has recovered enough to be sent home in the middle of June. Rabble is both happy and dismayed because she knows that when Mrs. Bigelow returns, she will lose her new home and family and will have to return to the cramped garage. But there are further surprises. Sweet-Ho tells Rabble that they will be moving. She has saved enough money so that, by taking a part-time evening job, she can enter the university at Clarksburg as a full-time student in the teacher's training program. Mr. Bigelow has given them an old car and Sweet-Ho has already rented a small apartment for them. Together they pack the car with their few belongings and set out for a new life.

Themes and Subjects

This novel contains a sensitive portrait of a charming, feisty, honest young girl who faces change and the problems of growing up with both humor and common sense. It is also a portrait of various kinds of love: romantic love that almost develops between Mr. Bigelow and Sweet-Ho; familial love as shown by the tender relationship between Sweet-Ho and Rabble and by the Bigelows; love that stems from deep friendship like that shared by Veronica and Rabble; and love that develops through nearness and compassion such as that felt by Rabble for Millie Bellows and Gunther. A realistic picture of mental illness and its effects on families is presented, and the novel also contains a touching portrayal of the meaning and importance of home and family in the lives of young children. The importance of growing up and moving on when necessary is underlined. The episodes involving Rabble, Veronica, and Norman illustrate the destructive power of jealousy and the constructive power of forgiveness.

Booktalk Material

Some passages that could be read or retold are: the family tree assignment (pp. 1–6); Sweet-Ho tells of her life with Ginger and the naming of Rabble (pp. 9–13); the Starkeys move into the garage (pp. 18–23); the incident at the creek with Mrs. Bigelow (pp. 38–45); Rabble uses a thesaurus for her composition about home (pp. 59–67); and trick-or-treating at Millie Bellows's house (pp. 78–86).

Additional Selections

Growing up in a small, secure community, fourteen-year-old Marley's life is shattered when she discovers that her "parents" are really her aunt and uncle in Angela Johnson's *Heaven* (Simon, 1998).

In Janet McDonald's *Spellbound* (Farrar, 2001), fifteen-year-old Raven, an unmarried mother, hopes to get out of the Brooklyn projects by winning a spelling bee.

Orphaned seventeen-year-old Arden investigates the disappearance of the older brother who has been raising her in *Thin Ice* (Dell, 1999) by Marsha Qualey.

When her mother discovers she has a brain tumor, sixteen-year-old Mindy assumes new responsibilities in Joan Abelove's *Saying It Out Loud* (Dorling, 1999), a coming-of-age novel.

About the Author and Book

Authors and Artists for Young Adults. Gale. Vol. 5, 1990; vol. 32, 2000.
Biography Today: Author Series. Vol. 4, Omnigraphics, 1998.
Bostrom, Kathleen Long. *Winning Authors: Profiles of the Newbery Medalists*. Libraries Unlimited, 2003.
Children's Books and Their Creators. Houghton, 1995.
Children's Literature Review. Gale. Vol. 6, 1984; vol. 46, 1998; vol. 72, 2002.
Contemporary Authors. Vol. 200, Gale, 2002.
Continuum Encyclopedia of Children's Literature. Continuum, 2001.
Drew, Bernard A. *100 Most Popular Young Adult Authors*. Libraries Unlimited, 1996.
Estes, Glenn E. "American Writers for Children Since 1960: Fiction." In *Dictionary of Literary Biography*. Vol. 52, Gale, 1986.
Favorite Children's Authors and Illustrators. Vol. 4, Tradition Books, 2003.
Fifth Book of Junior Authors and Illustrators. Wilson, 1983.
Gallo, Donald R. *Speaking for Ourselves, Too*. National Council of Teachers of English, 1993.
Gillespie, John T., and Corinne J. Naden. *Characters in Young Adult Literature*. Gale, 1997.
Haley-James, Shirley. "Lois Lowry," *Horn Book*, July/Aug., 1990, pp. 422–24.

Jones, Raymond E. *Characters in Children's Literature.* Gale, 1997.
Lives and Works: Young Adult Authors. Vol. 5, Grolier, 1999.
Lowry, Lois. "Impossible Promises," *School Library Journal,* April, 2000, pp. 56–60.
———. *Looking Back: A Book of Memories.* Houghton, 1998.
———. "The Zena Sutherland Lecture: The Remembered Gate and the Unexpected Door," *Horn Book,* March/April, 2002, pp. 159–77.
McElmeel, Sharron L. *100 Most Popular Children's Authors.* Libraries Unlimited, 1999.
Major Authors and Illustrators for Children and Young Adults (1st ed.). Vol. 4, Gale, 1993.
Major Authors and Illustrators for Children and Young Adults (2nd ed.). Vol. 5, Gale, 2002.
St. James Guide to Young Adult Writers (2nd ed.). St. James, 1999.
Something About the Author. Gale. Vol. 23, 1981; vol. 70, 1993; vol. 111, 2000; vol. 127, 2002.
Something About the Author Autobiography Series. Vol. 3, Gale, 1987.
Stevens, Jen. *The Undergraduate's Companion to Children's Writers and Their Web Sites.* Libraries Unlimited, 2004.
Twentieth-Century Young Adult Writers (1st ed.). St. James, 1994.
Writers for Young Adults. Vol. 2, Scribner, 1997.
www.loislowry.com (personal Web site)
See also listing "Selected Web Sites on Children's Literature and Authors."

Naylor, Phyllis Reynolds. *The Keeper.* Starfire, 1986. Pap. $3.95, 0-55326-882-1 (Grades 7–10).

Introduction

Phyllis Reynolds Naylor (1933–), the daughter of a salesman and a teacher, grew up during the Great Depression in an ordinary midwestern family for whom books and reading were part of everyday life. She published her first story at age sixteen and for twenty-five years wrote a humorous column for teenagers in a church newspaper. Perhaps some of the episodes in her very popular Alice series came from these columns. She has said about her writing, "I will do anything possible to save time in which to write. I shamelessly order meals to be divided, pay for secretarial and cleaning help, and if I could allocate my three-mile walk every morning to someone else, I would probably even pay for that." She has written more than 60 books for children of various ages. Among them are the Newbery Medal-winning *Shiloh* (Macmillan, 1991), the story of the Preston family of West Virginia and their efforts to adopt a young beagle that has been abused by its owner; and *The Keeper,* the story of a boy's adjustment to his father's mental illness. This story, which arose from the ordeal of the author's first marriage, is suitable for readers in grades seven through ten.

Principal Characters
    Nick Karpinsky, a teenager in Chicago
    Jacob and Wanda, his parents
    Thad Karpinsky, his uncle
    Danny, his best friend
    Lois, his girlfriend
    Karen, his friend in the apartment building
    Miss Etting, the school nurse

Plot Summary
For Nick Karpinsky, life seems pretty good. He lives in an apartment in Chicago with his father, Jacob, and his mother, Wanda. In his last year of junior high, Nick has taken a girl to the movies for the first time, and he and his best friend, Danny, get along just fine. In fact, everything would be just about perfect were it not for the problems with his father, who has been acting strange lately. More and more, he avoids his job at the post office, staying home because he can't bear to face the workplace. Nick and his mother have become used to his father's frequent job changes. At first, each change appeared to be for the best, but now the situation has worsened and Nick's father can't hold a job at all. Part of the reason, Jacob claims, is that the Communists are after him.

It is as though his father has become a stranger. Always known as a precise and meticulous man, Jacob now leaves bills unpaid and newspapers strewn around the apartment. Some days he does not shave at all. It becomes difficult to have a rational conversation with him. Nick and his mother do not know what to do or how to reach him.

Christmas was especially uncomfortable that year. Nick's grandparents came for dinner, but his father barely paid attention to anyone. He had to be reminded to come to the dinner table. When he got up to get the coffeepot, he never came back. Nick found him staring out the kitchen window.

Although they both try to deny it, Nick and his mother slowly begin to realize that Jacob is mentally ill. They try in various ways to get help for him, enlisting advice from the local priest, from Jacob's brother Thad, and from their doctor. But Jacob resists seeking treatment, and without his cooperation, they can't commit him to the VA hospital.

As his father's condition worsens, Nick gets a job after school to help the family and tries to hide the situation from Danny and Lois, whom Nick has begun to date, and from Karen, his friend who lives in the same apartment building. Finally, Jacob comes home with a rifle he has bought to protect himself from imagined enemies. He tells his family that "they're coming" and he must be ready. Nick's mother tells him she won't allow a gun in the house. His father replies that the Constitution allows it. Nick and his mother are able to get the gun away and Nick takes it back to the store. Nick now convinces his mother that something must be done.

Out in the car with his family, his father driving 40 miles an hour in a 25-mph zone, Nick boldly attracts the attention of a passing patrol car by pressing on the horn. Nick tells the police his father is sick, but Jacob stoutly denies it and acts normally. The police are reluctant to do anything. Finally, Nick calls the school nurse, Miss Etting, to whom he has confided his problems. She convinces the authorities of the seriousness of Jacob's condition. Finally, the doctors agree to admit Jacob against his will, and he is taken into the VA hospital.

The doctors can give Nick and his mother no assurances that his father will ever recover fully, but they hope he will improve enough to return home eventually. Nick wants to understand his father's illness and worries it might be inherited. The doctor says he would be very surprised if the same thing happened to Nick. Nick grieves for the father he will never have again, but he understands that he and his mother must build a new life for themselves.

Themes and Subjects

This is an honest and direct look at mental illness and the problems of those who confront it. Nick is a thoughtful teenager who wants to help his father but at the same time tries to hide the truth from his friends. Readers will sympathize with his efforts to get help, his protectiveness toward his mother, and his sadness as he watches his father descend further and further into his illness.

Booktalk Material

Christmas Day with the grandparents is a good introduction to Jacob's condition (pp. 9–12). Other important passages are: his father talks about Communists (pp. 36–38); Nick talks to Miss Etting (pp. 65–68); Jacob says he's not going back to the post office (pp. 95–98); Jacob brings home a gun (pp. 154–63); the scene in the car (pp. 176–79); Jacob is admitted to the VA hospital (pp. 189–92).

Additional Selections

Alice learns that her abusive father, who has physically injured her, is dying in Graham McNamee's *Hate You* (Dell, 2000).

In Randy Powell's *Run If You Dare* (Farrar, 2001), Gardner witnesses his father's descent into depression and apathy after he loses his job.

After two high school seniors move in together, the girl discovers that her boyfriend suffers from chronic depression in Margaret Willey's *Saving Lenny* (Bantam, 1991).

In her journal, Tish, a tenth-grader, reveals how she is bored with school and how she must care for her severely depressed mother in *Don't You Dare Read This, Mrs. Dunphrey* (Simon, 1996) by Margaret Peterson Haddix.

About the Author and Book
Authors and Artists for Young Adults. Gale. Vol. 4, 1990; vol. 29, 1991.
Bostrom, Kathleen Long. *Winning Authors: Profiles of the Newbery Medalists.* Libraries Unlimited, 2003.
Children's Books and Their Creators. Houghton, 1995.
Children's Literature Review. Vol. 17, Gale, 1989.
Contemporary Authors New Revision Series. Vol. 130, 2005.
Continuum Encyclopedia of Children's Literature. Continuum, 2001.
Drew, Bernard A. *100 Most Popular Young Adult Authors.* Libraries Unlimited, 1996.
Favorite Children's Authors and Illustrators. Vol. 4, Tradition Books, 2003.
Fifth Book of Junior Authors and Illustrators. Wilson, 1983.
Gallo, Donald R. *Speaking for Ourselves, Too.* National Council of Teachers of English, 1993.
Gillespie, John T., and Corinne J. Naden. *Characters in Young Adult Literature.* Gale, 1997.
Graham, Joyce, "An Interview with Phyllis Reynolds Naylor," *Journal of Youth Services in Libraries,* Summer, 1993, pp. 392–98.
Life and Works: Young Adult Authors. Vol. 6, Grolier, 1999.
McElmeel, Sharron L. *100 Most Popular Children's Authors.* Libraries Unlimited, 1999.
Major Authors and Illustrators for Children and Young Adults (1st ed.). Vol. 4, Gale, 1993.
Major Authors and Illustrators for Children and Young Adults (2nd ed.). Vol. 6, Gale, 2002.
Naylor, Phyllis Reynolds. *How I Came to Be a Writer.* Macmillan, 1989.
Naylor, Rex. "Phyllis Reynolds Naylor," *Horn Book,* July/Aug., 1992.
St. James Guide to Children's Writers (5th ed.). St. James, 1999.
St. James Guide to Young Adult Writers (2nd ed.). St. James, 1999.
Something About the Author. Gale. Vol. 12, 1977; vol. 66, 1991; vol. 102, 1999; vol. 152, 2005.
Something About the Author Autobiography Series. Vol. 10, Gale, 1990.
Twentieth-Century Children's Writers (4th ed.). St. James, 1995.
Twentieth-Century Young Adult Writers (1st ed.). St. James, 1994.

Writers for Young Adults. Vol. 2, Scribner, 1997.
See also listing "Selected Web Sites on Children's Literature and Authors."

Neufeld, John. *Lisa, Bright and Dark.* Puffin, 1999 (1969). Pap. $5.99, 0-14-130434-0 (Grades 7–9).

Introduction
John Neufeld (1938–), a Chicago native, never imagined he would be the writer of several innovative young adult novels even though he began writing while only in middle school. After an American education that included an undergraduate degree from Yale, he spent some time in Europe before beginning a career in publishing in this country. His first novel for young adults was *Edgar Allan* (Phillips, 1968), a book about interracial adoption based on actual events. The story of *Lisa, Bright and Dark* (which was originally titled *I'll Always Love You, Paul Newman*) is an agonizing cry for help from a young girl who is slowly but inexorably sinking into madness. What saves this novel from being simply a harrowing and unrelieved account of a descent into insanity is its hopeful ending and the devices used to tell the story. The title refers to the moods that alternate within Lisa Shilling, the sixteen-year-old heroine. On her good or bright days, she dresses gaily and is her normal, effervescent and friendly self, but on her dark days (which occur with increased frequency and intensity), Lisa is sullen, malicious, withdrawn, and lost in the imaginary voices she hears. The book has been popular with both junior and senior high school students since its first publication.

Principal Characters
Betsy Goodman, high school student and narrator
Lisa Shilling, a young girl sinking into madness
Mr. and Mrs. Shilling, her unresponsive parents
Brian Morris, Lisa's boyfriend
M.N. Fickett and Elizabeth Frazer, Lisa's friends
Mr. Burstein, a mealy-mouthed guidance counselor
Dr. Neil Donovan, a psychiatrist

Plot Summary
Except for an introductory scene in which Lisa tells her parents that she is going crazy and begs for help, the story is narrated by Betsy Goodman, a high school student who lives in an upper-middle-class community on

Long Island, New York. Although Betsy is very modest about her own capability, the reader soon realizes that she has a natural warmth and simplicity, not to mention a wild crush on Paul Newman, all of which immediately endear her to the reader. She quickly introduces the other principals in the story—Lisa Shilling; Lisa's unfeeling and stubborn father; her social-climbing mother; and Lisa's school friends: the All-American Girl, M.N. (short for Mary Nell) Fickett; the extremely wealthy and beautiful Elizabeth Frazer; and Brian Morris, Lisa's boyfriend and the eleventh-grade heartthrob.

M.N. is the first to mention Lisa's moodiness. At a party at the Ficketts', Lisa suddenly becomes enraged and orders everyone to stop dancing. Her insulting behavior toward Brian eventually leads to their breakup. Even worse, M.N. and Betsy one day discover Lisa crouching under the teacher's desk, sticking pins into her wrists and making them bleed. The girls tell Mr. Burstein, their somewhat mealy-mouthed guidance counselor, who in turn recommends to the Shillings that Lisa be sent away for a rest. She spends six weeks in Florida, but she comes back even more despondent and erratic. The girls become more fearful of the eventual outcome, and they appeal to Mr. Burstein and to Lisa's mother to get help for her, but without success.

It is M.N.'s idea to organize a group consisting of Elizabeth, Betsy, and herself to "group therapy-ize" Lisa by spending all their free time with her. In spite of their kindness and attention, the bouts of madness increase. M.N. persuades her father, a minister, and Mr. Milne, an understanding English teacher, to visit Mr. Shilling and make him aware of Lisa's plight. In the middle of the conversation, Lisa rushes in and also begs her father for help, but he is implacable, claiming that all Lisa needs is rest.

In her moments of clarity, Lisa tells the girls about the dreadful abyss into which she is sinking and the hopelessness she feels. But her moments of lucidity are becoming fewer and her bouts of depression more violent and destructive. During an outdoor barbecue, Lisa tries to push Elizabeth into the fire and then brutally attacks all three of the girls when they attempt to subdue her.

Later Lisa makes a desperate attempt to alert adults to her condition by jumping through a glass wall in the presence of Betsy's father. Lisa is taken to the hospital, but when Mr. Goodman approaches Mrs. Shilling, he is once more rebuffed. This time the girls are forbidden to see Lisa again.

Elizabeth contacts "a friend," Dr. Neil Donovan, a psychiatrist who is so wildly handsome and charming that Betsy momentarily forsakes Paul

Newman. In confidence, Elizabeth tells Betsy that Dr. Donovan had been *her* psychiatrist. At Elizabeth's pleading, her father has agreed to pay the costs of Lisa's treatment by Dr. Donovan, but first they must get the consent of the Shillings, which does not seem an easy task. However, it turns out to be less difficult than the girls expect.

After Lisa is released from the hospital, she once more attempts to take her life. This time she tries an overdose of barbiturates. She is returned to the hospital and this time her parents give in. But is it too late? Dr. Donovan and the girls visit Lisa in the hospital. At first there is no response, only blank stares, but when Dr. Donovan is introduced and Lisa is told that he will help her, she begins to sob. Her cry for help has been heard.

Themes and Subjects

Lisa, Bright and Dark shows the fine, often indistinct line between mental illness and sanity and that treatment for psychiatric disorders is as vital and natural as treatment for physical problems. The novel is remarkable in the sympathy and understanding that the young people show toward Lisa in contrast to the unfeeling, guilt-ridden attitudes of her parents. Betsy Goodman is an engaging heroine with disarming modesty and charm. Her presence lends much to the compassion and naturalness of this story.

Booktalk Material

Chapter 1 is a conversation out of context in which Lisa tells her family at the dinner table that she is going insane and needs help. A reading of this will certainly arouse interest (pp. 9–11), as will Betsy's retelling of Lisa's first overt signs of insanity (pp. 18–20), the incident with the pins under the teacher's desk (pp. 24–26), and Lisa with amateur psychiatrist M.N. (pp. 85–88).

Additional Selections

Terry Spencer Hesser's *Kissing Doorknobs* (Delacorte, 1998) is a realistic novel about a girl struggling with an obsessive-compulsive disorder.

Melinda is slowly sinking into depression and isolation because of a traumatic event she can't talk about in Laurie Halse Anderson's *Speak* (Farrar, 1999).

Francesca feels fat and starves herself to a point where not eating becomes an obsession in Steven Levenkron's *The Best Little Girl in the World* (Warner, 1979).

Subtitled *What Happened When My Big Sister Went Crazy*, Sonya Sones's *Stop Pretending* (HarperCollins, 1999) portrays in blank-verse poems a thirteen-year-old girl coping with her sister's strange behavior.

About the Author and Book
Authors and Artists for Young Adults. Vol. 11, Gale, 1993.
Children's Literature Review. Vol. 52, Gale, 1999.
Contemporary Authors New Revision Series. Vol. 56, Gale, 1997.
Eighth Book of Junior Authors and Illustrators. Wilson, 2000.
Gillespie, John T., and Corinne J. Naden. *Characters in Young Adult Literature.* Gale, 1997.
Major Authors and Illustrators for Children and Young Adults (1st ed.). Vol. 4, Gale, 1993.
Major Authors and Illustrators for Children and Young Adults (2nd ed.). Vol. 6, Gale, 2002.
St. James Guide to Young Adult Writers (2nd ed.). St. James, 1999.
Something About the Author. Gale. Vol. 6, 1974; vol. 81, 1995; vol. 131, 2002.
Something About the Author Autobiography Series. Vol. 3, Gale, 1987.
See also listing "Selected Web Sites on Children's Literature and Authors."

Peck, Richard. *Remembering the Good Times.* Dell, 1985. Pap. $5.99, 0-440-97339-2 (Grades 7–10).

Introduction
During the approximately forty years Richard Peck (1934–) has had a full-time writing career, he has produced about thirty highly praised novels for young people. His work falls into two categories. The first includes many serious novels that explore such adolescent concerns as loneliness, family problems, and relationships with peers, as well as emotional situations such as rape and death. *Remembering the Good Times* falls into this group. The second is generally for a slightly younger audience. These are lighter and filled with humorous situations. Some are adventure/fantasies; many are set in America in the first half of the twentieth century. *A Year Down Yonder* (Dial, 2000), Peck's Newbery Medal winner, is one of these. Regardless of the nature of the work, the author has stated, "Every young adult novel must be a chronicle of change. You've got to take a step forward or it doesn't work." This is true of *Remembering the Good Times*, a moving story of friendship and loss. It is suitable for readers in the seventh through tenth grades.

Principal Characters

Buck Mendenhall, who is adjusting to his parents' divorce
Kate Lucas, who lives with her mother and invalid great-grandmother
Polly Prior, Kate's great-grandmother
Trav Kirby, a perfectionist and compulsive worrier

Plot Summary

The story involves the friendship of three young people, Buck Mendenhall, Kate Lucas, and Trav Kirby. The action takes place in once-rural Slocum Township, now developing fast because of a new IBM plant and an influx of upper-middle-class professionals. The Kirbys belong to this group, but Kate is from the original farm stock and Buck's father is a construction worker newly arrived in the area.

Buck's parents have divorced and his mother has remarried, so he moves to Slocum Township to share a trailer with his father, whom he adores. At school he finds himself in the same eighth-grade class as attractive, hoydenish Kate, who lives with her working mother and invalid great-grandmother, Polly Prior; and a newcomer in town, the intelligent, highly sensitive Trav. The three begin hanging out every day after school at Kate's farmhouse, where they talk about their problems and play card games with Polly, the blunt, plain-spoken elder of the family.

The eighth-grade bully, Skeeter, steals Buck's father's hard hat and begins wearing it defiantly to school. For Buck, retrieving the hat becomes a matter of family honor. He confronts Skeeter and in the ensuing fight Buck is knocked unconscious. Skeeter is frightened off when Kate and Trav arrive and, in his haste, he leaves the hat behind. Buck, although badly beaten, feels a sense of triumph.

Their freshman year is a welter of confused class schedules and less-than-inspiring teachers. Trav is particularly disturbed by the confusion and lack of challenge. By accident, the three learn that their English teacher, the ineffective Mrs. Slater, has been receiving obscene phone calls from Skeeter. Kate realizes he must be stopped and secretly plans revenge.

The three decide to attend a costume party at school dressed in outfits Polly has kept in her storehouse of clothes dating back to World War I. During the festivities, Kate lures Skeeter down a dark road where he is attacked and beaten by Mrs. Slater's husband. Trav is horrified by this violence.

During the spring semester, Kate gains the coveted leading role of Laura in the school's production of *The Glass Menagerie*, but a tragedy occurs on opening night when Trav is arrested for shoplifting. It is a cry for help, but it goes unheeded. His parents send him away to spend the summer on a farm in Iowa.

When Trav returns, he appears rested but his calmness quickly disappears. One day he gives his friends two of his prized possessions: Buck receives his calculator and Kate, his stuffed Paddington bear. They are puzzled by his behavior. They later discover that it is actually Trav's last will and testament. Two days later he commits suicide by hanging himself from a tree in the orchard.

Everyone is stunned by his death. Buck and Kate are so numb that they are unable to grieve. At a public meeting to discuss the suicide, speakers try to place the blame on various agencies. Signs of acrimony are emerging when Polly Prior speaks from her wheelchair. First she asks everyone to stop bickering and trying to find a scapegoat and then she talks simply but movingly about the mild, loving Trav and what a void has been left by his death. Her gentle words release Buck and Kate's pent-up emotions and they weep openly.

In time, the friends' sorrow abates and life goes on, but in moments of reflection, they speak fondly of Trav and remember the good times.

Themes and Subjects

The two major themes of this novel are the nature of friendship and the causes and effects of suicide. Other themes involve adjusting to the death of a friend; differences in family relationships (particularly the contrast between Trav's distance from his parents and the closeness of Buck and his father); the difficulty of understanding another's feelings and emotions; the necessity of adjusting to change; and ways of handling a bully. Coping with new school situations and surmounting social barriers caused by wealth and position are also issues in this novel. Generational differences and how to overcome them are well depicted in the scenes with the youngsters and Polly.

Booktalk Material

This book could be introduced by describing the three protagonists, the nature of their friendship, and hinting at its disintegration. Specific passages for retelling are: Buck takes Kate to the trailer (pp. 5–8); Buck meets Polly Prior (pp. 9–12); Trav calms Skeeter (pp. 21–23); the party at the Kirbys (pp. 42–46); Buck and Kate talk about parents (pp. 46–48); and Skeeter and the hard hat (pp. 54–63).

Additional Selections

Three teenage friends seem to have it all, but they are inwardly drowning their pain in James Howe's *The Watcher* (Atheneum, 1997).

In his diary, seventeen-year-old Luke appears to be on top of everything but he is hiding a disability in Jackie French Koller's *The Falcon* (Atheneum, 1998).

In Rob Thomas's *Rats Saw God* (Simon, 1996), Steve, a brilliant but failing high school student and habitual dope smoker, reveals his past in a diary he keeps as an assignment.

In Sarah Dessen's *Someone Like You* (Viking, 1998), the friendship of Halley and Scarlett survives many crises including the death of Scarlett's boyfriend in an accident.

About the Author and Book

Authors and Artists for Young Adults. Gale. Vol. 1, 1989; vol. 24, 1998.
Biography Today: Author Series. Vol. 10, Omnigraphics, 2002.
Bostrom, Kathleen Long. *Winning Authors: Profiles of the Newbery Medalists.* Libraries Unlimited, 2003.
Brown, J. M. "A Long Way from Decatur," *Publishers Weekly,* July 21, 2003, pp. 169–70.
Children's Books and Their Creators. Houghton, 1995.
Children's Literature Review. Vol. 15, Gale, 1988.
Contemporary Authors New Revision Series. Vol. 129, Gale, 2004.
Drew, Bernard A. *100 Most Popular Young Adult Authors.* Libraries Unlimited, 1996.
Favorite Children's Authors and Illustrators. Vol. 5, Tradition Books, 2003.
Fifth Book of Junior Authors and Illustrators, Wilson, 1983.
Gallo, Donald R. *Presenting Richard Peck.* Twayne, 1989.
———. *Speaking for Ourselves.* National Council of Teachers of English, 1990.
Gillespie, John T., and Corinne J. Naden. *Characters in Young Adult Literature.* Gale, 1997.
Lives and Works: Young Adult Authors. Vol. 6, Grolier, 1999.
McElmeel, Sharron L. *100 Most Popular Children's Authors.* Libraries Unlimited, 1999.
Major Authors and Illustrators for Children and Young Adults (1st ed.). Vol. 5, Gale, 1993.
Major Authors and Illustrators for Children and Young Adults (2nd ed.). Vol. 6, Gale, 2002.
Rochman, Hazel. "Talking with Richard Peck," *Book Links,* Sept., 2004, pp. 44–45.
St. James Guide to Young Adult Writers (2nd ed.). St. James, 1999.
Something About the Author. Gale. Vol. 18, 1980; vol. 55, 1989; vol. 97, 1989; vol. 110, 2000; vol. 158, 2005.
Something About the Author Autobiography Series. Vol. 2, Gale, 1986.
Stevens, Jen. *The Undergraduate's Companion to Children's Writers and Their Web Sites.* Libraries Unlimited, 2004.
Talbert, Marc. "Richard Peck," *Horn Book,* July/Aug., 2001, pp. 403–09.
Twentieth-Century Young Adult Writers (1st ed.). St. James, 1994.

Writers for Young Adults. Vol. 3, Scribner, 1997.
www.richardpeck.smartwriters.com (personal Web site)
See also listing "Selected Web Sites on Children's Literature and Authors."

Sebestyen, Ouida. *Far from Home.* Dell, 1980. Pap. $5.99, 0-440-97339-2 (Grades 7–10).

Introduction

Ouida Sebestyen (1924–) was born in Vernon, Texas, and attended the University of Colorado at Boulder. On her road to becoming a successful writer she worked in a fast-food stand, cleaned houses, and watched children in her home. In her first novel for young adults, *Words by Heart* (Little, Brown, 1970), she explored the theme of racial prejudice through the experiences of the only black family living in a small southwestern town in 1910. *Far from Home*, her second book, is set in a northern Texas town in 1929 and explores various aspects of love, its dimensions and delimitations—as revealed by seven characters living together for a short time in a rundown boarding house. Of her work, she has said, "Most of my fiction has been set solidly in a home or a place someone longs to call home. These houses, or temporary rooms, or farms, or little towns where all sorts of people unite as families are rich, complex little worlds to write about." *Far from Home* explores such a rich, complex little world. It is suitable for readers in grades seven through ten.

Principal Characters

Salty Yeager, thirteen years old and homeless
Mam, his great-grandmother
Tom and Babe Buckley, who run a boarding house
Hardy and Rose Ann McCaslin, boarding house residents
Jo Miller, wife of a prohibition bootlegger

Plot Summary

It is 1929. Salty Yeager is thirteen, homeless, and, except for his great-grandmother, Mam, without a family since his mother died a few weeks ago. She had worked for many years at a boarding house called the Buckley Arms. His mother left Salty a note telling him to go to Tom Buckley, who would take in Salty and Mam. Tom and his wife Babe are less than enthusiastic about taking in two non-paying boarders, but they accept them, even Salty's pet Embden gander, Tollybosky. Mam gets an upstairs bedroom, Salty gets a tiny room in the basement, and Tolly gets the garage.

Salty meets two other residents: Babe's nephew, the wise-cracking, ne'er-do-well Hardy McCaslin, and his wife, Rose Ann. Hardy is unemployed and Rose Ann is newly pregnant.

On an errand for Babe, Salty meets a pregnant girl looking for a cheap hotel room. Her name is Jo Miller and she has left her husband, Kell, because he allowed an innocent man to be convicted of a crime for which he himself was guilty. Jo is given a room at the inn and she and Babe become friends.

Although things seem to be working out, Salty has an inner conflict. He has always wanted to know his father's identity. His mother, who was mute, never told him. Pieces of evidence now point to Tom as his father, and Salty talks about the evidence with Hardy, who says that Tom's silence on the matter is not a sign of lack of love for Salty but a sign of concern for Babe.

Jo visits Salty in his room for a talk, but before she can return upstairs labor pains begin and she gives birth on Salty's bed. The next morning, amid great bustle and fanfare, Jo and her baby boy, whom she names Micah, are triumphantly transported upstairs. Rose Ann, however, feels very differently about her pregnancy. She believes Hardy does not want the child, whom he flippantly refers to as the "bean." They quarrel and Rose Ann, trying to sort out her emotions, leaves to visit her sister.

At Tom's urging, Jo decides to return to her husband to give him another chance. She and Salty say a tearful farewell at the train station. But when Salty returns home, he finds that Tolly, his gander, has been given to a farmer because of a provoked attack on neighboring children. Furthermore, Babe and Mam have fought so violently that Babe wants her to leave. Feeling angry and betrayed, Salty tells the Buckleys that he has as much right as anyone to live in their home. Before he can tell Babe the truth, Tom orders him out of the house. Salty attacks his father but Hardy separates them, drags Salty outdoors, and forces him to join the Independence Day activities. During the parade Tom catches up with Hardy and delivers the horrifying news that Rose Ann has had an abortion and is in the hospital. Hardy is sickened at the news and, realizing he is partly to blame, decides he must see her. While waiting at the station with Hardy and Salty, Tom talks about his love for and guilt about Salty's mother and why had he had to reject Salty after his return from the war for Babe's sake.

On returning home, Tom and Salty find that Mam has wandered off alone. After frantic searching, they find her back on her old property. She has suffered a stroke and is disoriented.

On the way back to the Buckley Arms, Tom and Salty talk about the future. Tom says that he will not sell the boarding house and that there will always be room there for Salty and Mam. He also assures Salty that he will be able to visit Tolly, but Salty is afraid that the bird will feel unloved. Tom says, "Then he'll have to go on loving you on faith. Like people do when they can't tell each other." "Like us," Salty says. "Yes," Tom replies.

Themes and Subjects
Toward the end of the book, Tom asks the question, "Why do we have rules for loving?" This book explores life's rules for loving in several different relationships. It is also the story of one boy's search for identity and his birthright. Family relationships are well developed as are the concepts of responsibility toward others, facing the consequences of one's actions, and the nature of trust and friendship. Details of small-town life in 1929 are carefully interwoven into the plot to create an authentic picture of America at that time.

Booktalk Material
Paraphrasing Chapter 1, in which Salty first visits the Buckley Arms with his mother's note, should intrigue readers. Other passages are: Salty meets Tom and Babe and is accepted (pp. 17–23); some first adjustments (pp. 43–45); Salty encounters Jo (pp. 58–61); and Jo tells her story (pp. 73–76).

Additional Selections
In Joan Bauer's *Squashed* (Putnam, 2001), Ellie wishes she would stop growing and that her pumpkin would win the first prize at the county fair.

Sal and her grandparents set out from Ohio on a car trip to try to find Sal's mother, who has disappeared, in Sharon Creech's *Walk Two Moons* (HarperCollins, 1994).

Lara is riding high until she begins gaining weight because of a metabolic disorder in Cherie Bennett's *Life in the Fat Lane* (Dell, 1999).

In Bruce Brooks's *Midnight Hour Encores* (Harper, 1988) a sixteen-year-old girl drives with her father across the country searching for her mother.

About the Author and Book
Authors and Artists for Young Adults. Vol. 8, Gale, 1992.
Children's Books and Their Creators. Houghton, 1995.
Children's Literature Review. Vol. 17, Gale, 1989.
Contemporary Authors New Revision Series. Vol. 114, Gale, 2003.

Continuum Encyclopedia of Children's Literature. Continuum, 2001.
Drew, Bernard A. *100 Most Popular Young Adult Authors.* Libraries Unlimited, 1996.
Fifth Book of Junior Authors and Illustrators. Wilson, 1983.
Gallo, Donald R. *Speaking for Ourselves.* National Council of Teachers of English, 1990.
Gillespie, John T., and Corinne J. Naden. *Characters in Young Adult Literature.* Gale, 1997.
Lives and Works: Young Adult Authors. Vol. 7, Grolier, 1999.
Major Authors and Illustrators for Children and Young Adults (1st ed.). Vol. 5, Gale, 1993.
Major Authors and Illustrators for Children and Young Adults (2nd ed.). Vol. 7, Gale, 2002.
St. James Guide to Young Adult Writers (2nd ed.). St. James, 1999.
Something About the Author. Gale. Vol. 39, 1985; vol. 140, 2003.
Something About the Author Autobiography Series. Vol. 10, Gale, 1990.
Twentieth-Century Young Adult Writers (1st ed.). St. James, 1994.
Writers for Young Adults. Vol. 3, Scribner, 1997.
See also listing "Selected Web Sites on Children's Literature and Authors."

Taylor, Theodore. *The Cay.* Dell, 2002 (1969). Pap. $5.99, 0-440-41663-9 (Grades 6–9).

Introduction

Theodore Taylor (1921–) was born in Statesville, North Carolina, but at an early age moved with his family to Virginia, where he was educated and began his writing career while in high school, producing a column on school sports for the local newspaper. A nature lover and adventurer, he traveled widely and during World War II served in both the Merchant Marines and the U.S. Navy. He wrote two books for adults before entering the juvenile field. His first novel for young adults, *The Cay*, is a survival story involving two characters, a young white boy and old West Indian black man, who are shipwrecked on a Caribbean island during World War II. It contains many of the elements found in his work: strong characterization, plenty of action, and the exploration of themes involving inner strength, survival, environmental responsibility, self-reliance, and racial harmony. One young reader said its message is that "brotherhood can and should exist between men, regardless of race." This novel was followed by a prequel, *Timothy of the Cay* (Harcourt, 1993). Both books are enjoyed by readers in middle school and up.

Principal Characters

Phillip Enright, eleven, son of an American engineer living in the Netherlands Antilles
Timothy, lifeboat crew member
Phillip's parents
Stew, the cat

Plot Summary

In February 1942, German U-boats attack the Netherlands Antilles. For the narrator, eleven-year-old Phillip Enright, whose father is an American engineer working in the oil refineries, the attack sets off an amazing chain of events. Phillip's mother fears the attack will lead to shelling of civilian areas. She asks her husband to book passage on a freighter for Phillip and herself, and he reluctantly agrees. In early April they sail on a small Dutch freighter. Phillip's father is confident that the Germans would not waste a torpedo on such an old tub. He is wrong and the freighter is sunk.

Phillip and his mother are lowered into a lifeboat, but the boat capsizes and Phillip is knocked unconscious. He awakens some hours later in a life raft with a black West Indian crew member named Timothy and the cook's cat, Stew. Timothy is confident that Phillip's mother has been saved, and he is also confident that they will be saved because they have a small supply of water, biscuits, and matches. He tells Phillip he grew up on St. Thomas in the American Virgin Islands. Timothy protects the boy by building a shelter of his clothing and trying to keep up his spirits. He catches fish for them and rations the water supply. Phillip resents his leadership and remembers his mother's distrust of and scorn toward all blacks as being inferior.

Phillip suffers from headaches from the blow he received. On the second day, the pain disappears but he is blind. Timothy tries to reassure him that the blindness is temporary, but Phillip will not be consoled and he blames Timothy for separating him from his mother.

On the fourth day, Timothy sights land. Leaving Phillip on shore, Timothy explores their new home. He tells Phillip that they are on a small cay—maybe the Devil's Mouth Cay—shaped like a melon. There is no animal life. Timothy builds a shelter of palm fronds. Phillip learns Timothy cannot read or write when he asks for assistance in spelling "help" for the message he builds out of large stones on the shore.

With great patience and understanding, Timothy slowly breaks down Phillip's antagonism and his reluctance to help with chores. Then Timothy gets tropical fever, becomes delirious, and rushes into the ocean. Phillip is able to save him by dragging him back to the beach, but Timothy never fully recovers his strength. As though he senses his impending death, he works to make Phillip as self-sufficient as possible.

In July a hurricane strikes. Timothy lashes himself and Phillip to a tree. When the waves crash, Phillip loses consciousness. When he awakens, Stew, the cat, is gone and Timothy is unconscious. Phillip unties Timothy and realizes that, in his efforts to protect the boy, Timothy had placed his back to the storm and there is not a place on his legs and back that is not cut. Timothy dies and Phillip buries him in the sand.

Stew comes back, but Phillip is blind and alone on a forgotten cay. However, he has learned his lessons well from Timothy. He rebuilds the shelter, the signal fire, and the message. He is able to fish and gather food as Timothy taught him.

Early in August, he hears a plane overhead, but, in spite of his fire and shouting, the plane goes away. However, on the morning of August 20, Phillip hears thunderlike explosions and wonders if a battle is in progress. He lights a signal fire and throws vines of sea grapes on it to create a dense smoke. About noon a small boat lands on the cay. The sailors are from an American destroyer.

Phillip is reunited with his parents and sent to New York for operations to restore his sight. He often studies nautical maps to see where cays like the Devil's Mouth are located. Someday he knows that he must return to that tiny island where his friend Timothy is buried.

Themes and Subjects

The author dedicates this book to "Dr. King's dream which can only come true if the very young know and understand." The book will help to give young people the knowledge and understanding to combat racial prejudice and bigotry. Phillip's changes in feeling toward blacks develop logically and convincingly. There is also an interesting contrast of wisdom and strength versus innocence and weakness. The theme of a human being against nature is also important, with some parts of the book constituting a West Indies survival manual.

Booktalk Material

The Cay is largely episodic; therefore, there are many sections suitable for introducing the book: the *Hato* is torpedoed (pp. 39–41); life on the raft

126 • CLASSIC TEENPLOTS

and Phillip's prejudice (pp. 36–39); Phillip goes blind (pp. 46–48); constructing the signals on the island (pp. 70–72); and Phillip learns to work (pp. 74–76).

Additional Selections

In Hawaii's coastal waters, thirteen-year-old Mikey works as a deckhand on his stepfather's fishing boat in Graham Salisbury's *Lord of the Deep* (Delacorte, 2001).

When their plane makes a forced landing in the woods of Canada's Northwest Territories, Gabe and Raymond struggle to survive in Will Hobbs's *Far North* (Morrow, 1996).

In *Hatchet* (Macmillan, 1987) by Gary Paulsen, teenager Brian survives a plane crash in the Canadian wilderness but must fend for himself.

After her father dies of a heart attack while she is traveling with him in Italy, Jackie is kidnapped in Donna Jo Napoli's *Three Days* (Dutton, 2001).

About the Author and Book
Authors and Artists for Young Adults. Gale. Vol. 2, 1989; vol. 19, 1996.
Children's Books and Their Creators. Houghton, 1995.
Children's Literature Review. Vol. 30, Gale, 1993.
Contemporary Authors New Revision Series. Vol. 108, 2002.
Continuum Encyclopedia of Children's Literature. Continuum, 2001.
Drew, Bernard A. *100 Most Popular Young Adult Authors.* Libraries Unlimited, 1996.
Fourth Book of Junior Author and Illustrators. Wilson, 1978.
Gallo, Donald R. *Speaking for Ourselves, Too.* National Council of Teachers of English, 1993.
Gillespie, John T., and Corinne J. Naden. *Characters in Young Adult Literature.* Gale, 1997.
Jones, Raymond E. *Characters in Children's Literature.* Gale, 1997.
Lives and Works: Young Adult Authors. Vol. 7, Grolier, 1999.
McElmeel, Sharron L. *100 Most Popular Children's Authors.* Libraries Unlimited, 1999.
Major Authors and Illustrators for Children and Young Adults (1st ed.). Vol. 6, Gale, 1993.
Major Authors and Illustrators for Children and Young Adults (2nd ed.). Vol. 8, Gale, 2002.
St. James Guide to Young Adult Writers (2nd ed.). St. James, 1999.
Something About the Author. Gale. Vol. 5, 1975; vol. 54, 1989; vol. 83, 1996; vol. 128, 2002.
Something About the Author Autobiography Series. Vol. 4, Gale, 1987.
Twentieth-Century Young Adult Writers (1st ed.). St. James, 1994.
Writers for Young Adults. Vol. 3, Scribner, 1997.
See also listing "Selected Web Sites on Children's Literature and Authors."

Walker, Alice. *The Color Purple.* Harcourt, 1992 (1982). $23, 0-15-119154-9 (Grade 10–Adult).

Introduction

Alice Walker (1944–) was born in Eatonton, Georgia, and received her formal education at Spelman College in Atlanta and Sarah Lawrence College, in Bronxville, New York. She is a writer proficient in many genres: novels, short stories, essays, poetry, and juvenile literature. Often classified as a Southern writer, an African American writer, or a feminist, Walker really defies categorization in that her work deals with universal truths. *The Color Purple* became a successful 1985 film directed by Steven Spielberg. More recently (2005) it became a well-received Broadway musical. It is Alice Walker's third novel. It was preceded by *The Third Life of Grange Copeland* (Harcourt, 1970) and *Meridian* (Harcourt, 1976). All three have certain elements in common. The central characters are black women who share pain and hardship at the hands of stupid and weak men. Racism and sexism are two important themes in these powerfully moving novels. They are suitable for mature senior high school readers.

Principal Characters

Celie, a fourteen-year-old black girl in the South of many years ago
Nettie, her younger sister
Pa, her sexually abusive father
Mr., the man Celie is forced to marry
Pauline, Celie's daughter, whom she named Olivia
Harpo, Mr.'s oldest son
Sophia, the outspoken woman Harpo marries
Shug Avery, a blues singer

Plot Summary

It is the South of many years ago. Fourteen-year-old Celie has just faced the birth of her second child, a process she barely understands although she does tie it in some way with the fact that Pa has been forcing her to have sex with him for some time. Her mother is ill. Celie is too terrified of Pa to resist him and too terrified to tell her mother. Pa gets rid of both children. Celie suspects he killed one and sold the other.

Celie's mother dies and Pa brings a young girl into the house as his new wife. Celie vows to care for her younger sister, Nettie. A man named Mr., who has four children, asks Pa if he can marry Nettie. He says no but offers Celie instead since she is the oldest and, as he says, ugly and dumb.

Celie accepts that description, but Nettie does not. She goes to school and teaches Celie to read. Celie never lets on, but she learns.

Celie is married to Mr. and tends his four children. One day she sees a little girl named Pauline. She is almost seven and Celie knows it is her daughter, whom she called Olivia.

Nettie runs away from Pa and moves in with Celie and Mr. But she will not give in to Mr.'s demands. "You got to fight," she tells Celie. Because of Nettie's resistance, Mr. forces her to leave the home. Harpo, Mr.'s oldest boy, marries Sophia and when he hits her, she hits back. Their fights become the talk of the town. Celie is amazed. Sophia leaves Harpo, but the white folk of the town break her will—at least outwardly. She is jailed and savagely beaten, losing her sight in one eye.

The other woman to enter Celie's life is Shug Avery, a blues singer, the true love of Mr.'s life and the most beautiful woman Celie has ever seen. When Shug returns to town for a spell and becomes ill, Celie cares for her and to Celie's amazement, the glamorous Shug Avery takes a liking to her.

The years pass. Sophia gets out of jail, Shug marries and returns from time to time. She provides Celie with the love and closeness she is not yet aware she desperately craves. Then one day a letter arrives from long-lost Nettie. The letter tells Celie that Nettie has been writing to her all these years, so Celie knows that Mr. must have been keeping the letters from her. This prompts her to be courageous enough to search for Nettie's letters, which, with Shug's help, she finds in Mr.'s trunk. In the letters, Celie reads that Nettie went to Africa with missionaries and that she has found and is with both Celie's daughter, Olivia, and Celie's son. But perhaps even more shocking is Nettie's news about Pa. He is not their father. And that means that Celie's children are not the product of her own father.

With this new knowledge and Nettie's continuing letters, Celie at last finds the courage to fight. She leaves Mr. and goes to Memphis with Shug. She continues to correspond with Nettie and hopes that one day soon she will be able to return.

Then Celie learns that the man she called Pa has died, but that the house and land she thought was his actually belonged to her real father. It is now Celie's. With great joy, Celie writes to Nettie to come back; now they all have a home of their own.

Although it seems a lifetime later to Celie, one day as she sits on the porch of the house to which she has returned, a car drives up the road. At first Celie thinks it is Sophia; instead it is Nettie and Celie's children, now grown.

It has been a long and difficult road for Celie. She is a grown woman now, with a house to tend and people to care for. At last she has found a family and love and a sense of worth. As she says in her letter to God, "Matter of fact, I think this is the youngest us ever felt. Amen."

Themes and Subjects
This is a bittersweet tale of love and abuse, of a seemingly hopeless case of worthlessness struggling against a will to survive. *The Color Purple* is by turns funny, blunt, vivid, and touching in its portrayal of blacks and whites in the South of its time. But most of all, this is the story of the suffering and injustice brought about through bigotry and discrimination—whites against blacks, men against women, ignorance against dignity. There is poverty here, rape and incest, physical and mental abuses; but there is also friendship, the strength of hope, and the wonder of sweet love. The novel speaks of degradation, of despair, but also of courage and the freeing of the human mind. For all its sadness, *The Color Purple* is remarkably uplifting.

Booktalk Material
At the core of the book is the strong character of Celie, who perseveres even when she does not yet understand what she is searching for, who comprehends the evil that people can bring upon one another even though she cannot explain it. One of the many rewards of reading this novel is sensing the growth and determination of the central character, which can be seen in the following passages, all taken from Celie's letters to God. Before she is married to Mr., she writes of the man she thinks is her Pa: "Sometime he still be looking at Nettie, but I always git in his light. Now I tell her to marry Mr. I don't tell her why" (p. 15). Celie writes about her education, "The way you know who discover America, Nettie say, is think bout cucumbers. That what Columbus sounds like." But then she goes on to write that it is hard to concentrate on Nettie's schoolbooks when instead she must think about getting married to Mr. (pp. 19–20). Sophia tells a disbelieving Celie that she has got to fight (pp. 45–47). Shug sings Miss Celie's song, "first time somebody made something and name it after me" (pp. 73–75). Celie finally gets a letter from Nettie (pp. 112–13). Celie and Shug find Nettie's letters (p. 118).

Additional Selections
A black man is unjustly accused of rape and Atticus Finch defends him in the novel *To Kill a Mockingbird* (Harper, 1961) by Harper Lee.

The coming-of-age of a Chicano boy in New Mexico in the 1940s is the central subject of Rudolfo Anaya's *Bless Me, Ultima* (Warner, 1994).

Pecola tells of the many unspeakable events that she has experienced including being raped by her father in *The Bluest Eye* (Knopf, 1993) by Toni Morrison.

In Connie Rose Porter's *Imani All Mine* (Houghton, 2000), fourteen-year-old Tasha, who lives in a housing project in Buffalo, has just given birth to her first child.

About the Author and Book
Authors and Artists for Young Adults. Gale. Vol. 3, 1990; vol. 33, 2000.
Bloom, Harold. *Alice Walker.* Chelsea, 1990.
Contemporary Authors New Revision Series. Vol. 131, Gale, 2005.
Davis, Thadious M., and Harris Trudler. "Afro-American Fiction Writers After 1955." In *Dictionary of Literary Biography.* Vol. 33, Gale, 1984.
Early, Gerald. "The Color Purple as Everybody's Protest Art," *Antioch Review 44,* Summer, 1986.
Gentry, Tony. *Alice Walker.* Chelsea, 1983.
Gillespie, John T., and Corinne J. Naden. *Characters in Young Adult Literature.* Gale, 1997.
Kibler, James E. "American Novelists Since World War II, Second Series." In *Dictionary of Literary Biography.* Vol. 6, Gale, 1991.
Winchell, Donna H. *Alice Walker.* Twayne, 1992.
World Authors, 1975–1980. Wilson, 1985.
See also listing "Selected Web Sites on Children's Literature and Authors."

3

Science Fiction and Fantasy

Alexander, Lloyd. *Westmark.* Dutton 1981, o.p.; pap. Puffin, 2002. $5.99, 0-14-131068-5 (Grades 7–10).

Introduction
Lloyd Alexander (1924–) has long been considered a master of fantasy. He is perhaps best known for his five-volume Prydain cycle (for a slightly younger audience), which recounts the adventure of Taran, the Pigkeeper. Of *Westmark*, Alexander says, "It isn't a fantasy but it is, I hope, no less fantastic." However, the book does contain most of the elements of a first-class fantasy: mythical kingdoms, a hero's quest, and an epic struggle between good and evil. Missing is the use of magic or spells, either to solve or to thwart the plans of the central characters. In the richness and singularity of its setting and plot, *Westmark* transports the reader to a never-never land where one experiences simultaneously both magic and reality. *The Kestrel* (Puffin, 1982) and *The Beggar Queen* (Dell, 1984) complete the Westmark trilogy. Because the events and themes cumulate in this series, the three books should be read in sequence. Without giving away too much of the final ending, the forces of good finally triumph and Mickle marries Theo.

Principal Characters
    King Augustine and Queen Caroline of Westmark
    Cabbarus, the wicked chief minister
    Theo, a printer's devil
    Musket, a dwarf
    Dr. Absalam, alias Count Las Bombas
    Mickle, a street urchin
    Florian, a firebrand

Plot Summary

The king and queen of Westmark, a medieval-like kingdom, are so prostrate with grief at the disappearance of their only child, a daughter, six years earlier that they have given power to the wicked, tyrannical chief minister, Cabbarus. This villain stifles any criticism by requiring prior government approval for printing any publications in Westmark.

Theo, an idealistic young printer's devil who works for Anton, accepts an overnight printing commission from a dwarf named Musket on behalf of his master, Dr. Absalam. The press is raided by militiamen, and Theo and Anton flee. Anton is killed. Theo meets up with Musket and Dr. Absalam, alias Count Las Bombas, who lives by his wits. Theo reluctantly joins them. Las Bombas tries to sell elixir in the next town, but is disturbed by a young urchin girl named Mickle who later joins the group. Theo is attracted to her. She has frequent nightmares in which she is trying to remember her past. Theo is unhappy with the trickery of Las Bombas and sets out on his own. In the town of Freyborg he meets firebrand Florian and joins the student group he leads. Florian is intent on toppling Cabbarus.

Theo learns that Count Las Bombas and company have been discovered in their chicanery by the townspeople of Nierkeeping and are being held prisoners. Florian decides that he and his group should free the prisoners during their attack on Cabbarus's garrison. In a daring raid both are accomplished; Theo frees the Count, Mickle, and Musket, and all four flee the town.

In a neighboring inn, Las Bombas encounters the cheat Skeit. Realizing that their fraudulent act of clairvoyance might be of some value to Cabbarus's scheme to control the king through the search for his daughter, Skeit has all four brought to the palace where they are confronted by Cabbarus in a former torture chamber in the cellar. During the interrogation, filled with threats of imprisonment and instructions for a royal spiritualist performance, all notice that Mickle is transfixed with horror on the center of the floor where there is a narrow well, the shaft of which leads to water fathoms below.

Mickle continues to behave strangely during the evening's presentation and when she first speaks, the queen screams out that she is listening to her own child's voice. Like one possessed, Mickle falls into a trance, and through this trauma regains her memory. She recalls an incident when years before as a young princess she had disobeyed her parents and wandered into the torture chamber, where she toppled into the well. Clinging to the rim, she screamed for help. Cabbarus heard her calls, but instead of helping, dislodged her fingers so that she fell, he thought, to her death below. But she had survived and, suffering from amnesia, wandered the streets scavenging for food until years later, when she met Las Bombas.

In his attempt to escape, the now-unmasked villain, Cabbarus, is saved from falling to his death by Theo who, because he believes in the sanctity of human life, asks that banishment, not death, be Cabbarus's punishment. This is granted. Mickle, now Princess Augusta, is reunited with her parents. Las Bombas and Musket once more take to the road. As for Theo, he is made adviser to the king and will, as a result, be close to Mickle. But, best of all, he is accepted by Florian as one of his children.

In *The Kestrel*, Theo and a group of guerrillas led by Florian join forces with the royal troops to repel an invasion from neighboring Regia. In this novel, Theo changes from the peace-loving dove of *Westmark* to the predatory falconlike Kestrel of the title when he is forced to kill prisoners who might betray his cause. Mickle has become Queen Augusta in *The Beggar Queen* and Theo one of her consuls. Both, along with their friends, are forced into hiding when Cabbarus returns and seizes the government. In a dramatic confrontation, Mickle and Theo escape from Cabbarus through the same well that almost caused Mickle's death years before. Inevitably the forces of good triumph. Cabbarus is killed, but so is the gallant Justin. Mickle marries Theo, and both she and Florian—who has been revealed to be a member of the royal family—renounce their claims to the throne so that Westmark can at last become a democracy.

Themes and Subjects

Westmark is basically a tale of derring-do and hair-breadth escapes that could rival an Indiana Jones movie. It moves quickly with a challenging plot and memorable characters but also explores serious themes involving such political and ethical questions as who should rule and why; the nature of leadership; benevolent monarchy versus democracy; various forms of courage; loyalty to principles; and the nature of friendship. Most importantly, Lloyd Alexander explores the question of when, if ever, is one justified in taking another's life.

Booktalk Material

The covers of both the hardbound and paperback editions introduce two views of Theo and his friends. Theo's story until the encounter with Las Bombas would interest readers. Specific episodes: Anton's shop is raided (pp. 9–14; pp. 14–19, pap.); Theo joins Las Bombas (pp. 24–28; pp. 30–33, pap.); Skeit tricks Las Bombas (pp. 38–42; pp. 44–48, pap.); the troupe meets Mickle (pp. 46–59; pp. 52–55, pap.); Theo meets Florian and his children (pp. 83–88; pp. 87–92, pap.).

Additional Selections

On the death of the great wizard, Morenna finds that she possesses the last five wishes in the world in Avi's *Bright Shadow* (Simon, 1994).

In N. M. Browne's *Warriors of Alarna* (Bloomsbury, 2002), a historical fantasy, fifteen-year-olds Dan and Ursula fight against invaders in Roman Britain.

In the time of Richard the Lion-Hearted, a thirteen-year-old boy finds that his life mirrors that of King Arthur in Kevin Crossley-Holland's *The Seeing Stone* (Scholastic, 2001).

Set in Cornwall during the reign of King Mark, the coming-of-age novel *Juniper* (Demco, 1992), by Monica Furlong, involves the king's son Ninnoc.

About the Author and Book

Alexander, Lloyd. "Fools, Heroes and Jackasses: The 1995 Anne Carroll Moore Lecture," *School Library Journal*, March, 1996, pp. 114–16.
Authors and Artists for Young Adults. Gale. Vol. 1, 1989; vol. 27, 1997.
Biography Today: Author Series. Vol. 6, Omnigraphics, 2000.
Bostrom, Kathleen Long. *Winning Authors: Profiles of the Newbery Medalists*. Libraries Unlimited, 2003.
Children's Books and Their Creators. Houghton, 1995.
Children's Literature Review. Gale. Vol. 1, 1976; vol. 5, 1983; vol. 48, 1998.
Contemporary Authors New Revision Series. Vol. 113, Gale, 2003.
Continuum Encyclopedia of Children's Literature. Continuum, 2001.
Drew, Bernard A. *100 Most Popular Young Adult Authors*. Libraries Unlimited, 1996.
Eighth Book of Junior Authors and Illustrators. Wilson, 2000.
Estes, Glenn E. "American Writers for Children Since 1960: Fiction." In *Dictionary of Literary Biography*. Vol. 52, Gale, 1986.
Favorite Children's Authors and Illustrators. Vol. 1, Tradition Books, 2003.
Gallo, Donald R. *Speaking for Ourselves*. National Council of Teachers of English, 1990.
Gillespie, John T., and Corinne J. Naden. *Characters in Young Adult Literature*. Gale, 1997.
Jacobs, James S., and Michael O. Tunnell. *Lloyd Alexander: A Bio-Bibliography*. Greenwood, 1991.
Jones, Raymond E. *Characters in Children's Literature*. Gale, 1997.
Lives and Works: Young Adult Authors. Vol. 1, Grolier, 1999.
McElmeel, Sharron L. *100 Most Popular Children's Authors*. Libraries Unlimited, 1999.
Major Authors and Illustrators for Children and Young Adults (1st ed.). Vol. 1, Gale, 1993.
Major Authors and Illustrators for Children and Young Adults (2nd ed.). Vol. 1, Gale, 2002.
May, Jill. *Lloyd Alexander*. Twayne, 1991.
St. James Guide to Children's Writers. St. James, 1999.

St. James Guide to Young Adult Writers. St. James, 1999.
Something About the Author. Gale. Vol. 3, 1972; vol. 44, 1987; vol. 81, 1995; vol. 129, 2002; vol. 135, 2003.
Something About the Author Autobiography Series. Vol. 19, Gale, 1995.
Stevens, Jen. *The Undergraduate's Companion to Children's Writers and Their Web Sites.* Libraries Unlimited, 2004.
Third Book of Junior Authors. Wilson, 1972.
Twentieth-Century Children's Writers (4th ed.). St. James, 1994.
Wheeler, Jill C. *Lloyd Alexander.* Abdo and Daughter, 1997.
Writers for Young Adults. Vol. 1, Scribner, 1997.
See also listing "Selected Web Sites on Children's Literature and Authors."

Asimov, Isaac. *Foundation.* Spectra, 2004 (1951). $24, 0-5538-0371-9 (Grade 9–Adult).

Introduction

Isaac Asimov (1920–92) was born in 1920 in Russia but emigrated with his family to the United States in 1923 and became an American citizen in 1928. Although he was a professor of biochemistry at Boston University for many years, he is best known as a super-prolific writer of science fiction and of nonfiction titles that popularize many scientific subjects. With more than 200 books to his credit, his intended audiences range from the elementary grades to adult readers. In the realm of science fiction, he is perhaps best known for his basic Foundation trilogy, which consists of *Foundation, Foundation and Empire* (Gnome, 1952), and *Second Foundation* (Gnome, 1953). Additional books about the Foundation by Asimov include *Foundation's Edge* (Doubleday, 1982), *Foundation and Earth* (Doubleday, 1986), and *Prelude to Foundation* (Doubleday, 1988). Three of science fiction's most famous writers—Gregory Benford, Craig Bear, and David Brin, respectively—have each written separate volumes in the second Foundation trilogy. These titles are *Foundation's Fear* (Eos, 1997), *Foundation and Chaos* (Eos, 1998), and *Foundation's Triumph* (Eos, 1999). All of these books supply rich reading experiences, particularly for science fiction buffs in senior high.

Principal Characters

Gaal Dornick, from Synnax
Hari Seldon, legendary mathematician of Trantor
Salvor Hardin, mayor of Terminus City

Plot Summary

Gaal Dornick, from faraway Synnax, has come to Trantor to work with legendary mathematician Hari Seldon in the Galactic Era. Trantor is the most advanced world of the Galactic Empire. Dornick discovers that Seldon is out of favor with the authorities because he foresees the total destruction of Trantor.

During his trial for treason, Seldon says that not only Trantor but the entire Galactic Empire will fall—and this cannot be prevented. However, Seldon declares that he can prevent thousands of years of suffering by saving the knowledge of the human race. He can do this by completing the *Encyclopedia Galactica*. This encyclopedia, which 30,000 individuals in his employ are now working on, will be a giant summary of knowledge. It will be complete by the time Trantor falls, says Seldon, and will be in every major library in the galaxy. The human race will not have to start over to pick up the pieces of civilization.

The response is to banish Seldon and his entire project staff to Terminus, on the edge of the galaxy, where they can be left in peace to "complete their work." Fifty years pass; the first volume is due in five years. But Salvor Hardin, mayor of Terminus City, is now faced with trouble from other planets, such as Anacreon, whose royal governor has just assumed the title of king. Terminus is small and defenseless.

To Hardin's astonishment, the figure of Hari Seldon appears, now confined to a wheelchair and declaring that he is not really there. He tells Hardin that the entire encyclopedia project has been a fraud, part of a grand scheme. Seldon wanted to be banished to Terminus. The fall of the Galactic Empire has begun. In its place, the Foundation on Terminus and a companion foundation at the other end of the empire are the seeds of a new beginning—the start of the Second Galactic Empire.

Then Seldon declares that the Galactic Empire, although dying, is still mighty and must be overcome; there are still 920 years left for it to exist.

And so through the years emerge the Traders, who seek to establish economic fingerholds for the new Foundation on the edges of space. Traders become Master Traders and then Merchant Princes, bringing the power of money to the fledgling Foundation as it begins to rise to power and domination of the kingdoms on the outskirts of the galaxy.

Themes and Subjects

This is a science fiction classic, the first of three in the series, followed by *Foundation and Empire* (Gnome, 1952), which tells the story of how the Foundation becomes strong enough to finally defeat the First Empire, and *Second Foundation* (Gnome, 1953), which tells of the time after the defeat of the First Empire and the growth of a dangerous mutant. The thousand-year period covered in these three volumes includes the building of an ideal corporation that rules the universe. Good reading for all devotees of science fiction.

Booktalk Material
Some of the details of life in the worlds of the galaxy will be of special interest to science fiction readers: see the landing on Trantor (pp. 4–6) and the elevator ride (pp. 10–14). To gain an understanding of what Asimov has in mind for the basis of the Foundation, the reader should pay close attention to the speeches of Hari Seldon (see pp. 14–17, 22–29, and 72–75).

Additional Selections
In the many challenging Dune novels, Frank Herbert has created an amazing family, the Astreides, who are banished to the planet Dune. Two of the earliest are *Dune* (Putnam, 1984) and *Children of Dune* (Putnam, 1985).

Two rival groups send teams to Earth to recover lost technology in Arwen Elys Dayton's *Resurrection* (Roc, 2001).

A young girl lives outside the confines of time on a space station in *The Big Time* (Amereon, 1976) by Fritz Leiber.

In Jack Williamson's *Transforming Earth* (Tor, 2001), an asteroid destroys nearly all life on Earth.

About the Author and Book
Authors and Artists for Young Adults. Vol. 13, Gale, 1994.
Children's Books and Their Creators. Houghton, 1995.
Children's Literature Review. Vol. 79, Gale, 2002.
Contemporary Authors New Revision Series. Vol. 125, Gale, 2004.
Continuum Encyclopedia on Children's Literature. Continuum, 2001.
Gillespie, John T., and Corinne J. Naden. *Characters in Young Adult Literature.* Gale, 1997.
Lives and Works: Young Adult Authors. Vol. 1, Grolier, 1999.
Major Authors and Illustrators for Children and Young Adults (1st ed.). Gale, 1993.
Major Authors and Illustrators for Children and Young Adults (2nd ed.). Vol. 1, Gale, 2002.
St. James Guide to Young Adult Writers (2nd ed.). St. James, 1999.
Something About the Author. Gale. Vol. 1, 1971; vol. 26, 1982; vol. 74, 1991.
Third Book of Junior Authors. Wilson, 1972.
Twentieth-Century Science Fiction Writers (3rd ed.). St. James, 1991.
Twentieth-Century Young Adult Writers (1st ed.). St. James, 1994.
Writers for Young Adults. Vol. 1, Scribner, 1997.
See also listing "Selected Web Sites on Children's Literature and Authors."

138 • CLASSIC TEENPLOTS

Brin, David. *The Postman.* Spectra, 1997 (1985). Pap. $7.50, 0-5532-7874-6 (Grade 9–Adult).

Introduction
David Brin (1950–), at one time an electrical engineer and computer expert, has an impressive academic background in science. He holds bachelor's and master's degrees in science plus a Ph.D. in space science from the University of California in San Diego. Since beginning to write science fiction (*The Postman* was an early success), he has won all the major awards in the field, including both the Hugo and the Nebula awards and the Interstellar War Award. He is perhaps best known for a series of six novels that comprise two trilogies known as the Uplift series, described as dealing with "a huge galactic civilization responsible for 'uplifting' all known intelligent forms of oxygen breathing life." The first book, *Sundiver* (Spectra, 1984), is more science fiction mystery than pure science fiction. Its position in the series has been compared with that of *The Hobbit* as a prelude to *The Lord of the Rings*. These novels, like Brin's other works, are characterized by swift action, interesting character development, logical plot lines, and thought-provoking ideas. Unlike the Uplift novels, *The Postman* deals with our own world and its bleak but not unbelievable future.

Principal Characters
    Gordon Krantz, a wanderer following the nuclear holocaust
    Cyclops, a superintelligent computer
    Dr. Lazarensky, designer of Cyclops
    Dena Spurgen, archfeminist
    George Powhatan, leader of an antisurvivalist group
    General Macklin, leader of the Holnists, a survivalist group

Plot Summary
Sixteen years after the Doomwar of the mid-1990s, much of the world is destroyed by a global nuclear holocaust. Most of the United States is desolate, although some communities in the western states are still able to maintain life. But they are subject to raids by the Holnists, those who follow a neo-Fascist philosophy of deceased survivalist Nathan Holn.

    Gordon Krantz, now thirty-four, was eighteen years old when the Doomwar began. He still maintains a belief in the ideals that once guided life in the United States. He wanders from community to community, holding audiences spellbound as he retells stories, including some from Shakespeare.

As Gordon enters Oregon, he is attacked by bandits who steal all his belongings. Wandering in the wilderness, he comes upon the remains of a postal service jeep and finds the skeleton of a postman at the wheel. Gordon dons the postman's uniform and shoes. He then enters Pine View and becomes friendly with the leader of the community. He consents to sleep with a young married woman so that she and her sterile husband can have a child. Gordon leaves Pine View with letters from the residents, hoping to make contact with other survivors.

To gain admission to Oak Ridge, he tells a story that he is courier from the Restored United States and he is given the responsibility of organizing a mail route to the East. As he moves from community to community, the story he has created about himself becomes more complex. He also learns of a benevolent force known as Cyclops.

In the remains of Eugene, Oregon, he hears of a plot by the Holnists to attack communities in the North. Two captives are left behind—a young boy and his dying mother, who says "North, take boy, warn Cyclops."

Cyclops's headquarters are in Cornvallis in the Williamette Valley, where there is a higher level of prosperity and well-being. There he meets an archfeminist Dena Spurgen; Cyclops itself, which is a superintelligent computer; and its designer, Dr. Lazarensky. Gordon warns of the impending attacks. He decides to remain and help defend these communities against the Holnists. During this period he becomes attracted to Dena, with whom he has a love affair.

When the savage raids begin, Gordon takes a perilous journey to get help from George Powhatan, leader of an anti-survivalist group. Powhatan is sympathetic but refuses to submit his people to another bloody conflict. Disheartened, Gordon and his men leave. They are ambushed and Gordon is taken prisoner. He is offered a position of power by the Holnist leader General Macklin, but Gordon refuses.

After a failed escape attempt, Gordon is once more thrown in prison, where he is reunited with Dena. She was gravely wounded when leading a group of gallant female warriors in an attempt to rescue him, and dies in his arms.

When Powhatan learns about the courageous efforts of the women of Cornvallis, he is shamed into action. His men attack the Holnist stronghold and in single-handed combat he kills Macklin and frees Gordon.

With the Holnist threat ended, Gordon packs his belongings and sets out alone. He heads south. After all, there are many post offices to be established in California.

Themes and Subjects
This is more than a fast-moving adventure story set in the future. In its many layers of symbolism, it explores such themes as the importance of ideals in life and the need for hope. The conflict between belief and truth is explored in the effects of the positive mythology of Gordon and Cyclops and the destructive perversions of fact by the Holnists. The nature of liberty, the necessity to act against oppression and evil, and courage through adversity are important themes. Individual bravery and heroism are often depicted as the strength that comes with sharing and cooperation. Gordon is a believable character who, although beset by doubts, sacrifices his own well-being to fight for his ideals. This is also a cautionary tale about the awesome destructive power that humankind now controls and the catastrophic results, should it be unleashed.

Booktalk Material
This book could be introduced with a discussion of the nature of life after a "limited" nuclear war. It is also filled with exciting episodes suitable for reading or retelling. A few are: Gordon's camp is attacked (pp. 4–9); he finds the jeep and the postman's uniform (pp. 20–24); his discovery of a house containing medicines (pp. 61–66); gaining admission to Oak Ridge by lying (pp. 73–80); his adventure in Eugene (pp. 112–21); and meeting Cyclops (pp. 142–46).

Additional Selections
Only two small communities survive after a comet hits Earth in Samuel C. Florman's *The Aftermath: A Novel of Survival* (St. Martin's, 2001).

George Orwell's *Nineteen Eighty-Four* (Signet, pap., 1950) is a prophetic novel, first published in 1945, that tells of a future world where complete mind control is practiced.

A teenage girl raised in an alien world discovers that there is another human living in her complex in Pamela Sargent's *Alien Child* (Harper-Collins, 1988).

In the future world, there are three feuding groups, including the genetically altered ruling elite, in Nancy Kress's *Beggars and Choosers* (Tor, 1994).

About the Author and Book
Authors and Artists for Young Adults. Vol. 21, Gale, 1991.
Contemporary Authors New Revision Series. Vol. 127, Gale, 2004.
Something About the Author. Vol. 65, Gale, 1991.
Twentieth-Century Science Fiction Writers (3rd ed.). St. James, 1991.
See also listing "Selected Web Sites on Children's Literature and Authors."

Brooks, Terry. *Magic Kingdom for Sale—Sold!* Del Rey, 1986. Pap. $7.99, 0-345-31758-0 (Grade 9–Adult).

Introduction
From Terry Brooks's Web site (www.terrybrooks.net/bio.html) one can garner some interesting facts about this writer. He was born in Illinois in 1944 and, though majoring in English literature, he went on to get a law degree and become a lawyer. He had always dabbled in creative writing and found after reading *The Lord of the Rings* in college that writing fantasies could give him the outlet to "explore ideas about life, love, truth, redemption, and the wonder that fills the world." He first gained prominence in the world of fantasy with his Shannara trilogy, which began with *The Sword of Shannara* (Del Rey, pap.) first published in 1977. These books were so successful that Brooks was able to move to Seattle and devote himself full-time to writing. Next came *Magic Kingdom for Sale—Sold!*, the first of a humorous fantasy series that was continued in *The Black Unicorn* (Del Rey, 1987) and *Wizard at Large* (Del Rey, 1988). In *The Black Unicorn*, Ben Holiday loses the royal medallion that can summon Paladin, is betrayed by his wizard, and loses Lady Willow on a search for a mysterious black unicorn.

Principal Characters
Ben Holiday, a wealthy Chicago lawyer
Questor Thews, chief adviser to the throne of Landover
Iron Mark, a demon lord

Plot Summary
Since the death of his wife, Annie, Ben Holiday, a wealthy Chicago lawyer, has no interest in living. He sees a Christmas catalog ad from Rosen's in New York that says "Magic Kingdom for Sale" for $1 million. Preposterous as it seems, the ad haunts Ben, so much so that he flies to New York City and Rosen's, Ltd. to inquire of a Mr. Meeks, as the ad instructs. Mr. Meeks tells him that if he decides to purchase Landover, he will be given ten days to examine his new kingdom and decide if he wants to stay. If he does not, the purchase price will be refunded. If he decides to stay, the purchaser must agree to spend at least a year in Landover; if not, he will lose the $1 million.

Following instructions, Ben goes to the Blue Ridge Mountains of Virginia and is given a medallion to wear. He enters a tunnel in the mountains and is transported to Landover, where he meets Questor Thews, chief adviser to the throne. The kingdom is very dilapidated, and he is told about Iron Mark, a demon lord who now and then strays into Landover.

Ben stays the ten days and is committed for a year. He learns how the kingdom came to be in such a sorry state. Questor says Ben could restore it and also tells him about Paladin, once the kingdom's protector. But Paladin has disappeared. Questor also tells Ben that once a year the king will be challenged by demon Iron Mark. Ben also meets Willow, a sylph, who tells him of her love, but he still grieves for Annie.

But as Ben walks off into the mist, he finds himself back in Chicago! Ten years have passed, his astonished law partner tells him. Ben is but a memory to everyone. He doesn't exist in his own world any longer. And then Been sees his beloved Annie, who tells him she is only a ghost. She admonishes him for leaving his world, telling him that they are separated forever.

And just as suddenly Ben is back in Landover. But this time the kingdom is desolate and his friends are dying because their king has abandoned them. He decides he must confront the demon Iron Mark.

When Ben confronts the 8-feet-tall Iron Mark, he remembers the medallion and realizes that it will save him. He places it outside his tunic for all to see.

As Iron Mark charges with his terrible sword, Ben stands fast. And suddenly, out of the light comes Paladin!

Iron Mark is defeated and Paladin disappears once more. Who is he? the people ask, but Ben knows the answer. Ben himself was, just now, Paladin when he brought forth the courage of the legendary hero when he committed himself to the new kingdom. All the knights and nobles unite under the new king. Ben has committed himself to a new life in this strange land, with Willow at his side.

Themes and Subjects

This fantasy mixes the real world with the enchantment and magic of a fairy tale place. It shows how the pressures, and sometimes sorrows, of life can make individuals lose all interest in people and things around them. But it also says that a commitment to what one believes in, backed by determination and strength and the willingness to reach out to others, can bring rewards that surpass even one's most fantastic dreams.

Booktalk Material

Descriptions of this magic kingdom are a good introduction to this fantasy. See: Ben arrives in Landover (pp. 51–58); the meeting with Questor

SCIENCE FICTION AND FANTASY • 143

(pp. 62–66); Ben first sees the castle and staff (pp. 78–86); Ben's coronation (pp. 109–17); and Ben meets Willow (pp. 174–77).

Additional Selections
A young factory worker's daydreams become reality when a leprechaun transports him to a fairy realm in R. A. Salvatore's *The Woods Out Back* (Berkeley, pap., 1993).

In Neal Shusterman's *Downsiders* (Simon, 1999), a teenage boy ventures into the Downside, a subterranean world beneath New York City.

Anna is transported in time to the land of Erde, where she can use her beautiful voice to create magic in L. E. Modesitt, Jr.'s *The Soprano Sorceress* (Tor, 1997).

A clumsy, lanky girl meets the prince of her dreams in the fantasy *Far Harbor* (Tor, 1989) by Melisa C. Michaels.

About the Author and Book
Authors and Artists for Young Adults. Vol. 18, Gale, 1996.
Contemporary Authors New Revision Series. Vol. 135, Gale, 2005.
Gillespie, John T., and Corinne J. Naden. *Characters in Young Adult Literature.* Gale, 1997.
Lives and Works: Young Adult Authors. Vol. 1, Grolier, 1999.
St. James Guide to Young Adult Writers (2nd ed.). St. James, 1999.
Something About the Author. Vol. 60, Gale, 1990.
Twentieth-Century Young Adult Writers (1st ed.). St. James, 1994.
See also listing "Selected Web Sites on Children's Literature and Authors."

Christopher, John. *When the Tripods Came.* Simon Pulse, 2003 (1988). Pap. $5.99, 0-689-85762-4 (Grades 6–10).

Introduction
In the first of the Tripods Trilogy (also called the White Mountains trilogy), *The White Mountains* (Simon Pulse, pap., 1967), three boys in the twentieth century try to escape both the domination of malevolent machines known as the Tripods and the coming-of-age operation known as Capping that will destroy their self-will. They travel to the isolated mountains in a land once known as Switzerland, where a band of humans still live a free life. From there, guerrilla warfare is launched that inevitably leads to the defeat of the Tripods. This sort of tale forms the exciting subject matter of the other two books in the series, *The City of Gold and Lead* (Simon Pulse, pap., 1967) and *The Pool of Fire* (Simon Pulse,

pap., 1968). This series has been read extensively ever since its first appearance almost 40 years ago and was turned into a highly successful British television series. *When the Tripods Came* is set in contemporary England and serves as a prequel to the White Mountains series. It tells about the first appearance of the Tripods, how they came to dominate the earth, and the formation of the resistance movement. It is a first-person narrative told by Laurie Cordray, the young hero of the novel.

Principal Characters
> Laurie Cordray, fourteen
> His friend Andy
> Laurie's Pa, a real estate agent
> Angela, Laurie's half-sister
> Ilse, his stepmother
> His wealthy Uncle Ian
> "Wild Bill" Hockey, a teacher
> Ian's teenage son, Nathanael

Plot Summary
Fourteen-year-old Laurie (short for Laurence) Cordray and his friend Andy take the wrong turn during a camping expedition on the moors of Dorset and are forced to spend the night in a deserted shed. About five in the morning, they are awakened by a series of loud explosions. From the window of the hut, they see something unbelievable—a giant hemispherical capsule with three mechanical legs has landed on a nearby farm. Using huge tentacles that issue from the underside of its body, it destroys the farmhouse and takes its terrorized occupant aboard. Airplanes from the Royal Air Force attack and destroy this marauder from outer space.

For a time, Laurie and Andy are celebrities in the media and at school, where even their gruff physics teacher "Wild Bill" Hockey wants any insider information they can provide about these space vehicles now known as Tripods.

Laurie lives in a Dorsetshire town with his pa, his father's second wife, the Swiss-born Ilse, and their daughter Angela. They all live with Pa's feisty mother, Martha. When Ilse is called back suddenly to Switzerland, Laurie and Angela are cared for by Pa and Martha.

All of Britain, indeed the world, is abuzz with speculation about the Tripods. A half-animated/half-real-life television show about them, called "The Trippy Show," becomes an international sensation, though in Laurie's household only Angela is a fan. Within weeks, it becomes apparent that this show is casting a sinister influence over its viewers, now known as Trippies.

Soon the rallying cry of "Hail the Tripod" and echoes of brainwashing slogans about peace and harmony for humankind are heard everywhere. Several teachers at Laurie's school, including "Wild Bill," have Tripped. When Andy's mother leaves to join a commune, he comes to live with the Cordrays. During the next invasion, the Tripods distribute "Caps," rubber helmets equipped with electronic devices, which induce slavish compliance to the Tripods' will.

One day when Laurie is alone in the house, his very wealthy Uncle Ian and his teenage son, Nathanael, arrive. Soon Laurie realizes this is not a social call. Both have become Tripod fanatics and they have brought four Caps to turn the Cordrays into converts. The two pin Laurie to the floor and are about to Cap him when Martha arrives, brandishing her revolver.

This incident, coupled with a national situation comparable to civil war, forces Pa to make a grim assessment of their future. All avenues of communication, including the news media and the airlines, are under the control of the Trippies, who have cut off information from outside England. Under Pa's leadership, the family, with Andy, decide to escape on their yacht, the *Edelweiss*, to the Channel Island of Guernsey, where Martha owns some property. After a rough crossing, they are greeted in port by the dockmaster, who shouts "Hail the Tripods." Realizing that they cannot stay, they plan to get to Switzerland and reunite with Ilse. Pa disconnects the electronic device in the Caps left behind by Uncle Ian and they all don this disguise. Martha sells some of her jewelry and the five are grudgingly allowed to buy airplane tickets to London. In midair, Pa uses Martha's pistol to hijack the plane and directs the pilot to land in Geneva.

Laurie and family are joyfully reunited with Ilse along with Swigram and Swigramp, although everyone realizes the old man is failing fast and that Tripod invasion is imminent.

The invasion comes within a few weeks and there are mass Cappings of the Swiss people, including the residents of Fernohr, the little town near Ilse's home. Andy is captured and held for Capping. When Laurie is also captured in an abortive rescue mission, Pa engineers a daring escape. That night Swigramp dies and the family, now joined by a faithful farmhand named Yone and a young village boy, Rudi, flees into the mountains and takes refuge in an unused train tunnel where they can take advantage of the supplies left in a nearby abandoned ski resort. As the winter passes, they are joined by a few others who tell them that the Tripods are replacing the mind-controlling Cap with a permanent steel plate that cannot be removed. Eventually a small resistance movement is formed with Pa as its leader. Their first act of defiance is to destroy a reconnoitering Tripod by causing an avalanche that buries it. This signifies the beginning of a war of liberation against the Tripods that may take generations.

Themes and Subjects
Although this is basically a thrilling science fiction adventure, it portrays an evil that is found in contemporary life in totalitarian regimes and sometimes in religious cults—the tyranny of brainwashing and mind control. This novel describes both the frightening effects of such control and the accompanying struggle people endure to remain free. Laurie is an average teenager who through adversity rises to acts of daring and courage. This is also a story of friendship and one that explores the bonds of family and the meaning of freedom.

Booktalk Material
Some thrilling episodes that can be used are: Andy and Laurie witness the landing of the first Tripod (pp. 1–11); Angela overreacts when Laurie forgets to tape "The Trippy Show" (pp. 29–34); Angela is hypnotized (pp. 39–44); Laurie is almost Capped by Uncle Ian and Nathanael (pp. 55–61); and the flight to Guernsey (pp. 78–84).

Additional Selections
In Garth Nix's *Shade's Children* (HarperCollins, 1997), children, when they are sixteen, are sent to the Meat Factory where body parts are turned into hideous creatures.

A pet smuggled to Earth never stops growing in Robert A. Heinlein's *The Star Beast* (Macmillan, 1977).

In H. G. Wells's *The War of the Worlds* (Bantam, pap., 1988), a classic science fiction novel first published in 1898, strange creatures from Mars invade England.

The fate of humankind rests in Thomas's hands when he discovers his parents are really aliens in Terence Blacker's *The Angel Factory* (Simon, 2002).

About the Author and Book
(Many of the following citations are under John Christopher's real name, Sam Youd.)

Authors and Artists for Young Adults. Vol. 22, Gale, 1997.
Children's Books and Their Creators. Houghton, 1995.
Children's Literature Review. Vol. 2, Gale, 1976.
Contemporary Authors New Revision Series. Vol. 114, Gale, 2003.

Continuum Encyclopedia of Children's Literature. Continuum, 2001.
Drew, Bernard A. *100 More Popular Young Adult Authors.* Libraries Unlimited, 2002.
Fourth Book of Junior Authors and Illustrators. Wilson, 1978.
Gallo, Donald R. *Speaking for Ourselves, Too.* National Council of Teachers of English, 1993.
Major Authors and Illustrators for Children and Young Adults (1st ed.). Vol. 6, Gale, 1993.
Major Authors and Illustrators for Children and Young Adults (2nd ed.). Vol. 8, Gale, 2002.
St. James Guide to Young Adult Writers (2nd ed.). St. James, 1999.
Something About the Author. Gale. Vol. 47, 1987; vol. 135, 2003.
Something About the Author Autobiography Series. Vol. 6, Gale, 1988.
Stevens, Jen. *The Undergraduate's Companion to Children's Writers and Their Web Sites.* Libraries Unlimited, 2004.
Twentieth-Century Young Adult Writers (1st ed.). St. James, 1994.
See also listing "Selected Web Sites on Children's Literature and Authors."

Clarke, Arthur C. *Rendezvous with Rama.* Spectra, 1990 (1973). Pap. $7.99, 0-5532-8789-3 (Grade 9–Adult).

Introduction

The English writer Arthur C. Clarke was born in 1917. A scientist by education and profession, he began his writing career with nonfiction works in some of which he accurately predicted future scientific developments. For example, in a magazine article published in 1945, he predicted the use of communication satellites. He began writing science fiction in 1951 and now moves comfortably from one genre to another, with more than 60 books to his credit. Perhaps his most famous work remains the screenplay for *2001: A Space Odyssey,* which he wrote with director Stanley Kubrick. He also novelized it (NAL, 1968) and later produced three sequels: *2010: Odyssey Two* (Del Rey, 1982); *2061: Odyssey Three* (Del Rey, 1988); and in 1997, *3001: The Final Odyssey* (Del Rey, 1997). Like *Rendezvous with Rama,* which was first published in 1973, many of his novels deal with the exploration of other worlds and the search for a superior intelligence. All of these novels are popular with science fiction enthusiasts in grades nine and up.

Principal Characters

   William Norton, captain of spaceship *Endeavor*
   Joe Calvert, navigator
   Karl Mercer, lieutenant commander
   Boris Rodrigo, communications officer

Laura Ernst, surgeon commander
Jimmy Pak, crewman

Plot Summary
In the year 2130, a large asteroid outside Jupiter's orbit is named Rama. William Norton in spaceship *Endeavor* is assigned to explore it. The ship lands near three boxlike structures. After unscrewing the top of the one of the pillboxes, the space travelers find themselves in a completely dark world. Using flares, they see tall skyscraper-like structures that look like New York or London in the distance. Many entries are made into Rama, trying to discover its purpose.

Surgeon Commander Laura Ernst travels from base camp Alpha to the edge of the frozen Cylindrical Sea and suddenly it is spring. The ice melts and dazzling light appears, as does oxygen. Rama is undergoing an evolution that took millions of years on Earth.

By raft, the "city of New York" is explored. Young crewman Jimmy Pak encounters three robotlike creatures (it seems everything appears in threes on Rama), but is rescued. At base camp other three-legged beings begin infesting the plain. Laura dissects the brain of one of them and discovers only a giant battery.

At a meeting of the United Planets, the ambassador from Mercury admits that a missile with a bomb has been sent to Rama because he is afraid the asteroid is headed their way. But Norton and his crew do not think Rama is warlike. The bomb is intercepted.

Rama's exploration continues. When night descends, it is as though one phase in the evolution of this planet has been completed.

The *Endeavor* flies off. From afar the crew sees Rama pass dangerously close to the sun and suddenly the purpose of this intrusion into the solar system becomes clear. This is simply a refueling stop. Its source of energy renewed, Rama again heads into the universe, leaving behind many questions and few answers.

Norton is now vindicated for preventing the destruction of Rama, and it appears that his rendezvous with Rama is complete. But is it? After all, Ramans do everything in threes.

Themes and Subjects
Clarke affords the reader the opportunity to explore a new world as the English adventurer Captain Cook did centuries earlier on his ship the *Endeavor*. The possibility that a superior intelligence exists in the universe and could visit our solar system is an intriguing idea, and Clarke explores the various reactions from excitement and wonder to suspicion and hos-

SCIENCE FICTION AND FANTASY • 149

tility that could accompany this event. That this intelligence is indifferent to humans and their accomplishments adds an ironic twist. Politics, religion, teamwork, and human relationships are additional subjects explored. The wealth of astrological information given by the author adds authenticity and excitement.

Booktalk Material
An introduction to UFOs in general and Rama in particular, plus the discussion of possible reasons for their visits should fascinate prospective readers. Important passages are: Rama is first sighted (pp. 4–9); data are collected concerning its size (pp. 10–12); the landing on Rama (pp. 19–22); the interior is described (pp. 38–40); the descent into Rama (pp. 48–56); and dawn comes to Rama (pp. 101–07).

Additional Selections
In Piers Anthony's *Split Infinity* (Ballantine, pap., 1987), the first of the Apprentice Adept series, someone is trying to kill Stile on the planet Proton.

Orion the Hunter realizes that he and his human clone soldiers are pawns of the gods in Ben Bova's *Orion Among the Stars* (Tor, 1995).

A mysterious capsule from space brings the threat of a deadly epidemic in *The Andromeda Strain* (Knopf, 1969) by Michael Crichton.

In Philip K. Dick's 1968 novel *Do Androids Dream of Electric Sheep?* (Ballantine, pap., 1996), after a brutal war, androids are so sophisticated that it is hard to distinguish them from humans.

About the Author and Book
Authors and Artists for Young Adults. Gale. Vol. 4, 1990; vol. 33, 2000.
Contemporary Authors New Revision Series. Vol. 130, Gale, 2002.
Fourth Book of Junior Authors and Illustrators. Wilson, 1978.
Gillespie, John T., and Corinne J. Naden. *Characters in Young Adult Literature.* Gale, 1997.
Hollow, John. *The Science Fiction of Arthur C. Clarke.* Ohio University, 1987.
Major Authors and Illustrators for Children and Young Adults (1st ed.). Gale, 1993.
Major Authors and Illustrators for Children and Young Adults (2nd ed.). Vol. 2, Gale, 2002.
Olander, Joseph D., and Martin H. Greenberg. *Arthur C. Clarke.* Taplinger, 1977.
Rabkin, Eric S. *Arthur C. Clarke.* Starmont, 1980.
St. James Guide to Young Adult Writers (2nd ed.). St. James, 1999.
Something About the Author. Gale. Vol. 13, 1978; vol. 70, 1993; vol. 115, 2000.
Twentieth-Century Science Fiction Writers (2nd ed.). St. James, 1986.
Twentieth-Century Science Fiction Writers (3rd ed.). St. James, 1991.
Twentieth-Century Young Adult Writers (1st ed.). St. James, 1994.
See also listing "Selected Web Sites on Children's Literature and Authors."

Dickinson, Peter. *Eva.* Delacorte, 1989. $15.95, 0-385-29702-5 (Grades 7–12).

Introduction
In the world of contemporary English literature, Peter Dickinson (1927–) has a dual place of importance because he writes both highly acclaimed adult thriller-fantasies and equally exciting, thought-provoking books for young adults. In the first genre, *The Poison Oak* (o.p.) is an *Eva* in reverse. This mystery involves a scientist who is able to teach a chimpanzee to communicate with humans. Among his many books for junior-high readers is the famous Changes trilogy, an exciting fantasy series that chronicles the dire happenings after the seal of an ancient tomb in Wales is broken and the bones of Merlin the magician are accidentally unearthed. Described as "a breathtaking epic fantasy that explores the relationship between man and machine," the work consists of three separate titles—*The Devil's Children, Heartease,* and *The Weathermonger*—all now available in a single omnibus edition (Dell, pap., 1991). *Eva* is set in the unspecified future and covers a period of slightly more than two years—from Eva's awakening to her finding refuge on the island of St. Hilaire. There is a brief epilogue that takes place about twenty years later. Each chapter begins with a few stream-of-consciousness lines that express Eva's inner feelings.

Principal Characters
Eva, who suffers a terrible accident
Dr. Dan Adamson, her father
Grog, who becomes her friend

Plot Summary
Eva awakens after a terrible car accident to find that, in an effort to save her life, her brain has been transplanted into the body of a young female chimpanzee. Her father is Dr. Dan Adamson, director of primate zoology and manager of the International Chimpanzee Pool. To pay for her long months in the hospital, sponsored by a shaper company called SMI and World Fruit, producers of the popular Honeybear drink, she is required to appear on shaper programs and commercials. The shaper is a provider of three dimensional environments, like a sophisticated television.

Gradually she adjusts to life as a chimp, but when she returns from the hospital, her life becomes a media nightmare. There is no privacy and she feels humiliated. Only Grog, the son of her volatile shaper director Mimi Venturi, seems to understand her misery and loneliness.

As Eva visits the chimp pool more and more, she begins to feels at peace with herself and with them. Grog begins to think she will be happy only with them and tries to devise a plan to transport Eva and her friends to one of the few remaining natural environments left on Earth.

When further brain transplants using animal brains fail, Eva publicly denounces these procedures and some animal rights activists begin to support her. Grog now persuades SMI and World Fruit to transport Eva and twenty other chimps to St. Hilaire, a deserted island off the coast of Madagascar, once owned by World Fruit.

Eva and her friends arrive on St. Hilaire, and Eva periodically visits the media crews and her father, who has accompanied the expedition. When a typhoon hits and the electric current is broken, Eva, two females and their babies, and Sniff, a young intelligent male, escape. The activists, including Grog, force SMI and World Fruit to give in. They allow Eva and all the chimps to live on the island. In exchange, shaper crews can occasionally come in for filming.

Twenty years later, Eva is dying of old age surrounded by her children and other members of the chimp colony. The news from outside is discouraging. Many humans, unable to cope with the rampant nihilism in the world, are committing mass suicide. Eva's reply, using the antiquated keyboard of her youth, is only that she and her group are grateful to be left alone to live by nature's laws. When the humans depart, her followers carry her on a litter that she has constructed into the woods, where one by one they touch a part of her body as a farewell gesture.

Themes and Subjects

With flawless detail, the author has created a nightmarish future world governed by greed, ambition, and selfishness. Central to this decline is the growing exploitation of all forms of life by humans intent only on immediate gratification of needs. Humans are depicted as unable to see outside themselves or to realize that humanity is only part of a larger natural world. As the epilogue points out, the inevitable consequence of this egocentrism is nihilism and eventual self-destruction. The dehumanizing effects of technology, the dangers of mass media unleashed without control, and the increasing decline of ethics and respect for human dignity form other important themes. The reader not only learns a great deal about the lifestyles of chimpanzees but also learns to admire their behavior and respect for each other. The rights of animals and the consequences of ecological indifference are also well-developed themes. The reader will also empathize with the courageous Eva and her struggle to find peace in two conflicting worlds.

Booktalk Material

An explanation of the unusual operation Eva has undergone should interest young readers. Specific passages are: Eva wakes up (pp. 5–10); Eva sees herself in the mirror (pp. 14–17); with the help of Robb, a physiotherapist, she tries to use her new body (pp. 33–38); the shaper interview with Dirk Ellan (pp. 49–53); Eva gets permission to visit the pool (pp. 84–86); and her first visit with the chimpanzees (pp. 89–95).

Additional Selections

In Philip Pullman's *The Golden Compass* (Knopf, 1995), the first volume of His Dark Materials trilogy, Lyra searches for her father in a northern stronghold guarded by armed bears.

Fire Bringer (Dutton, 2000) by David Clement-Davies is an animal fantasy about a deer hero and a fawn who try to overthrow a harsh dictatorship.

Jack, a high school junior, moves with his family to Paradise, a town where things are not as they seem in Steven L. Layne's *This Side of Paradise* (North Shore, 2001).

Corgan's peaceful life is disturbed by the arrival of a pair of quite different clones in *The Clones* (Simon, 2002) by Gloria Skurzynski.

About the Author and Book

Authors and Artists for Young Adults. Gale. Vol. 9, 1992; vol. 49, 2003.
Children's Books and Their Creators. Houghton, 1995.
Children's Literature Review. Vol. 29, Gale, 1993.
Contemporary Authors New Revision Series. Vol. 134, Gale, 2005.
Continuum Encyclopedia of Children's Literature. Continuum, 2001.
Dickinson, Peter. "Fantasy: The Need for Realism in Children's Literature," *Education,* Spring, 1986.
Drew, Bernard A. *100 Most Popular Young Adult Authors.* Libraries Unlimited, 1997.
Fourth Book of Junior Authors and Illustrators. Wilson, 1978.
Gallo, Donald R. *Speaking for Ourselves, Too.* National Council of Teachers of English, 1993.
Gillespie, John T., and Corinne J. Naden. *Characters in Young Adult Literature.* Gale, 1997.
Lives and Works: Young Adult Authors. Vol. 3, Grolier, 1999.
Major Authors and Illustrators for Children and Young Adults (1st ed.). Vol. 2, Gale, 1993.
Major Authors and Illustrators for Children and Young Adults (2nd ed.). Vol. 3, Gale, 2002.
St. James Guide to Young Adult Writers (2nd ed.). St. James, 1999.
Something About the Author. Gale. Vol. 5, 1973; vol. 62, 1990; vol. 95, 1998; vol. 150, 2005.
Twentieth-Century Science Fiction Writers (3rd ed.). St. James, 1991.

Twentieth-Century Young Adult Writers (1st ed.). St. James, 1994.
Writers for Young Adults. Vol. 1, Scribner, 1997.
See also listing "Selected Web Sites on Children's Literature and Authors."

Garner, Alan. *The Owl Service.* Magic Carpet Books, 1999 (1967). Pap. $7.95, 0-15-201798-4 (Grades 6–9).

Introduction

In this, as in his other highly-acclaimed novels for young adults, Alan Garner (1934–) has intertwined overtones of fantasy and the supernatural with realism and legend. The rugged Welsh setting, the brooding atmosphere, and conflict involving young lives separated by background and temperament reminds readers of Emily Brontë's English romance *Wuthering Heights*. Prevading the novel is a Welsh legend for the valley where the story takes place, in which the wizard Gwydion fashions from flowers a bride, Blodeuwedd, for Lleu Llan Gyffes. However, the girl falls in love with Gronw Peyr, who slays Lleu. The wizard restores life to Lleu, who kills Gronw by throwing a spear with such force that it passes through a large rock slab that Gronw has used for protection. As punishment, Blodeuwedd is turned into an owl. It is rumored that the legend is fated to repeat itself in different variations from generation to generation. *The Owl Service* won the Carnegie Medal in England in 1967. The extensive use of English and Welsh expressions and references sometimes causes problems for American readers, but the effort is worth the reward of reading this rich, imaginative fantasy.

Principal Characters

Alison, who inherits a large home
Margaret, her remarried mother
Clive Bradley, Alison's stepfather
Roger, Bradley's son
Nancy, the housekeeper
Gwyn, her son
Huw Hannerhob, the groundsman

Plot Summary

By her father's will, Alison has been left a large home in a secluded valley in Wales. She is spending the summer with her mother, Margaret; Clive

Bradley, Margaret's new husband; Roger, Clive's teenaged son; the housekeeper, Nancy, and son Gwyn; and Huw Hannerhob, the groundsman.

Gwyn investigates some scratching coming from the attic and finds owl droppings and a whole dinner service of dishes. He brings a dish to Alison, who sees that under the floral design is the shape of an owl. When Nancy hears of the discovery, she demands the plate, which Alison gives to her, but the design has disappeared. Nancy tells Gwyn to board up the attic entrance, but first the young people rescue the dinner set.

Alison begins tracing the designs on paper and cutting them into owl-like figures, but the patterns keep disappearing. Other mysterious events occur, such as a vanishing painting and the sound of a motorbike passing back and forth.

Tensions mount. Nancy tells the Bradleys that she and Gwyn must leave. Gwyn runs away and is found by Huw, who admits that he is the boy's father and that years ago, as in the recurring legend, his mother, then Huw's wife, fell in love with Bertram, the previous owner of Alison's house. Huw's jealousy drove him to tamper with the brakes on Bertram's motorbike, causing his death. Through the centuries, everyone tried to hide the power of the legend by trying to encase it in such objects as dishes and paintings.

Roger and Alison, meanwhile, break into a room above the stable and see a huge glass case containing an owl. Nancy enters the room and smashes the case. Alison faints and her body becomes covered with falling owl feathers, while clawlike markings appear on her face and legs. Huw murmurs that it should be flowers not owls, and Roger suddenly realizes how he can help Alison. He tells her she is flowers, not owls, and that the pattern was flowers instead of owls. Over and over he repeats flowers, and suddenly the room is filled with petals. The markings disappear and Alison awakens. She has been saved; the strength of the legend has passed.

Themes and Subjects

Through fact and fantasy, the author connects past and present in a supernatural novel of mounting suspense and terror. The concept of fate and its power over the destiny of others is well explored in this multilayered novel. The reader is also introduced to the rugged Welsh countryside, its people, and its legends. The cultural differences between the wealthy English visitors and the poor townspeople and servants are sharply delineated.

SCIENCE FICTION AND FANTASY • 155

Booktalk Material

An explanation of the title could be used to introduce the book. Some interesting passages are: Gwyn finds the dishes (pp. 3–6); Roger's discovery of Gronw's stone (pp. 7–8); the painting begins to appear (pp. 28–29); the room in the stable (pp. 56–57); Alison compulsively traces the owl patterns (pp. 81–83); and Roger develops the pictures (pp. 100–03).

Additional Selections

A collie exists in two worlds, one realistic and the other magical, but both are linked by a mysterious ravine in Janet Hickman's *Ravine* (Greenwillow, 2002).

In John Herman's *Labyrinth* (Philomel, 2001), Gregory lives in the real world and the dream world of Greek mythology and the maze of the Minotaur.

While caring for her dying grandfather, seventeen-year-old Cassie and her mother find themselves in a battle between two clans of fairy people in Midori Snyder's *Hannah's Garden* (Viking, 2002).

In Philip Pullman's *Clockwork* (Scholastic, 1998), reality and fantasy interact when characters in a storyteller's tale come to life.

About the Author and Book

Authors and Artists for Young Adults. Vol. 18, Gale, 1996.
Children's Books and Their Creators. Houghton, 1995.
Children's Literature Review. Vol. 20, Gale, 1990.
Contemporary Authors New Revision Series. Vol. 178, Gale, 2000.
Continuum Encyclopedia of Children's Literature. Continuum, 2001.
Gallo, Donald R. *Speaking for Ourselves.* National Council of Teachers of English, 1990.
Jones, Raymond E. *Characters in Children's Literature.* Gale, 1997.
Major Authors and Illustrators for Children and Young Adults (1st ed.). Vol. 3, Gale, 1993.
Major Authors and Illustrators for Children and Young Adults (2nd ed.). Vol. 3, Gale, 2002.
St. James Guide to Young Adult Authors (2nd ed.). St. James, 1999.
Something About the Author. Gale. Vol. 18, 1980; vol. 69, 1992; vol. 108, 2000.
Third Book of Junior Authors. Wilson, 1972.
Twentieth-Century Young Adult Writers (1st ed.). St. James, 1994.
See also listing "Selected Web Sites on Children's Literature and Authors."

Hamilton, Virginia. *Sweet Whispers, Brother Rush.* Philomel, 1982. $21.99, 0-399-20894-1 (Grades 7–10).

Introduction
While still a young girl growing up in Ohio, Virginia Hamilton (1936–2002), decided to become a writer and in 1967 began writing children's books. During her subsequent writing career she wrote over 60 distinguished books of contemporary fiction, historical fiction, fantasy, nonfiction, and retellings of folktales for both children and young adults. She has won every major award in the field of children's literature including the Newbery Medal, the Boston Globe-Horn Book Award, and the National Book Award for *M. C. Higgins the Great* (Macmillan, 1974). *Sweet Whispers, Brother Rush* was given both the Coretta Scott King Award and the Boston Globe-Horn Book Award. Like many of her works, this book uses black children as central characters in situations that effectively combine realism with fantasy. It is interesting to note that the author lived much of her life in a part of Ohio connected to her family's history: she was the granddaughter of a fugitive slave who traveled with his mother via the Underground Railroad from Virginia to Jamestown, Ohio. Better readers in junior and senior high school enjoy this haunting novel.

Principal Characters
Teresa (Tree) Pratt, fourteen
Vi, her mother
Dab, her retarded brother
Brother Rush, Vi's brother
Silversmith, Vi's boyfriend

Plot Summary
Fourteen-year-old Tree Pratt is old for her years. Her mother Vi is a practical nurse and sometimes away from their apartment for days or longer. Tree's major responsibility is to care for her eighteen-year-old retarded brother Dab, who has been experiencing severe stomach pains. Both go to school. Tree has a special playroom, a walk-in closet. One Friday she looks at the table in the room and sees a vision. She is in a house in the country with a two-year-old girl and her mother, Vi. Vi's brother, Brother Rush, a numbers man, enters. When he leaves, upstairs in the bedroom a young boy is cruelly tied to a bed.

Later, Tree brings Dab into the room, but he has a different vision in which he attends his uncle's funeral. That night Vi comes home and tells

Tree she has a new boyfriend nicknamed Silversmith and he will help her to buy a new car. Tree tells Vi about the vision, but she is unable to see it.

Vi becomes so alarmed at Dab's condition, particularly after finding hidden barbiturates in his room, that she phones Silversmith and together the three take Dab to the hospital where his condition worsens. Vi explains that Dab has a hereditary ailment called porphyria, a disease that surfaces when the victim takes drugs or alcohol. This is what killed her other brother and, because he drank excessively, would have killed her Brother Rush had he not died in an automobile accident. Tree now realizes that through the mirror she was reliving experiences from her own life and that she is the little girl in these visions. After further questioning, she learns that somewhere she has a real father who survived the crash but disappeared after Vi left him. She also knows that Vi's cruel behavior toward Dab as a child shows that she never really accepted him or his condition.

Feelings of hostility and rejection against her mother well up inside Tree. Silversmith proves to be a kindly, understanding man who tries to help Tree forgive and forget. Tree tells him about the table and he says that perhaps such visions are intended only for the guiltless.

Dab dies, and Tree, in a dramatic confrontation, blames Vi for his death and decides to leave home after the funeral. In one last encounter with Brother Rush, she sees him together with Dab. Her brother looks beautiful. The two are laughing and enjoying themselves with their faces full of sunlight and without pain. Perhaps Brother Rush's visit was to take Dab to a better place.

Before the funeral Miss Pricherd moves in to relieve Tree of all the housework. She is also thankful for this new home and tells the girl about the horrors of the street life Tree would face should she run away.

By funeral time, Tree has become more reconciled to her brother's death. After the funeral she talks to Silversmith's eighteen-year-old son Don, who shamelessly flirts with her and invites her to a movie. Vi announces that sometime in the future when their business is established she and Silversmith will marry and be able to establish a proper home for Tree. The young girl is torn about her future, but finally decides to stay. Working things out will be difficult but at least possible.

Themes and Subjects
Although the supernatural elements in this story supply fascination and suspense for the reader, this is basically a novel of human relationships that involve a commingling of present and past. It deals with the power of love, of family ties and devotion, and guilt and acceptance. The sister-brother

interdependence and later the mother-daughter situation are brilliantly portrayed in their complexity. The reader learns to know and understand all of the characters and their individual struggles and conflicts.

Booktalk Material

Telling about Tree's first encounters with Brother Rush should interest readers, as well as perhaps a discussion of ghosts and ghost stories. Some important passages are: an introduction to the main characters, including Brother Rush (pp. 9–13); Tree discovers that Brother Rush is a ghost (pp. 18–23); Tree's first journey into the past (pp. 27–34); Tree reads to Dab (pp. 58–61); and Vi comes home (pp. 90–98).

Additional Selections

The power of love to transcend time and space is one of the themes in Madeleine L'Engle's *A Wrinkle in Time* (Farrar, 1962).

Remi, a thirteen-year-old immigrant from Haiti, sees a ghost train and witnesses an unsolved murder that occurred fifty years ago in *Ghost Train* (Holt, 1996) by Jess Mowry.

After Nick meets Marina, a surfer, he realizes that she is an immortal who has plotted against the males in his family for generations in Linda Cargill's *The Surfer* (Scholastic, pap., 1995).

In Charles Butler's *The Darkling* (Simon, 1998), Petra is taken over by the spirit of the dead love of a hermit she has just met.

About the Author and Book

Authors and Artists for Young Adults. Gale. Vol. 2, 1989; vol. 21, 1997.
Biography Today: Author Series. Omnigraphics. Vol. 1, 1995; vol. 12, 2002.
Bostrom, Kathleen Long. *Winning Authors: Profiles of the Newbery Medalists.* Libraries Unlimited, 2003.
Children's Books and Their Creators. Houghton, 1995.
Children's Literature Review. Gale. Vol. 1, 1976; vol. 11, 1986; vol. 40, 1996.
Contemporary Authors New Revision Series. Vol. 126, Gale, 2004.
Continuum Encyclopedia of Children's Literature. Continuum, 2001.
Drew, Bernard A. *100 Most Popular Young Adult Authors.* Libraries Unlimited, 1996.
Estes, Glenn E. "American Writers for Children Since 1960: Fiction." In *Dictionary of Literary Biography.* Vol. 52, Gale, 1986.
Favorite Children's Authors and Illustrators. Vol. 3, Tradition Books, 2003.
Fourth Book of Junior Authors and Illustrators. Wilson, 1978.
Gallo, Donald R. *Speaking for Ourselves.* National Council of Teachers of English, 1990.
Gillespie, John T., and Corinne J. Naden. *Characters in Young Adult Literature.* Gale, 1997.
Hamilton, Virginia. "Laura Ingalls Wilder Medal Acceptance," *Horn Book,* July/Aug., 1995, pp. 436–41.

———. "Looking for America," *School Library Journal,* May, 1999, pp. 28–31
———. "Sentinels in Long Still Rows," *American Libraries,* June/July, 1999, pp. 68–71.
Jones, Raymond E. *Characters in Children's Literature.* Gale, 1997.
Lives and Works: Young Adult Authors. Vol. 4, Grolier, 1999.
McElmeel, Sharron L. *100 Most Popular Children's Authors.* Libraries Unlimited, 1999.
Major Authors and Illustrators for Children and Young Adults (1st ed.). Vol. 3, Gale, 1993.
Major Authors and Illustrators for Children and Young Adults (2nd ed.). Vol. 4, Gale, 2002.
Mikkesen, Nina. *Virginia Hamilton.* Twayne, 1992.
Ninth Book of Junior Authors and Illustrators. Wilson, 2004.
St. James Guide to Young Adult Writers (2nd ed.). St. James, 1999.
Something About the Author. Gale. Vol. 4, 1973; vol. 56, 1989; vol. 79, 1995; vol. 123, 2001; vol. 132, 2002.
Stevens, Jen. *The Undergraduate's Companion to Children's Writers and Their Web Sites.* Libraries Unlimited, 2004.
Twentieth-Century Young Adult Writers (1st ed.). St. James, 1994.
Wheeler, Jill. *Virginia Hamilton.* Abdo and Daughter, 1997.
Writers for Young Adults. Vol. 2, Scribner, 1997.
www.virginiahamilton.com (personal Web site)
See also listing "Selected Web Sites on Children's Literature and Authors."

Heinlein, Robert A. *Stranger in a Strange Land.* Putnam, 1961, o.p.; pap. Ace, $16.95, 0-44-178838-6 (Grade 10–Adult).

Introduction

When Robert A. Heinlein (1907–88) died in May 1988, at age eighty, he was considered one of the three greatest science fiction writers of the time, along with Arthur C. Clarke and Isaac Asimov. His output was extremely large: at the time of his death, sixty-four of his books were listed in *Books in Print.* They range in scope from many titles written for teenagers to the present volume, which was written originally for adults. He was recipient of every major award given to science fiction writers, including the Grand Master Nebula Award, and he was a four-time winner of Hugo award (one was for this volume). The prophetic nature of his writing is sometimes uncanny. For example, this novel, though first published in 1961, anticipated the philosophy and lifestyle of the flower children and hippies of some years later. It also introduced a new verb into our vocabulary—"to grok"—which means approximately to comprehend fully and assimilate inwardly the essence of an idea, situation, or person as in "science fiction fans grok Heinlein."

Principal Characters
>Captain Willem van Tromp, leader of spacecraft *Champion*
>Mike Smith, born on Mars
>Ben Caxton, newspaperman
>Secretary General Joseph Douglas, leader of the Federation
>Jill Boardman, Ben's fiancée
>Jubal Harshan, Ben's friend
>Madame Becky Vesant, astrologer

Plot Summary
Twenty-five years after the first unsuccessful attempt to colonize Mars from our planet, Terra, the spacecraft *Champion*, commanded by Willem van Tromp, lands, returning to Terra with Mike Smith, son of two of the original colonists. Mike was born on Mars and, after all the remaining colonists died, was raised as a Martian. He knows little English and has never seen a woman or been exposed to sex (Martians are three-legged unisexuals). But he does have unusual mental powers such as the ability to move the mind from place to place while the body remains stationary, the ability to move objects mentally, and the ability to enter another's mind.

Mike is held for observation at Bethesda Medical Center and newspaperman Ben Caxton realizes he might be in danger. As sole survivor of the first expedition, he is not only heir to the accumulated wealth of the participants but could claim ownership of Mars. The Federation, a political union of many nations including the U.S., led by Secretary General Joseph Douglas, would find this awkward and would like to dispose of Mike.

Mike is held under tight security but Jill, Ben's fiancée, disguises Mike as a nurse and escapes from the hospital to the mansion of Jubal Harshan, Ben's friend. Ben is kidnapped by members of the Federation. But in time an agreement is reached; Ben is released, Mike gives up his rights to Mars, and Douglas becomes Mike's financial adviser.

Mike decides to enter the world with Jill, now his lover. The jobs that Mike tries are no good. Finally, he realizes that his mission on Earth is to guide humans into the caring and sharing ways of Martians. He forms a large commune called "the Nest" that practices nudity and free love.

The general public becomes outraged. An angry mob comes after Mike and his followers. Although he is able to make them disappear, he realizes that he must provide his group with a lasting inspirational act. He confronts the mob, which kills him with rocks and fists. His last words are "thou art god." The members continue to spread the teachings of Mike and the Martians to the far corners of the Federation.

Themes and Subjects

In his life and death, Mike represents a Christ-like figure passing on a modern message of love and unselfishness, but he is derided and scorned and eventually martyred for his beliefs. His fate is that of many contemporary great people who have died for humanity. The author presents a sardonic and disturbing picture of such modern institutions as organized religion, marriage, and power politics. It is also an inspiring story of faith, honor, and friendship that explores the depth and variety of human love. The author has also created a fascinating and believable picture of the alien, morally advanced culture of the Martians and contrasts this tellingly with our own.

Booktalk Material

An introduction to the Man from Mars and his arrival on Earth should interest readers. Some good passages are: Jill first visits Mike in the hospital (pp. 21–24; pp. 14–17, pap.); Mike's parentage and possible future (pp. 30–33; pp. 24–27, pap.); Ben contemplates Mike's possible murder (pp. 33–38; pp. 27–32, pap.); Ben interviews Mike and is kidnapped (pp. 49–56; pp. 44–51, pap.); and Mike's escape from the hospital (pp. 60–63; pp. 56–58, pap.).

Additional Selections

Chris Stone, who lives in darkness because of a rare disease, explores his town's deadly secret to save his world in Dean Koontz's *Fear Nothing* (Bantam, 1998).

Stephen King's *The Stand* (Doubleday, 1990) traces the lives of several characters who have survived the "super flu" that has killed ninety percent of the world's population.

Billy Pilgrim, a World War II veteran, becomes unstuck in time and encounters, among others, a writer named Kilgore Trout in Kurt Vonnegut's *Slaughterhouse-Five* (Dell, pap., 1991).

In a different world called Winter, one's sex can change from season to season in Ursula K. Le Guin's *The Left Hand of Darkness* (Ace, pap., 1969).

About the Author and Book

Authors and Artists for Young Adults. Vol. 17, Gale, 1996.
Biography Today: Author Series. Vol. 4, Omnigraphics, 1998.

Children's Literature Review. Vol. 75, Gale, 2002.
Contemporary Authors New Revision Series. Vol. 53, Gale, 1993.
Continuum Encyclopedia of Children's Literature. Continuum, 2001.
Drew, Bernard A. *100 More Popular Young Adult Authors.* Libraries Unlimited, 2002.
Gillespie, John T., and Corinne J. Naden. *Characters in Young Adult Literature.* Gale, 1997.
Major Authors and Illustrators for Children and Young Adults (1st ed.). Vol. 3, Gale, 1993.
More Junior Authors. Wilson, 1963.
St. James Guide to Young Adult Writers (2nd ed.). St. James, 1999.
Something About the Author. Gale. Vol. 9, 1976; vol. 56, 1989; vol. 69, 1992.
Twentieth-Century Young Adult Writers (1st ed.). St. James, 1994.
See also listing "Selected Web Sites on Children's Literature and Authors."

Jones, Diana Wynne. *Castle in the Air.* Greenwillow, 1990, o.p.; pap. HarperTrophy, $6.99, 0-06-447345-7 (Grades 7–10).

Introduction

Diana Wynne Jones (1934–) was born in London but spent the World War II years in the north of England where she met, as a child, two legends of English children's literature, Arthur Ransom and Beatrix Potter, and was shocked to discover that both disliked children. She chose to write fantasies because she claimed this element was absent from her childhood. Her books are characterized by complex plots, plenty of suspense, humorous situations, romance, and exciting adventures involving castles (some of which move), demons, witches, and wizards. Although this book is labeled a sequel to *Howl's Moving Castle* (Greenwillow, 1986), it can be read quite independently of the first volume. Two of the characters from the first book, Sophie and the Wizard Howl, do make appearances late in the second book, but a knowledge of their former adventures is not necessary. *Castle in the Air* is the story of Abdullah, his pursuit of lady love, Flower-in-the-Night, and the constant help he receives from a tired but loyal magic carpet.

Principal Characters

Abdullah, a carpet merchant in Zanzib
Princess Flower-in-the-Night, whom he sees on a magic carpet
Prince of Ochinstan, whom the princess is to marry
Kabul Aqba, a desert bandit
Hasruel, who sold Abdullah the carpet
Dalzel, who has Hasruel under his power

Plot Summary

In the magical city of Zanzib, a young carpet merchant named Abdullah buys a worn-looking carpet from a stranger who says it is magic. That night when he sleeps on it, he meets Princess Flower-in-the-Night, who says she is betrothed to the ugly Prince of Ochinstan. Abdullah gives her the impression that he is a prince, too. After a few meetings, Abdullah is convinced he loves the princess. He tells her to jump onto the carpet beside him, but a flying djinn drops out of the sky and grabs her. The carpet refuses his command to follow her.

Abdullah is taken prisoner and the sultan, father of the princess, wants to know what Abdullah has done with his daughter. Abdullah says they did not have time to marry, which pleases the sultan because the prophecy says she will marry the first man she sees outside of her father.

Abdullah escapes and lands in the desert in the arms of a world-famous bandit, Kabul Aqba. Abdullah convinces the bandit that he is a magician. Luckily, he finds a bottle that contains a genie. With help from this genie and the carpet, Abdullah escapes and asks the genie to take him to the princess. But the genie says she is nowhere on Earth. Abdullah asks to be taken to the nearest person who can help find her. He finds an old soldier and this unlikely pair team up. Along the way, they meet a cat who goes with him. She is called Midnight.

They meet Hasruel, who sold the magic carpet to Abdullah in the first place. Hasruel's brother Dalzel, the evil djinn who stole Flower-in-the-Night, has ordered him to steal every princess in the world because Dalzel wants to marry a princess. Abdullah now knows that Flower-in-the-Night must be Dalzel's prisoner because she is a princess. Once in Dalzel's floating palace, Abdullah and the soldier meet an astounding number of princesses, including Flower-in-the-Night. They all conspire to break the cruel Dalzel's spell. When they succeed and Hasruel is about to send his brother away forever, Dalzel breaks down and cries because he is going to be so lonely. Enter Abdullah's two fat nieces. Wonder of wonders, Dalzel is enchanted with both of them. The loneliness problem is solved!

The wedding of Abdullah and Flower-in-the-Night is quite a grand affair. Although the sultan gives them land to build a palace, they actually build a rather modest house with a thatched roof—and the most beautiful gardens in the world.

Themes and Subjects

A delightfully wacky fantasy filled with prophecies that are fulfilled, tantalizing twists and turns, magic carpets and lovely princesses, and all manner of surprises. An action-packed, fun-filled, humorous, impossible adventure on a grand scale.

Booktalk Material
A number of amusing incidents will make a delightful introduction to this charming fantasy. See: Abdullah meets the seller of the magic carpet (pp. 4–10, pap.); Abdullah and the princess discuss whether he is a woman (pp. 12–16, pap.); Abdullah tries to get the carpet to fly (pp. 21–23, pap.); the prophecy is read (pp. 31–38, pap.); Abdullah becomes the sultan's prisoner (pp. 42–47, pap.).

Additional Selections
Young wizard Nita travels to other universes seeking a cure for her mother's cancer in Diane Duane's *The Wizard's Dilemma* (Harcourt, 2001).

In Ursula K. Le Guin's *A Wizard of Earthsea* (Bantam, pap., 1968), an apprentice wizard accidentally unleashes an evil power into the land of Earthsea.

In Patricia C. Wrede's *Magician's World* (Tor, 1997), Kim, a former thief who is now an apprentice magician, continues her lessons while investigating a burglary.

Because of the violence and pollution, a family builds a large ship and fills it with animals just before the rain starts in Barbara Cohen's *Unicorns in the Rain* (Atheneum, 1980).

About the Author and Book
Authors and Artists for Young Adults. Vol. 12, Gale, 1994.
Children's Books and Their Creators. Houghton, 1995.
Children's Literature Review. Vol. 23, Gale, 1991.
Contemporary Authors New Revision Series. Vol. 120, Gale, 2004.
Continuum Encyclopedia of Children's Literature. Continuum, 2001.
Drew, Bernard A. *100 Most Popular Young Adult Authors.* Libraries Unlimited, 1997.
Fifth Book of Junior Authors and Illustrators. Wilson, 1983.
Gallo, Donald R. *Speaking for Ourselves, Too.* National Council of Teachers of English, 1993.
Gillespie, John T., and Corinne J. Naden. *Characters in Young Adult Literature.* Gale, 1997.
Major Authors and Illustrators for Children and Young Adults (1st ed.). Vol. 3, Gale, 1993.
Major Authors and Illustrators for Children and Young Adults (2nd ed.). Vol. 4, Gale, 2002.
St. James Guide to Young Adult Writers (2nd ed.). St. James, 1999.
Something About the Author. Gale. Vol. 9, 1976; vol. 70, 1993; vol. 108, 2000; vol. 160, 2005.
Something About the Author Autobiography Series. Vol. 7, Gale, 1989.
Twentieth-Century Young Adult Writers (1st ed.). St. James, 1994.
See also listing "Selected Web Sites on Children's Literature and Authors."

McCaffrey, Anne. *Dragonsong.* Atheneum, 1976, o.p.; pap. Aladdin, 2003, $5.99, 0-689-86008-0 (Grades 7–12).

Introduction

Anne McCaffrey's (1926–) world is a planet named Pern that circles about the star Rukbat. Readers first read about this astral system in a trilogy, *The Dragonriders of Pern* (Del Rey, pap., 1988), now available in an omnibus volume consisting of *Dragonflight* (Del Rey, 1968), *Dragonquest* (Del Rey, 1971), and *The White Dragon* (Del Rey, 1978). *Dragonsong* is the fourth book about Pern and the first one in the Harperhall trilogy. It is not necessary to have read the previous volumes to understand this one, but certain background facts are important. Life on Pern is conducted largely underground because a neighboring malevolent rogue planet, Red Star, periodically emits silvery spore strands that eat anything in their way. This rain of ravenous Threads can be destroyed only by the flaming breath of the giant dragons that have been trained by their riders since birth through a system of "impressing" to comb the skies of Pern, destroying the Threads. The dragonriders and their entourage live in five communities known as Weyrs, but the general population inhabits many smaller subterranean communities called Holds. Time is measured in Pern by "turns," corresponding to our years, but dragons and their much smaller distant relatives, fire lizards, can move through time by a process called "Between."

Principal Characters

Menolly, almost fifteen, who lives on a remote coast on the planet Pern
Yanus, her father
Mavi, her mother
Alemi, her favorite brother
Petiron, the Harper, a minstrel
Elgion, the new Harper
Robinton, the Masterharper

Plot Summary

Menolly lives in Half Circle Sea Hold on a remote eastern coast on Pern in a gigantic, partially manmade cave. Life is very primitive. The community's leader is her father, Yanus, a harsh man. Her favorite brother is Alemi. In each community, the place of honor is that of the Harper, a minstrel who keeps the records. In Sea Hold, the Harper is Petiron. When Petiron dies and the community awaits a new Harper—Harpers can never be women—Menolly is allowed to play music as long as she doesn't sing or compose her own songs. The new Harper is tall, handsome Elgion.

While gutting fish one day, Menolly wounds her hand and thinks she may not be able to play her music. Completely discouraged, she runs away for one night and hides in a cave with the fire lizards. That night their eggs hatch at the same time as the deadly Thread begins dropping. To save them from the Thread, she keeps them safe and inadvertently becomes their surrogate mother. She continues to nourish them and care for them over the next weeks. Her favorite is the female, Beauty. They all accompany her singing with sounds.

Menolly's family thinks she has been lost in the Thread attack, so they don't search for her, but Elgion is curious about the person who wrote the songs he has grown to love. Yanus tells the family that a man was the composer.

Meanwhile, while Menolly is on the beach, another Thread attack occurs, and Menolly is saved by a dragonrider who takes her to the lower caverns where her wounds are cared for. She has never experienced such kindness before. In time, she heals and returns to her music and singing, but begs not to be sent back to the Sea Hold and her cruel father.

At dragon hatching time, there is a great gathering of people and by accident, Menolly meets Elgion and the Masterharper, Robinton. Slowly her true identity as the talented balladeer is discovered. Robinton insists she accompany him to to Harperhall, the great music conservatory of Pern. Menolly accepts ecstatically.

Themes and Subjects
Pern is a fully conceived, believable fantasy world and Menolly's journey from outcast to secure womanhood is convincingly portrayed. Her courage and resoluteness make her particularly appealing. The oppression and unfairness of a male-dominated society and the close relationship between humans and animals are well portrayed. The power and importance of music, even in this primitive society, are an interesting subtheme.

Booktalk Material
A description of Pern, the Sea Hold, the Thread, and the Between phenomenon should intrigue readers. Some important passages are: Menolly gets instruction about teaching from Yanus (pp. 11–15; pp. 8–11, pap.);

her disobedience (pp. 24–26; pp. 19–21, pap.); she sees her first fire lizards (pp. 27–30; pp. 22–24, pap.); taking care of Old Uncle (pp. 37–43; pp. 31–36, pap.).

Additional Selections

The classic battle between black and white magic is at the center of Marion Zimmer Bradley's exciting fantasy *Heartlight* (Tor, 1998).

In Patricia A. McKillip's *The Forgotten Beasts of Eld* (Magic Carpet, 1996), an ageless enchantress who has mastered many magical beasts, including dragons, takes in an abandoned child.

Aerin, the daughter of the King of Damon, nurses a warhorse to health in preparation for her becoming a dragon slayer in Robin McKinley's *The Hero and the Crown* (Berkley, pap., 1987).

Harry enters the Hogwarts School of Witchcraft and Wizardry in *Harry Potter and the Sorcerer's Stone* (Scholastic, 1998), the first volume in the amazing series by J. K. Rowling.

About the Author and Book

Authors and Artists for Young Adults. Gale. Vol. 6, 1991; vol. 34, 2000.
Brizzi, May T. *Anne McCaffrey.* Starmont, 1986.
Children's Books and Their Creators. Houghton, 1995.
Children's Literature Review. Vol. 49, Gale, 1998.
Contemporary Authors. Vol. 227, Gale, 2005.
Cowart, David, and Thomas L. Wymer. "Twentieth-Century American Science Fiction Writers." Vol. 8. In *Dictionary of Literary Biography,* Gale, 1981.
Drew, Bernard A. *100 Most Popular Young Adult Authors.* Libraries Unlimited, 1996.
Fifth Book of Junior Authors and Illustrators. Wilson, 1983.
Fonstad, Karen Wynn. *The Atlas of Pern.* Ballantine, 1984.
Gallo, Donald R. *Speaking for Ourselves.* National Council of Teachers of English, 1990.
Gillespie, John T., and Corinne J. Naden. *Characters in Young Adult Literature.* Gale, 1997.
Lives and Works: Young Adult Authors. Vol. 5, Grolier, 1999.
Major Authors and Illustrators for Children and Young Adults (1st ed.). Vol. 4, Gale, 1993.
Major Authors and Illustrators for Children and Young Adults (2nd ed.). Vol. 5, Gale, 2002.
St. James Guide to Young Adult Writers (2nd ed.). St. James, 1999.
Something About the Author. Gale. Vol. 8, 1976; vol. 70, 1993; vol. 116, 2000; vol. 152, 2004.
Something About the Author Autobiography Series. Vol. 11, Gale, 1991.
Stevens, Jen. *The Undergraduate's Companion to Children's Writers and Their Web Sites.* Libraries Unlimited, 2004.
Twentieth-Century Science Fiction Writers (3rd ed.). St. James. 1991.
Twentieth-Century Young Adult Writers (1st ed.). St. James, 1994.

Writers for Young Adults. Vol. 2, Scribner, 1997.
www.annemccaffrey.com (personal Web site)
See also listing "Selected Web Sites on Children's Literature and Authors."

O'Brien, Robert C. *Z for Zachariah.* Heinemann, 1975, $13.52, 0-43512211-8; pap. Simon Pulse, 1987, $5.99, 0-02044650-0 (Grades 7–10).

Introduction
Robert C. O'Brien (1918–73) was the pseudonym of Robert Leslie Conly, an American writer who was educated in such prestigious institutions as Williams College, the Juilliard School of Music, Columbia University, and the University of Rochester in New York State where he received his bachelor's degree in 1940. During his relatively short writing career, he produced three novels for young people. The first, *The Silver Crown* (Atheneum, 1968), is an adventure/survival novel set in contemporary America, which deals with a malevolent sect allied to St. Jerome who perpetrate destructive acts on society hoping to gain control of people's minds. The second was the Newbery Medal winner, *Mrs. Frisby and the Rats of NIMH* (Atheneum, 1971), a mixture of animal fantasy and science fiction involving a group of super-intelligent rats. In 1986, the author's daughter, Jane Leslie Conly wrote a sequel, *Rasco and the Rats of NIMH* (Harper, pap., 1990). *Z for Zachariah* was left uncompleted at the author's death and the last few chapters were written by his wife and daughter from the notes he left. This is the story, told in diary form, of a fifteen-year-old girl who believes, for a time, that she is the sole survivor of a nuclear war, and of the four months that elapse between sighting a stranger in her valley and their final confrontation.

Principal Characters
Ann Burden, survivor of the atomic holocaust
Mr. and Mrs. Klein, grocery store proprietors
John R. Loomis, chemist

Plot Summary
After the atomic holocaust, Ann Burden is left alone in a secluded valley near Amish country, while her family and Mr. and Mrs. Klein, grocery store proprietors, go to look for survivors. When they never return, she

thinks she may be the last survivor on Earth because of the fall of radiation. She survives through the year with supplies from the grocery store and the family farm.

One day she sees smoke from a campfire on a nearby hill. Fearful of strangers, she retreats into a cave. Soon a man in a green plastic suit appears, pulling a wagon. He sets up a camp and settles in. The next day he is joined by Faro, Ann's dog, who has amazingly returned home. But the man makes the mistake of bathing in the contaminated creek and becomes ill from radiation. Carrying her gun, Ann approaches the tent.

When he gains strength, she moves him into the house. He is John R. Loomis, age thirty-two, a chemist from Cornell University. He was wearing a suit that stops radiation when the war broke out. He tells Ann that the second stage of his exposure, from the creek, is about to begin and he may die. During the next week, in a high fever, he reveals many things to Ann, such as the fact that when the bombs were dropping, he shot his colleague, Edward, to prevent him from leaving the lab in the safe suit. Sometimes Ann prays for the man's recovery. She remembers from childhood her biblical ABC book, beginning with "A is for Adam" and ending with "Z is for Zachariah." If Adam was the first man maybe Zachariah is the last.

Loomis recovers but is very weak. Ann plays hymns for him but he is unmoved and says they must plan scientifically for the future. After her sixteenth birthday, he tries to make love to her but she fights him and runs away. When she returns, hoping to work out a compromise, he shoots his rifle at her, wounding her in the heel. He locks up the food, hoping to starve her into submission.

Ann realizes her only hope of escape is to get the safe suit and leave the valley. She tricks Loomis into leaving the house unguarded for a few moments. However, her sense of honesty and integrity does not allow her to leave under such circumstances. In the safe suit, she confronts Loomis and tells him that to stop her from leaving, he will have to shoot her as he did Edward. Shaken by this reminder of his guilt, Loomis allows her to go. Pulling the wagon behind her, the girl sets out alone, hoping to find another valley where there may be other survivors.

Themes and Subjects

This is not only a chilling glimpse of what could result from a nuclear war, but also an inspiring, suspenseful story of a girl fighting to retain her set of values. In it, Ann's wholesomeness and honesty are pitted against another's self-interest.

Booktalk Material
A retelling of the story until the arrival of the stranger will interest readers. Some passages from the diary that could be used are: Ann and her journal (pp. 3–6; pp. 10–13, pap.); Loomis explores the house and bathes in the creek (pp. 25–31; pp. 25–30, pap.); Ann leaves the cave to help Loomis (pp. 45–49; pp. 41–43, pap.); Loomis's past (pp. 59–62; pp. 51–53, pap.); and his quarrel with Edward (pp. 114–18; pp. 91–94, pap.).

Additional Selections
Eric Campbell's *The Shark Callers* (Harcourt, 1994) contains parallel stories of two boys who survive a volcanic eruption and tidal waves in Papua, New Guinea.

A war game turns serious when a gunman begins picking off the participants in Philip Kerrigan's *Survival Game* (Avon, pap., 1999).

After the Bomb (Scholastic, pap., 1987) by Gloria D. Miklowitz describes the experiences of a group of young people after an atomic bomb falls on Los Angeles.

While on the run from killers, a teenage boy must survive in an Alaskan wilderness in Walt Morey's *Death Walk* (Blue Heron, 1991).

About the Author and Book
(Many of these entries are under the author's real name, Robert Leslie Conly.)

Authors and Artists for Young Adults. Vol. 6, Gale, 1991.
Bostrom, Kathleen Long. *Winning Authors: Profiles of the Newbery Medalists.* Libraries Unlimited, 2003.
Children's Books and Their Creators. Houghton, 1995.
Children's Literature Review. Vol. 2, Gale, 1976.
Continuum Encyclopedia of Children's Literature. Continuum, 2001.
Favorite Children's Authors and Illustrators. Vol. 4, Tradition Books, 2003.
Fourth Book of Junior Authors and Illustrators. Wilson, 1978.
Gillespie, John T., and Corinne J. Naden. *Characters in Young Adult Literature.* Gale, 1997.
Jones, Raymond E. *Characters in Children's Literature.* Gale, 1997.
Major Authors and Illustrators for Children and Young Adults (1st ed.). Vol. 2, Gale, 1993.
Major Authors and Illustrators for Children and Young Adults (2nd ed.). Vol. 2, Gale, 2002.
St. James Guide to Young Adult Writers (2nd ed.). St. James, 1999.
Something About the Author. Vol. 23, Gale, 1981.
Stevens, Jen. *The Undergraduate's Companion to Children's Writers and Their Web Sites.* Libraries Unlimited, 2004.
Twentieth-Century Guide to Young Adult Writers (1st ed.). St. James, 1994.
See also listing "Selected Web Sites on Children's Literature and Authors."

SCIENCE FICTION AND FANTASY • 171

Pascal, Francine. *Hangin' Out with Cici.* Dell, 1985 (1977). Pap. $4.95, 0-440-93364-1 (Grades 6–8).

Introduction
Although she had always been interested in writing, New York-born Francine Pascal (1938–) didn't begin to write seriously until after she married John Pascal, a journalist. Afterward, they collaborated on many projects, including soap opera scripts, and Francine branched out into writing for popular magazines. *Hangin' Out with Cici* was her first novel for young adults. Set in Jamaica, Queens, where Francine grew up, it tells the story of a self-centered girl named Victoria who time-travels to the year 1944, where she meets and becomes friends with Cici, her mother at age thirteen. It is a witty, often uproarious comedy that utilizes zingy remarks, slang, exaggeration, understatement, and pure slapstick to produce a laugh-aloud farce with serious undertones. Victoria's story is continued in *My First Love and Other Disasters* (Simon Pulse, pap., 1979), in which she falls hopelessly in love with Jim and spends time on Fire Island, and *Love and Betrayal and Hold the Mayo* (Simon Pulse, pap., 1981), which tells of Victoria, now sixteen, and her crush on a handsome camp counselor. Pascal is perhaps best known as the author and editor of the popular Sweet Valley High series, featuring Jessica and Elizabeth, a pair of attractive, popular identical twins.

Principal Characters
Victoria Martin, an eighth-grader
Nina, her eleven-year-old sister
Her mother and father
Aunt Hildy
Cici, a girl she meets at Penn Station

Plot Summary
Eighth-grader Victoria Martin had thought that when she turned thirteen, she would be treated as an adult. No way. Life stays the same. She argues with her younger sister, Nina, with whom she lives in their comfortable apartment in New York City with her mother, a well-known sculptor, and her father, a successful real estate lawyer. In addition, Victoria is always getting into trouble at school because of her practical jokes. This time she gets herself suspended and her mother grounds her for a week. However, her grandmother does get her to attend Cousin Elizabeth's party in Philadelphia. But that is a disaster, too. When Victoria is caught

on the back porch with some boys who are passing joints around, everyone is sent home and Victoria is dumped on a train for New York.

When the train gives a sudden lurch, she bumps her head and she has a momentary blackout. When she wakes up, the train is in Penn Station. But everything looks different and her mother is not there to greet her. She meets a girl her age named Cici who looks familiar. When Victoria can't get in touch with her mother, Cici invites her home to Queens.

Victoria is amazed how much Cici is like herself, even to engaging in some petty shoplifting. Victoria likes her new friend, but Cici doesn't seem to comprehend things such as frozen food and television and uses expressions like "hubba-hubba." When Victoria sees that the date on a newspaper is May 19, 1944, she realizes that Cici—short for Felicia—is her own mother and that she has time-traveled into the past.

Cici explains that she is in serious trouble. If she flunks her science test Monday, she will not graduate. She arranges to buy a copy of the test from Ted Davis, son of her science teacher. When that fails, she is forced to tell her parents the truth.

Later that night there is an air raid alarm. In the dark, Victoria bumps her head and awakes on the train to New York. Never has she been more pleased and happy than to be greeted at the station by her mother and Nina. The next day at school, Victoria recognizes the new principal as the grown-up Ted Davis. Felicia gets Victoria reinstated at school after the young girl promises to mend her ways. Felicia tells Victoria about the test paper incident and how she later reached an agreement so she could graduate. Mother and daughter seem to have reached a new understanding and peace reigns in the Martin household. Well, at least temporarily.

Themes and Subjects

This is basically a wonderfully comic novel with an appealing, self-deprecating gamine as heroine. The elements of fantasy are well integrated into the plot. Conflicts even within happy families and the agonies of adolescence are well portrayed, as are problems involving the generation gap, reaching maturity, and accepting responsibility. Life in 1944 New York City is nicely recreated, and the contrast between that relatively safe, secure, more simple life and that of the present day is both amusing and revealing.

Booktalk Material

A discussion of the question "Did you ever wonder what your parents were like at your age?" could introduce Victoria and her unique situation. Some amusing passages are: the incident during the school movie (pp.

11–14); the quarrels with Nina at the train station (pp. 31–35); pot smoking at the party (pp. 37–38); shoplifting at Woolworth's (pp. 62–65); and the riot at the movie theater (pp. 66–73).

Additional Selections

Graeme Base's *The Discovery of Dragons* (Abrams, 1996) is a humorous account of three pioneers in dragon research.

Maddy knows she will be a real vamp if she follows Dr. Dudley's program in Ellen Conford's *Seven Days to a Brand New Me* (Scholastic, pap., 1990).

Susanna, a flirt, makes a bet she can give up guys for three months in June Foley's *Susanna Siegelbaum Gives Up Guys* (Scholastic, pap., 1992).

In Claudia Mills's *Alex Ryan, Stop That!* (Farrar, 2003), seventh-grader Alex has problems with attractive Marcia and his father-son relations.

About the Author and Book
Authors and Artists for Young Adults. Gale. Vol. 1, 1989; vol. 40, 2001.
Children's Literature Review. Vol. 25, Gale, 1991.
Contemporary Authors New Revision Series. Vol. 97, Gale, 2001.
Drew, Bernard A. *100 Most Popular Young Adult Authors.* Libraries Unlimited, 1996.
Fifth Book of Junior Authors and Illustrators. Wilson, 1983.
Gallo, Donald R. *Speaking for Ourselves, Too.* National Council of Teachers of English, 1993.
Major Authors and Illustrators for Children and Young Adults (1st ed.). Vol. 5, Gale, 1993.
Major Authors and Illustrators for Children and Young Adults (2nd ed.). Vol. 6, Gale, 2002.
St. James Guide to Young Adult Writers (2nd ed.). St. James, 1999.
Something About the Author. Gale. Vol. 51, 1986; vol. 80, 1995; vol. 143, 2004.
See also listing "Selected Web Sites on Children's Literature and Authors."

Sleator, William. *House of Stairs.* Puffin, 1991 (1974). Pap. $5.99, 0-14-034580-9 (Grades 7–9).

Introduction
William Sleator (1945–), the son of a college professor and a physician, was born in Maryland but grew up in University City, Missouri. It is ironic that Harvard, his alma mater, should be the university where B. F. Skinner conducted his experiments on behavior modification through conditioning responses in animals and birds, because this novel deals with the horrifying results of similar experiments, this time with human subjects. This

subject is typical of the topics handled by Sleator, in which established scientific theories are applied to situations where conditions become extreme and uncontrollable. Two other of his popular titles are *Singularity* (Puffin, pap., 1985) about twins who discover a playhouse where time proceeds at an alarmingly fast rate, and *Interstellar Pig* (Puffin, pap., 1984) in which sixteen-year-old Barney becomes involved with three strangers in a board game where each player becomes a creature from outer space trying to get possession of a card marked "Piggy." Sleator once said, "I can't seem to keep outer space, time travel, and aliens out of my work." Although *House of Stairs* doesn't deal with aliens, it explores an original and daring theme full of horror and suspense.

Principal Characters
Peter and Lola, who are the first to arrive on the flights of stairs
Blossom, Abigail, and Oliver, who arrive next
Dr. Lawrence, head of the experiment

Plot Summary
Shy Peter is the first to arrive to this place of no walls, ceilings, or windows after being called into the orphanage office, blindfolded, and transported by car. In his new environment, there are only flights and flights of stairs, all without banisters, intersected with occasional small landings. Peter is joined by brash, outspoken Lola. They find a girl on one of the landings. She is fat, selfish Blossom. Soon, they meet Abigail, a naïve girl of great beauty, and Oliver, a boy of great ego and bravado. Although all different, they are all sixteen and orphans, and all have been brought to this strange place under the same mysterious circumstances.

Blossom is the first to discover the food machine, a small red dome that gives food when she sticks out her tongue. But when the food supply no longer operates according to her behavior, the five try various responses, which develop into a kind of ritualistic dance for survival.

The stressful environment causes all sorts of tensions and changes among the young people. The red machine again begins to deny them food, which brings on arguments between different pairs. Slowly they realize they are being programmed to hate and distrust, and their reward for attacking each other is food and, thus, survival.

Lola convinces Peter that it is better to starve than live as subhumans. They leave the security of the landing with its red machine.

After a few days, Peter and Lola return out of curiosity to find the other three healthy and well fed. The machine has been giving food solely on the basis of increased acts of cruelty among the three. The various forms of behavior they have devised constitute a horrifying chronicle of mental and physical abuse. Now they turn on the half-starved pair and commit physical violence. Lola realizes she is about to die and tells Peter her will to live is stronger than a total loss of humanity, and she wants to give in to the machine. Peter agrees and at that moment the experiment is over.

After recuperating in the hospital, all five are taken to Dr. Lawrence. He explains they have been in a reinforcement center undergoing conditioning as part of a plan to supply the president of the country with young people who will obey him without question. Three have passed the initial steps and are ready for further conditioning, but Peter and Lola will be sent to the outside world as misfits.

The briefing over, Blossom, Abigail, and Oliver leave and cross the hospital grounds. They see a blinking traffic light and immediately begin to dance.

Themes and Subjects

The misapplication of scientific theories and practices to control and change human behavior is an important theme. Peter's conduct demonstrates that the seemingly weak can often amass the greatest amount of inner resources. As happens to many who undergo severe emotional ordeals, Peter and Lola emerge stronger and more confident. The interaction of five very different people in an isolated and forced situation makes a fascinating character study.

Booktalk Material

An explanation and discussion of the concept of behavior modification might precede an introduction to the situations and characters in this book. Some interesting passages are: Chapter 1 with Peter alone in the house of stairs (pp. 9–11); Lola and Peter find Blossom (pp. 24–28); they get the machine to work (pp. 62–64); and performing the dance (pp. 68–69).

Additional Selections

Fifteen-year-old Tess must choose whether to remain human or assume a permanent animal form in Kate Thompson's *Midnight Choice* (Hyperion, 1999).

Scott and Becka discover that a local bookstore is the hub of a Ouija board cult in Bill Myers's *The Society* (Tyndale, 2001).

In Carol M. Tanzman's *The Shadow Place* (Millbrook, 2002), friendship and peer pressure are themes in this story of Lissa and the choices she makes.

Accidentally Tony reveals his problems to the school's weirdo, who then makes Tony her pet project in Ron Koertge's *Confess-O-Rama* (Orchard, 1996).

About the Author and Book
Authors and Artists for Young Adults. Gale. Vol. 5, 1990; vol. 39, 2001.
Children's Books and Their Creators. Houghton, 1995.
Children's Literature Review. Vol. 29, Gale, 1993.
Contemporary Authors New Revision Series. Vol. 97, Gale, 2002.
Continuum Encyclopedia of Children's Literature. Continuum, 2001.
Davis, James, and Hazel Davis. *Presenting William Sleator.* Twayne, 1991.
Drew, Bernard A. *100 Most Popular Young Adult Authors.* Libraries Unlimited, 1996.
Fifth Book of Junior Authors and Illustrators. Wilson, 1983.
Gallo, Donald R. *Speaking for Ourselves.* National Council of Teachers of English, 1990.
Gillespie, John T., and Corinne J. Naden. *Characters in Young Adult Literature.* Gale, 1997.
Lives and Works: Young Adult Authors. Vol. 7, Grolier, 1999.
Major Authors and Artists for Children and Young Adults (1st ed.). Vol. 5, Gale, 1993.
Major Authors and Illustrators for Children and Young Adults (2nd ed.). Vol. 7, Gale, 2002.
St. James Guide to Young Adult Writers (2nd ed.). St. James, 1999.
Something About the Author. Gale. Vol. 3, 1972; vol. 68, 1992; vol. 118, 2001; vol. 161, 2006.
Stevens, Jen. *The Undergraduate's Companion to Children's Writers and Their Web Sites.* Libraries Unlimited, 2004.
Twentieth-Century Young Adult Writers (1st ed.). St. James, 1994.
Writers for Young Adults. Vol. 3, Scribner, 1997.
See also listing "Selected Web Sites on Children's Literature and Authors."

Tolkien, J. R. R. *The Hobbit.* Harper, 2001 (1938). $23.31, 0-26110-328-8 (Grades 6–12).

Introduction
John Ronald Reuel Tolkien (1892–1973) was orphaned at the age of twelve, but his guardian provided ample financial and spiritual help so that he was able to pursue an Oxford education, where he received both his bachelor's and master's degrees. For the next forty years, he lived the academic life of a professor and lecturer. He was always keenly interested in language and literature and began writing at an early age. In structure and content, his *The Lord of the Rings* cycle resembles Richard Wagner's operatic work, *The Ring of the Nibelung.* Here, too, we have an introductory prelude (*The Hobbit*) followed by a trilogy that completes the saga. In

1938, *The Hobbit* won the New York Herald Tribune prize for the best children's book of the year. Since that time, it has provided enchantment and delight to thousands of readers. Although it was written for children in grades four through eight, like *Alice in Wonderland*, it can be enjoyed by a much older audience. In *The Hobbit*, the author introduces the readers to a land peopled by gnomes, dwarves, goblins, and elves (some friendly and others as mean and avaricious as even humans can be). The hero of the story is a hobbit named Mr. Bilbo Baggins of Bag-End, Underhill, Hobbiton.

Principal Characters
  Mr. Bilbo Baggins of Bag-End, a hobbit
  Gandalf, a wizard
  Smaug, a wicked dragon
  Gollum, a slimy reptile
  Beorn, a woodsman
  Thorin, leader of the dwarves

Plot Summary
The hero is Mr. Bilbo Baggins of Bag-End, Underhill, Hobbiton. He is a hobbit. Hobbits are smaller than dwarves but larger than Lilliputians. They are gentle and peace-loving. Gandalf, a wizard, persuades Bilbo to join thirteen dwarves on a dangerous mission to Lonely Mountain to recapture a vast treasure that once belonged to their ancestors. Now it is guarded by a wicked dragon named Smaug.

   They have many adventures and narrow escapes. They are captured by trolls and taken prisoner by goblins; encounter Gollum, a slimy reptile; and they are also captured by giant spiders. But, at last in the territory of Smaug, the group finds a secret entrance into the mountain. Yet they are powerless to recapture the treasure because Smaug, the fire-breathing dragon, keeps a constant vigil over it. However, Smaug is aware that there are strangers in this cave, but he is unable to find them.

   One night the dragon mysteriously disappears. He has accidentally discovered that the people of Lake Town have aided these intruders and has left to seek his revenge. During his attack on Lake Town, Smaug is killed by an enchanted arrow shot from the bow of Bard, a hero of the Lake People.

   The treasure is now free, but soon greed and avarice take over. The Lake People, accompanied by the Wood-elves, arrive at Lonely Mountain to demand their share. They are followed by the goblins and the Wargs. A great struggle—the Battle of the Five Armies—takes place in which the leader of the dwarves, Thorin, is killed. The goblins and Wargs are driven off and, helped by Bilbo's sacrifice of his share of the treasure, a truce is arranged between the other parties. Bilbo Baggins wants only to return to his quiet hobbit hole in Hobbiton, where he hopes he will live out the rest of his days in peace and quiet.

Themes and Subjects
The world of the hobbit bears a striking and at times disturbing resemblance to the world of humans. In this tale of fantasy, wonder, and quiet humor are revealed human foibles and basic moral principles.

Booktalk Material
How this book is introduced will depend largely on the audience. Here are some excerpts from which to choose: what is a hobbit? (pp. 11–12); details of the quest for treasure (pp. 32–36); the incident with the trolls (pp. 44–52); imprisonment by the goblins (pp. 74–79); riddles with Gollum (pp. 85–94); capture by giant spiders (pp. 162–69); and the escape in barrels (pp. 183–90).

Additional Selections
Four children enter the kingdom of Narnia through the back of a wardrobe in the first book of the Narnia series, *The Lion, the Witch, and the Wardrobe* (Macmillan, 1988) by C. S. Lewis.

In Anne Lindbergh's *Three Lives to Live* (Pocket, pap., 1995), a teenager discovers that her laundry chute is a conduit through time.

Intelligent sheep take over control of the world after the humans have left in David Macaulay's *Baaa* (Houghton, 1985).

Chip, a white-footed mouse, is chosen to lead his people against an invasion of brown rats in Gilbert Morris's *Journey to Freedom* (Crossway, 2000).

About the Author and Book
Authors and Artists for Young Adults. Vol. 10, Gale, 1993.
Becker, Alida. *The Tolkien Scrapbook.* Running Press, 1978.
Carpenter, Humphrey. *J. R. R. Tolkien: A Biography.* Houghton, 1977.
Children's Books and Their Creators. Houghton, 1995.
Children's Literature Review. Vol. 56, Gale, 1999.
Contemporary Authors New Revision Series. Vol. 134, Gale, 2005.
Continuum Encyclopedia of Children's Literature. Continuum, 2001.
Crabbe, Katharyn F. *J. R. R. Tolkien.* Ungar, 1981.
Day, David. *A Tolkien Bestiary.* Ballantine, 1978.
Drew, Bernard A. *100 Most Popular Young Adult Authors.* Libraries Unlimited, 1996.
Favorite Children's Authors and Illustrators. Vol. 5, Tradition Books, 2003.

Fonstad, Karen Wynn. *The Atlas of Middle Earth.* Houghton, 1981.
Giddings, Robert. *J. R. R. Tolkien: This Far Land.* Barnes and Noble, 1983.
Gillespie, John T., and Corinne J. Naden. *Characters in Young Adult Literature.* Gale, 1997.
Green, William, *The Hobbit: A Journey to Maturity.* Twayne, 1994.
Hammond, Wayne G., and Christina Scull. *J. R. R. Tolkien: Artist and Illustrator.* Houghton, 2000.
Isaacs, Neil D., and Rose A. Zimbardo. *Tolkien: New Critical Perspectives.* University of Kentucky, 1981.
Johnson, Judith Anne. *J. R. R. Tolkien: Six Decades of Criticism.* Greenwood, 1986.
Jones, Raymond E. *Characters in Young Adult Literature.* Gale, 1997.
Lives and Works: Young Adult Authors. Vol. 8, Grolier, 1999.
Major Authors and Illustrators for Children and Young Adults (1st ed.). Vol. 6, Gale, 1993.
Major Authors and Illustrators for Children and Young Adults (2nd ed.). Vol. 8, Gale, 2002.
More Junior Authors. Wilson, 1963.
Niemark, Anne, and Brad Weinman. *Myth Maker: J. R. R. Tolkien.* Harcourt, 1996.
Oldsey, Brian. "British Novelists, 1930–1959." In *Dictionary of Literary Biography.* Vol. 15, Gale, 1983.
Rogers, Deborah W. *J. R. R. Tolkien.* Twayne, 1980.
St. James Guide to Children's Writers (5th ed.). St. James, 1999.
St. James Guide to Young Adult Writers (2nd ed.). St. James, 1999.
Something About the Author. Gale. Vol. 2, 1971; vol. 24, 1991; vol. 32, 1983; vol. 100, 1999.
Stevens, Jen. *The Undergraduate's Companion to Children's Writers and Their Web Sites.* Libraries Unlimited, 2004.
Twentieth-Century Guide to Children's Writers (4th ed.). St. James, 1995.
Twentieth-Century Guide to Young Adult Writers (1st ed.). St. James, 1994.
White, Michael. *Tolkien: A Biography.* Little, Brown, 2001.
Writers for Young Adults. Vol. 3, Scribner, 1997.
http://gollum.usask.ca/tolkien (Tolkien timeline)
www.barrowdowns.com/Welcome.asp (includes The Middle-Earth Encyclopedia)
www.tolkiensociety.org/index.html (Tolkien Society home page)
See also listing "Selected Web Sites on Children's Literature and Authors."

Yolen, Jane. *Dragon's Blood.* Delacorte, 1982, o.p.; pap. Magic Carpet Books, 2004, $6.95, 0-15-205126-0 (Grades 7–9).

Introduction

Jane Yolen (1939–) is a writer of many and varied talents. Her output extends from alphabet and counting books for the very youngest readers to sophisticated science fiction for adults. She also spans a variety of genres, with books of poetry, drama, picture books, short stories, folklore, and full-length novels. She was born in New York City and began writing at an early age (in junior high school she wrote a nonfiction book about pirates). For younger readers she is best known for her easy-to-read books featuring Commander Toad and, for the middle grades, the young Merlin Trilogy. *Dragon's Blood* is volume one of the Pit Dragon Trilogy. In volume two, *Heart's Blood* (Magic Carpet Books, pap., 1984), Jakkin Stewart, now a Dragon Master, is plunged into a web of intrigue when Akki, the daughter of his former master Sarkkhan, becomes involved with a rebel group and disappears in the capital city. The third volume, *A Sending of Dragons* (Magic Carpet Books, pap., 1987), follows Jakkin and Akki as they try to survive in the mountains of the desert planet Austar IV. As expected, our heroes are triumphant and, after their rescue, plan to bring peace and freedom to the planet.

Principal Characters
   Jakkin, who works on a dragon farm
   Master Sarkkhan, farm owner
   Likkarn, overseer
   Akki, a young nurse

Plot Summary
The principal tourist attraction on the planet Austar IV is visiting the gaming pits, where large fights are staged between 13-foot-long dragons native to the planet. Jakkin, fifteen, works on a dragon farm owned by Master Sarkkhan. Under the supervision of the cruel overseer Likkarn, Jakkin and his friends Slakk and Errikin clean the stables and bathe the male dragons. Jakkin was actually born into the Master caste, but after his parents' sudden deaths, he was sold into bondage. Each worker, including Jakkin, wears a leather bond bag around his neck, hoping to collect enough coins to buy freedom.

Jakkin has his own plan to buy his freedom. He plans to steal a fertile egg and raise his own fighting dragon. But at hatching time he is attacked by a dragon and spends time in the hospital under the care of Akki, a young, attractive nurse. When he is released, he visits the hen dragon's room and finds the hatchlings have been miscounted. There are ten, not nine. He takes the strongest one and hides it. With every free moment, he tends to the fledgling and then spends months training his dragon to be a fighter. Akki helps him in training the dragon they call Red. At one year, he is ready for his first fight.

Red is matched against a veteran, but he emerges victorious. Jakkin learns that Sarkkhan realized Jakkin's potential and deliberately falsified the count, hoping the boy would steal the hatchling to obtain his freedom as Sarkkhan had done years before. Furthermore, Sarkkhan reveals that, although Akki refuses to acknowledge it, she is his daughter.

Jakkin's dragon is renamed Heart's Blood and, as a result of his victory, the boy now has enough coins to buy his freedom, and has the hope of taking Akki as his bride. But the girl has other plans. Believing that she can be of no further use to Jakkin, she leaves the nursery. Jakkin swears he will wait for her return.

Themes and Subjects
The galaxy that the author has created may be exotically futuristic, but such eternal verities as courage, resourcefulness, and justice are still present. The necessity of freedom to lead a dignified life is stressed, as is the binding relationship of human beings and nature as seen through the interdependence of the boy and his dragon. The details of dragon lore given by the author are fascinating and believable, as is the society she has created. Jakkin's growing maturity and his tender feelings toward Akki are interesting subthemes.

Booktalk Material
A description of Austar IV and Sarkkhan's dragon nursery should fascinate readers. A mock encyclopedia article and a map appear as frontispieces. Some exciting passages are: Jakkin takes Blood Brother into its bath (pp. 21–30); Jakkin is injured because of Likkarn's rage (pp. 34–39); he steals a hatchling (pp. 69–72); the drakk hunt (pp. 94–103); Jakkin begins working with the dragon (pp. 109–14); and the male drakk attacks (pp. 140–45).

Additional Selections
Shimmer, a dragon, in the company of a boy, Thorn, sets out to destroy the villain Civet in Laurence Yep's *Dragon of the Lost Sea* (HarperCollins, pap., 1982).

In Vivian Vande Velde's *Dragon's Bait* (Harcourt, 1992), a girl sentenced to be killed by a dragon becomes friends with a shape-changer.

In *The Book of Dragons* (Scholastic, pap., 1998), edited by Michael Hague, there are several stories about dragons by such writers as Tolkien and Kenneth Grahame.

Young Merlin faces the threat of the dragon Valdearg, who is preparing to conquer Finayra, in T. A. Barron's *The Fires of Merlin* (Putnam, 1998), part of a series.

About the Author and Book
Authors and Artists for Young Adults. Gale. Vol. 4, 1990; vol. 22, 1997.
Children's Books and Their Creators. Houghton, 1995.
Children's Literature Review. Vol. 44, Gale, 1997.
Contemporary Authors New Revision Series. Vol. 29, Gale, 1990.
Continuum Encyclopedia of Children's Literature. Continuum, 2001.
Drew, Bernard A. *100 Most Popular Young Adult Authors.* Libraries Unlimited, 1996.
Estes, Glenn E. "American Writers for Children Since 1960: Fiction." In *Dictionary of Literary Biography.* Vol. 52, Gale, 1978.
Favorite Children's Authors and Illustrators. Vol. 6, Tradition Books, 2003.
Fourth Book of Junior Authors and Illustrators. Wilson, 1978.
Gallo, Donald R. *Speaking for Ourselves.* National Council of Teachers of English, 1990.
Gillespie, John T., and Corinne J. Naden. *Characters in Young Adult Literature.* Gale, 1997.
Jones, Raymond E. *Characters in Children's Literature.* Gale, 1997.
Lives and Works: Young Adult Authors. Vol. 8, Grolier, 1999.
McElmeel, Sharron L. *100 Most Popular Children's Authors.* Libraries Unlimited, 1999.
Major Authors and Illustrators for Children and Young Adults (1st ed.). Vol. 6, Gale, 1993.
Major Authors and Illustrators for Children and Young Adults (2nd ed.). Vol. 8, Gale, 2002.
St. James Guide to Children's Writers (5th ed.). St. James, 1999.
St. James Guide to Young Adult Writers (2nd ed.). St. James, 1999.
Something About the Author. Gale. Vol. 4, 1973; vol. 40, 1986; vol. 75, 1994; vol. 111, 2000; vol. 112, 2000; vol. 158, 2005.
Stevens, Jen. *The Undergraduate's Companion to Children's Writers and Their Web Sites.* Libraries Unlimited, 2004.
Twentieth-Century Children's Writers (4th ed.). St. James, 1995.
Twentieth-Century Young Adult Writers (2nd ed.). St. James, 1994.
Writers for Young Adults. Vol. 3, Scribner, 1997.
Yolen, Jane. *A Letter from Phoenix Farm.* R. C. Owen, 1992.
www.janeyolen.com (personal Web site)
See also listing "Selected Web Sites on Children's Literature and Authors."

4

Historical Fiction and Other Lands

Aiken, Joan. *Midnight Is a Place.* Houghton Mifflin, 2002 (1974), $16, 0-618-19626-9; pap. $5.95, 0-618-19625-0 (Grades 6–10).

Introduction

Although Joan Aiken (1924–2004) was the daughter of the esteemed American poet Conrad Aiken, she was born and spent most of her life in England. Being raised in a literary household, she soon began reading Kipling, de la Mare, and Frances Hodgson Burnett and, while still a teenager, began writing stories and poems. She was a prolific author and used an imaginary setting of nineteenth-century England as a setting for many of her exciting, fast-paced historical novels. Among her most famous creations are the novels for the middle grades set in the time of the fictitious James III, beginning with the entertaining melodrama, *The Wolves of Willoughby Chase* (Dell, 1963). It is the story of two young girls held captive by an evil governess, Miss Slighcarp, who will stop at nothing, including murder, to secure the title to the vast estate known as Willoughby Chase. In the succeeding five volumes in the series, the reader meets the ingenious Dido Twite, a resourceful young girl who fights intolerance and evil. Many critics have compared Aiken's writing to that of Dickens. Certainly this holds true with *Midnight Is a Place,* a tale that features many Dickensian-style characters and a tightly-knit suspenseful plot, and like the Master's work, it expresses outrage at the appalling class structure and the squalid living and working conditions of nineteenth-century English industrial cities. This book is popular with both adults and young readers.

Principal Characters

Lucas Bell, thirteen, who lives in a decaying mansion
Sir Randolph Grimsby, his usually drunk guardian

Mr. Oakapple, Lucas's tutor
Bob Bludward, a mill worker
Anna-Marie Murgatroyd, who comes to live at the mansion
Tom Gudgeon, a "togher"

Plot Summary
It is 1842 and Lucas Bell, thirteen, is living in a decaying mansion, Midnight Court, with his usually drunk guardian, Sir Randolph Grimsby, since both his parents died. His brittle tutor, Mr. Oakapple, explains that Grimsby had won the mill in town, known as the Murgatroyd Carpet, Rug and Matting Manufactury, on a bet, which many think was rigged, from the scion of the Murgatroyd family, Denzil. According to Lucas's father's will, he must live with Grimsby and learn the mill business. On his first trip to the mill, he is sickened by the working conditions and notices that the employees are terrorized by a gang of ruffians led by Bob Bludward, a mill worker.

Grimsby is faced with the loss of the mill or the house for nonpayment of back taxes, but suddenly there is a new mouth to feed. She is eight-year-old Anna-Marie Murgatroyd, whose father Denzil has died. The girl, who knows no English, is stubborn and arrogant. Then Grimsby dies in a fire that destroys the mansion. Lucas and Anna-Marie are unharmed but Mr. Oakapple is severely burned.

The two young waifs rent lodgings in a run-down waterfront rooming house. Anna-Marie learns to speak English and begins to sell discarded cigar stubs, rolled into new ones, in a market stall. Lucas goes to work for Tom Gudgeon, a "togher," a man who fishes through the slime of underground sewers for discarded valuables. Lucas finds a jewel-studded saddle on his first day. In this way, they are able to maintain themselves and visit Mr. Oakapple in the hospital. When he gets out, they all move to larger quarters in a house occupied by Anna-Marie's grandmother.

Local toughs harass Anna-Marie, so she has to give up the cigar business and go to work in the carpet factory. Lucas narrowly escapes death in the sewers and also goes to the factory to work. Because Anna-Marie won't pay protection money to Bob Bludward, he tries to kill her at the factory, but Lucas is able to save her.

A packet of legal papers that Lucas found in the sewers shows that Grimsby illegally acquired the factory. The Murgatroyd property must now be returned to its rightful owners. Although the factory has already been bought by a new company, Anna-Marie's grandmother knows the new owner and is assured that Lucas will enter the training program as his father wished. Lucas hopes that someday he will be able to improve working conditions in the mill, but for now it is comforting to know that his adopted family is safe and secure in their new home.

Themes and Subjects
The author uses the familiar mystery staples of coincidence, mistaken identity, and forgotten family secrets to produce a novel of suspense, melodrama, and unexpected twist of plot. The plight of the factory workers and the dismal living conditions during the Industrial Revolution are memorably recreated. The strength and fortitude of the children in their struggle for survival are also an important theme.

Booktalk Material
A verse of a song from Anna-Marie's father reads "nights' winged horse / No one can outpace / But midnight is no moment / Midnight is a place." An explanation of this in the context of the novel could be used as an introduction. Some interesting passages are: Lucas sees the press room (pp. 27–29; pp. 20–22, pap.); he meets Anna-Marie for the first time (pp. 38–39; pp. 30–32, pap.); the history of the wager (pp. 53–58; pp. 44–50, pap.); and in the sewers (pp. 150–54; pp. 141–45, pap.).

Additional Selections
   Michael Crichton in *The Great Train Robbery* (Knopf, 1975) has written a thriller about an actual robbery that shocked Victorian England.
   Jamaica Inn (Avon, pap., 1977) by Daphne du Maurier is a suspenseful yarn set on the coast of England during the days of pirates.
   Fifteen-year-old Emmeline goes to London in Victorian England to search for her deaf brother in Linda Holeman's *Search of the Moon King's Daughter* (Tundra, 2002).
   Several of Charles Dickens's novels would also be suitable, including *Oliver Twist* (NAL, pap., 1961) and *Great Expectations* (NAL, pap., 1998).

About the Author and Book
Authors and Artists for Young Adults. Gale. Vol. 1, 1989; vol. 25, 1998.
Children's Books and Their Creators. Houghton, 1995.
Children's Literature Review. Vol. 90, Gale, 2004.
Contemporary Authors. Vol. 182, Gale, 2000.
Continuum Encyclopedia of Children's Literature. Continuum, 2001.
   Drew, Bernard A. *100 Most Popular Young Adult Authors.* Libraries Unlimited, 1996.
Favorite Children's Authors and Illustrators. Tradition Books, 2003.
   Gallo, Donald R. *Speaking for Ourselves,* National Council of Teachers of English, 1990.
   Hunt, Caroline C. "British Children's Writers Since 1960." In *Dictionary of Literary Biography.* Vol. 160, Gale, 1996.

Jones, Raymond E. *Characters in Children's Literature*. Gale, 1997.
Lives and Works: Young Adult Authors. Vol. 1, Grolier, 1999.
Major Authors and Illustrators for Children and Young Adults (1st ed.). Vol. 1, Gale, 1993.
Major Authors and Illustrators for Children and Young Adults (2nd ed.). Vol. 1, Gale, 2002.
St. James Guide to Young Adult Writers (2nd ed.). St. James, 1999.
Something About the Author. Gale. Vol. 2, 1971; vol. 30, 1983; vol. 73, 1993; vol. 109, 2000; vol. 152, 2005.
Something About the Author Autobiography Series. Vol. 1, Gale, 1986.
Stevens, Jen. *The Undergraduate's Companion to Children's Writers and Their Web Sites*. Libraries Unlimited, 2004.
Third Book of Junior Authors. Wilson, 1972.
Twentieth-Century Young Adult Writers (1st ed.). St. James, 1994.
Writers for Young Adults. Vol. 1, Scribner, 1997.
See also listing "Selected Web Sites on Children's Literature and Authors."

Avi. *The True Confessions of Charlotte Doyle*. Scholastic, 1990. $16.95, 0-531-05893-X (Grades 6–9).

Introduction

Avi Wortis (1937–), the son of a psychiatrist and a social worker, was nicknamed Avi because that is how his younger sister pronounced his given name. As a youngster, he developed a keen interest in reading, which later turned into the development of his writing skills. Avi has become a prolific and versatile author of books for young people. While some are thrillers and others deal with social issues, he has also written a number of fine historical novels, like the present volume. Two others are *The Fighting Ground* (Harper, 1984), which tells of one eventful day in the life of thirteen-year-old Jonathan when he marches off to fight the British during the Revolutionary War, and *The Man Who Was Poe* (Harper, 1989), an engrossing story set in Providence, Rhode Island, during 1848, when a young boy named Edmund elicits the help of Edgar Allan Poe to find his missing sister. *The True Confessions of Charlotte Doyle*, a Newbery Honor Book, is a rousing sea adventure told in the first person and set in the days of the trans-Atlantic sailing ships. See also *Wolf Rider* in Chapter 5.

Principal Characters

Charlotte Doyle, thirteen
Zachariah, ship's cook

Jaggery, ship's captain
First Mate Hollybrass

Plot Summary
It is 1832, and the Doyle family is moving back to Providence, Rhode Island, after eight years in England. Thirteen-year-old Charlotte stays to finish the school term and leaves on the *Seahawk* for a two-month crossing. Mysteriously, she is the only passenger aboard. None of the crew is friendly except for Zachariah, the old, black ship's cook. He gives her a small dagger for protection, which she reluctantly takes. He does so because, he tells Charlotte, Captain Jaggery behaved so cruelly on the last voyage that he flogged a seaman named Cranick, who lost his arm as a result. Charlotte finds it hard to believe the stories about the captain, who seems stern but fair.

When Charlotte overhears talk of mutiny and a stowaway, she reports to the captain. The stowaway is found and turns out to be Cranick. He wants Jaggery to give up command of the ship. In reply, the captain shoots him and tosses the body overboard. Then he declares that Zachariah is the scapegoat for the planned mutiny and beats him unmercifully. Later that night, Charlotte sees the crew conduct a service on deck and throw a stitched hammock overboard. She believes that Zachariah has been buried at sea.

During a hurricane, Jaggery commands Charlotte to climb the foremast to cut a sail. She is yanked to safety by a sailor and she sees that it is Zachariah. Later the body of First Mate Hollybrass is found on deck with Charlotte's dagger in his back. She is condemned to death by hanging in twenty-four hours.

Zachariah visits her in the brig and tells her that the crew staged his funeral. Jaggery killed Hollybrass to get rid of an insubordinate mate and also to get rid of Charlotte, who could testify against him in Providence. Charlotte escapes the brig but is confronted by Jaggery. She climbs out on the bowsprit and is followed by Jaggery, who loses his balance and falls into the sea.

At home in Providence, Charlotte cannot adjust to the prim life of her parents. Her father chastises her for an overactive imagination when she relates her adventures. She begins to feel like a prisoner. When she reads that the *Seahawk* is leaving for England, she climbs out her window and heads for the dock and her true home. She is greeted by an incredulous but delighted Zachariah.

Themes and Subjects
This is basically a swashbuckler told at breakneck speed, but there are other important elements to the novel. A prim, protected, somewhat prissy young lady becomes a self-reliant, responsible woman who now understands life's true values. The friendship and devotion between Charlotte and Zachariah are presented logically and are not oversentimentalized. Avi has captured an authentic feeling of life at sea during the early nineteenth century, including details of the ship and its construction. Other developed themes are the importance of friendship and devotion; the danger of accepting first impressions; the need to fight injustice; and tyranny, courage, and the nature of evil.

Booktalk Material
The first three pages of the novel (labeled "An Important Warning") foreshadow the thrilling events to come and will capture the interest of most readers. Some other important passages are: Charlotte sees her cabin (pp. 16–18) and meets Zachariah, who gives her the knife (pp. 18–24); Charlotte's first impressions of Captain Jaggery (pp. 27–30); Zachariah explains why she might need the knife (pp. 36–38); Jaggery tells Charlotte about a possible mutiny (pp. 41–48); and Charlotte sees the face while at her trunk (pp. 49–55).

Additional Selections
A spoiled teenager learns about life after he falls from an ocean liner and is rescued by common fishermen in Rudyard Kipling's *Captains Courageous* (Amereon, 1964).

There are eight compelling sea stories that involve a wide range of characters and situations found in Theodore Taylor's *Rogue Wave and Other Red-Blooded Sea Stories* (Harcourt, 1991).

Told by an eleven-year-old stowaway, Karen Hesse's *Stowaway* (Simon, 2000) is the story of Captain Cook's two-and-a-half-year voyage around the world, beginning in 1768.

Delia, her mother, and her new stepfather encounter trauma and murder when they vacation on a remote Canadian lake in Jan O'Donnell Klaveness's *Ghost Island* (Dell, pap., 1987).

About the Author and Book
(Some of these entries are under Avi's real name, Avi Wortis.)

Authors and Artists for Young Adults. Gale. Vol. 10, 1993; vol. 37, 2001.
Bloom, S. P., and C. M. Mercier. *Presenting Avi.* Twayne, 1997.

Bostrom, Kathleen Long. *Winning Authors: Profiles of the Newbery Medalists.* Libraries Unlimited, 2003.
Bray D. "Avi," *Horn Book,* July/Aug., 2003, pp. 415–18.
Children's Books and Their Creators. Houghton, 1995.
Children's Literature Review. Gale. Vol. 24, 1991; vol. 68, 2001.
Contemporary Authors New Revision Series. Vol. 120, Gale, 2004
Continuum Encyclopedia of Children's Literature. Continuum, 2001.
Cooper, Ilene. "The Booklist Interview—Avi," *Booklist,* May 15, 2002, p. 1609.
Drew, Bernard A. *100 Most Popular Young Adult Authors.* Libraries Unlimited, 1997.
Favorite Children's Authors and Illustrators. Vol. 1, Tradition Books, 2003.
Fifth Book of Junior Authors and Illustrators. Wilson, 1983.
Gallo, Donald R. *Speaking for Ourselves.* National Council of Teachers of English, 1990.
Gillespie, John T., and Corinne J. Naden. *Characters in Young Adult Literature.* Gale, 1997.
Lives and Works: Young Adult Authors. Vol. 1, Grolier, 1999.
McElmeel, Sharron L. *100 Most Popular Children's Authors.* Libraries Unlimited, 1999.
Major Authors and Illustrators for Children and Young Adults (1st ed.). Vol. 6, Gale, 1993.
Major Authors and Illustrators for Children and Young Adults (2nd ed.). Vol. 8, Gale, 2002.
Markham, Lois. *Avi.* Learning Works, 1996.
St. James Guide to Young Adult Writers (2nd ed.). St. James, 1999.
Something About the Author. Gale. Vol. 14, 1987; vol. 71, 1993; vol. 108, 2000; vol. 156, 2005.
Stevens, Jen. *The Undergraduate's Companion to Children's Writers and Their Web Sites.* Libraries Unlimited, 2004.
Twentieth-Century Young Adult Writers (1st ed.). St. James, 1994.
Writers for Young Adults. Vol. 1, Scribner, 1997.
www.avi-writer.com (personal Web site)
See also listing "Selected Web Sites on Children's Literature and Authors."

Collier, James Lincoln, and Christopher Collier. *My Brother Sam Is Dead.* Simon, 1984 (1974), $17.95, 0-02-722980-7; pap. Scholastic, $5.99, 0-439-78360-7 (Grades 6–9).

Introduction

With *My Brother Sam Is Dead,* James Lincoln Collier (1928–) and his brother Christopher Collier (1930–) made a particularly auspicious debut as a writing team. The novel received a Newbery Honor Book award in 1975 and has been in print since its original publication. James is a professional writer who, when this book was published, already had several juvenile titles to his credit, and brother Christopher is a professor of history whose area of specialization is the same period as this novel, the American Revolution. In an interesting postscript to the book, the authors state that, although the Meeker family, as depicted in the book, is fictitious, most of the other characters and events are real. A later book by the Colliers, *The Bloody Country* (Scholastic, 1976), uses the same theme of divided allegiances during the Revolution, but the setting is Wilkes-Barre, Pennsylvania, rather than Connecticut. It is the story of a family that manages to eke out a living in spite of floods, a massacre, and savage battles. Again there is an "afterword" that explains the factual elements in the story.

Principal Characters
　　Tim Meeker, eleven years old
　　Eliphalet and Susannah Meeker, his parents
　　Sam Meeker, sixteen, his brother
　　Betsy, Sam's girlfriend

Plot Summary
Eleven-year-old Tim Meeker is confused about his loyalties in the gathering crisis that will become the American Revolution. He and his parents, Eliphalet and Susannah, live in the southern Connecticut town of Redding. His parents are opposed to the war, but Tim's brother, Sam, sixteen, has joined the rebel army. He returns home in April 1775 to get his father's musket Brown Bess, which he takes despite his father's protest that his taking it will leave the family defenseless.

　　In the fall of 1776, Mr. Meeker and Tim set out to trade cattle and pigs. On the way back from Peekskill, New York, there is a severe snowstorm and Tim's father rides ahead to make sure the road is clear. When he doesn't return, Tim finds clues that his father has been taken prisoner by a gang of marauding cowboys. He gets home safely with no word of his father.

　　In the spring, British troops raid the town, killing rebel sympathizers and burning their homes. Later the family learns that Mr. Meeker has died of cholera on a prison ship. Tim becomes sickened by the war and the wanton destruction and death it has brought.

　　At the end of 1778, Sam's regiment is sent to Redding for winter encampment. One evening he steals away from his post to visit his family. A noise is heard in the barn. Sam intercepts two soldiers from his regiment stealing cattle. The soldiers take Sam prisoner and accuse him of being the thief. He is court-martialed and sentenced to death. Tim witnesses his brother's execution by firing squad.

　　Years later when Tim has become a successful merchant in Pennsylvania, he looks back at all the tragic events of the Revolution that he experienced and how they destroyed his family. He speculates that there might have been a way besides war to achieve the same ends. But now it's too late; all has become history.

Themes and Subjects
From this novel, readers gain a different perspective on the American Revolution than history texts convey. Through Tim's experiences, war becomes a senseless, destructive force that brings tragedy regardless of allegiances. Besides the futility of aggression, the book graphically portrays, through one family's misfortunes, the agony of a country divided against itself. The authentic details of colonial life add immediacy and realism to the story. Tim's courage and perseverance form an important subplot.

Booktalk Material
The basic conflict between Sam and his father is revealed in conversations on pp. 3–7 (pp. 3–8, pap.) and pp. 20–22 (pp. 23–35, pap.). Other important episodes are: Tim trics to save his father from the rebels (pp. 51–60; pp. 60–70, pap.); Tim's first brush with the cowboys (pp. 93–98; pp. 108–13, pap.); and Tim tricks them on the homeward journey (pp. 123–25; pp. 143–47, pap.).

Additional Selections
Thirteen-year-old Jonathan marches off to fight the British in Avi's *The Fighting Ground* (HarperCollins, 1984).

In Howard Fast's *April Morning* (Bantam, pap., 1961), Adam Cooper, a fifteen-year-old boy, becomes a man during the early stages of the Revolutionary War.

The daughter of Paul Revere recalls the years of the American Revolution in Ann Rinaldi's *The Secret of Sarah Revere* (Harcourt, 1995).

During the Revolutionary War, a young Scottish refugee and her grandparents are torn by conflicting loyalties in Kathleen Ernst's *Betrayal at Cross Creek* (Pleasant, 2004).

About the Author and Book
Authors and Artists for Young Adults. Vol. 13, Gale, 1994.
Children's Books and Their Creators. Houghton, 1995.
Children's Literature Review. Vol. 3, Gale, 1978.
Contemporary Authors New Revision Series. Vol. 102, Gale, 2002.
Continuum Encyclopedia of Children's Literature. Continuum, 2001.
Drew, Bernard A. *100 Most Popular Young Adult Authors.* Libraries Unlimited, 1996.
Fifth Book of Junior Authors and Illustrators. Wilson, 1983.
Gallo, Donald R. *Speaking for Ourselves.* National Council of Teachers of English, 1990.

Gillespie, John T., and Corinne J. Naden. *Characters in Young Adult Literature.* Gale, 1997.
Lives and Works: Young Adult Authors. Vol. 2, Grolier, 1999.
McElmeel, Sharron L. *100 Most Popular Children's Writers.* Libraries Unlimited, 1999.
Major Authors and Illustrators for Children and Young Adults (1st ed.). Vol. 2, Gale, 1993.
Major Authors and Illustrators for Children and Young Adults (2nd ed.). Vol. 2, Gale, 2002.
St. James Guide to Young Adult Writers (2nd ed.). St. James, 1999.
Something About the Author. Gale. Vol. 8, 1976; vol. 16, 1979; vol. 70, 1993.
Something About the Author Autobiography Series. Vol. 21, Gale, 1996.
Twentieth-Century Young Adult Authors (1st ed.). St. James, 1994.
See also listing "Selected Web Sites on Children's Literature and Authors."

Fox, Paula. *One-Eyed Cat.* Simon, 2003 (1984). $16.95, 0-689-86193-1 (Grades 6–8).

Introduction

Paula Fox (1923–) is primarily known as a writer of novels for young readers, but she is also the author of numerous books for adults, including a revealing autobiography, *Borrowed Finery: A Memoir* (Holt, 2001). In her juveniles, Fox often has a central character, a lonely, misunderstood young person—a boy in the case of *One-Eyed Cat*—who has difficulty communicating with others but, through a singular, out-of-the-ordinary occurrence, is able to make contact with others. In her most famous novel, *The Slave Dancer* (Bradbury, 1973), the hero also undergoes rapid character development as a result of harrowing experiences. It is the story of Jessie Bollier, a young man kidnapped from his family in New Orleans and conscripted into becoming a "slave dancer," one who plays the flute on a slave ship to help exercise the slaves. Though permanently scarred by this experience, Jessie escapes and begins building a new life in the North. *One-Eyed Cat*, a Newbery Honor Book in 1985, takes place in upstate New York in the mid-1930s. Its action spans an autumn, winter, and spring in the lives of James Wallis, a Congregational minister, his wife, Martha, and their son, Ned. (See also *The Moonlight Man* in Chapter 1, p. 29.)

Principal Characters

Ned Wallis, nearly eleven
James, his father, a Congregational minister
Martha, his mother, mostly confined to a wheelchair

Mr. Scully, a neighbor
Uncle Hilary

Plot Summary
It is September 1935 and Ned Wallis is nearly eleven years old. He and his father, a Congregational minister, and his mother, mostly confined to a wheelchair because of arthritis, live modestly in an old farmhouse on the Hudson River in New York. Ned gets thirty-five cents a week from his eighty-year-old neighbor, Mr. Scully, to do chores. On Ned's birthday, his Uncle Hilary gives him a Daisy air rifle, which his father, a kindly, highly-respected man who dislikes guns, puts in the attic.

Ned takes it from the attic that night and shoots at a shadow near the barn. The shadow disappears and Ned thinks he sees a face staring down at him from the house.

During the summer, Ned and Mr. Scully, who tells him many stories of times past, sees a gray feral cat in the backyard with only one eye. Ned is convinced that the cat is the victim of his disobedience. He begins to care for the cat, who is too wild to be coaxed inside and Mr. Scully contributes food, which Ned leaves outdoors for it to eat.

One day, Ned finds Mr. Scully on the floor. He has suffered a stroke and is taken to a nursing home, where Ned often visits him. Ned continues to care for the cat. During his last visit, Ned confesses that he shot the cat. The old man tenderly encloses the boy's hand in his own as a gesture of understanding and forgiveness. A few days later Mr. Scully dies.

With Mr. Scully's death and the sale of his house, Ned can no longer secure food for the cat. But one night with his mother, who has responded well to a new arthritis treatment, he goes for a walk outdoors. They see the one-eyed cat, his mate, and two kittens. As they walk home, Ned confesses what he did with the air rifle. Mama says she was the one at the window. She decided to keep silent about the incident. She also makes a confession, saying that when Ned was only three she left her husband for three months because she felt unable to live up to his goodness. At home, they are greeted by Papa in the doorway. He was worried about them and welcomes them back.

Themes and Subjects
This is a mood piece that deals with timeless values and conflicts. It is the story of the goodness of one man and the obligations and guilt that this produces in others. It also deals with a friendship gained and lost that transcends the ages of the friends involved, with the strength of the family unit, and with gentleness and kindness. Ned's acceptance of the conse-

quences of his action and the eventual expiation of his guilt are powerful themes. This novel also masterfully recreates a quiet, more temperate time when poverty was commonplace but neighborliness and trust were more prevalent.

Booktalk Material
The significance of the title could be explained. Some interesting passages are: Ned visits his mother (pp. 28–32); he receives Uncle Hilary's air gun (pp. 36–40) and retrieves it from the attic (pp. 43–46); Mr. Scully reminisces and they spot the cat (pp. 49–68); an electrical storm (pp. 77–80); and the cat's illness (pp. 135–36, pp. 139–40).

Additional Selections
In a story set in New York during the 1920s, Greer and her spiritualist mother become involved in the occult in Kathleen Karr's *Playing with Fire* (Farrar, 2001).

Thirteen-year-old Thad, who lives with his mother in rural Mississippi during the Depression, operates an illegal still in Gary L. Blackwood's *Moonshine* (Marshall Cavendish, 1999).

Josh must assume responsibilities far beyond his years in Irene Hunt's *No Promises in the Wind* (Berkeley, pap., 1987), a novel set in the Depression.

During the Depression, Henry leaves his foster home to ride the rails to Chicago to find his father in Adrienne Wolfert's *Making Tracks* (Silver Moon, 2000).

About the Author and Book
See entry for *The Moonlight Man* (p. 29).

Greene, Bette. *The Summer of My German Soldier.* Dial, 1974, $18.99, 0-8037-2869-7; pap. Puffin, $6.99, 0-14-130636-X (Grades 6–12).

Introduction
This quote from Carruth's *Young Reader's Companion* (Bowker, 1993, o.p.) succinctly summarizes two high points in the writing career of Bette Greene (1934–).

> Best known for her *Summer of My German Soldier*, Greene was born in Memphis, Tennessee, and grew up there and in a small town in Arkansas. Her childhood experiences in Arkansas are reflected in this novel, about a girl who shelters an escaped German prisoner of

war during World War II, and in her other novels. *Philip Hall Likes Me, I Reckon Maybe* (Puffin, 1974), for a younger audience, is set in rural Arkansas and tells about Beth Lambert, an 11-year-old black girl who has a crush on Philip Hall, the cutest, smartest boy in her school, yet finds herself competing against Philip both in and out of school. A warm family story, it is also a touching tale of first love and friendship.

Greene has received many distinctions for her writing, including the Golden Kite Award; she is also a National Book Award finalist and one of her novels is a Newbery Honor Book. *Summer* is read and enjoyed by students from the sixth grade through senior high.

Principal Characters
Patty Bergen, the twelve-year-old narrator
Ruth, the Bergens' maid
Sharon, Patty's six-year-old sister
Anton Reiker, an escaped German prisoner
Mr. Bergen, Patty's abusive father

Plot Summary
Patty Bergen, the twelve-year-old daughter of the local department store owner in Jenkinsville, Arkansas, is a nervous, unhappy girl growing up in the 1940s. Her parents ignore her or nag her; her father is abusive and often beats her. She escapes her loneliness by entering a world of her imagination. One day, a group of German prisoners of war, who have arrived in town, are marched into Bergens' Department Store for shopping. Patty is intrigued by a handsome young prisoner who speaks flawless English. She waits on him and he introduces himself as Anton Reiker, son a university professor and an English-born mother.

Later that week, she discovers Anton furtively wandering by railroad tracks. He has escaped. She takes him to her hideaway—the unused servants' quarters above the family's garage. She brings him food and clothing and has long talks with him. Anton tells her that he hates Hitler. He also takes an interest in Patty and draws her out. For the first time, she feels like a person of some value.

One day a slightly retarded neighbor, Freddie Dowd, wanders into the Bergen yard. Mr. Bergen thinks that Patty has allowed this trespassing as a deliberate defiance to his authority and begins to beat Patty. Anton leaves his hiding place to protect her just as the beating stops, but Ruth, the Bergens' maid, has seen him.

Ruth agrees to help Patty feed and shelter Anton, but she makes Patty realize that one day he must leave. Patty plans to go with him, but Anton says no. Before he leaves, he gives her his only prized possession, his great-grandfather's gold ring.

In the fall, Patty carelessly shows the ring to friends and later is questioned by FBI men about the ring. They produce a shirt with holes in it that Patty had given to him. Anton has been shot and killed in New York City. Stunned, Patty blurts out the truth, but does not involve Ruth. However, the maid is fired by her father.

Patty is arraigned in court on a charge of delinquency and sentenced to four to six months in a state reformatory. She is visited only by Ruth and wonders forlornly what the future will bring. She decides to live one day at a time and hopes that somehow things will get better.

Themes and Subjects
Patty's painful search for strength and a feeling of worthiness is well portrayed, as is the theme that one should evaluate humans as individuals, not as a group. Also well depicted are the townspeople's bigotry and hypocrisy that stem from their ignorance and narrowmindedness. These are brought into sharp contrast with the truth and honesty of the "losers" in the novel, Patty, Ruth, and Anton.

Booktalk Material
A brief introduction to the historic period might be necessary. Some interesting passages are: the prisoners arrive by train (pp. 3–7; pp. 1–4, pap.); Patty's first encounter with Anton (pp. 40–46; pp. 32–38, pap.); the game with Freddie and its consequences (pp. 63–69; pp. 53–59, pap.); and Patty helps Anton escape (pp. 80–82; pp. 69–70, pap.).

Additional Selections
The effects of war are covered in Cynthia Rylant's *I Have Seen Castles* (Harcourt, 1993), the story of John, a Canadian adolescent who is growing up during World War II.

Tilara, the fourteen-year-old child of a mixed marriage, finds love when she volunteers in a West Virginia home for the elderly in Sandra Belton's *McKendree* (Greenwillow, 2000).

Mary Christner Borntrager's *Rebecca* (Herald Press, pap., 1989) is a coming-of-age novel about an Amish girl who falls in love with a Mennonite young man.

In a city slum, Vernon forms a friendship with an eccentric woman and helps her care for her disabled teenage son in *Crazy Lady* (HarperCollins, 1993) by Jane L. Conly.

About the Author and Book
Authors and Artists for Young Adults. Vol. 7, Gale, 1992.
Children's Books and Their Creators. Houghton, 1995.
Children's Literature Review. Vol. 2, Gale, 1976.
Contemporary Authors New Revision Series. Vol. 4, Gale, 1981.
Continuum Encyclopedia of Children's Literature. Continuum, 2001.
Drew, Bernard A. *100 Most Popular Young Adult Authors.* Libraries Unlimited, 1996.
Fifth Book of Junior Authors and Illustrators. Wilson, 1983.
Gallo, Donald R. *Speaking for Ourselves.* National Council of Teachers of English, 1990.
Gillespie, John T., and Corinne J. Naden. *Characters in Young Adult Literature.* Gale, 1997.
Lives and Works: Young Adult Authors. Vol. 3, Grolier, 1999.
Major Authors and Illustrators for Children and Young Adults (1st ed.). Vol. 2, Gale, 1993.
Major Authors and Illustrators for Children and Young Adults (2nd ed.). Vol. 4, Gale, 2002.
St. James Guide to Children's Writers (5th ed.). St. James, 1999.
St. James Guide to Young Adult Writers (2nd ed.). St. James, 1999.
Something About the Author. Gale. Vol. 8, 1976; vol. 102, 1999; vol. 161, 2006.
Something About the Author Autobiography Series. Vol. 16, Gale, 1993.
Twentieth-Century Guide to Young Adult Writers (1st ed.). St. James, 1994.
Writers for Young Adults. Vol. 2, Scribner, 1997.
See also listing "Selected Web Sites on Children's Literature and Authors."

Levitin, Sonia. *The Return.* Fawcett, 1987. Pap. $5.99, 0-44-970280-4 (Grades 7–9).

Introduction
Sonia Levitin has been closely associated with the most devastating events in Jewish history. She was born in 1934 in Germany to an upper-middle-class Jewish family who fled the Nazi Jewish persecution to come to the United States in 1938. Because her family left everything behind, she grew up in poverty and faced many related problems with her family. After college and some years as a teacher, she married and turned to full-time writing, specializing in historical fiction. Another of her popular works is *Escape from Egypt* (Little, Brown, 1994), the story of Moses and the exodus of the Hebrews from Egypt in biblical times as seen from the standpoint of Jesse, a young Hebrew slave who becomes a follower of Moses. In *The Return*, she writes of another traumatic experience in the history of the Jews. It is the story of a poor, black, Ethiopian Jewish girl who journeys to join Operation Moses, a secret maneuver in 1984 and 1985 that rescued

Jews fleeing genocide in the Sudan and transported them to freedom in Israel.

Principal Characters
Desta, an Ethiopian Jew
Joas, her brother
Dan, the man her elders have decided she will marry
Almaz, her little sister

Plot Summary
Desta is an Ethiopian Jew who is poor, black, African, little educated, and parentless. Other Ethiopians treat her people as outcasts. Despite this, Desta loves her homeland and the kindness of her aunt and uncle who have provided a home for her, her brother Joas, and her little sister Almaz. Desta wants to go to school but cannot. She is waiting for the elders to decide when she will marry quiet Dan from another village.

Joas tells Desta that he is going to make the long trek to the Sudan, where he has heard it is possible to escape to Israel, and he begs Desta and Almaz to go with him. Desta is terrified, but when soldiers approach the village for plunder, her aunt and uncle urge them to leave, and the three young people set out on a harsh journey of courage, fear, faith, and determination.

To her horror and despair, Joas is killed on the journey. Now Desta has only her faith in the promise of her religion to get her and sister Almaz to the Promised Land.

The long, arduous trip to the refugee camp in the Sudan is even more harrowing for Desta than the beginning of the journey. They are hounded and shot at, starved, sore, and bleeding. Yet, when they reach the refugee camp, more horror awaits, for famine has touched the thousands who are there.

Although Desta loses track of the time spent in the wretchedness of the refugee camp, at last she hears that a rescue operation is in progress to remove Jews from the camp at night and fly them to Israel.

Frightened and unsure of whom to trust, Desta and Almaz become two of the lucky Ethiopian Jews to be spirited away from the camps into the safety of Israel, where, if a land of milk and honey does not await them, at least there is freedom and help, and hope.

The Return is the story of one young girl's courage and faith, of her modern-day exodus to Israel, and of her decision not to marry Dan, to whom she has been promised. This tale of personal bravery and courage is based on the secret airlifting, called Operation Moses, of Ethiopian Jews to Israel in 1984–85.

Themes and Subjects
Sonia Levitin tells this story of Operation Moses and the Ethiopian Jews with stark realism. She presents a grim picture of life for a people who live in constant hardship and fear of persecution, who cling to their age-old beliefs as a beacon of light in an uncompromising world. Discerning young readers, however, will find much to admire in this story of one young girl's bravery and refusal to give in to despair.

Booktalk Material
The character of this young Ethiopian girl comes through vividly, and her curiosity and awakening mind, plus her love of small pleasures, will make an interesting introduction to the people of this little known or understood land. Specific passages are: Desta wonders about Jews in America (pp. 28–29); Desta and Joas discuss leaving for the Sudan (pp. 32–36); Desta and her aunt talk about marriage (pp. 40–41); Desta goes to the marketplace (pp. 49–54); and she makes a decision (pp. 54–57).

Additional Selections
A Chinese boy migrates to America in Laurence Yep's historical novel *Mountain Light* (HarperCollins, 1985), a sequel to *The Serpent's Children* (HarperCollins, 1984) about the Taiping Rebellion and battle against the Manchus.

David Kherdian tells about his mother's childhood in Turkey, where she was persecuted as a member of the Christian Armenian minority and eventually deported, in *The Road from Home* (Greenwillow, 1979). In *Finding Home* (Greenwillow, 1981), she arrives in America as a mail-order bride.

A young Vietnamese boy tells about his family's journey to Australia in Jack Bennett's *The Voyage of the Lucky Dragon* (Prentice, 1982).

In *So Far from the Bamboo Grove* (Lothrop, 1986) by Yoko Kawashima Watkins, a Japanese girl escapes from Korea during World War II.

About the Author and Book
Authors and Artists for Young Adults. Gale. Vol. 13, 1994; vol. 4, 2003.
Children's Literature Review. Vol. 53, Gale, 1999.
Contemporary Authors New Revision Series. Vol. 79, Gale, 1999.
Continuum Encyclopedia of Children's Literature. Continuum, 2001.
Drew, Bernard A. *100 More Popular Young Adult Authors.* Libraries Unlimited, 2002.
Fifth Book of Junior Authors and Illustrators. Wilson, 1983.
Gallo, Donald R. *Speaking for Ourselves, Too.* National Council of Teachers of English, 1993.
Lives and Works: Young Adult Authors. Vol. 5, Grolier, 1999.

Major Authors and Illustrators for Children and Young Adults (1st ed.). Vol. 4, Gale, 1993.
Major Authors and Illustrators for Children and Young Adults (2nd ed.). Vol. 5, Gale, 2002.
St. James Guide to Young Adult Writers (2nd ed.). St. James, 1999.
Something About the Author. Gale. Vol. 4, 1973; vol. 68, 1992; vol. 119, 2001; vol. 131, 2002.
Something About the Author Autobiography Series. Vol. 2, Gale, 1986.
Twentieth-Century Young Adult Writers (1st ed.). St. James, 1994.
See also listing "Selected Web Sites on Children's Literature and Authors."

Morrison, Toni. *Beloved.* Knopf, 1987. $19.95, 0-394-53597-9 (Grade 10–Adult).

Introduction

Toni Morrison (1931–) is one of the most highly regarded of contemporary black writers. Her first book, published in 1970, *The Bluest Eye* (Knopf, 1970), tells the story of an eleven-year-old black girl, Pecola Breedlove, who, after being raped by her father, becomes pregnant and retreats into insanity. In *Beloved*, her Pulitzer Prize-winning novel, she continues to explore the frequent tragedy and heartbreak of being born black. The epigraph of the novel is a verse from the Bible's Book of Romans, "I will call my people which were not my people, and her beloved which was not beloved." This message of rejection is transformed in the next verse, however, to one of hope when all of the unloved and unwanted of the world are nevertheless "children of a living god." *Beloved* is a historical novel that deals with the abomination of slavery and spans several years surrounding the American Civil War. Although it begins in a black community outside Cincinnati in 1873, much of the action occurs before the war in the slave state of Kentucky. The novel is suitable for mature senior high school readers.

Principal Characters

   Sethe, a slave
   Baby Suggs, whose son Halle has purchased her freedom
   The Garners, who own Sethe
   Amy Denver, a white indentured servant girl
   Denver, Sethe's daughter
   Beloved, a twenty-year-old waif
   Paul D, a slave

Plot Summary

The book's episodes are told through flashbacks. Sethe's childhood is one of unrelenting horror and deprivation. She saw her mother hanged. At age thirteen in 1849, she is sold to the Garners on a small farm called Sweet Home in northern Kentucky close to the Ohio River. She takes the place of Mrs. Garner's servant, the crippled Baby Suggs, whose son Halle, also a slave at Sweet Home, has purchased her freedom by working extra hours off the farm. Baby Suggs has lost contact with all her eight children except Halle. She lives alone in a rural black community outside of town.

Although marriage is denied to slaves, Sethe and Halle are joined, with the Garners' blessing. In time they have three children, but things change when Mr. Garner dies and his sadistic brother-in-law, referred to as "schoolteacher," takes charge. Slaves are sold and for those who remain, life is a series of beatings and hardships.

Two slaves try to escape and are burned alive. Sethe, pregnant with her fourth child, is trapped in the barn by schoolteacher's two nephews who strip her and suck her milk. Halle witnesses this outrage and goes insane, but remains on the farm in a state of numbness.

When Sethe tells Mrs. Garner of the attack, schoolteacher retaliates by beating her so that she nearly bleeds to death. She sends her three children ahead and escapes to Baby Suggs's with the help of two blacks. In the woods she meets a white indentured servant girl, Amy Denver, who is also escaping. Amy dresses her wounds and aids the birth of her daughter, whom Sethe names Denver.

Sethe heals, but when slave hunters arrive to take her and her children back, she tries to kill the children to keep them from slavery. The baby is saved, both boys are injured, and the two-year-old dies of a slit throat. The slave hunters retreat and Sethe prostitutes herself to a gravestone maker to pay for a gravestone for her child. Instead of "dearly beloved," he engraves only the word "beloved" as payment.

Sethe is taken into custody and given a prison sentence. After her release, she returns to her family and Baby Suggs, but the house becomes haunted by the angry ghost of her dead daughter, causing her teenage sons to flee. The following year, Baby Suggs dies, leaving Sethe and Denver alone.

In 1873, eighteen years after Sethe's escape from Sweet Home, a stranger appears at their door. It is the slave Paul D, whose life has been a continuous history of wretchedness, including a stretch in a Georgia chain gang. With his arrival the ghost is silenced and love returns to Sethe's life.

One day a mysterious twenty-year-old waif appears who calls herself Beloved. Sethe thinks she is the embodiment of her dead child. Soon Beloved becomes the center of the family's attention. She seduces Paul D, who after learning from a co-worker in the slaughterhouse about the murder years before, is so filled with revulsion for Sethe and shame for his affair with Beloved that he leaves.

Sethe devotes her entire life to Beloved, trying to lessen her guilt and gain expiation for her transgression. Without money for food, Denver finds that she must leave the security of the house and find work.

Through Denver, the town ladies learn about Beloved's presence and they appear at the door to exorcise the spirit. Fearful of losing Beloved, Sethe attacks them with an ice pick but is subdued before doing any harm. The women pray and, just as mysteriously as she appeared, Beloved vanishes.

When everyone has left, Sethe is alone in the quiet, now peaceful house. Paul D appears and, hoping to start life again with the woman he loves, gently takes Sethe into his arms.

Themes and Subjects

This book is one of the most powerful indictments of slavery and its legacy ever written. In its description of the horror inflicted on the black race, it is reminiscent of Nazi death camps, although this takes place in the United States. The dehumanizing aspects of slavery are best described in Sethe's words when she says (on p. 131) that "[the worst part is] that anybody white could take your whole self or anything that came to mind, not just work, kill, or maim you, but dirty you, dirty you so badly that you couldn't like yourself anymore." Mere survival is not enough unless it is accompanied with honor and dignity. Besides telling of the near-destruction of a race, this novel deals with the deliberate shattering of family unity, the passion of motherhood, and the limits to which maternal feelings can extend. The burden that guilt produces, its eventual expiation, and the need for self-acceptance are explored. Even in torment, Sethe is by turns gallant, pathetic, courageous, and a universal earth mother.

Booktalk Material

Perhaps because the story is too horrifying to be narrated sequentially, the author has instead used jagged shards of memory too painful to be seen chronologically to tell her story. Some episodes of importance are: Paul D arrives and, after exposition about Sweet Home, drives away the ghost (pp. 6–19); the meeting with Amy and the birth of Denver (pp. 31–35, 78–85); the arrival of Beloved (pp. 51–54); and Paul D on the chain gang (pp. 106–13.)

Additional Selections

A first-person account of being born a slave and living to participate in the twentieth-century civil rights movement is told in Ernest Gaines's novel *The Autobiography of Miss Jane Pittman* (Doubleday, 1971). In the author's *A Gathering of Old Men* (Doubleday, 1982), each member of a group of elderly black men claims to have committed a murder to prevent racial conflicts.

The story of the abortive slave revolt in 1831 and its courageous leader is told in the novel *The Confessions of Nat Turner* (Random, 1967) by William Styron.

Alex Haley traces his family history back to the days of slavery in *Roots* (Doubleday, 1976).

The story of a black woman's childhood in the rural South, her loveless marriage, and her departure to the North are told in Sara Brooks's *You May Plow Here* (Norton, 1986).

About the Author and Book
Authors and Artists for Young Adults. Gale. Vol. 1, 1989; vol. 22, 1997; vol. 61, 2005.
Bjork, Patrick Price. *The Novels of Toni Morrison.* Peter Land, 1994.
Bloom, Harold. *Toni Morrison.* Chelsea House, 1991.
Century, Douglas, *Toni Morrison: Author.* Chelsea House, 1994.
Charmean, Karen. *Toni Morrison's Work of Fiction.* Whitson, 1993.
Children's Literature Review. Vol. 99, Gale, 2005.
Contemporary Authors New Revision Series. Vol. 124, Gale, 2004.
Davis, Thadius M., and Trudier Harris. "Afro-American Fiction Writers After 1955." In *Dictionary of Literary Biography.* Vol. 33, Gale, 1984.
Giles, James R., and Wanda H. Giles. "American Novelists Since World War II, Third Series." In *Dictionary of Literary Biography.* Vol. 143, Gale, 1994.
Gillespie, John T., and Corinne J. Naden. *Characters in Young Adult Literature.* Gale, 1997.
McKay, Nellie Y. *Critical Essays on Toni Morrison.* Hall, 1988.
Rigney, Barbara. *The Voices of Toni Morrison.* Ohio State University, 1991.
St. James Guide to Young Adult Writers (2nd ed.). St. James, 1999.
Samuels, Wilfred D., and Clenora Hudson. *Toni Morrison.* Macmillan, 1990.
Something About the Author. Gale. Vol. 1, 1989; vol. 22, 1997; vol. 61, 2005.
Twentieth-Century Young Adult Writers (1st ed.). St. James, 1994.
See also listing "Selected Web Sites on Children's Literature and Authors."

Myers, Walter Dean. *Fallen Angels.* Scholastic, 1988. Pap. $5.99, 0-590-40943-3 (Grades 9–12).

Introduction

Although Walter Dean Myers (1937–) was born in West Virginia, he spent most of his youth in Harlem and has never lost touch with that environment, which helped shape his character. Many of his young adult novels are set in Harlem, such as *Monster* (HarperCollins, 1999), the winner of the first Michael L. Printz Award for excellence in literature for young adults. This story of the central character's trial for felony murder is told through a personal journal and a movie script. In *Fallen Angels*, the author shifts locales and subjects and deals with a conflict many wish to forget—the Vietnam War. If readers regard this as a series of daredevil adventures, this novel will disabuse them of these feelings. Its portrayal of warfare is often sickeningly real in detail and description. The language is adult and graphic, recapturing the conversations of men at war. It is told in the first person by Richie Perry, a most likable and sensitive hero who, though sickened by the brutality and death he sees around him, remains a loyal soldier and faithful friend. This novel, not for the squeamish, is read in grades nine through twelve. (See also *Now Is Your Time!* in Chapter 8.)

Principal Characters

Richie Perry, seventeen, on the way to Vietnam
Judy Duncan, a nurse from Texas
Harry (Peewee) Gates, from Chicago
Jenkins, Monaco, Lobel, Walowick, Brewster, and Corporal Brunner, all in Perry's outfit
Sergeant Simpson, squad leader
Lieutenant Carroll, platoon leader

Plot Summary

Richie Perry, seventeen, is from Harlem and on his way to Vietnam, despite a trick knee that is supposed to keep him out of combat. On the plane are Judy Duncan, a nurse from Texas, and Harry (Peewee) Gates, a wisecracking guy from Chicago. They join an outfit in Vietnam that includes Jenkins, another black from Georgia; Monaco, an Italian kid; Lobel from Hollywood; Walowick, pimply faced and Polish; Brewster, a religious youngster; and unpopular, crude Corporal Brunner. The squad leader is Sergeant Simpson and the platoon leader is well-liked Lieutenant Carroll.

During a routine operation, Jenkins steps on a mine and is killed, an experience that sickens and frightens Richie. After that, life becomes a series of deadly encounters with the Viet Cong. At one point, Richie is cornered but the guerrilla's gun jams, and Richie kills him. That night he sobs uncontrollably until Peewee puts his arms around him and cradles him until he sleeps. During another operation, the gentle Brewster is killed and Richie is wounded in the legs.

After a two-week stay in the hospital, where he sees Judy Duncan again, he returns to his outfit, fearful of what is to come. On a raid into enemy territory, Peewee and Richie are separated from the rest of the squad. Surrounded by the enemy, they take refuge in a hole on the side of a ridge. All night they cower in their hiding place, certain it will be the end of their lives. When the rescue chopper finally appears in the morning, Richie and Peewee are wounded by enemy gunfire, but they manage to board the chopper and be flown to safety. Peewee's wounds are so severe that he must be sent back permanently to the States, and Richie, though less severely injured, will also be sent home because the medical records about his trick knee have finally arrived.

After some investigation, Richie learns that nurse Duncan was killed when her field hospital was bombed. As Richie and Peewee board the C-47 to take them back to "the World," they see lines of silver caskets being loaded into the tail end of the plane and think of the buddies they left behind and of the dead comrades they will never see again.

Themes and Subjects

This novel gives the cliché "war is hell" a new meaning and dimension. The terrible waste in lost and shattered lives, the inhumanity and barbarism that war produces, and the endless carnage it brings are graphically portrayed. The book also vividly creates the paralyzing fear of facing near-certain death, the submerged questions concerning the rightness of waging war, and the inner strength and courage that even the most ordinary soldier must possess. It also depicts well the camaraderie of war buddies and shows that in crises where one must rely on one's friends, the really important values surface and differences concerning race and religion become irrelevant.

Booktalk Material

Some of the interesting passages: Richie meets Peewee and Judy Duncan (pp. 3–7); the death of Jenkins and the angel warrior speech (pp. 40–44); the pacification project and meeting An Linh, an eight-year-old war refugee (pp. 50–53); Lobel and Richie talk about home (pp. 70–77); the episode with the television crew (pp. 77–80); the death of Lieutenant Carroll (pp. 124–28); and Richie kills his first Viet Cong (pp. 176–81).

Additional Selections

Lisa's life in haunted by the Vietnam War where her father was killed and her mother was a nurse in Nancy Antle's *Lost in the War* (Dial, 1998).

Three Utah teenagers have a growing interest in the Vietnam War in Margaret Rostowski's *The Best of Friends* (HarperCollins, 1989), a novel that traces how the war affects each of them.

In an effort to find out about his father who was killed in Vietnam, Sam tries to find out about the war in Bobbie Ann Mason's *In Country* (HarperCollins, 1985).

The hell of trench warfare in World War I is re-created in the now-classic novel by Erich Maria Remarque, *All Quiet on the Western Front* (Little, 1929).

About the Author and Book

Authors and Artists for Young Adults. Gale. Vol. 4, 1990; vol. 23, 1998.
Children's Books and Their Creators. Houghton, 1995.
Children's Literature Review. Gale. Vol. 4, 1982; vol. 16, 1989; vol. 35, 1995.
Contemporary Authors New Revision Series. Vol. 108, Gale, 2002.
Continuum Encyclopedia for Children's Literature. Continuum, 2001.
Drew, Bernard A. *100 Most Popular Young Adult Authors.* Libraries Unlimited, 1997.
Favorite Children's Authors and Illustrators. Vol. 4, Tradition Books, 2003.
Fifth Book of Junior Authors and Illustrators. Wilson, 1983.
Gallo, Donald R. *Speaking for Ourselves.* National Council of Teachers of English, 1990.
Gillespie, John T., and Corinne J. Naden. *Characters in Young Adult Literature.* Gale, 1997.
Jordan, Denise. *Walter Dean Myers.* Enslow, 1999.
Lives and Works: Young Adult Authors. Vol. 6, Grolier, 1999.
McElmeel, Sharron L. "A Profile—Walter Dean Myers," *Book Report,* Sept./Oct., 2001, pp. 42–45.
Major Authors and Illustrators for Children and Young Adults (1st ed.). Vol. 4, Gale, 1993.
Major Authors and Illustrators for Children and Young Adults (2nd ed.). Vol. 6, Gale, 2002.
Myers, Walter Dean. *Bad Boy—A Memoir.* HarperCollins, 2001.
———. "Escalating Offenses," *Horn Book,* n.d., 2001, pp. 701–02.
———. "Pulling No Punches," *School Library Journal,* June, 2001, pp. 44–47.
Rochman, Hazel. "The Booklist Interview—Walter Dean Myers," *Booklist,* Jan. 1–15, 2000, pp. 932–33.
St. James Guide to Young Adult Writers (2nd ed.). St. James, 1999.
Something About the Author. Gale. Vol. 27, 1982; vol. 41, 1985; vol. 71, 1993; vol. 109, 2000; vol. 157, 2005.
Something About the Author Autobiography Series. Vol. 2, Gale, 1986.

Stevens, Jen. *The Undergraduate's Companion to Children's Writers and Their Web Sites.* Libraries Unlimited, 2004.
Twentieth-Century Young Adult Writers (1st ed.). St. James, 1994.
Writers for Young Adults. Vol. 2, Scribner, 1997.
www.walterdeanmyers.com (personal Web site)
See also listing "Selected Web Sites on Children's Literature and Authors."

Paterson, Katherine. *Lyddie.* Dutton, 1991. $17.99, 0-525-67338-5 (Grades 7–10).

Introduction

Katherine Paterson (1932–) was born in China to missionary parents who originally hailed from the American South. At the outbreak of World War II, they fled to North Carolina, where she spent her childhood. As an adult, she spent time as a missionary in Japan, the locale of her first two novels for young readers. She is one of the very few authors to have been awarded the Newbery Medal twice. She received the first in 1978 for *Bridge to Terabithia* (Harper, 1977), a tender story of the friendship of two young people that is interrupted by death. Her second was in 1981 for *Jacob Have I Loved* (Harper, 1981). In it, the central character, Louise, is overshadowed by her popular, beautiful sister but, through her courage and determination, she is able to find fulfillment and conquer the resentment that has been destroying her. Louise is somewhat like Lyddie, who also overcomes adverse conditions to achieve self-reliance. *Lyddie* is the story of a plucky young girl who is unable to pay off the debt on the family farm and goes to work in the textile mills in Lowell, Massachusetts, during the 1840s, where she endures both loneliness and harsh working conditions.

Principal Characters

Lyddie, a plucky young girl
Her mother
Charles, Agnes, and Rachel, her siblings
Diana, a radical thinker
Quaker Luke Stevens
Mr. Marsden, the mill supervisor

Plot Summary

In 1843, Lyddie, her mother, and her siblings Charles, Agnes, and Rachel are trying to keep their debt-ridden Vermont farm together after their father left. When a bear nearly wrecks the place, Mama insists on taking the two younger children to the home of her sister, but Lyddie and Charles refuse to go. They will try to keep the farm together.

In the spring, Mama writes to say that she has hired them out to pay off the farm debts. Charles goes to work in a mill and Lyddie is sent to work at Cutler's tavern, where she feels like a slave. So, she goes to Lowell, Massachusetts, and gets a job at the mill, where she meets Diana, a radical thinker who urges the girls to sign a petition for better working conditions. Although Lyddie saves her money, she learns the farm has been sold, Charles now has a home with a family who owns the mill where he works, young Agnes has died, and Mama is in an institution. Rachel goes to live with Charles's new family, and Lyddie is alone.

Lyddie has a chance to escape her dreary existence when she gets a letter from her former neighbor Quaker Luke Stevens, asking her to marry him. But Lyddie knows she does not love him and does not respond.

After Lyddie saves a young girl at the mill from attack by the supervisor, she is dismissed without a certificate of honorable discharge, meaning she can't get another job in Lowell. She travels to Boston to see Diana, who now has her own family. Discouraged, she goes again to Vermont to see the farm once more.

It is November again as she stands at the door of what was once her home. Suddenly she hears a voice. It is Luke Stevens. He asks her to come stay with his family for the night and he apologizes for writing a letter asking her to marry him—but where will she go? he asks. Suddenly, Lyddie knows what she will do. "I'm off to Ohio," she says, "to a college that will take a woman just like a man."

Lyddie knows in her heart that it may be many years before she will return to Vermont. However, she will return, and not because she has been beaten down with nowhere else to go. She will not be a slave, even to herself. Yet, as she looks at the kind face of Luke Stevens, she thinks that this gentle Quaker is the man she will one day love. Perhaps, just perhaps, he will wait.

Themes and Subjects

This is in many ways a grim story of the hard life endured by children in factories and farms in early America. But Lyddie is painted as a resourceful, believable heroine whose determination to succeed overcomes all obstacles. Life may be hard, the story warns, but there is always hope for a better future. Lyddie's strength and devotion to family and friends make her an inspiring role model.

Booktalk Material
Incidents on the farm and in the factory provide a good contrast in this story of the deplorable conditions in many working towns in early America. See: the bear intrudes at the Vermont farm (pp. 1–4); Lyddie and Charles make it through the winter (pp. 18–26); Lyddie goes to Lowell and the mill (pp. 53–61); and Lyddie meets Diana (pp. 68–73).

Additional Selections
Set in upstate New York in 1816, twelve-year-old Mem struggles to keep her family together in spite of her mother's depression in Mary Jane Auch's *Frozen Summer* (Holt, 1998).

Fifteen-year-old Annie Steele contends with the harsh life of mill workers in Connecticut in 1810 in *The Clock* by James Lincoln and Christopher Collier (Dell, pap., 1995).

In the mid-1800s, orphan Lucas becomes an apprentice to the local dentist/barber/undertaker in Cynthia DeFelice's *The Apprenticeship of Lucas Whitaker* (Farrar, 1996).

In Trudy Krisher's *Uncommon Faith* (Holiday, 2003), ten residents of Millbrook, Massachusetts, describe life in their town during the 1830s.

About the Author and Book
Authors and Artists for Young Adults. Gale. Vol. 1, 1989; vol. 31, 2000.
Biography Today: Author Series. Vol. 3, Omnigraphics, 1997.
Bostrom, Kathleen Long. *Winning Authors: Profiles of the Newbery Medalists.* Libraries Unlimited, 2003.
Brodie, C. S. "Katherine Paterson," *School Library Media Activities Monthly.* May, 2001, pp. 45–47.
Cary, Alice. *Katherine Paterson.* Learning Works, 1997.
Children's Books and Their Creators. Houghton, 1995.
Children's Literature Review. Vol. 50, Gale, 1999.
Contemporary Authors New Revision Series. Vol. 111, Gale, 2003.
Continuum Encyclopedia of Children's Literature. Continuum, 2001.
Drew, Bernard A. *100 Most Popular Young Adult Authors.* Libraries Unlimited, 1996.
Estes, Glenn E. "American Writers for Children Since 1960: Fiction." In *Dictionary of Literary Biography.* Vol. 52, Gale, 1986.
Favorite Children's Authors and Illustrators. Vol. 5, Tradition Books, 2003.
Fifth Book of Junior Authors and Illustrators. Wilson, 1983.
Gallo, Donald R. *Speaking for Ourselves.* National Council of Teachers of English, 1990.
Gillespie, John T., and Corinne J. Naden. *Characters in Young Adult Literature,* Gale, 1997.
Jones, Raymond E. *Characters in Children's Literature.* Gale, 1997.
Lives and Works: Young Adult Authors. Vol. 6, Grolier, 1999.
McElmeel, Sharron L. *100 Most Popular Children's Authors.* Libraries Unlimited, 1999.

Major Authors and Illustrators for Children and Young Adults (1st ed.). Vol. 5, Gale, 1993.
Major Authors and Illustrators for Children and Young Adults (2nd ed.). Vol. 6, Gale, 2002.
Paterson, Katherine. "Confusion at the Crossroads: The Forces that Pull Children and Reality Apart (1997 Anne Carroll Moore Lecture)," *School Library Journal*, May, 1998, pp. 34–37.
———. *Gates of Excellence: On Reading and Writing Books for Children*. Elsevier, 1981.
———. "Historical Fiction: Some Why's and How's," *Booklist*, April 15, 1999, pp. 1430–31.
———. "In Search of Wonder (May Hill Arbuthnot Honor Lecture)," *Journal of Youth Services in Libraries*, Summer, 1997, pp. 378–91.
———. *A Sense of Wonder: On Reading and Writing Books for Children*. Plume, 1995.
———. *The Spying Heart: More Thoughts on Reading and Writing Books for Children*. Lodestar, 1989.
St. James Guide to Children's Writers (5th ed.). St. James, 1999.
St. James Guide to Young Adult Writers (2nd ed.). St. James, 1999.
Schmidt, Gary D. *Katherine Paterson*. Twayne, 1990.
Something About the Author. Gale. Vol. 13, 1978; vol. 53, 1989; vol. 133, 2002.
Stevens, Jen. *The Undergraduate's Companion to Children's Writers and Their Web Sites*. Libraries Unlimited, 2004.
Sutton, Roger. "An Interview with Katherine Paterson," *Horn Book*, Nov./Dec., 2001, pp. 689–99.
Twentieth-Century Children's Writers (4th ed.). St. James, 1995.
Twentieth-Century Young Adult Writers (1st ed.). St. James, 1994.
Writers for Young Adults. Vol. 2, Scribner, 1997.
www.terabithia.com (personal Web site)
See also listing "Selected Web Sites on Children's Literature and Authors."

Portis, Charles. *True Grit.* Overlook, 2003 (1968). Pap. $15.95, 1-5856-7369-2 (Grade 7–Adult).

Introduction

Charles Portis was in born in 1933, in El Dorado, Arkansas, where his father was a school superintendent. After a stint in the Marine Corps and receiving a bachelor's degree in journalism from the University of Arkansas, he worked as a reporter for different newspapers before pursuing a full-time career as a fiction writer. He has been described as "one of the most inventively comic writers of western fiction. With an unerring ear for the rhythms of speech and idiosyncrasies of language, he delivers deadpan humor as his characters strive to come to terms with their own limitations and an increasingly cockeyed world." In *True Grit*, the author has created two outrageously overdrawn yet believable characters that readers will long remember. They are the shrewd, indomitable, fourteen-year-old heroine, Mattie Ross, and her tarnished Galahad, the one-eyed gunfighter, Marshal Rooster Cogburn. This mismatched pair have one quality in common—true grit. The novel takes place in the 1870s, but is told in flashbacks by Mattie fifty years later. Originally written for adults, it is enjoyed by readers in the junior high grades and up.

Principal Characters
Mattie Ross
Rooster Cogburn, meanest federal marshal in the territory
Tom Chaney, who killed Mattie's father
Sergeant LeBoeuf, who is trailing Chaney

Plot Summary
The Ross family, including Mattie and two siblings, farm a large stretch on the Arkansas River. When Tom Chaney, a newly hired hand, kills Frank Ross after a business deal, he steals his horses and flees to Oklahoma. Mattie goes to Fort Smith to claim the body and decides to stay there to avenge her father's death. She approaches the meanest federal marshal in the territory, Rooster Cogburn, to hunt down Chaney for one hundred dollars.

Sergeant LeBoeuf of the Texas Rangers is also after Chaney because he has learned that there is a reward for his capture for a previous murder. Even though Mattie has reached an agreement with Rooster, LeBoeuf outbids her with his offer to share the reward. The following morning the two men leave for the territory, but they are followed by Mattie riding her small horse. She is carrying some provisions and her father's revolver. The men try to lose her, but she sticks with them, and they finally let her join them.

They learn that Chaney has joined Ned Pepper's gang. Rooster plans an ambush but some of the gang escape, including Chaney. Later, on the trail Mattie accidentally meets up with Chaney and tries to shoot him, but she only wounds him and is captured by the gang. Rooster charges the gang and kills four of them. Mattie grabs a gun and shoots Chaney again, but the gun's kick is so strong that she falls into a pit of rattlesnakes and is bitten on the arm. Rooster rescues her and Chaney dies.

Mattie's arm must be amputated, and she is sent home. Through the years she loses touch with Rooster, until twenty-five years later, now a successful unmarried businesswoman, Mattie learns he has joined a Wild West show. She travels to Memphis where the show is playing, but it is too late. Rooster has died a few days before. Mattie brings back his body to her home and Rooster is buried next to her father.

Themes and Subjects
Portis has written a moving and often uproarious tale that is also a rousing adventure story filled with suspense and action. Mattie's singleminded innocence, along with her courage and resourcefulness, reminds one of the legendary spirit of the Old West and the "true grit" responsible for opening up the country. The matter-of-fact writing style matches the tale to perfection.

Booktalk Material
Here are a few of the many wonderful passages that could be used: Mattie witnesses the hanging (pp. 20–23); she talks to Rooster for the first time (pp. 51–56); Mattie meets LeBoeuf (pp. 62–66); and she follows the two men until they accept her (pp. 90–96).

Additional Selections
Outlaws who are trying to free their leader who is a prisoner in a mission school are fought off by a marshal, a cowboy, and the school's staff and students in Clifford Blair's *The Guns of Sacred Heart* (Walker, 1981).

Set in California in the 1870s, Margaret S. McClain's *Bellboy: A Mule Train Mystery* (Univ. of New Mexico, 1989) tells the story of a twelve-year-old boy and his first job on a mule train.

Meg Brennon and a group of friends and relatives try to eke out a living in rural Kansas during pioneer days in *The Long Road Turning* (Macmillan, 2000) by Irene Bennett Brown.

Cindy Bonner's *Lily* (Algonquin, 1992) is an old-fashioned Western romance about an innocent girl who falls for a worldly man from an outlaw family.

About the Author and Book
Connaughton, Michael E. "American Novelists Since World War II, Second Series." In *Dictionary of Literary Biography*. Vol. 6, Gale, 1980.
Contemporary Authors New Revision Series. Vol. 1, Gale, 1981.
Contemporary Fiction Writers of the South: A Bio-Bibliographical Sourcebook. Greenwood, 1993.
Twentieth-Century Western Writers. Gale, 1982.
World Authors, 1980–1985. Wilson, 1991.
See also listing "Selected Web Sites on Children's Literature and Authors."

Pullman, Philip. *The Ruby in the Smoke.* Laurel Leaf, 1987 (1985).
Pap. $6.50, 0-394-89589-4 (Grades 8–12).

Introduction
With the publication of *The Golden Compass* (Knopf, 1995), the first volume of the trilogy, His Dark Materials, Philip Pullman (1946–) gained a new and greater audience than he had before. His previous novels, like *The Ruby in the Smoke*, are also very entertaining and of literary merit. On the first page of this novel set in nineteenth-century London, Pullman introduces his plucky heroine with the words, "She was a person of sixteen or so, alone and uncommonly pretty. Her name was Sally Lockhart, and within fifteen minutes she would have killed a man." With this, most readers are hooked into completing one of the best adventure mysteries in years, complete with bloody murders, cliff-hanging chapter endings, seedy Victorian flophouses and opium dens, and the search for a fabulous ruby that people would and do kill to possess. At the end of this novel, Sally mistakenly believes that she has killed her arch-enemy Henrik van Eiden, alias Ah Ling, the leader of an international smuggling ring, but she discovers otherwise in the book's two sequels, *The Shadow in the North* (Knopf, 1988) and *The Tiger in the Well* (Knopf, 1990).

Principal Characters
Sally Lockhart
Caroline Rees, her aunt
Jim Taylor, a cockney office boy
Mrs. Holland, proprietress of a rooming house and opium den
Major George Marchbanks
Matthew Bedwell, an opium-addicted sailor
Adelaide, an orphaned servant
Fred Garland, a young photographer
Mr. Reynolds, alias van Eiden, alias Ah Ling, a villain

Plot Summary
It is early October 1872 and to the office of Lockhart and Selby, the shipping agents in Cheapside, London, Sally has come to inquire about a mysterious message received in the post from her deceased father, but written by a second, almost illiterate person. It warns her to beware of the "Seven Blessings" and to seek help from a certain Marchbanks. Her father,

Matthew Lockhart, had served as a British officer in the Indian mutiny some fifteen years before, during which time Sally believes her mother was murdered. The violence and horror of these incidents have left Sally with a recurring unfinished nightmare she is unable to explain.

On his return to England, Lockhart had become a shipping agent with his partner, Selby. Hearing stories from the Far East of smuggling and mismanagement and interference by a Mr. van Eiden involving their shipments, Lockhart went to investigate. Scarcely three months ago Sally learned that her beloved father drowned when the schooner *Lavinia* sank in the South China Sea. Since then she has been living in London like an outcast with an unfeeling distant relative, Aunt Caroline Rees. Now this strange note has arrived and she is anxious to learn its meaning.

Selby is absent and Sally is taken by the saucy cockney office boy Jim Taylor to see Mr. Higgs, the company secretary. When Sally mentions the Seven Blessings, Higgs falls dead of a heart attack. Shocked and shaken, Sally explains her mission to Jim and gives him her address should he be able to help.

Meanwhile in the slums of the East End, a wicked crone named Mrs. Holland, proprietress of a squalid combination rooming house and opium den, is plotting with her lawyer to gain possession of a precious ruby from a man named Marchbanks. To her lodging house comes Matthew Bedwell, an opium-addicted sailor newly returned from the South Seas and seeking a floor to sleep on and a drug fix. He is escorted to a filthy room by Mrs. Holland's pathetic young girl servant, an orphaned slave named Adelaide. Here in his opium-induced delirium, Bedwell raves about the Seven Blessings, the firm of Lockhart and Selby, and the sinking of the *Lavinia*. At each session Mrs. Holland listens and soon realizes that this information can be used to blackmail Selby. During his lucid moments when alone with Adelaide, Bedwell tells her that he has a twin brother, Nicholas, a respected clergyman, and also that she must secretly contact Sally Lockhart through her father's firm and tell her the story.

With great fear and trepidation, Adelaide visits the company office and meets Jim, who promises to arrange a meeting with Sally.

Via the newspaper account of Higgs's autopsy, Major George Marchbanks learns of Sally's whereabouts and writes a letter urgently inviting her to visit him at his coastal home on the outskirts of Swaleness. On the walk from the train to his house, Sally encounters a young photographer named Fred Garland who is busy taking pictures of the landscape.

Marchbanks hurriedly gives Sally a handwritten document and tells her that he has another visitor, an evil lady named Mrs. Holland, awaiting him. He bids Sally goodbye and warns her that she is in great danger.

On her way back to the station, Sally realizes that she is being followed by Mrs. Holland. She eludes her by hiding in the photographer's tent. Inside the train carriage, she begins reading the document that deals with the fate of the famed ruby of Agrupur and how it fell into the hands of Marchbanks. Before finishing it, Sally falls asleep. She awakens to find that the document has been stolen, except for the last page, which had fallen on the floor. It contains a series of cryptic clues that deal with the present whereabouts of the ruby.

Mrs. Holland, who engineered the robbery, is furious at her loss. She sends her henchman to steal the page from Sally's room at Mrs. Rees's. The robbery is successful, but fortunately not before Sally had copied the contents into her diary and shared them with her friend Jim.

Life with Mrs. Rees becomes increasingly intolerable, so Sally moves out, collects a few pounds owed to her from her father's lawyer (the bulk of her inheritance has mysteriously disappeared), and sets out on her own. She calls on the young photographer, who lives in spacious quarters behind his studios with his young assistant, a failed pickpocket named Trembler, and Fred's sister, a struggling young actress, Rosa Garland. Not only is Sally made welcome, but also she is hired as their business manager.

Sally tells them her story. News reaches them that Marchbanks has been murdered, and after Sally learns Bedwell's story from Adelaide, and about his virtual imprisonment by Mrs. Holland, the group decides to contact his twin brother. With the reverend's help, an exciting rescue is carried out that frees both Bedwell and a terrified Adelaide. Upon recovery, Bedwell tells his story. He had been mate on the *Lavinia* on which Mr. Lockhart had sailed, convinced that his partner, Selby, was part of an international conspiracy involving an insurance racket that included both the ship and its cargo. He was right. The day of sailing, the ship was boarded by a group of pirates known as the Seven Blessings under their leader, the villainous Ah Ling. Mr. Lockhart was murdered, the cargo transferred to the pirates' junk, and the ship was sunk.

Fortunately, Bedwell and Lockhart's native servant, Perak, escaped. It was Perak who had copied down Lockhart's dying words and sent them to Sally.

In another part of London, a stranger checks into the fashionable Warwick Hotel under the name Mr. Reynolds. Within the next days both Selby and Matthew Bedwell are murdered and an advertisement appears in the *Times* from Reynolds requesting a meeting with Sally. She ignores it and takes the precaution of purchasing a revolver. Jim is convinced that Reynolds is involved with the Seven Blessings.

In the interim, Mrs. Holland has been busy. By using her cunning, she has solved the riddle of the whereabouts of the ruby. She follows each direction only to discover that someone has preceded her—the hiding place is empty. It was Jim. When Sally gets the ruby, she decides that she must confront Mrs. Holland to determine the truth behind the half-revealed horror of her nightmare.

At midnight they meet on London Bridge. Sally places the gem on the parapet between them. To secure the ruby, Mrs. Holland talks. In India many years back, Mrs. Holland, then Polly Andrews, was the mistress of the maharajah, who once promised her the ruby. Instead he gave it to Lockhart to ensure protection during the mutiny. Unfortunately, because of Marchbanks's opium habit, the maharajah was betrayed and murdered. Marchbanks and Lockhart quarreled violently—this was Sally's recurring nightmare. Marchbanks, a widower, begged Lockhart for the ruby to repay his growing drug debts. In exchange he offered his daughter. Filled with disgust, Lockhart agreed, and in that instant Sally Marchbanks became Sally Lockhart.

Sally throws the cursed ruby into the water and the half-crazed Mrs. Holland jumps after it, only to be killed on the pilings below. Within minutes a cab drives up and a voice invites Sally in. The stranger identifies himself as Reynolds, alias van Eiden alias Ah Ling, leader of the Seven Blessings. He threatens her with either immediate death or enslavement in the Far East. His ship is about to sail. Sally remembers the gun in her purse. She shoots and amid the sight of gushing blood, she escapes from the cab.

Although no body is found by the police, Sally and company are convinced that van Eiden could not survive such a serious wound. Within a few days there is a final surprise, this time a pleasant one. It comes in a letter from Nicholas Bedwell. Shortly before his murder, his brother had remembered one last message to Sally from Mr. Lockhart. It was "tell her to look under the clock."

Sally returns to their former home in the country and following directions, finds in large bills her inheritance plus a final note from Matthew Lockhart begging her forgiveness for not telling her the truth of her origins.

At last Sally's future is bright. The missing inheritance ensures financial security for herself and her new-found friends, and soon perhaps a new business, Garland and Lockhart.

Themes and Subjects
This is a tense, intricately plotted, very entertaining thriller, but it also effectively evokes the atmosphere and living conditions in the London of Dickens's time. Surface prosperity and gentility contrast with invasive inner squalor and violence. The author also supplies horrifying details on the conduct and effect of the government-sponsored opium trade in the

nineteenth century. Sally is portrayed as an intrepid, resourceful heroine, at times unsure of herself but usually mature beyond her years. Several other characters, like Mrs. Holland, could have stepped out of Dickens, but basically this is a story in which in spite of fantastic odds, right triumphs over might.

Booktalk Material
After a brief introduction to the time and locale of the novel, the first few pages (pp. 3–7) introduce Sally and the Seven Blessings and conclude with the sudden death of Mr. Higgs, which should grab the attention of most readers. Other interesting passages are: the story of Sally's background and the nightmare (pp. 12–15); Mrs. Holland and the ruby are introduced (pp. 20–25); Matthew Bedwell finds shelter at Mrs. Holland's (pp. 25–27); Sally visits Mr. Marchbanks and meets both Fred Garland and Mrs. Holland (pp. 30–38); and she reads from the manuscript before it is stolen (pp. 39–43).

Additional Selections
Set in the Old West, a tale of romance and mystery, Claudia Dain's *A Kiss to Die For* (Leisure, pap., 2003) features the hunt for a killer of a young woman.

A young heroine is trapped on a desert island with a murderer in Victoria Holt's *The Captive* (Fawcett, pap., 1990).

On the eerie Ravensmore estate, teenage Clare gets involved in adventure, a motorcycle gang, psychic visions, and a trip to Stonehenge in Liz Berry's *China Garden* (Fawcett, pap., 1990).

In Arthur Conan Doyle's *The Hound of the Baskervilles* (Buccaneer, 1983), Sherlock Holmes investigates strange deaths on the moors close to the Baskerville estate.

About the Author and Book
Authors and Artists for Young Adults. Gale. Vol. 15, 1995; vol. 41, 2001.
Children's Books and Their Creators. Houghton, 1995.
Children's Literature Review. Gale. Vol. 20, 1990; vol. 62, 2000; vol. 84, 2003.
Contemporary Authors New Revision Series. Vol. 134, Gale, 2005.
Cooper, Ilene. "Darkness Visible—Philip Pullman's *Amber Spyglass,*" *Booklist,* Oct., 2000, pp. 354–55.
Drew, Bernard A. *100 More Popular Young Adult Authors.* Libraries Unlimited, 2002.
Favorite Children's Authors and Illustrators. Vol. 5, Tradition Books, 2003.
Gallo, Donald R. *Speaking for Ourselves, Too.* National Council of Teachers of English, 1993.
Gillespie, John T., and Corinne J. Naden. *Characters in Young Adult Literature.* Gale, 1997.
Lives and Works: Young Adult Authors. Vol. 5, Grolier, 1999.

Major Authors and Illustrators for Children and Young Adults (1st ed.). Vol. 5, Gale, 1993.
Major Authors and Illustrators for Children and Young Adults (2nd ed.). Vol. 6, Gale, 2002.
Odean, Kathleen. "The Story Master—Philip Pullman," *School Library Journal,* Oct., 2000, pp. 50–54.
Pullman, Philip. "Gotterdammerung or Bust," *Horn Book,* Jan.–Feb., 1999, pp. 31–33.
———. "The Republic of Heaven," *Horn Book,* Nov./Dec., 2001, pp. 655–67.
St. James Guide to Young Adult Writers (2nd ed.). St. James, 1999.
Sixth Book of Junior Authors and Illustrators. Wilson, 1989.
Something About the Author. Gale. Vol. 65, 1991; vol. 103, 1999; vol. 150, 2004.
Something About the Author Autobiography Series. Vol. 17, Gale, 1994.
Stevens, Jen. *The Undergraduate's Companion to Children's Writers and Their Web Sites.* Libraries Unlimited, 2004.
Twentieth-Century Young Adult Writers (1st ed.). St. James, 1994.
Writers for Young Adults. Supplement 1, Scribner, 1999.
See also listing "Selected Web Sites on Children's Literature and Authors."

Speare, Elizabeth. *Calico Captive.* Houghton Mifflin, 2001 (1957). $16, 0-618-15075-7 (Grades 6–9).

Introduction

Elizabeth Speare (1908–94) was born in Massachusetts but moved to Connecticut, where she lived for many years. She had an unusual record of success in the field of children's literature. Of her four historical novels written for young people, *The Witch of Blackbird Pond* (Houghton, 1958) and *The Bronze Bow* (Houghton, 1961), both won Newbery Medals and a third, *The Sign of the Beaver* (Houghton, 1983), was chosen as an Honor Book in 1984. She often used New England as a setting for her novels. For example, she chose Wethersfield, a town on the Connecticut River 10 miles south of Hartford, as the setting of *The Witch* because it had once been a bustling river port in colonial times and because she had once lived there. *Calico Captive,* her first book, is based on the diary of Susanna Johnson, published in 1807, which tells of a family of New England settlers who are captured by Indians in 1754 and later bartered to French captors. The novel's narrative concentrates on Susanna's high-spirited younger sister, Miriam, who was also one of the prisoners.

Principal Characters
  Miriam Willard
  Susanna Johnson, her older sister

Phineas Whitney, a divinity student
Mehkoa, a Native American boy
Hortense, a maid
Pierre, a young Quebec adventurer

Plot Summary
Because of the Indian raids, Miriam Willard has spent the hot, grueling summer of 1754 in Fort Number Four with her older sister Susanna Johnson and the three Johnson children. But when Captain Johnson returns from his journey down the Connecticut River they move back to their cabin outside the fort. Here, during one last gay party, Phineas Whitney, a young divinity student, declares his love to the shy Miriam before leaving for Harvard College.

At dawn on the following day, Indians surround the cabin. Each Indian takes one person as his captive. When Susanna Johnson gives birth to a daughter on the trail, no one is more pleased than the dark savage who then has two prisoners to ransom to the French in Canada. Only the little children fare well on the brutal forced march. Miriam is continually tormented by Mehkoa, an Indian boy about her age. But when she rescues Susanna's baby from the swirling waters of a deep stream, Mehkoa stops his mischief and returns Miriam's blue calico dress.

The Indians bring the captives to their village, whereupon Mehkoa asks the Chief to give him Miriam for his squaw. Repelled, Miriam runs from the scene, bringing dishonor to the young brave and trouble to her family, who are parceled out as slaves to the Indian families. In time, Susanna persuades the Chief to sell her husband, children, and sister to the French in Quebec. She and her six-year-old son Sylvanus remain with the Indians as prisoners.

Miriam begins a new life as a servant in a wealthy French home where she becomes fast friends with the young maid, Hortense, and a sometime playmate of the pretty young daughter of the house, Felicité. Here, too, she meets Pierre, a rich, worldly, young adventurer, who proposes marriage. But even this opportunity to end her hard circumstances cannot change Miriam's belief that she loves Phineas and his way of life far more than all the worldly things that Pierre can give her.

After many discouraging months, Susanna makes her way to Quebec. She and Miriam finally arrange passage to England through the influence of the Governor's wife. From England, these valiant colonists will then attempt to find passage to their home in Massachusetts.

The word "calico" in the title refers to the cherished blue dress in which Miriam first learned of Phineas's love and in which she sustained the horrors of Indian captivity.

Themes and Subjects
Wholesome relationships are well presented in this book, as is Miriam's friendship with a young girl that she meets in the wealthy Quebec home. The themes of self-reliance and perseverance are also stressed.

Booktalk Material
To captivate an audience, the story could be introduced by reading aloud the third paragraph on page 9, followed by a description of the raid (pp. 15–19). The romantic vignette in which Pierre tricks Miriam into going to a fancy dress ball for which she has sewn many of the gowns will interest readers (pp. 244–53).

Additional Selections
In 1849, fourteen-year-old Meribah leaves her home in Pennsylvania to accompany her father on a wagon train to California in Kathryn Lasky's *Beyond the Divide* (Simon, 1983).

In Jackie F. Koller's *The Primrose Way* (Harcourt, 1996), sixteen-year-old Rebekah falls in love with Mishannock, a Pawtucket holy man.

Lynda Durrant's *The Beaded Moccasins* (Clarion, 1998) is a fictional account of the true story of twelve-year-old Mary Campbell, who was captured by Delaware Indians in 1759.

The story of a fourteen-year-old whose family is killed during an Indian raid on their cabin in 1676 is told in Madge Harrah's *My Brother, My Enemy* (Simon, 1997).

About the Author and Book
Apseloff, Marilyn. *Elizabeth George Speare*. Twayne, 1992.
Bostrom, Kathleen Long. *Winning Authors: Profiles of the Newbery Medalists*. Libraries Unlimited, 2003.
Children's Books and Their Creators. Houghton, 1995.
Children's Literature Review. Vol. 8, Gale, 1985.
Continuum Encyclopedia of Children's Literature. Continuum, 2001.
Cosgrave, Mary Silva. "Elizabeth George Speare," *Horn Book*, July/Aug., 1989, pp. 465–68.
Drew, Bernard A. *100 More Popular Young Adult Authors*. Libraries Unlimited, 2002.
Favorite Children's Authors and Illustrators. Vol. 6, Tradition Books, 2003.
Gallo, Donald R. *Speaking for Ourselves, Too*. National Council of Teachers of English, 1993.
Gillespie, John T., and Corinne J. Naden. *Characters in Young Adult Literature*. Gale, 1997.
Jones, Raymond E. *Characters in Children's Literature*. Gale, 1997.
McElmeel, Sharron L. *100 Most Popular Children's Authors*. Libraries Unlimited, 1999.

Major Authors and Illustrators for Children and Young Adults (1st ed.). Vol. 5, Gale, 1993.
Major Authors and Illustrators for Children and Young Adults (2nd ed.). Vol. 7, Gale, 2002.
More Junior Authors. Wilson, 1963.
St. James Guide to Young Adult Writers (2nd ed.). St. James, 1999.
Something About the Author. Gale. Vol. 2, 1973; vol. 62, 1991; vol. 83, 1996.
Speare, Elizabeth George. "Laura Ingalls Wilder Award Acceptance," *Horn Book,* July/Aug., 1989, pp. 460–64.
Stevens, Jen. *The Undergraduate's Companion to Children's Writers and Their Web Sites.* Libraries Unlimited, 2004.
Twentieth-Century Young Adult Writers (1st ed.). St. James, 1994.
See also listing "Selected Web Sites on Children's Literature and Authors."

Spiegelman, Art. *Maus: A Survivor's Tale—My Father Bleeds History.* Pantheon, 1986. Pap. $14, 0-394-74723-2 (Grade 10–Adult).

Introduction

Art Spiegelman was born in Stockholm, Sweden, in 1948, the son of two survivors of the Nazi Holocaust. The family emigrated to the United States in 1951. In his teens, Spiegelman began writing, printing, and distributing his own comics magazines and was influenced by such satirical comics as *Mad* magazine. Since 1965, he has been a freelance artist and author. In 1980, he published the first issue of *Raw,* an anthology magazine that published adult comics from around the world. Based on his parents' past histories, Spiegelman began working on *Maus.* In 1972, it was originally just a three-page script, but by the 1980s, he began to expand it into the full-length book that is now considered an epic parable of the Holocaust that substitutes mice and cats for human Jews and Nazis. In the second volume, *Maus: A Survivor's Tale II—And Here My Troubles Began* (Pantheon, pap., 1992), Art, a mouse, visits his father in his summer home in the Catskills, and the story of the horrors of concentration camp life continues, with his father and mother being reunited after the war and traveling to Sweden, and subsequently the story of his mother's suicide in 1968. This graphic novel ends with Art visiting Vladek, his father, just before his death in 1982.

Principal Characters

Vladek Spiegelman
His son, Art
His wife

Various family members
Various Nazi military

Plot Summary

In this original story told in cartoon form, Vladek Spiegelman relates to his son, Art, the details of his astonishing story of survival, which took him to the gates of the Auschwitz gas chamber in World War II. It is terrifying all the more because it is history. The Jews in the book are depicted as mice and the Nazis are cats. As in life, cats prey on mice, so in this story do the Nazis prey on the Jews.

Two stories are related throughout the book. One is the harrowing tale of survival as Vladek and his family in Poland live through the terror of confinement, of betrayal by people they thought were friends, and of those who risked their lives to help them escape. Vladek tells his son that they never would have made it had it not been for those who gave them aid as they brushed with death time and again. The father's story takes the family through the chain of events that led to the Final Solution and right up the steps of the gas chamber. Each day was a desperate struggle just to survive.

The second concurrent story concerns the always-troubled relationship of Vladek and his son as they try to live a normal life in Rego Park, New York. As Art hears the harrowing story of his father's survival, he finds it difficult to grasp and to understand as the two men try to develop a closer relationship.

Through all the reality, *Maus* is also a magical story, made gentle by the language of an old Eastern European family and filled with humor and life's daily trials in the midst of unspeakable horror and terror all about them.

Themes and Subjects

The theme of those who prey on others is a good opening to the device used by the author to portray a horror story in cartoon form. Also, what are the incidences of humor in this story that help the participants live through each day?

Booktalk Material

Art's crying day (pp. 5–6); Art's parents fall in love (pp. 16–17); the beginning of the war (pp. 32–33); the Nazis kill people in the forest (p. 61); the Jews are told to register (pp. 88–89); a Jew walks in the ghetto (p. 118); the Gestapo search (p. 143–49).

Additional Selections

In Jacob Boas's *We Are Witnesses: Five Diaries of Teenagers Who Died in the Holocaust* (Holt, 1995), the author talks about being a Holocaust survivor and the deaths of five other young inmates.

Joseph Freeman, a survivor of a Polish ghetto and Auschwitz, tells of what he witnessed in *Job: The Story of a Holocaust Survivor* (Paragon House, pap., 1995).

Mordecai Paldiel's *Saving the Jews* (Scribner, 2000) contains forty-seven accounts of Gentiles from different parts of Europe who saved Jews during World War II.

A Jewish teenager joins forces with a notorious Polish criminal to escape the Holocaust in the nonfiction *A Match Made in Hell* (Univ. of Wisconsin, 2003) by Larry Stillman.

About the Author and Book

Authors and Artists for Young Adults. Gale. Vol. 10, 1994; vol. 46, 2002.
Contemporary Authors. Vol. 125, Gale, 1989.
Contemporary Authors New Revision Series. Vol. 124, Gale, 2004.
Something About the Author. Vol. 109, Gale, 2002.
Spiegelman, Art. "Maus and Man," *Village Voice,* June 6, 1989, pp. 21–22.
See also listing "Selected Web Sites on Children's Literature and Authors."

Taylor, Mildred D. *Let the Circle Be Unbroken.* Dial, 1981, $17.99, 0-8037-4748-9; pap. Puffin, $5.99, 0-140-34892-1 (Grades 6–9).

Introduction

The Logan family was first introduced in *Song of the Trees* (Dial, 1975) and the Newbery Medal winner, *Roll of Thunder, Hear My Cry* (Dial, 1976). In these novels many of the plot threads are introduced that are later tied together in this, the third volume of the series. The Logan family members are Mama and Papa, grandmother Big Ma, and four children: Stacey, the beloved older brother, now fourteen; ten-year-old Cassie, the narrator; and two young boys, Christopher-John and Big Boy. Their hired hand, gigantic Mr. Morrison, has become like one of the family. It is during the Depression in rural Mississippi and, though the Logans fortunately own their own land, most of their neighbors are sharecroppers whose land is owned by the heartless Harlan Granger. Some of the Logans' friends include Mrs. Lee Annie, a feisty sixty-three-year-old woman who lives with her grandson, fourteen-year-old Wardell. Another grandson,

Russell Thomas, has just joined the army. The Averys are also good friends. They have a son named T.J., who became involved with two trashy white boys, R.W. and Melvin Simms, and was caught after a robbery attempt of a local store during which the owner was killed by one of the Simms boys. The brothers have escaped, but T.J. is in jail awaiting trial for murder. The Logans have many other friends, such as the Wiggins and Ellis families. Though they are all dirt-poor and are completely at the mercy of their white overseers, they live dignified, moral lives filled with love and compassion. The novel begins a few months after *Roll of Thunder, Hear My Cry* ended and spans the time from late 1935 through the beginning of 1937.

Principal Characters
   Cassie Logan, ten-year-old narrator
   Mama and Papa
   Grandmother Big Ma
   Stacey, Christopher-John and Big Boy, Cassie's brothers
   Mr. Morrison, a hired hand
   Harlan Granger, a heartless landowner
   Mrs. Lee Annie, a friend
   Wardell and Russell, her grandsons
   The Averys, good friends, and son T.J.

Plot Summary
It is during the Depression in rural Mississippi and one day, the Logan youngsters, including Cassie, the narrator, skip school to attend the trial of T.J. Avery. He was involved in a robbery attempt in which the store owner was killed. His lawyer is a liberal white man who gives legal aid to blacks. T.J. is sentenced to death, and the Logans never see their friend again.

There is much trouble on the land between sharecroppers and landowners and labor troubles continue. As summer approaches, Papa is forced to take a job on the railroad far from home. They are visited by Uncle Hammer from Chicago in his Ford car, and later, Suzella. She is the daughter of Bud Rankin, Mama's cousin, who married a white woman. She is so fair that she could pass for white and when some white boys try to date her, Mama tells her she will always be colored.

In the fall, Stacey, Cassie's fourteen-year-old brother, feels he must do more to help the family. One night, he and friend Moe Turner steal away, leaving only a short note of explanation. The family is devastated and Mama sends for her husband to return home and search for their son. Uncle Hammer and Mr. Logan, thinking that Stacey might have gone to Louisiana to work on plantations cutting sugarcane, set out to find the boy without success.

Bud comes to visit at Christmas to take Suzella back to New York. But they, including the Logan children, are accosted by white teenagers. Luckily, big Mr. Morrison comes along in time.

Mrs. Lee Annie, almost sixty-five, decides she wants to vote. Her friends try to deter her, afraid she will be lynched, but she is adamant. But when she enters the courthouse for the test, which Mrs. Logan helped her to study for, she is made to fail. To teach her a lesson, her landlord then orders her off her property within twenty-four hours.

Only in the Logan household is there good news. They learn that two black boys who fled a sugar plantation are being held in jail in a town called Shokesville. In Uncle Hammer's Ford, they drive through the night and into the next day. Their prayers are answered. Although more dead than alive, Stacey and Moe are rescued and released from jail. The Logan family is together again.

Themes and Subjects

This is a bleak, unremitting picture of poverty among people who are denied basic human rights. The novel brilliantly depicts the injustice, oppression, and humiliation forced on people solely because of skin color and also gives indications of the civil rights movement to follow. Although filled with bitterness and disillusionment, Cassie's family and friends have the dignity and sense of values that never allow their souls to be enslaved. This is also a portrait of a loving family and the strong ties that keep them together. Cassie is a resourceful, courageous girl who could serve as a role model for children of any race.

Booktalk Material

Introducing the Logan family is a good opening to this book. Some specific passages are: the first marble game (pp. 11–16; pp. 9–14, pap.) and the second (pp. 16–23; pp. 14–20, pap.); in the courthouse Cassie learns about segregated washrooms (pp. 54–59; pp. 47–51, pap.); T.J.'s trial (pp. 60–86; pp. 52–74, pap.); a typical day for Cassie at school (pp. 107–09; pp. 92–94, pap.); and Suzella arrives (pp. 211–15; pp. 181–85, pap.).

Additional Selections

Set in a small Vermont town in the 1920s, Karen Hesse's *Witness* (Scholastic, 2001) reveals various views on race as well as a murder mystery and the Ku Klux Klan.

In 1921 Oklahoma, a fifteen-year-old boy helps an African American man who is injured during race riots in Anna Myers's *Turning Burning* (Walker, 2002).

In 1807, Ajeemah and his son are taken by slave traders from their African home to Jamaica where they are separated in James Berry's *Ajeemah and His Son* (Harper, 1969).

The moving tragedy of a black sharecropper and his dog is told in William H. Armstrong's Newbery Medal winner, *Sounder* (Harper, 1969).

About the Author and Book
Authors and Artists for Young Adults. Gale. Vol. 10, 1993; vol. 47, 2003.
Biography Today: Author Series. Vol. 1, Omnigraphics, 1995.
Bostrom, Kathleen Long. *Winning Authors: Profiles of the Newbery Medalists*. Libraries Unlimited, 2003.
Children's Books and Their Creators. Houghton, 1995.
Children's Literature Review. Vol. 9, Gale, 1985.
Contemporary Authors New Revision Series. Vol. 136, Gale, 2005.
Continuum Encyclopedia of Children's Literature. Continuum, 2001.
Drew, Bernard A. *100 Most Popular Young Adult Authors*. Libraries Unlimited, 1996.
Estes, Glenn E. "American Writers for Children Since 1960: Fiction." In *Dictionary of Literary Biography*. Vol. 52, Gale, 1986.
Favorite Children's Authors and Illustrators. Vol. 6, Tradition Books, 2003.
Fifth Book of Junior Authors and Illustrators. Wilson, 1983.
Gillespie, John T., and Corinne J. Naden. *Characters in Young Adult Literature*. Gale, 1997.
Lives and Works: Young Adult Authors. Vol. 7, Grolier, 1999.
McElmeel, Sharron L. *100 Most Popular Children's Authors*. Libraries Unlimited, 1999.
Major Authors and Illustrators for Children and Young Adults (1st ed.). Vol. 6, Gale, 1993.
Major Authors and Illustrators for Children and Young Adults (2nd ed.). Vol. 8, Gale, 2002.
Rochman, Hazel. "The Booklist Interview: Mildred Taylor," *Booklist*, Sept. 15, 2001, p. 221.
St. James Guide to Young Adult Writers (2nd ed.). St. James, 1999.
Something About the Author. Gale. Vol. 15, 1979; vol. 70, 1993; vol. 135, 2003.
Something About the Author Autobiography Series. Vol. 5, Gale, 1988.
Stevens, Jen. *The Undergraduate's Companion to Children's Writers and Their Web Sites*. Libraries Unlimited, 2004.
Twentieth-Century Young Adult Writers (1st ed.). St. James, 1994.
See also listing "Selected Web Sites on Children's Literature and Authors."

Westall, Robert. *The Machine Gunners.* HarperTrophy, 1997 (1976). Pap. $6.99, 0-688-15498-0 (Grades 7–9).

Introduction
The British author Robert Westall (1929–93) was born in Newcastle upon Tyne, the setting of many of his novels. After studying art at Durham University, he became an art teacher in various English public (i.e., private in U.S.) schools. His first book for young readers was *The Machine Gunners*. It was first published in England in 1975 and won the Carnegie Medal for excellence in literature for older children. It gives an authentic picture of World War II life as experienced by ordinary adults and children. In it, a teenager, Chas McGill, happens on a machine gun that he and his friends decide to use to deter enemy bombers. In a sequel, *Fathom Five* (Random, 1977, o.p.), Chas, his friend Cem Jones, and girlfriend Sheila come across a strange object after a U-boat has been sunk. This discovery leads to uncovering the identity of the villain in their sleepy coastal village who is feeding information to the Germans. Westall won a second Carnegie Medal for the novel *The Scarecrows* (Morrow, 1981, o.p.), the chilling story of a teenager who, while visiting his mother and stepfather whom he detests, is terrorized by three scarecrows that seem to embody the spirits of people who have met violent deaths.

Principal Characters
Chas McGill, a fourteen-year-old British schoolboy
Sicky Nicky, a boy everyone teases
Sergeant Rudi Gerlath, a German rear gunner

Plot Summary
It is 1941 in Garmouth, England. The British are bombarded daily by German bombers and there are rumors of an imminent invasion by Nazi forces. Like his friends, fourteen-year-old Chas McGill has grown used to spending nights in an air raid shelter. His out-of-school hours are usually spent looking for bits of shrapnel and other litter from the air raids.

After one raid, Chas comes upon a bit of luck—a German Heinkel has been shot down in a wood near town. The dead pilot is still in his plane, and the pilot's hand in still on an intact machine gun. What a prize for his collection! It takes some effort, but Chas is able to wrest the gun from the plane.

A plan forms in Chas's mind: Instead of turning in the gun, he will use it to shoot at the hated German hit-and-run bombers. Such a scheme requires careful planning. How can he conceal the gun from the authorities? Chas first carefully removes the cartridge cases, wraps the gun in cloth, and stows it in the end of a large water pipe in his father's greenhouse.

It doesn't take the British authorities long to realize that someone has removed the machine gun from the German plane. They even suspect that it might be some boys up to mischief. But suspicions are one thing; finding the gun and proving the suspicions are quite another.

After the roof is bombed off his grandparents' home—luckily they are unharmed—Chas is more determined than ever to fight the Germans with his hidden weapon. He and his friends decide that the place to make an encampment for the gun is the garden of nerdy Sicky Nicky, because nobody ever goes there. Sicky Nicky is the boy everyone teases, and he is at first quite surprised to find himself the object of so much attention.

Chas and his friends build the secret encampment. When they finally shoot at a German bomber, the plane isn't hit but the pilot is startled, to say the least. The Messerschmitt is then hit by three Spitfires. Its German rear gunner, Sergeant Rudi Gerlath, parachutes to safety but injures his ankle. He lands in a garden and crawls into a shed. The boys, of course, think it is their gunfire that has blown up the German plane.

A few days later Rudi leaves his garden shed in search of food and chances on an abandoned house. As luck would have it, he stumbles right into the machine gun encampment of the young Britishers!

Both Rudi and his captors are terrified. The boys realize he's a Nazi; he realizes they are just youngsters. He also realizes they have a real gun. For the next few days Rudi is attended by a girl-child, one of the group, who feeds him medicine and soup. Slowly Rudi and the youngsters begin to communicate. They learn he will be able to repair the machine gun, which is damaged. He agrees to this if they agree to get him a boat, which he thinks they cannot do. But the youngsters convince Nicky to let them have his father's boat.

Soon the whole area is in turmoil about rumors of a supposed German invasion. The boys get Rudi in the patched-up boat, but he soon realizes there is no invasion and returns to shore. By the next morning, the Garmouth citizens also realize there is no invasion. However, the boys in their encampment don't know this. When they see a corps of foreign soldiers—in this case Polish—marching toward them, they fire, luckily not hitting anyone. In the confusion, an English official sees a German waving a white flag. It is Rudi Gerlath, Sergeant, Luftwaffe, giving himself up. He tells the bewildered official that six schoolchildren are back in the encampment.

The missing machine gun is found, Rudi is taken prisoner, and Chas and his friends receive a stern warning from their parents. However, they are promised that perhaps they will be able to write letters to their friend Rudi.

Themes and Subjects
This is a wonderful, offbeat story of youngsters and grow-ups in war. All of the characters, children and adults, are portrayed in a most realistic, understandable way, showing them caught up in the hysteria of wartime but reaching out to each other as people and friends. It is a fast-paced adventure story that is also a tribute to the unflappable British spirit and will.

Booktalk Material
A number of incidents can be used as an introduction to this lively adventure. See: Chas finds the machine gun (pp. 7–9); Chas and his friends go back to the wood (pp. 17–20); Chas hides the gun (pp. 25–26); and the roof goes off Nana's house (pp. 51–57).

Additional Selections
Carrie relives her days during World War II when she and her brother were evacuated to Wales in Nina Bawden's *Carrie's War* (HarperCollins, 1973).

During World War II, a sixth-grade girl makes a difficult decision on whether or not to help a pacifist deserter in Mary D. Hahn's *Stepping on the Cracks* (Houghton, 1991).

The Silver Sword (Phillips, 1959) by Ian Serraillier is a World War II story of Polish children who are separated from their parents and finally reunited.

In Elizabeth Van Steenwyk's *A Traitor Among Us* (Eerdmans, 1998), a thirteen-year-old boy living in Nazi-occupied Holland hides a wounded American Soldier.

About the Author and Book
Authors and Artists for Young Adults. Vol. 12, Gale, 1994.
Children's Books and Their Creators. Houghton, 1995.
Children's Literature Review. Vol. 13, Gale, 1987.
Contemporary Authors New Revision Series. Vol. 68, Gale, 1998.
Continuum Encyclopedia of Children's Literature. Continuum, 2001.
Drew, Bernard A. *100 Most Popular Young Adult Authors.* Libraries Unlimited, 1996.
Fifth Book of Junior Authors and Illustrators. Wilson, 1983.
Gallo, Donald R. *Speaking for Ourselves, Too.* National Council of Teachers of English, 1993.
Gillespie, John T., and Corinne J. Naden. *Characters in Young Adult Literature.* Gale, 1997.

Lives and Works: Young Adult Authors. Vol. 8, Grolier, 1999.
Major Authors and Illustrators for Children and Young Adults (1st ed.). Vol. 6, Gale, 1993.
Major Authors and Illustrators for Children and Young Adults (2nd ed.). Vol. 8, Gale, 2002.
St. James Guide to Young Adult Writers (2nd ed.). St. James, 1999.
Something About the Author. Gale. Vol. 23, 1981; vol. 69, 1992; vol. 75, 1994.
Something About the Author Autobiography Series. Vol. 2, Gale, 1986.
Twentieth-Century Young Adult Writers (1st ed.). St. James, 1994.
Writers for Young Adults. Vol. 3, Scribner, 1997.
See also listing "Selected Web Sites on Children's Literature and Authors."

5
Adventure and Mystery Stories

Alexander, Lloyd. *The El Dorado Adventure.* Puffin, 2001 (1987). Pap. $5.99, 0-14-130463-4 (Grades 7–10).

Introduction
Readers of Lloyd Alexander (1924–) first met the intrepid teenager Vesper Holly in *The Illyrian Adventure* (Puffin, 1986), in which—with her bumbling loyal guardian, the narrator Brinton (Brinnie) Garrett—she travels from her home in Philadelphia in Illyria, a tiny kingdom on the Adriatic, to continue an archaeological investigation begun by her deceased father, D. Benjamin Rittenhouse Holly. Vesper and Brinnie become involved in a revolutionary plot to murder the king, plus an exciting search for treasure. *The El Dorado Adventure* is the second volume in the series. In the third volume, *The Drackenberg Adventure* (Puffin, 1988), while attending the diamond jubilee of the grand duchess of Drackenberg, Brinnie's wife, Mary, is kidnapped, Vesper lives with a gypsy band, and a hitherto unknown da Vinci painting is rescued. These novels take place in the mid- to late 1980s and, in each, Vesper and Brinnie eventually confront the archvillain Dr. Helvitius. Each adventure brims with breathless adventure and sly humor, often caused by Brinnie's overly proper, convention-bound attitudes. Others in the series include *The Philadelphia Adventure* (Puffin, 1990), *The Jedera Adventure* (Puffin, 1989), and *The Xanadu Adventure* (Dutton, 2005). See also *Westmark* on p. 131.

Principal Characters
  Vesper Holly, seventeen
  Brinnie, her guardian
  Blazer O'Hara, ship's captain
  Alain de Rochefort, who wants the land Vesper has inherited
  Acharro, an Indian chief

Plot Summary

Seventeen-year-old Vesper Holly has inherited a tract of land in the tiny Central American republic of El Dorado. She receives a telegram from an Alain de Rochefort, including tickets for her and her guardian, Brinnie, to go to El Dorado to attend to this property.

When they arrive in El Dorado, the captain of a decrepit riverboat called the *Libertador,* Blazer O'Hara, tells them that de Rochefort is a scoundrel who wants Vesper's land. He is an engineer and plans to build a canal that will destroy great stretches of arable land, driving the few remaining Indians, Chiricas, from their homes.

When Vesper and Brinnie meet de Rochefort, he appears charming. But on a rail trip to visit his jungle work camp, the two realize they are being kidnapped. Vesper breaks a carriage window and they escape into the jungle, where they are eventually rescued by the *Libertador* crew. Vesper meets the Indian chief Acharro and several of the Chirica women; she learns about their customs and handicrafts.

Vesper devises a plan to save the village, but she and Brinnie are again captured by de Rochefort, who now plans to kill her. And once again, they escape.

On board the *Libertador,* they are pursued by the evil Dr. Helvitius, who is de Rochefort's boss and the real power. He orders de Rochefort to kill Vesper and Brinnie, but he refuses, as he has come to admire Vesper.

At that tense moment, the Chirica women, who have witnessed the boarding from their canoes, silently creep up on Helvitius's men and attack them from behind with their paddles. The villains are forced back. They give chase to the *Libertador* but it gets away.

Back at the Indian village, there is general rejoicing. As a reward for her efforts, Vesper requests and receives permanent places on the council for the gallant women who effected their rescue. De Rochefort will stay behind to make a new life, and Vesper, her mission completed, gives her lands to the Indians. She and Brinnie return to Philadelphia, where more adventures await her.

Themes and Subjects

This is basically a rollicking, high adventure novel of good versus evil, but it does have some serious underlying themes. The heroine, a women's libber before her time, continually refuses to compromise her beliefs in sexual equality and fights to rectify the injustices that gender discrimination brings. The novel also deals with the disgraceful exploitation of native populations for wealth. When most adventure novels feature male central

ADVENTURE AND MYSTERY STORIES • 233

characters, it is refreshing to meet Vesper—intelligent, courageous, independent, and totally appealing.

Booktalk Material
Introduce the central characters, Vesper and Brinnie, to readers and then use one or more of these passages to develop the plot elements: they journey to El Dorado (pp. 3–9); Captain O'Hara talks about de Rochefort (pp. 22–28); the escape (pp. 36–41); the reunion with Dr. Helvitius (pp. 96–103); and the two futile attempts to escape from him (pp. 113–18, 121–26).

Additional Selections
Two eighth-graders find they are not alone when they take up residence in a shopping mall in Richard Peck's *Secrets of the Shopping Mall* (Dell, 1979).

While his mother is away, teenager Martin takes off and finds himself penniless in a small Idaho town in *Ten Miles from Winnemucca* (HarperCollins, 2002) by Thelma Hatch Wyss.

A boy is abducted and taken on the road by a man he believes is a bank robber in Peg Kehret's *Night of Fear* (Dutton, 1994).

In Lois Duncan's *I Know What You Did Last Summer* (Dell, 1995), four teenagers try to cover up a hit-and-run accident. Another title by this popular author is *Locked in Time* (Dell, 1985), about a girl trapped by a family who has found the secret of eternal life.

About the Author and Book
See under *Westmark*, p. 131.

Avi. *Wolf Rider.* Simon Pulse, 1993 (1986). Pap. $5.99, 0-02-041513-3 (Grades 7–10).

Introduction
Avi, the pen name of Avi Wortis (1937–), was born into a family of writers, real and aspiring, and numerous storytellers. For a time, he was a librarian and a teacher of children's literature but when his own children were born he became interested in writing for young readers. He once remarked, "One aspect of my work that seems to attract particular attention is the variety of my books." This variety is shown in three ways: in the span of reading levels from picture books to young adult novels; in the

different genres, from historical novels to those with contemporary settings; and in their formats, ranging from straight narratives to documentary novels. The diversity is also apparent in the three titles singled out over the years by the Newbery committee. Chosen as Honor Books were *The True Confessions of Charlotte Doyle* (Orchard, 1990), a rip-roaring sea adventure set in the 1830s (see p. 186), and *Nothing but the Truth* (Orchard, 1991), a powerful contemporary story about the manipulation of truth as told through a collection of documents and conversations. His 2003 Newbery Medal winner *Crispin: The Cross of Lead* (Hyperion, 2002) again switches settings, this time to England in the late fourteenth century, during the last year of the reign of Edward III. Subtitled *A Tale of Terror*, *Wolf Rider* explores another genre, the suspenseful mystery story.

Principal Characters
Andy Zadinski, fifteen
His father, a college teacher
Paul, Andy's friend
Zeke, a stranger
Nina Klemmer, a college girl

Plot Summary
Andy Zadinski and his father have just moved into a new apartment following the death of Andy's mother. One evening Andy takes a call. The voice says, "I just killed someone." The stranger says his name is Zeke and that he has just killed a student at the college where Andy's father teaches. Her name is Nina Klemmer. The stranger tells Andy that he just happened to dial Andy's number because he needed someone to talk to.

No one takes the call seriously, including the police, but Andy goes to the college to see if Nina does exist. She does and she is alive. Again, Andy tells the police, but they are not interested. Andy goes to see Nina and tells her about the strange call. She says he is harassing her and threatens to call the police. When the police and Andy's father find out what he has done, they are convinced he is emotionally unbalanced because of the death of his mother. In other words, he is crying wolf.

But Andy is convinced that the stranger named Zeke plans to kill Nina. He decides the stranger might be a member of his father's department at the college. He phones all the department members in turn; when Dr. Lucas answers the phone, Andy hears Zeke's voice. When Andy's father hears about this development, he says Andy is more disturbed than he thought and decides Andy should leave school early and go visit his aunt in the South.

Andy calls Lucas and says Nina wants to meet him. A meeting is set and Andy waits in the bushes. But Lucas pulls a knife, orders Andy into a car, and drives off into the mountains. Andy manages to get away when the car stops. As he runs away from the car, he picks up something that is glittering on the ground. It is Lucas's cufflink, which Andy puts it in his pocket.

Later, when Andy's father takes him to the airport, Dr. Zadinski tells him Lucas is dead, and from the elaborate steps he took to disguise his whereabouts on the night he died, police believe it to be suicide. But Andy realizes that Lucas was protecting himself because he intended to murder Andy.

As Andy leaves his father for the summer, he decides not to tell him the story of what happened. He reasons that his father would be too hurt if he found out the truth; better that he think his friend has committed suicide.

As Dr. Zadinski leaves the airport, he takes the cufflink he found in his son's room from his pocket and drops it in the trash. It is wet with his tears.

Themes and Subjects
This is a fast-paced thriller. Andy is presented as an average, likable teenager who is, perhaps, a little more sensitive to people's emotions due to the fairly recent death of his mother and others in his family. His relationship with his father is warm and true, and both characters are believable as they struggle to deal with Andy's growing obsession. However, the true sadness of the tale is that both father and son decide not to communicate fully, for now each will bear a secret forever and the closeness between the two will never be the same.

Booktalk Material
How Andy reacts to the phone call and how he struggles to vindicate himself and convince others that he is telling the truth are good beginnings for a discussion of how such a situation could best be handled. Did Andy overreact? What would you have done? See: the phone call (pp. 1–9); Andy tells his father (pp. 15–21); Andy finds Nina (pp. 24–26); Andy talks to the police (pp. 41–46); and Andy discovers Lucas (pp. 91–93).

Additional Selections
Strange deadly happenings occur to Mary Elizabeth Rafferty at the health club where she works in Joan Lowery Nixon's *The Dark and Deadly Pool* (Dell, 1987).

Bobby and Lauri are convinced that their new neighbor is a murderer in Paul Zindel's *The Undertaker's Gone Bananas* (Bantam, 1984).

236 • CLASSIC TEENPLOTS

In Christopher Pike's *Gimme a Kiss* (Pocket, 1991), a girl fakes her own death in a wild plot to get revenge.

In the mystery *Liars* (Simon, 1992) by P. J. Peterson, Sam, fourteen, discovers he can tell when someone is lying.

About the Author and Book
See under *The True Confessions of Charlotte Doyle*, p. 186.

Bennett, Jay. *The Haunted One.* Fawcett, 1987. Pap. $5.95, 0-449-70314-2 (Grades 7–12).

Introduction
Jay Bennett was born in New York on December 24, 1912. After graduating from New York University, he took a variety of jobs and spent the World War II years in the Office of War Information in Washington. After the war, he held positions as an editor, feature writer, and senior editor of an encyclopedia until he turned to the full-time writing of fast-paced, suspenseful murder mysteries for teenage readers. His first novel in this genre, *Deathman, Do Not Follow Me* (Meredith, o.p.), was published in 1968. It is the story of a young man pursued by art forgers after he accidentally discovers a fake Van Gogh. Two of his more than twenty mysteries for young adults were recipients of the Mystery Writers of America's Edgar Allan Poe Award for the best juvenile mystery novel of the year. He received the first, in 1974, for *The Long Black Coat* (Delacorte, 1973, o.p.) which tells how Phil Brant is hounded by the two accomplices who took part in a robbery with Phil's brother, who is now in Vietnam; the accomplices believe that Phil knows the location of the loot. In the second winner, *The Dangling Witness* (Delacorte, 1974, o.p.), Matt, an usher in a movie theater, witnesses a murder and is afraid of going to the police and of the killer, who is aware that Matt knows his identity. Like these novels, *The Haunted One* is a powerful, thrilling reading experience.

Principal Characters
 Paul Barrett, eighteen and a champion swimmer
 Joe Carson, Paul's boss at his lifeguard job
 Jody Miller, a dancer

Plot Summary
Eighteen-year-old Paul Barrett, a champion swimmer, is spending the summer as a lifeguard at the Jersey shore before entering Syracuse University

in the fall. His chief, Joe Carson, assigns Paul to a fairly deserted stretch of beach. One day a young woman appears. She looks like a goddess and Paul is fascinated by her as she returns day after day. Finally, he summons the courage to talk to her and finds out that her name is Jody Miller and she is a ballet dancer at the famed Lincoln Center in New York City.

Paul falls in love with Jody. But the day after he kisses her for the first time, she suddenly returns to New York City. Bored and sad, he sits on the beach and—even though he is on duty—smokes some grass. Then he hears someone calling to him. By the time he recognizes that it is Jody and she is in distress, it is too late. Although he does finally respond, Jody drowns. He later learns that Jody planned to swim to him and surprise him. Carson tells Paul he did all he could, but Paul must live with his guilt.

Paul returns to school, but the image of Jody is with him always. Then a woman calling herself Jody Miller starts calling him. She tells him to meet her at the Ferris wheel. When he gets there, he sees Jody herself, high above the ground. Paul confides in his friend Joan and she responds that someone must be playing a trick on him.

Distraught, Paul thinks of drowning himself. Carson confesses that after Jody's death he sent a harsh report about the drowning to Jody's twin sister. He says the twin is almost insane with grief.

Paul waits on the beach, knowing she will come. And she does. Jody's twin tells Paul that Jody loved him and that he is responsible for her death. Jody would have become a great ballerina, the twin says, but Paul destroyed it all. Then she takes a gun from her purse. Paul tells her to kill him if that will bring her rest—but it won't work, he asserts, for like him she will forever be haunted.

Paul reaches out and takes the gun. He holds Jody's twin sister close against him for a moment and then watches as she disappears into the darkness.

Themes and Subjects

This is a taut and suspenseful story with overtones of melancholy and an air of the supernatural. The relationship between Paul and Jody Miller takes on an almost mystical quality. Paul is presented as a likable, self-assured young man who is confident of his future and content with his world. But he becomes totally captivated by this somewhat secretive young woman. His descent into a life forever haunted by his mistake is touched with sadness. The lesson of Paul's dereliction of duty may be harsh but will not be lost on the reader.

238 • CLASSIC TEENPLOTS

Booktalk Material
The key to understanding the haunting of one young man lies in his character (see pp. 20–22, 25–28). Readers will also be interested in Paul's feelings about Jody Miller from the very beginning of their relationship (see pp. 31–41, 49–51, 53–58).

Additional Selections
   An unpopular teacher suffers mysterious accidents and Carter decides she must investigate in Diana Shaw's *Lessons in Fear* (Little, Brown, 1987).
   Cici helps seventeen-year-old Jake clear his brother of a murder charge in Willo Davis Roberts's *Twisted Summer* (Simon, 1996).
   In Theodore Taylor's *Lord of the Kill* (Scholastic, 2002), sixteen-year-old Ben is involved in a murder mystery in which the suspects include big-game hunters and an organized crime ring.
   Barrie's mother runs a hair salon called Killer Looks in which all of the employees have done time for murder in Marsha Qualey's *Close to a Killer* (Bantam, 2000).

About the Author and Book
Authors and Artists for Young Adults. Vol. 10, Gale, 1993.
Contemporary Authors. Vol. 79, Gale, 1999.
Drew, Bernard A. *100 Most Popular Young Adult Authors.* Libraries Unlimited, 1996.
Gallo, Donald R. *Speaking for Ourselves.* National Council of Teachers of English, 1990.
Gillespie, John T., and Corinne J. Naden. *Characters in Young Adult Literature.* Gale, 1997.
Lives and Works: Young Adult Authors. Vol. 1, Grolier, 1999.
St. James Guide to Young Adult Writers (2nd ed.). St. James, 1999.
Sixth Book of Junior Authors and Illustrators. Wilson, 1989.
Something About the Author. Gale. Vol. 41, 1986; vol. 87, 1996.
Something About the Author Autobiography Series. Vol. 4, Gale, 1987.
Twentieth-Century Young Adult Writers (1st ed.). St. James, 1994.
Writers for Young Adults. Vol. 1, Scribner, 1997.
See also listing "Selected Web Sites on Children's Literature and Authors."

Clark, Mary Higgins. *Weep No More My Lady.* Pocket, 1998 (1987). Pap. $7.99, 0-671-02558-9 (Grade 10–Adult).

Introduction
Mary Higgins Clark (1929–), a master storyteller of novels with suspenseful, tightly woven plots and believable characters, was born in New York

City, where she attended school and college. She graduated from Fordham University summa cum laude. She held many positions in the media world, including that of scriptwriter and producer of radio programs. Her earliest mystery was *Where Are the Children?* (Dell, 1975). In it, Nancy Eldridge was almost convicted of the deaths of her two children some years before. Now she has remarried and again has two children. When they mysteriously vanish, the finger of guilt again points to her, and in the course of unraveling the plot the author reveals solutions to both past and present mysteries. This situation is typical of Clark's taut, suspenseful stories, in which the present is often used to solve mysteries of the past. Clark has written about two dozen thrillers, some of her latest being collaborations with her talented daughter. Each ends with an amazing plot twist, leaving the reader begging for more.

Principal Characters
  Elizabeth Lange, an actress
  Leila LaSalle, murdered sister of Elizabeth
  Ted Winters, Leila's lover
  Baroness Minna von Schreiber, Elizabeth's friend
  Craig Babcock, Ted's friend
  Henry Bartlett, Ted's lawyer
  Cheryl Manning, actress
  Syd Melnick, Leila's former agent
  Scott, the sheriff
  Alvirah Meehan, housewife from Queens

Plot Summary
Leila LaSalle, a beautiful and talented stage and screen star, is dead and her lover, wealthy Ted Winters, is charged with her murder. Leila's beloved sister, Elizabeth Lange, herself an actress, will be a witness for the prosecution. The state claims Leila's body was thrown from the balcony of her New York apartment. It is Elizabeth, via a phone call at the time of her sister's death, who can place Ted Winters in the apartment. Although Ted denies killing Leila, he admits he was drunk and cannot remember the events of that tragic evening. Elizabeth, subconsciously in love with Ted, is determined to make him pay for Leila's death.

Before the trial begins, Elizabeth receives a call from Baroness Minna von Schreiber, an old friend who owns a luxurious California spa. Minna persuades Elizabeth to fly out to relax for a few days.

Min does not warn Elizabeth about the other guests: Ted Winters, with his business partner Craig Babcock and lawyer Henry Barlett; actress

Cheryl Manning, who kept losing parts to Leila and should benefit from her death; and Leila's former agent Syd Melnick, whom Leila once humiliated. In addition, there is Alvirah Meehan from Queens in New York City, winner of millions in the state lottery. She is an avid movie fan who is "bugged" to record conversations of the rich and famous for a magazine article.

Elizabeth is furious at being tricked into going to the spa, but decides to wait for the return of Sammy, an elderly woman who works for Minna and has sent a message that she wants to see Elizabeth. But before the two can meet, Sammy is murdered. Sammy had discovered poison pen letters sent to Leila that indicated that Ted was in love with someone else.

Next, Alvirah Meehan is nearly murdered and lies in a coma. Elizabeth finds her tapes and realizes what she has been doing.

Elizabeth now believes that Ted is not the murderer, so she sets a trap. She takes her nightly solitary swim in the pool, and is attacked by someone wearing scuba equipment. The sheriff and Ted rescue her at the last minute and the real killer is uncovered as Craig Babcock. Jealous of Ted's relationship with Leila, Craig also knew that if Ted went to prison, he would become the top man in the Winters financial empire.

Alvirah had started Elizabeth on the right track when her tapes revealed that Craig used to imitate Ted's voice at parties. Elizabeth realized it was Craig, not Ted she heard the night of Leila's death.

With the murder solved, Elizabeth and Ted look forward to a future together.

Themes and Subjects
This is an intriguing mystery set against a backdrop of luxury and wealth on the beautiful coast of California. The suspense gradually builds toward its final climax as more and more of the characters come under the umbrella labeled "suspect."

Booktalk Material
An introduction to the characters in this mystery is a good orientation to this novel. See: Leila's and Elizabeth's childhood (pp. 33–40); Elizabeth meets Alvirah (pp. 61–65); the baron and baroness (pp. 71–73); and Ted, Craig, and the lawyer arrive at the spa (pp. 80–84).

Additional Selections
Murder and espionage combine in Margaret Truman's *Murder in the CIA* (Fawcett, 1987), one of her many mysteries set in Washington that

include murder in such institutions as the Supreme Court, FBI, and the White House.

Elizabeth Peters has written a delightful series of mysteries featuring Victorian archaeologist Amelia Peabody. Two titles are *The Mummy Case* (Tor, 1987) and *The Deeds of the Disturber* (Tor, 1988).

Emily Pollifax is the grandmotherly CIA agent in Dorothy Gilman's amusing adventure series that includes *Mrs. Pollifax and the Golden Triangle* (Fawcett, 1988) and *The Amazing Mrs. Pollifax* (Fawcett, 1985).

Ann Waverly, a theology professor, is called in to conduct an undercover investigation of an international cult group in *A Darker Place* (Bantam, 1999) by Laurie R. King.

About the Author and Book
Authors and Artists for Young Adults. Gale. Vol. 10, 1993; vol. 55, 2004.
Contemporary Authors New Revision Series. Vol. 133, Gale, 2005.
St. James Guide to Young Adult Writers (2nd ed.). St. James, 1999.
Something About the Author. Vol. 46, Gale, 1987.
Twentieth-Century Young Adult Writers (1st ed.). St. James, 1994.

Cormier, Robert. *After the First Death.* Dell, 1991 (1979). Pap. $6.50, 0-440-20835-1 (Grades 8–12).

Introduction
Robert Cormier (1925–2000) was born and raised in the town of Leominster, Massachusetts, a community peopled mainly by French Canadian immigrants. Renamed Monument, this town became the setting for many of his novels, in which the theme of an individual in conflict with some aspect of society is often explored. For example, in *The Chocolate War* (see p. 15) and its sequel *Beyond the Chocolate War*, the social institution is the parochial school and its administrative structure; in *I Am the Cheese* (Dell, 1977) and *After the First Death*, it is various aspects of the government. The title of the latter is from a poem by Dylan Thomas, "After the first death there is no other." *After the First Death* is told from the standpoint of three teenage protagonists who become involved in the hijacking of a school bus by terrorists: Ben Marchand, the son of an army general; Kate Forrester, a substitute bus driver; and Miro a young terrorist. The main action tales place over a period of about twenty-four hours. In alternating chapters, two points of view are explored. The first is Ben's and tells of the army's resistance to the terrorist attack; the second is that of the terrorists and their captives on the bus.

Principal Characters

Kate Forrester, a blond, attractive teenager
Artkin and Miro, two thugs who stop the school bus she is driving
Stroll and Antibbe, their accomplices
General Mark Marchand, leader of Inner Delta
Ben, his son

Plot Summary

Kate Forrester, a blond, attractive teenager, has consented to help her sick uncle by driving his school bus with sixteen preschoolers to a summer day camp situated on the outskirts of their small Massachusetts town, close to the large army base at Fort Delta. On a lonely stretch of road, the bus is stopped by a van. Two of the four passengers in the van enter the bus brandishing pistols. The leader, a man about forty, is named Artkin. He is followed by a youth, Miro. They feed the children candy laced with drugs to tranquilize them and then force Kate to drive the bus to the middle of a rickety, abandoned railroad bridge. Kate is unaware that Artkin had promised Miro that at this point the young man could commit his first murder by killing the bus driver. However, to Miro's disappointment, Artkin decides that Kate should have a temporary reprieve so that she can help care for the children.

Gradually a terrified Kate is able to piece together details of the plot. Artkin and Miro, together with their colleagues Stroll, a black man, and brutish Antibbe, are on a terrorist mission to strike a blow for the liberation of their homeland. They have already been involved in similar deadly attacks in other American cities. Particularly vivid in Miro's memory is the one in which his beloved brother Aniel was killed. Their present plan is to establish contact with Fort Delta and make three demands involving the release of political prisoners, payment of ten million dollars, and the dismantling of a secret international brainwashing operation named Inner Delta that has its headquarters at Fort Delta. If these conditions are not met, it will mean death for Kate and the children.

The demands have been sent to the leader of Inner Delta, General Rufus L. Briggs, actually the code name for General Mark Marchand, the renowned behavioral psychologist who has joined the army at his country's request to head this special project.

Soon army units and helicopters buzz around the hijacking site, but they cannot act for fear of reprisals. The first death is accidental, but it gives the terrorists a psychological edge. One of the children dies from the drugged candy. After displaying the body publicly, Artkin lowers it from the bridge to the soldiers below.

Miro is left in charge of the bus while the others remain in the van negotiating with the army and awaiting further instructions from Sedeete, the chief of their central terrorist command. Kate uses this opportunity to try to break Miro's reserve and perhaps arouse some spark of humanity in this bitter teenager who, like his comrades, seems devoid of human feeling. She learns that Miro knows nothing about his parents and that he and his brother were found in a refugee camp by Artkin and were recruited into the terrorist organization. Artkin demanded and received slavish obedience from his two charges and instilled in them the idea that theirs was a holy crusade for freedom. Today Miro still regards Artkin as part savior and part god but Kate detects a glimmer of tenderness in this would-be killer.

Kate discovers that she has an extra key to the bus. Although filled with self-doubt concerning her own inner strength, she devises an audacious plan. When Miro makes one of his brief departures from the bus, she will back it off the bridge and drive to safety. She is fearful that she lacks the courage to carry out her plan, but when the opportunity comes, she rises to the situation and is able to move the bus back several feet before the engine stalls. The terrorists retake the bus. Kate's last hope of saving herself and the children is gone.

A trigger-happy soldier loses control and accidentally kills Antibbe. Artkin retaliates by taking one of the children—Kate's favorite, Benjamin—from the bus and performing a public execution.

By early morning, both sides are becoming increasingly desperate. Luckily, the army has been able to capture the ringleader, Sedeete, in Boston, but the hijackers refuse to believe this news, which, if true, would seriously weaken their position to negotiate. Artkin wants visual proof; he wants one of Sedeete's possessions, a small stone from their homeland, delivered to the van by some neutral unarmed person. General Marchand, who is anxious at all costs to save Inner Delta, can think of only one person to fulfill this operation: his son Ben. He summons Ben and explains what is needed of him. Ben, a sensitive, trusting young man, agrees. Although the army plans to attack the bus and van at 8:35 A.M., General Marchand gives the boy a series of incorrect clues to make him believe he has secret information that the attack will occur at 9:30.

In the early morning light, Ben approaches the van. Inside he is strip-searched and tortured unmercifully until he reveals what his father had known he would—the wrong information concerning the attack. As planned, the terrorists are taken by surprise. In the ensuing shootout, the bus is captured and the children are saved. Stroll is killed first, followed by Artkin, who before dying shoots Ben in the shoulder. Miro, using Kate

244 • CLASSIC TEENPLOTS

as his shield, flees into the woods. In one last attempt to awaken some feelings of humanity in Miro, Kate again questions him about his past. She tells him that she believes Artkin is really his father. Miro realizes that this could be true. Suddenly the full significance of this concept registers, and he begins wailing like a mortally wounded beast. As Kate cradles him like a mother, he shoots her in the heart, before making his successful escape to the highway and freedom.

Ben survives his physical wound but his psychological wounds will not heal. He can neither cope with his belief that he acted like a coward under torture nor accept the extent of his father's duplicity and betrayal and the fact that he was willing to sacrifice his own son for an army security project. Ben unsuccessfully attempts suicide by taking sleeping pills. When he recovers he is enrolled in his father's military school, Castleton Academy, where it is hoped he will resume a normal life. But the extent of his disillusionment is not understood. General Marchand, hoping for reconciliation and forgiveness, goes to see his son at Castleton for a weekend. During the first brief meeting in his son's room, he is able to express his true feelings. When he returns for a second visit, it is too late. Ben's second suicide attempt has been successful.

Themes and Subjects
This brutal story of terror and deception contains scenes of almost unbearable suspense and tension. However, each time the reader's hopes are aroused, the powers of evil triumph. It is a tale of deception and betrayal. Both Ben and Miro have been cruelly deceived by their fathers. Each father has placed his country's well-being over that of his son's and each father, in a sense, is in turn a victim of his own society. The novel questions how far basic human values can be sacrificed in the name of duty and patriotism. The vulnerability of the young and weak when challenging the existing power structure is explored as is the destructive potential of brainwashing. Various aspects of courage and bravery are well-depicted—particularly when Kate, an average girl, successfully conquers her fears to defy the terrorists. In the end, however, this novel delivers the cynical truth that sometimes in life there are no winners, only survivors.

Booktalk Material
This novel can be introduced by a brief discussion of international terrorism and the ethical questions it poses. Some passages of importance are: Miro and Artkin are introduced (pp. 17–23); hijacking the school bus

(pp. 23–31); the death of the first child (pp. 41–46) and Artkin's display of the body (pp. 73–77); and Ben and his father discuss the hijacking (pp. 85–90).

Additional Selections

Laura devotes her energy to finding the terrorist responsible for her brother's death in London in Caroline B. Cooney's *The Terrorist* (Scholastic, 1997).

In Clive Cussler's *Treasure* (Pocket, 1989), Dirk Pitt combats terrorists to rescue hostages in a frozen wilderness in Greenland.

A tough Welshman sets out to find the identity of a terrorist who has murdered his child in Jack Higgins's *Solo* (Pocket, 1989).

In *The One Who Came Back* (Houghton. 1992) by Joann Mazzio, a New Mexico teen must prove he didn't kill his best friend.

About the Author and Book
See under *The Chocolate War* p. 15.

Du Maurier, Daphne. *Rebecca.* Avon, 1994. Pap. $7.50, 0-380-77855-6 (Grade 9–Adult).

Introduction

Daphne du Maurier (1907–1989) was born in London, the daughter of the famous actor Gerald du Maurier and the granddaughter of the famous novelist and artist George du Maurier. She lived most of her adult life in Cornwall. The violent weather and untamed scenery of this area were often used as an atmospheric setting in her most successful novels. Manderley, Maxim de Winter, and Mrs. Danvers are three names that conjure up the suspense-filled world of *Rebecca* and the birth of the modern gothic novel. The story has survived many incarnations since it first appeared in 1938, including a television series and a fine film directed by Alfred Hitchcock and starring Lawrence Olivier and Joan Fontaine. In another of her best-sellers and a good companion volume, *My Cousin Rachel* (Warner, 1971), Philip Ashley falls under the spell of his deceased uncle's widow, but events point to the fact that she may have poisoned his beloved relative. Du Maurier also wrote extensively about her own illustrious family, including an autobiography, *Myself When Young: The Shaping of a Writer* (Time Warner, 1977).

Principal Characters

The second Mrs. de Winter, a shy young girl
Maxim de Winter, a brooding, mysterious Englishman
Mrs. Van Hopper, an obnoxious American
Rebecca, the deceased first Mrs. de Winter
Mrs. Danvers, the ghoulish housekeeper
Jack Favell, Rebecca's cousin and lover

Plot Summary

While in Monte Carlo, a shy young girl who is employed by an obnoxious and vulgar American, Mrs. Van Hopper, meets a mysterious, brooding, and wealthy Englishman, the widower Maxim de Winter. The poor and awkward young woman falls hopelessly in love with de Winter. Despite their obvious differences, a friendly relationship develops. The young woman is delighted, although surprised, when this fascinating man seems to be interested in her, and she is even more amazed when he proposes marriage. The wedding is held in Venice, and the second Mrs. de Winter, which is the only name she is given throughout the novel, looks forward to living at her husband's grand English country estate of Manderley.

The second Mrs. de Winter is many years younger than her handsome husband.

She not only looks up to him but is completely in love with him, and she is thrilled and eager to being their new life together at Manderley. The young woman's happiness, however, is soon tempered by the constant reminders of her husband's first wife, Rebecca. The dead woman's beauty, an image enhanced by a magnificent ball gown, haunts the second Mrs. de Winter with every step she takes inside the mansion.

Manderley's housekeeper, the ghoulish Mrs. Danvers, keeps the second Mrs. de Winter informed about Rebecca's sophistication and charm, which the young girl feels she desperately lacks. Mrs. Danvers spares no feelings as she describes the attributes of the late Rebecca. The new Mrs. de Winter learns that Rebecca died a year earlier in a boating accident. Her husband later identified her body. This tragedy caused him to take a long absence from Manderley, during which he met his new wife.

Although the second Mrs. de Winter tries to make her husband forget Rebecca, she finds it is not an easy task, and she begins to fear that the beautiful woman's memory will forever haunt him. She must also contend with Mrs. Danvers, who makes no secret of the fact that she feels Rebecca will forever be mistress at Manderley and that the newcomer can never replace her.

During Rebecca's life at Manderley, the de Winters gave a great ball each year to which the surrounding country folk were invited. Maxim is now urged to renew the practice, and, surprisingly, he agrees. Anxious to please him, the second Mrs. de Winter dresses in a replica of the gown worn by Rebecca in the portrait. Mrs. Danvers is most helpful with this suggestion. But Maxim is furious when his young wife, wearing the white gown of Rebecca's portrait as well as a dark wig to match her hair, descends the staircase. He rushes from the house. When he returns, he learns that a boat has been found with Rebecca's body in it.

The truth comes out when Maxim de Winter admits that he murdered his first wife. Far from loving her, he hated her for her selfishness and constant affairs with other men. When she confronted him down at the boathouse with her pregnancy, flaunting the fact that the child was not his, he killed her and set her body adrift in the boat. Later, he identified another body as Rebecca's. It is also learned from a Dr. Baker that Rebecca de Winter had cancer and would have died soon anyway. Favell, Rebecca's cousin and one of her lovers, vows revenge on Maxim for what he has done. Maxim and his wife return to Manderley only to discover that Mrs. Danvers has fled and the mansion is on fire. In no time, Manderley is no more.

Maxim and the second Mrs. de Winter now spend their days in quiet, simple contentments, far from their beloved English countryside, traveling from inn to inn, somewhat homeless perhaps and sometimes a bit bored, but together with their past, their memories, and their love.

Themes and Subjects
The dead Rebecca is a central figure in this classic gothic novel. Maxim de Winter is a fine example of the tortured gothic hero, and the second Mrs. de Winter is the naïve young girl, the only one to grow in stature and character throughout the tale. The brooding, mysterious quality of the novel and its characters is in the finest gothic tradition.

Booktalk Material
The first meeting between the naïve young woman and brooding Maxim de Winter is a fine introduction to this gothic novel (pap., pp. 12–20). Other intriguing passages are: Maxim asks her to marry him (pap., pp. 51–56); she meets Mrs. Danvers (pap., pp. 71–79); the ball gown (pap., pp. 213–18); Rebecca's body is found (pap., pp. 265–68); Maxim confesses all (pap., pp. 275–88); and Manderley burns (pap., pp. 385–86).

Additional Selections

In Beth Gutcheon's *More Than You Know* (Morrow, 2000), there are two love stories—one contemporary and the other historical—both with a touch of the supernatural.

A modern-day romance is combined with the life of Emily Brontë as seen through the eyes of one of her descendants in Jill Jones's *Emily's Secret* (St. Martin's, 1995).

In Barbara Delinsky's *Three Wishes* (Simon, 1997), a near-fatal accident brings Bree and Tom together in a love that transcends time and death.

The classic romantic gothic about a governess and her enigmatic employer is Charlotte Brontë's *Jane Eyre* (Bantam, 1988).

About the Author and Book
Authors and Artists for Young Adults. Vol. 37, Gale, 2001.
Contemporary Authors New Revision Series. Vol. 55, 1997.
Cook, Judith A. *Daphne: A Portrait of Daphne du Maurier.* Ulverscroft, 1992.
Gillespie, John T., and Corinne J. Naden. *Characters in Young Adult Literature.* Gale, 1997.
Kelly, Richard Michael. *Daphne du Maurier.* Twayne, 1987.
Shallcross, Martyn. *The Private World of Daphne du Maurier.* Robson, 1991.
Something About the Author. Gale. Vol. 27, 1982; vol. 60, 1990.

Duncan, Lois. *The Twisted Window.* Delacorte, 1987, $14.95, 0-385-29566-9; Dell, pap. 1988, $5.99, 0-440-20184-5 (Grades 7–10).

Introduction

Lois Duncan (1934–) was born in Philadelphia and from an early age showed a proficiency in writing. Before she graduated from college she was a three-time winner of *Seventeen* magazine's annual short story contest. It was as a writer of teenage suspense mystery stories that Duncan became popular. She was a runner-up five times for the Edgar Allan Poe Award (once for *The Twisted Window*) and, in 1992, became the fourth winner of the prestigious Margaret A. Edwards Award for her lasting contributions to young adult literature. Some of her mysteries use elements of the supernatural. For example, in *Locked in Time* (Dell, 1985), a young girl spends a summer with her father and discovers that her new stepfamily is ageless, literally locked in time, and will resort even to murder to protect this secret. Others, like the present novel and the controversial *Killing Mr. Griffin* (Dell, 1978), are more firmly grounded in reality. The latter tells how a group of disgruntled high school students led by a psychopathic malcontent is responsible for the death of a disliked teacher. *The Twisted Window* employs two points of view, one of the heroine, Tracy and the other that of her newfound friend, Brad. The action takes place over approximately one week.

Principal Characters
  Tracy Lloyd, seventeen, a junior at Winfield High
  Her friend Gina Scarpelli
  Brad Johnson, a newcomer
  Mindy, Brad's missing stepsister
  Gavin Brummer, Mindy's father
  Doug and Sally Carver, whom Brad believes have taken Mindy
  Jamie Hanson, Brad's best friend

Plot Summary
Seventeen-year-old Tracy Lloyd, a junior at Winfield High School, and her friend Gina Scarpelli one day become aware in the school cafeteria that a handsome young man neither has seen before is staring intently at them. He introduces himself as Brad Johnson and soon makes it clear that his interest lies only with Tracy. He asks her if he might get in touch with her that evening at her home. Tracy, who is both flattered and intrigued by this attention, tells him that she lives with her aunt and uncle, Cory and Irene Stevenson. On her way home from school, she is convinced that someone is following her and as she reaches her home she sees a car speeding away.

  Tracy's life has been marred by tragedy. For three years she had lived alone with her mother after her parents, both New York actors, were divorced. However, a few months ago her mother was murdered by a mugger outside their Brooklyn Heights apartment. Since then Tracy has lived with the loving but overly protective Stevensons in Winfield, Texas. Although outwardly she is trying to adjust to her new home and surroundings, she is still in a vulnerable state since her mother's death and filled with resentment toward her father, whom she incorrectly believes pays more attention to his successful motion picture career than to her well-being.

  That evening, Brad arrives and the two go for a walk. He confesses that in his anxiety he had followed Tracy home earlier that day and further explains that he has traveled to Winfield from Albuquerque during his school's spring break to effect a special mission. Shortly after his father died of a heart attack while he and Brad were camping in the family's isolated mountain cabin, his mother married Gavin Brummer. They had one daughter, Mindy, but the marriage ended in divorce, with Brad's mother gaining custody. Four months ago, Gavin visited them in Albuquerque and kidnapped his two-and-a-half-year-old daughter. Knowing Gavin has a sister living in Winfield, Brad believes he has relocated here with Mindy. He is determined to find his sister and bring her back home. Knowing there would be opposition to this unusual rescue operation, he told his mother and his best friend Jamie Hanson that he was spending the week at the mountain retreat. Fearful of being recognized by his former stepfather, he visited the local high school looking for an innocent, attractive girl to act as his accomplice and found in Tracy the person he believes can help him. The young girl has some misgivings but is so moved by Brad's story that she agrees.

The next day after school, Tracy goes with Brad to an apartment complex, the Continental Arms, where, according to the telephone directory, a Mr. Brummer lives. Using the excuse that she is a new tenant and needs to use a telephone, she gains access to the Brummer apartment and is greeted by Brummer's apartment mate, Jim Tyler. While Tyler is on the phone she secretly explores the apartment and in one of the bedrooms sees a photograph that matches the one of Mindy that Brad carries in his wallet. She also overhears Jim tell a friend that his roommate will be having dinner that evening at the home of his sister and brother-in-law, Doug and Sally Carver.

When darkness falls, Brad and Tracy find the Carver house and, peering through a kitchen window, see the Carvers seated with a young girl and Gavin around the dining table. Brad is ecstatic that he has found Mindy.

To gain access to the young girl, Tracy calls the Carvers and offers her services as a baby-sitter. The Carvers, who refer to the child as Cricket, think they are in luck because that evening they have theater plans and their regular sitter has just called in sick. After the couple leave, Brad joins Tracy and they rouse a sleeping Mindy. Unfortunately for them, Mr. Carver, who has forgotten the tickets, returns before they can make their escape. Brad rushes to his car and returns with a shotgun. Carver is locked in a closet at gunpoint and the two, with a protesting Mindy, flee in Brad's car. Tracy, fearful of facing the Stevensons after all she has done, agrees to accompany Brad to Albuquerque.

When changing the child's clothes in the car, she notices that Mindy does not have the scars from a childhood accident that Brad had once mentioned. Her suspicions are further aroused when the child stoutly refuses to answer to any name other than Julianne or her nickname Cricket.

ADVENTURE AND MYSTERY STORIES • 251

Brad drives all night. In the morning, when they are just two hours from their destination, he allows Tracy to take the wheel while he sleeps. On the car radio, she hears an emergency news bulletin that sends terror into her heart: Three-year-old Julianne Carver has been kidnapped by her baby-sitter, Tracy Lloyd, and an unidentified accomplice. Warrants have been issued for their arrest. In a panic, Tracy excuses herself when they stop for breakfast and calls Brad's mother. Mrs. Brummer is stupefied at the news and immediately sends Brad's lifelong buddy, Jamie, to go the restaurant to intercede. However, unknown to Tracy, Brad sees her make the telephone call, and, sensing danger, drives off with Cricket.

When Jamie arrives, Tracy is amazed to see that Brad's dearest friend is actually a girl who looks so much like herself that she now realizes why Brad chose her as a helper. Jamie obviously loves Brad deeply and tells Tracy something of his troubled past. He blamed himself for his father's death in the cabin and was slowly sinking into mental confusion when, four months ago, he accidentally ran over and killed his young sister, Mindy. After that he sank into deeper despondency until, unable to accept the ghastly truth, his tortured brain fabricated the kidnapping story.

Jamie is convinced that he has gone to the mountain shack, his favorite haunt when troubled. While Tracy enters the cabin from behind to rescue Cricket, Jamie approaches the front of the cabin where Brad is sitting alone on the steps. After a tense confrontational scene, Brad surrenders to Jamie and, sinking to his knees, says quietly that he now accepts the truth of his sister's death. Inside the cabin, Tracy comforts a frightened Cricket with promises of an early return to her parents.

Themes and Subjects
This page-turning novel combines elements of breathtaking suspense with an exploration of the meaning of reality. Brad's twisted view of the past and Tracy's feelings of rejection by her father represent reality seen through a distorting window. Various aspects of family ties and devotion, as well as the nature of guilt, are depicted in this mystery story.

Booktalk Material
Some interesting passages are: Brad chooses Tracy as his accomplice (pp. 2–11); he follows her home (pp. 15–18); Brad explains why he is in Winfield (pp. 33–37); Tracy looks for clues (pp. 49–56); and outside the Carvers' kitchen (pp. 61–66).

Additional Selections

Fifteen-year-old Macey investigates the burning of a barn and the death of a black school teacher in the suspenseful novel about racism *Burning Up* (Delacorte, 1999) by Caroline B. Cooney.

In Eve Bunting's *Someone Is Hiding on Alcatraz Island* (Berkeley, 1986), a teenager makes the mistake of choosing Alcatraz Island as a place to hide from a gang of toughs.

Stacy wakes from a four-year coma that was caused by a shooting in which her mother was killed in the mystery *The Other Side of Dark* (Dell, 1987) by Joan Lowery Nixon.

In Rob MacGregor's *Hawk Moon* (Simon, 1996), sixteen-year-old Will Lansa returns to Aspen and finds himself at the center of an investigation of his girlfriend's murder.

About the Author and Book

Authors and Artists for Young Adults. Gale. Vol. 4, 1990; vol. 34, 2000.
Children's Books and Their Creators. Houghton, 1995.
Children's Literature Review. Vol. 29, Gale, 1993.
Contemporary Authors New Revision Series. Vol. 45, Gale, 1995.
Continuum Encyclopedia of Children's Literature. Continuum, 2001.
Drew, Bernard A. *100 Most Popular Young Adult Authors*. Libraries Unlimited, 1996.
Favorite Children's Authors and Illustrators. Vol. 2, Tradition Books, 2003.
Fifth Book of Junior Authors and Illustrators. Wilson, 1983.
Gallo, Donald R. *Speaking for Ourselves*. National Council of Teachers of English, 1990.
Gillespie, John T., and Corinne J. Naden. *Characters in Young Adult Literature*. Gale, 1997.
Lives and Works: Young Adult Authors. Vol. 3, Grolier, 1999.
McElmeel, Sharron L. *100 Most Popular Children's Authors*. Libraries Unlimited, 1999.
Major Authors and Illustrators for Children and Young Adults (1st ed.). Vol. 2, Gale, 1993.
Major Authors and Illustrators for Children and Young Adults (2nd ed.). Vol. 3, Gale, 2002.
St. James Guide to Young Adult Writers (2nd ed.). St. James, 1999.
Something About the Author. Gale. Vol. 1, 1971; vol. 36, 1984; vol. 75, 1994; vol. 133, 2002; vol. 141, 2003.
Something About the Author Autobiography Series. Vol. 2, Gale, 1986.
Stevens, Jen. *The Undergraduate's Companion to Children's Writers and Their Web Sites*. Libraries Unlimited, 2004.
Twentieth-Century Young Adult Writers (1st ed.). St. James, 1994.
Writers for Young Adults. Vol. 1, Scribner, 1997.
http://loisduncan.arquettes.com (personal Web site)
www.teenreads.com/authors/au-duncan-lois.asp (author profile)
See also listing "Selected Web Sites on Children's Literature and Authors."

Forsyth, Frederick. *The Day of the Jackal.* Bantam, 1971. Pap. $7.99, 0-553-26630-6 (Grade 10–Adult).

Introduction

British writer Frederick Forsyth was born in Ashford, Kent, on August 25, 1928, and later attended the University of Granada in Spain. At the age of nineteen, he became one of the youngest pilots in the Royal Air Force and served until 1958, when he became a reporter working for a small newspaper before joining Reuters in 1961. Later, he decided to use the same techniques he employed in his journalism and wrote his first novel. The result was *The Day of the Jackal,* which was first published in 1971. It became an instant best-seller and later was made into a successful movie. The story involves a complicated assassination plot to kill Charles de Gaulle. In has been followed by a series of quality thrillers. One is *The Devil's Alternative* (Bantam, 1975), which weaves together such threads as the assassination of the KGB chairman, a Russian security agent spying for the British, a hijacked Swedish tanker, and a mysterious man found in the ocean off the coast of Turkey. Another is *The Odessa File* (Bantam, 1972) in which a young German reporter infiltrates an organization of former Nazi S.S. members. Although written for an adult audience, these thrillers are also enjoyed by high school readers.

Principal Characters

Jackal, code name for the assassin
Charles de Gaulle, president of France
Deputy Commissaire Claude Lebel

Plot Summary

It is 1963, and Charles de Gaulle has taken France out of Algeria. Although many of the French are displeased with the general's decision to withdraw, no group is so enraged as the fanatical right-wing Secret Army Organization, sworn to a man to kill de Gaulle and bring down his government. In their eyes, the withdrawal of their beloved country from what they consider their territory has brought disgrace and dishonor to France. De Gaulle must be assassinated.

However, in six attempts, the organization has not been able to accomplish its objective. Now it seeks outside help. The members contact a professional killer-for-hire, who is unknown to the French police. When the blond, gray-eyed Englishman meets three of the leaders in Vienna, his creed is contained in these words: "A professional does not act out of fervour and is therefore more calm and less likely to make elementary errors."

The code name of the killer is Jackal. For a half-million dollars, he demands total secrecy, even from his employers, and promises that their objective will be met.

So begins the hair-raising, step-by-step anatomy of an assassination, made not one whit less exciting by the reader's knowledge that President Charles de Gaulle died later of natural causes, not an assassin's bullet.

Part of the excitement, and almost admiration, comes from the exacting methods of the killer-for-hire. His plan is meticulous and excruciating in detail. The reader is swept along as the Jackal methodically goes about his business of forging identification papers, falsifying passports, giving himself alternate identities, and most important, perhaps, building for himself a collapsible, powerful, incredibly accurate rifle, with its specially made bullet. Finally, the Jackal plans his approach to the time and place where he knows the general will be and will be assassinated. No one stands in the Jackal's way; without regard for life and totally without compassion, he leaves no trace as he prepares for his work.

What can stand in the way of this finely tuned professional? Almost laughably, his only opposition seems to be a rather short, rumpled French policeman, Deputy Commissaire Claude Lebel. He is given police assistance from as far away as the United States and from all over Europe, along with much support from within his own country, where he is highly regarded.

And yet how can even the best of detectives track down a killer about whom he knows absolutely nothing? In fact, what has he to go on? There is no crime—yet; only the word that an attempt will be made on the general's life. There are no clues, no witnesses—to what? He has nothing.

But in his own way, Lebel is as professional as the Jackal and certainly as methodical. After he reasons that the attempt on the president's life will be made by a foreigner rather than a Frenchman, he begins his hunt by contacting all the top crime officials in the United States and Europe, swearing them to secrecy and asking them to search their files for a political assassin with several successful kills. And from this flimsy beginning follows one of the most fascinating hunts—by both hired killer and dogged detective—in modern-day fiction.

As the assassin completes his plans and nears his destination, the French detective ever so slowly amasses clues. A young Scotland Yard inspector's offhand thought that perhaps so professional a killer, if English, would operate only outside the country leads to England's Foreign Office. And that leads to the remembrance of an extraordinary assassination of a killer rumored to have been English . . . and so it goes.

Through painstaking sifting of the smallest clues, Lebel tracks the unknown killer until he learns his code name and that he is inside France. The Jackal himself realizes how much the authorities know of him as well; perhaps it just makes the task more exciting.

Eventually, the chase comes down to Sunday, August 25, 1963. The Jackal stands before a window on the sixth floor of a house that looks down onto a square where de Gaulle is about to bestow medals on deserving veterans. As the Jackal squints down the telescopic sight and slowly pulls the trigger, the French president does something that no Englishman—even the Jackal—would expect; de Gaulle stoops to kiss the veteran on both cheeks. The bullet barely misses, but it does miss.

The Jackal is astonished at his error. But the few seconds it takes to reload the rifle gives Lebel the time he needs to break into the room. The two men acknowledge each other by name. But this time the detective is faster.

The next day the body of an unknown man is buried in a Paris cemetery. The death certificate states that a foreign tourist was the victim of a hit-and-run accident.

"The day of the Jackal is over."

Themes and Subjects

This is an edge-of-your-seat thriller with all the elements of good detective/spy fiction. It has great adventure, fascinating details of deception and master planning, believable characterizations, a background of history to add the authenticity that is needed to build suspense, and a breath-stopping ending that makes the reader want to tell President de Gaulle to "watch out" or detective Lebel to "hurry up."

Booktalk Material

The Jackal's beginning preparations and the detective's beginning search are good introductions to this work; see: the Englishman sets the terms (pp. 39–50) and Lebel begins his seemingly hopeless manhunt (pp. 190–96, 211–19). Readers who enjoy knowing the details behind an intricate plot will be especially interested in how the Jackal goes about obtaining a weapon and a disguise (see pp. 54–63, 64–80).

256 • CLASSIC TEENPLOTS

Additional Selections
In *Eye of the Needle* by Ken Follett (Avon, 2000), a Nazi spy threatens a young couple on an isolated Scottish island. Also use Follett's *The Key to Rebecca* (NAL, 1980).

During World War II, prisoner of war Joseph Ryan plans on hijacking a train to escape in David Westheimer's *Von Ryan's Express* (NAL, 1985).

In *The Charm School* (Warner, 1988), Nelson DeMille has written a first-rate thriller about Russian spies infiltrating the United States.

Eric Ambler is an old-time master of the novel of intrigue and suspense. Two of his classics are *A Coffin for Dimitrios* (Vintage, 1995) and *Journey into Fear* (Vintage, 1995).

About the Author and Book
Contemporary Authors New Revision Series. Vol. 137, Gale, 2005.
World Authors, 1975–1980. Wilson, 1985.

Francis, Dick. *Bolt.* Fawcett, 1987. Pap. $7.95, 0-449-21239-4 (Grade 10–Adult).

Introduction
Dick Francis was born Richard Stanley Francis in South Wales on October 31, 1920. Before becoming a writer of successful mystery stories, Francis served in the Royal Air Force and, after World War II, followed in his father's footsteps and became a jockey. During this career he won more than 350 races and, from 1953 to 1957, he was jockey to Queen Elizabeth the Queen Mother. After a serious fall in 1957, he retired and took up "racing journalism," which in turn led to writing a number of top-flight mysteries that combine a horse-racing setting with fast-paced suspense. In *Break In* (Berkley, 1986), a smear campaign directed at a millionaire gradually involves Kit Fielding, a championship steeplechase jockey. The story of how a crippled ex-jockey solves the mystery of the deaths of four thoroughbred horses is told in *Whip Hand* (Berkley, 1989). Dick Francis's novels are read and enjoyed by both sports and mystery fans in the high school grades and up.

Principal Characters
    Kit Fielding, tall steeplechase jockey
    Danielle de Brescou, his fiancée
    Princess Casilia, her aunt
    Count Litsi, nephew of Princess Casilia

Roland de Brescou, husband of Princess Casilia
Henri Nanterre, descendant of de Brescou's business partner

Plot Summary
Christmas (Kit) Fielding is the tallest English jockey in steeplechase racing. He is engaged to Danielle de Brescou, niece of Princess Casilia's husband, French aristocrat Roland de Brescou.

The princess asks him to stay at her elegant home for a time because she is frightened for the safety of her husband, who is wheelchair-bound. He is threatened by Henri Nanterre, a descendant of de Brescou's business partner, who demands that de Brescou sign papers to allow their company in France to make arms.

When Kit discovers that two of the princess's top horses have been killed by a "bolt," a so-called humane killer, he realizes that Nanterre means business. He orders dog patrols around the stables. But trouble continues. A third horse is killed and Count Litsi, the princess's nephew, is nearly killed in a fall. Another relative, Cousin Beatrice, arrives and informs Kit that Nanterre has threatened to kill him and disfigure Danielle.

As Kit tries to protect Danielle, he learns why she has been somewhat cool to him of late. She is unsure whether she can live a life of fearing for his safety on the track.

Kit comes up with a plan, which ends with Nanterre being caught planting a bomb in his car. Faced with a witness to his act, Nanterre signs a contract that Kit had drawn up by de Brescou's lawyers. It changes the name of the firm and requires that both partners sell their interests. That takes care of that crisis.

But then Kit learns that Nanterre could not have been at the stables the night the horses were killed. He may have been responsible for everything else, but he was not the killer of the horses!

Kit arrives at the stables too late to save another horse, but he learns the horse-killer's identity—Maynard Allardeck, who had long carried on a feud with Kit's family and begrudged him any success. Allardeck is dead.

With the mystery solved and the princess's family no longer in danger, Kit can resume his relationship with Danielle. She assures him that living in fear for his safety is better than living without him at all.

Themes and Subjects
This is a fast-paced mystery with the added action of steeplechase racing. Kit Fielding is presented as an intelligent, dedicated, and, above all, honorable man. The book also nicely portrays the sense of honor that often governs people's lives. And for readers who enjoy a look into the lives of

the wealthy, in this case the "English" aristocracy, the scenes of home life with the princess are especially interesting.

Booktalk Material
Readers who like sports and action will be especially interested in descriptions of the races and racing stables; see the details of racing (pp. 9–13, 58–66, 130–37). See also the description of the "bolt" (pp. 74–85).

Additional Selections
A young lawyer who likes surfing gets a case involving parents who are accused of selling their newborn son in John DeCure's *Reef Dance* (St. Martin's, 2001).

Computers seem to be the only link in a series of murders by a psychopathic killer in Jeffery Deaver's *The Blue Nowhere* (Simon, 2001).

Edgar Rice Burroughs and his son solve a murder mystery just before the bombing of Pearl Harbor in *The Pearl Harbor Murders* (Berkeley, 2001) by Max Allan Collins.

K. J. Erickson's *Third Person Singular* (St. Martin's, 2001) involves the murder of a teenage girl and is told from four different points of view.

About the Author and Book
Authors and Artists for Young Adults. Gale. Vol. 5, 1990; vol. 21, 1997.
Contemporary Authors New Revision Series. Vol. 100, Gale, 2002.
World Authors, 1970–1975. Wilson, 1980.
See also listing "Selected Web Sites on Children's Literature and Authors."

Konigsburg, E. L. *Father's Arcane Daughter.* Aladdin, 1999 (1976). Pap. $6.95, 0-689-82680-X (Grades 6–9).

Introduction
When E. L. Konigsburg (1930–) was awarded the Newbery Medal in 1997 for *The View from Saturday* (Aladdin, 1996), she became the fifth author in the history of the award to receive it twice. The others are Joseph Krumgold, Elizabeth Speare, Katherine Paterson, and Lois Lowry. Her first award was for *From the Mixed-up Files of Mrs. Basil E. Frankweiler* (Dell, 1967). Like many of her novels, including *The View from Saturday*, *Father's Arcane Daughter* deals with family relationships complicated by special conflicts within the chief protagonist. Dictionaries define *arcane* as "mysterious, secret" and "known or understood only by those having secret,

special knowledge." Reading this book, one wonders whether the title refers to Caroline, the mysterious woman who appears after an absence of seventeen years, or to young Heidi, the troubled product of a second marriage. The surprise ending reveals the truth. The intricately structured plot shifts between two time periods. The first takes the form of a recollection by the narrator, Winston, of events that took place in 1952. The second is told in fragments of a conversation between Winston and his sister Heidi, more than twenty-five years later in the 1970s.

Principal Characters
    Winston Eliot Carmichael, a wealthy seventh-grader
    Heidi, his younger sister
    Their father and mother
    Caroline, the daughter of Mr. Carmichael's first marriage

Plot Summary
Seventh-grader Winston Eliot Carmichael and his family—mother, father, and younger sister, Heidi, who at age ten is strangely underdeveloped—live a life of luxury in Pittsburgh, complete with butler, chauffeur, and the rest. Winston worries about his unusual sister, although his parents usually ignore her erratic behavior. Another subject that is not discussed is Caroline, Mr. Carmichael's daughter by his first marriage. She was kidnapped while a freshman in college and is believed to have died in the fire that destroyed the kidnappers' hideout during a shootout with the police.

Winston is a precocious but lonely child, who has developed a sensitivity and wisdom beyond his years.

On what would be Caroline's thirty-fifth birthday, the deadline for her to claim her inheritance, a strange woman appears at the Carmichael mansion saying she is Caroline. She passes test after test and there can be no doubt that she really is Caroline. She explains that after the nightmare of the kidnapping, she wanted a new life. She changed her name to Martha Sedgewick and went to Ethiopia.

Caroline and Winston become friends. She secretly has Heidi tested and discovers that she is above average intelligence but suffers physical disabilities including deafness. Before Caroline leaves for college, she gives Winston a letter and tells him the contents will reveal whether she really is his half-sister.

Twenty-five years later, the envelope is still sealed. Caroline has just died. Winston, a writer, and Heidi, now a successful business executive, make funeral plans and decide to open the letter. They learn that Caroline was really Martha Sedgewick, an orphan who had indeed worked in

Ethiopia. She had been the personal nurse of Caroline's grandmother, who had confused Martha with her dead granddaughter; to please the dying woman, Martha gradually assumed Caroline's identity and in the process gained a lot of intimate details about the Carmichael family. After the old lady's death, Martha decided to present herself as Caroline, not because of the inheritance, but as a way to help this tortured family.

Brother and sister decide to keep Martha's secret and bury these documents with her. To them, she will always be their sister Caroline, the first of Mr. Carmichael's two arcane daughters.

Themes and Subjects

This novel explores the nature of truth, as both an abstract and a pragmatic entity. Defining truth as "that which works" explains the decision to hide the deception involving Caroline's reappearance. Complex family relationships are explored in the interaction among a mother who, driven by concern for social status, is damaging her family's future, a father eager to believe lies to assuage ghosts from the past, a son who feels guilt that he is normal when his sister is not, and an intelligent daughter trapped in a malfunctioning body. The extent to which the past can dominate the present is explored, as is the theme that wealth does not necessarily produce happiness. This novel also depicts how the intervention of a single individual can change and reshape the lives of others.

Booktalk Material

A definition of the word *arcane* and brief explanation of the family situation when Caroline appears should interest readers. Some interesting episodes are: a typical Saturday for Winston and Heidi (pp. 26–29); Winston tells about his only friend, Barney (pp. 24–26); a description of the kidnapping and its effects (pp. 14–19); Caroline and Winston get to know one another (pp. 37–40); and Caroline passes some truth tests administered subtly by Mrs. Carmichael (pp. 43–45).

Additional Selections

When sixteen-year-old Ivy begins working on her family history, the trail leads to the Adirondacks and the talented Aunt Jo in Joan Bauer's *Backwater* (Putnam, 1999).

Popular fourteen-year-old Lori, her overweight brother, and their mother share guilt after the death of their father in *Takeoffs and Landings* (Simon, 2001) by Margaret Peterson Haddix.

The Newbery Medal winner *Jacob Have I Loved* (HarperCollins, 1980) by Katherine Paterson deals with rivalry between two sisters in a Chesapeake Bay setting.

On her fourteenth birthday, Julie secretly discovers who her birth mother really is but hides this information from her stepparents in Ingrid Tomey's *The Queen of Dreamland* (Simon, 1996).

About the Author and Book
Authors and Artists for Young Adults. Gale. Vol. 3, 1990; vol. 41, 2001.
Biography Today: Author Series. Vol. 3, Omnigraphics, 1997.
Bostrom, Kathleen Long. *Winning Authors: Profiles of the Newbery Medalists.* Libraries Unlimited, 2003.
Children's Books and Their Creators. Houghton, 1995.
Children's Literature Review. Gale. Vol. 1, 1976; vol. 47, 1998; vol. 81, 2002.
Contemporary Authors New Revision Series. Vol. 106, Gale, 2002.
Continuum Encyclopedia of Children's Literature. Continuum, 2001.
Drew, Bernard A. *100 Most Popular Young Adult Authors.* Libraries Unlimited. 1996.
Eighth Book of Junior Authors and Illustrators. Wilson, 2000.
Estes, Glenn E. "American Writers for Children Before 1990." In *Dictionary of Literary Biography.* Vol. 52, Gale, 1985.
Favorite Children's Authors and Illustrators. Vol. 3, Tradition Books, 2003.
Gallo, Donald R. *Speaking for Ourselves, Too.* National Council of Teachers of English, 1993.
Hanks, Dorrel Thomas. *E. L. Konigsburg.* Twayne, 1993.
Jones, Raymond. E. *Characters in Children's Literature.* Gale, 1997.
Lives and Works: Young Adult Authors. Vol. 5, Grolier, 1999.
McElmeel, Sharron L. *100 Most Popular Children's Authors.* Libraries Unlimited, 1999.
Major Authors and Illustrators for Children and Young Adults (1st ed.). Vol. 4, Gale, 1993.
Major Authors and Illustrators for Children and Young Adults (2nd ed.). Vol. 5, Gale, 2002.
St. James Guide to Children's Writers (5th ed.). St. James, 1999.
St. James Guide to Young Adult Writers (2nd ed.). St. James, 1999.
Something About the Author. Gale. Vol. 4, 1973; vol. 48, 1987; vol. 94, 1998.
Stevens, Jen. *The Undergraduate's Companion to Children's Writers and Their Web Sites.* Libraries Unlimited, 2004.
Third Book of Junior Authors. Wilson, 1972.
Twentieth-Century Children's Writers (4th ed.). St. James, 1995.
Twentieth-Century Young Adult Writers (1st ed.). St. James, 1994.
See also listing "Selected Web Sites on Children's Literature and Authors."

Nixon, Joan Lowery. *The Séance.* Harcourt, 2004 (1980). Pap. $5.95, 0-15-205029-9 (Grades 7–9).

Introduction
Joan Lowery Nixon (1923–2003) was a prolific writer of fiction, nonfiction, and picture books for children and young adults. Born in Los Angeles and

educated in southern California, she was an elementary school teacher before she began writing fiction at the insistence of her three daughters and son. She wrote in a number of genres, including historical novels such as the Orphan Train Quartet and stories of contemporary teen problems such as *Maggie, Too* (Harcourt, 1985, o.p.), about a young girl's search for identity. But she is best known as a writer of more than fifty complicated thrillers that contain unusual characterizations, complex plotting, and thrilling climaxes. She won the coveted Edgar Allan Poe Award for best juvenile novel from the Mystery Writers of America three separate times: in 1980, for *The Kidnapping of Christina Lattimore* (Harcourt, 1979), in which the kidnappers of a young journalist claim that she was their accomplice; in 1981 for *The Séance*, a locked-door mystery involving six girls who gather for a test of psychic powers that ends in a disappearance and murder; and in 1987 for *The Other Side of Dark* (Dell, 1988), the story of Stacy, who wakens after being in a coma for four years, remembering the identity of the man who shot her and killed her mother.

Principal Characters
    Lauren, the seventeen-year-old narrator
    Aunt Mel, Lauren's aunt with whom she lives
    Sara Martin, who comes to live with them
    Jep Jackson, sheriff's deputy
    Carley Hughes, school baseball hero
    Fant Lester, across-the-fence neighbor
    Roberta Campion, who supposedly has psychic powers
    Ila Hughes, Carley's grandmother
    Doris Martin, Sara's mother
    Sheriff Ashe Norvell

Plot Summary
Lauren has lived in a small East Texas town with her Aunt Mel since the age of four; she is now a senior in high school. Sara Martin, also seventeen, has been sent from the foster care agency to live with them. She is beautiful and boy-crazy. Sara persuades mousy Roberta Campion, who supposedly has psychic powers, to hold a séance for some of the girls. Lauren reluctantly attends with her friends. During the séance, Sara begins shrieking. When the lights are turned on, she is missing, even though both the front and back doors are locked.

    The next morning, Sara's body is found in a forest area. She has drowned in a swamp. Some people—such as Ila Hughes, grandmother of attractive baseball star Carley—think it is the work of evil spirits. Sara's mother arrives from Houston, but leaves after the funeral. The sheriff questions Lauren and others, convinced that Sara left the séance for an assignation and that one of them is Sara's accomplice.

The sheriff tries to re-create the séance and all but Roberta show up. Two days later, Roberta's body is found. Now everyone knows it is murder. When the sheriff confronts Lauren again, she admits that Sara was planning to run away with a man the night of her murder and that Lauren helped her escape from the locked house.

Several nights later, Carley visits Lauren and says he was the person with whom Sara was going to run away. But Sara had already left the meeting place when he got there. He and Lauren decide to do some investigating.

After Carley leaves, Lauren is attacked at gunpoint and ordered to a car parked in her driveway. The assailant is Carley's grandmother, who confesses that she committed the murders to prevent her grandson from being bewitched and losing both his soul and bright future to devilwoman Sara.

She forces Lauren into the driver's seat of her car. Frantically, the girl thinks of a method of escape. She has no alternative but to drive headlong into the side of a brick building. Later, recovering in the hospital, she learns that Mrs. Hughes is undergoing psychiatric tests, but, best of all, Aunt Mel has been making plans for her entrance into college next year.

Themes and Subjects
This basically an edge-of-the-seat thriller that successfully creates an atmosphere of growing danger and terror. The story of the relationship between Aunt Mel and Lauren shows how adversity can bring people together. Small-town pettiness and gossip are also well portrayed.

Booktalk Material
Discussing the subject of séances should serve as a brief introduction to the book. Some useful passages are: Sara and Lauren quarrel (pp. 16–22,); the séance (pp. 32–39); Sheriff Norvell investigates (pp. 40–47); and Lauren reviews Sara's boyfriends and learns of her death (pp. 55–58).

Additional Selections
While staying with a great-aunt, three children learn about the family curse in *House of Shadows* (Tor, 1984) by Andre Norton.

In David Gifaldi's *Yours Till Forever* (HarperCollins, 1989), a high school senior sees disturbing similarities between his friends and his dead parents.

A scuba-diving vacation in Hawaii turns into an adventure involving murder, ghosts, and underwater thrills in Christopher Pike's *Bury Me Deep* (Pocket, 1991).

Fourteen-year-old Drew is convinced there is a ghost in her crusty grandfather's house in Stephanie Tolan's *Who's There?* (Morrow, 1994).

About the Author and Book
Authors and Artists for Young Adults. Gale. Vol. 12, 1994; vol. 54, 2004.
Biography Today: Author Series. Vol. 1, Omnigraphics, 1995.
Children's Books and Their Creators. Houghton, 1995.
Children's Literature Review. Vol. 24, Gale, 1991.
Contemporary Authors New Revision Series. Vol. 135, Gale, 2005.
Continuum Encyclopedia of Children's Literature. Continuum, 2001.
Drew, Bernard A. *100 Most Popular Young Adult Authors*. Libraries Unlimited, 1996.
Favorite Children's Authors and Illustrators. Vol. 4, Tradition Books, 2003.
Fifth Book of Junior Authors and Illustrators. Wilson, 1983.
Gallo, Donald R. *Speaking for Ourselves,* National Council of Teachers of English, 1990.
Gillespie, John T., and Corinne J. Naden. *Characters in Young Adult Literature*. Gale, 1997.
Lives and Works: Young Adult Authors. Vol. 6, Grolier, 1999.
Major Authors and Illustrators for Children and Young Adults (1st ed.). Vol. 4, Gale, 1993.
Major Authors and Illustrators for Children and Young Adults (2nd ed.). Vol. 6, Gale, 2002.
St. James Guide to Young Adult Writers (2nd ed.). St. James, 1999.
Something About the Author. Gale. Vol. 8, 1976; vol. 44, 1986; vol. 78, 1994; vol. 115, 2000; vol. 146, 2004.
Something About the Author Autobiography Series. Vol. 9, Gale, 1990.
Twentieth-Century Young Adult Writers (1st ed.). St. James, 1994.
See also listing "Selected Web Sites on Children's Literature and Authors."

Paulsen, Gary. *Hatchet.* Atheneum, 2000 (1987). $16.95, 0-689-84092-6 (Grades 7–10).

Introduction
Gary Paulsen was born in Minnesota and grew up as an "army brat." His childhood was marred by disruptive family situations, a painful shyness, and unpopularity with both teachers and fellow students. His one salvation as a youngster was finding joy and escape in the books from his local libraries. After working in a variety of jobs including farmer, rancher, singer, soldier, trapper, archer, sailor, teacher, engineer, and sled dog

worker, he became a technical writer. By 1977, he had written a number of fiction works including his first children's book *Mr. Tucket* (Dell, 1969), which eventually became a five book series about Francis Tucket's exploits in the Old West. Paulsen is primarily known for a series of harrowing adventure stories often involving miraculous outdoor survival narratives, near-death experiences, encounters with wild animals, and unsupportive parents. Many are also coming-of-age stories in which the young central characters take a journey, sometimes real, sometimes figurative, to greater self-knowledge and maturity. This is true of the superior survival novel *Hatchet*, which also reveals Paulsen's love and respect for nature and the outdoors. It has been followed by several sequels, *The River* (Dell, 1991), *Brian's Winter* (Dell, 1996) *Brian's Return* (Dell, 1998) and *Brian's Hunt* (Dell, 2003).

Principal Characters
    Brian Robeson, thirteen
    His just-divorced mother and father

Plot Summary
Brian Robeson, age thirteen, thinks the hatchet his mother gives him for his scout belt is a little hokey but doesn't say so. He is getting ready to stay with his father for the summer in the Canadian north woods. His parents are newly divorced. Brian has been angry with his mother since he saw her kissing another man. He knows why she wanted the divorce; that's The Secret and he can't wait to tell his father.

Flying north to his father as the only passenger in a Cessna, the pilot lets him take the controls. Then the unthinkable happens. The pilot has a heart attack, the plane crashes, and Brian survives with nothing but the clothes he is wearing and the hatchet.

So begins Brian's fifty-four days of struggle in the wilderness. At first, the panic-stricken boy has no idea how to begin to survive. But slowly the will to live begins to surface. He drinks water from the lake, starts to search for food, and then learns how to catch fish. One day he hears the drone of a plane but it flies off without seeing him. That night Brian tries to cut himself with the hatchet, hoping he will die.

But after that, he decides that no matter what happens, he will not give in. That is easier said than done. But he rescues the survival kit from the plane. It contains freeze-dried food and a transmitter. Just as he is settling down to his first "home cooked" meal in fifty-four days, he is astonished to see a plane appearing. It lands on the lake; a pilot jumps out and says he heard the emergency transmitter. Brian is rescued.

After Brian's ordeal, he is a celebrity for a few days, and in their joy at having him alive, his parents almost seem as though they will get back together . . . almost. But things soon return to normal, except that Brian is forever changed. It's not just that his body has become lean and wiry, not just that all kinds of food are still a wonder to him, not just that he becomes more thoughtful, or that he has quiet, reflective times about his period of survival, but Brian knows that he has come of age; he is tough now, tough where it counts—in the head.

And although he thinks about it, Brian never tells his father about The Secret.

Themes and Subjects

This is a realistic story of strength, toughness, survival, and a boy's growing up in almost impossible conditions. Brian is a likable boy who, when faced with true terror and almost insurmountable odds, finds strength and courage within himself, although at times he almost gives in to despair. It is also an exciting picture of survival in the wilderness and how the small, seemingly inconsequential lessons learned in some almost forgotten classroom can make the difference between survival and death.

Booktalk Material

The ways in which Brian tries to reason out his problems and struggles to remember techniques of survival are a good introduction to this tale. See: Brian tries to land the plane (pp. 13–15); should he drink the lake water? (pp. 43–45); the search for berries (pp. 60–66); building a fire (pp. 84–86); and the first plane brings despair (pp. 115–18).

Additional Selections

A now-classic story of survival is Jean Craighead George's *Julie of the Wolves* (HarperCollins, 1972), which tells of Miyax's lonely trek across 300 miles of Alaskan wilderness.

Howie and Laura must struggle to survive when their fellow campers leave them naked and alone on an island in Brock Cole's *The Goats* (Farrar, 1987).

Jack McCaskill's fourteenth summer is enlivened by a forest fire in Montana's wilderness, an alcoholic ex-forest ranger, and an older brother with personal problems in *English Creek* (Penguin, 1984) by Ivan Doig.

In Farley Mowat's *Lost in the Barrens* (Starfire, 1956), two boys are lost in Canada's barren northlands.

About the Author and Book
Authors and Artists for Young Adults. Gale. Vol. 2, 1984; vol. 17, 1995.
Biography Today: Authors Series. Vol. 1, Omnigraphics, 1995.
Children's Books and Their Creators. Houghton, 1995.
Children's Literature Review. Vol. 82, Gale, 2003.
Contemporary Authors New Revision Series. Vol. 129, Gale, 2004.
Continuum Encyclopedia of Children's Literature. Continuum, 2001.
Drew, Bernard A. *100 Most Popular Young Adult Authors.* Libraries Unlimited, 1996.
Favorite Children's Authors and Illustrators. Vol. 5, Tradition Books, 2003.
Gale, David. "The Maximum Expression of Being Human: A Talk with Gary Paulsen," *School Library Journal,* June, 1997, pp. 24–29.
Gallo, Donald R. *Speaking for Ourselves.* National Council of Teachers of English, 1990.
Gillespie, John T., and Corinne J. Naden. *Characters in Young Adult Literature.* Gale, 1997.
Jones, Raymond E. *Characters in Children's Literature.* Gale, 1997.
Lives and Works: Young Adult Authors. Vol. 6, Grolier, 1999.
McElmeel, Sharron E. *100 Most Popular Children's Authors.* Libraries Unlimited, 1999.
Major Authors and Illustrators for Children and Young Adults (1st ed.). Vol. 5, Gale, 1993.
Major Authors and Illustrators for Children and Young Adults (2nd ed.). Vol. 6, Gale, 2002.
Paulsen, Gary. *My Life in Dog Years.* Delacorte, 1998.
St. James Guide to Children's Writers (5th ed.). St. James, 1999.
St. James Guide to Young Adult Writers (2nd ed.). St. James, 1999.
Sixth Book of Junior Authors and Illustrators. Wilson, 1989.
Something About the Author. Gale. Vol. 22, 1981; vol. 50, 1988; vol. 54, 1989; vol. 111, 2000; vol. 158, 2005.
Twentieth-Century Children's Writers (4th ed.). St. James, 1995.
Twentieth-Century Young Adult Writers (1st ed.). St. James, 1994.
Writers for Young Adults. Vol. 2, Scribner, 1997.
See also listing "Selected Web Sites on Children's Literature and Authors."

Thompson, Julian. *The Grounding of Group 6.* Holt, 1997 (1983). $16.95, 0-8050-5085-X (Grades 7–10).

Introduction
Julian F. Thompson (1927–), the author of many prize-winning books for young people, worked exclusively with teenagers before devoting his full-time efforts to writing. As an example, in the early 1970s, he founded an alternative school in northern New Jersey and spearheaded efforts to champion the rights of teenagers. He and his wife, the artist Polly Thompson, live in Burlington and West Rupert, Vermont. When it appeared in

1983, *The Grounding of Group 6* was a trailblazer in at least two ways: first, its subject was shocking, and second, it was one of the first high-quality novels to appear first in paperback. Since this auspicious beginning, Thompson has written many other successful novels for this group, many of which explore new subjects. For example, *Simon Pure* (Scholastic, 1987, o.p.) pokes fun at academe by way of a wacky plot to turn a liberal arts college into a profitable business school. A more conventional title is *Terry and the Pirates* (Atheneum, 2000, $17), a humorous adventure story about a girl captured by pirates on a remote island in the Bermuda Triangle. About teenagers and readers, the author has said, "It's natural and proper for kids to want to read [and discuss] books about people like themselves. It's right for them to value and enjoy such books—books whose characters are asking the same questions they're asking. . . . This is values education at its best, when kids are discussing, even arguing about books and the suitability of this behavior over that one."

Principal Characters
Six boarders at the Coldbrook Country School:
Coleman DeCoursey, Arthur Robey Sullivan, Sara Slayman Winfrey, Marigold, Louisa Rebecca Locke, and their leader, Nat Rittenhouse.

Plot Summary
Some parents send their teenagers to expensive, discreet, remote Coldbrook Country School because they don't conform. For a fee, the school will ground them, which means dropping their bodies into one of the limestone faults near the school. None of the bodies has ever been discovered.

The five sixteen-year-olds who arrive at Coldbrook and are assigned to Group 6 are only aware that their parents have shipped them off for some kind of test. The group consists of two boys and three girls. Coleman DeCoursey, called Coke, is a kid whose hair never stays in place; he has been a loser from the word go. His parents have taken his name out of the school register so he doesn't embarrass them.

Arthur Robey Sullivan, or Sully, is a smallish kid who people think is a nerd, although he isn't. He has been a pain to his mother because he gets in the way of all the "uncles" who come to stay at the house.

Sara Slayman Winfrey embarrassed her parents by being thrown out of school for plagiarism. Marigold grew up in a household that was very open about sex. Then she told her mother she was pregnant. When her mother asked who the father was, Marigold mentioned her mother's lover . . . hence Coldbrook.

Louisa Rebecca Locke sees things in a different way from most people. Her mother understood, but then her mother died and her father thinks she is out of step with everything.

The Group 6 leader is Nat Rittenhouse. The school dean told him he is in charge of the "ultimate bad seeds." He is to lead them off on a camping expedition and then poison them. The faculty will take care of the "grounding." Why is Nat willing to do this?

It has to do with a father who is unwilling to pay his son's gambling debts. Nat is in so deep, it seems the only way out is this assignment.

But the misfits become real to Nat on the trail and he decides he cannot go through with the plan. He secretly returns to Coldbrook, where he discovers that he will be the next to be grounded. Then he tells the group that their families are planning to have them killed. When the shock wears off, they discuss their options. Eventually they decide to return to the school to find proof of the conspiracy between the school and the parents. But before they do, Sara is nearly killed by one of the faculty who has been searching for them. Sully saves her life and shoots the man with a bow and arrow.

Nat and Group 6 do gain access to the school files and finally come upon the Group 6 folder containing letters from all their families. Before they have time to congratulate themselves, the door opens and in walk the four remaining teachers. They are all armed.

Through the conversations and explanations that follow, Nat fixes the four a drink, which they accept as a toast to their victory. The drinks are poisoned, just as the five members of Group 6 were to be poisoned.

The rest of it goes according to the Group 6 plan: remove any evidence, dispose of the bodies in the way Group 6 was supposed to be grounded, call their respective parents and let them know what they've discovered, then show up at the school as though they've been out in the wilderness all these weeks.

And that is just what they do.

Themes and Subjects

Julian Thompson has written an offbeat, suspenseful, yet comic novel that pulls no punches in its depiction of the depths to which humans can succumb. And yet the characters of the Group 6 members and of the young leader are sympathetically and interestingly drawn, as is their gradual blossoming into adulthood and responsibility under the most harrowing of circumstances.

Booktalk Material
An introduction to the members of Group 6 is a good orientation to this novel (see pp. 6–12). See also: how Nat gets involved (pp. 18–20, 52–60); Nat tells the five about their "grounding" (pp. 92–100); the Group decides on a plan for survival (pp. 114–22); Group 6 goes into training (pp. 137–41); and the Group discusses getting back at their parents (pp. 155–57).

Additional Selections

In Claudio Apone's *My Grandfather Jack the Ripper* (Herodias, 2000), thirteen-year-old Andy Dobson, a clairvoyant Londoner, travels back in time to discover the true identity of the legendary murderer.

In the thriller *Spy High: Mission One* (Little, Brown, 2004) by A. J. Butcher, set in the year 1960, a group of students at a school known as Spy High are training to become secret agents.

Sharon's beach party at a resort with a reputation for being haunted ends in murder in Linda Cargill's *Pool Party* (Scholastic, pap., 1996).

In Alane Ferguson's *Overkill* (Bradbury, 1992), Lacey is arrested for a murder she has dreamed about committing.

About the Author and Book
Authors and Artists for Young Adults. Vol. 9, Gale, 1992.
Children's Literature Review. Vol. 24, Gale, 1991.
Contemporary Authors New Revision Series. Vol. 102, Gale, 2002.
Gallo, Donald R. *Speaking for Ourselves.* National Council of Teachers of English, 1990.
Lives and Works: Young Adult Authors. Vol. 8, Grolier, 1999.
Major Authors and Illustrators for Children and Young Adults (1st ed.). Vol. 6, Gale, 1992.
Major Authors and Illustrators for Children and Young Adults (2nd ed.). Vol. 8, Gale, 2002.
Something About the Author. Gale. Vol. 55, 1989; vol. 99, 1999.
Something About the Author Autobiography Series. Vol. 13, Gale, 1992.
Writers for Young Adults. Vol. 3, Scribner, 1997.
See also listing "Selected Web Sites on Children's Literature and Authors."

Voigt, Cynthia. *Homecoming.* Simon Pulse, 2002 (1981). Pap. $6.99, 0-689-85132-4 (Grades 6–9).

Introduction
Cynthia Voigt (1942–) has created a literary landmark with the seven novels she has written about the Tillerman family. In the first, *Homecoming,*

the reader meets the four Tillerman children: Dicey, the courageous, indomitable thirteen-year-old heroine, who assumes family leadership when their mother abandons them; ten-year-old James; quiet Maybeth, age nine; and Sammy, a boisterous, stubborn boy of six. This novel tells of their harrowing but finally successful odyssey in search of a new home with their maternal grandmother. The first sequel, the Newbery Medal-winning *Dicey's Song* (Fawcett, 1982), begins "And they lived happily ever after. Not the Tillermans." It chronicles the adjustment of the children to life with Gran. For example, Dicey has trouble letting go of the maternal responsibilities she had assumed while trying to get along at school and make new friends. In the last in the series, *Seventeen Against the Dealer* (Atheneum, 1989), Dicey, now twenty-one, decides to become independent and begins a career as a boat builder.

Principal Characters
   Dicey Tillerman, thirteen
   Her mother, who is acting strangely
   Her siblings, James, ten; Maybeth, nine; Sammy, six
   Aunt Cilla
   Runaways Louis and Edie
   Father Joseph
   Mrs. Abigail Tillerman, their grandmother

Plot Summary
Thirteen-year-old Dicey Tillerman notices that her mother is acting increasingly vague and distant, as though all the problems of caring for her four fatherless children have suddenly overpowered her reason. As well as Dicey, there is ten-year-old precocious James; sweet Maybeth, age nine; and boisterous Sammy, age six. One night Mamma packs the family in their beat-up jalopy and heads for Aunt Cilla's in Bridgeport, Connecticut. She parks in a shopping mall on the way, leaves the car, and never returns. Dicey gathers the family together and they set off to walk to Aunt Cilla's.

   Their journey, lasting more than two weeks, is a saga of courage and devotion to each other. They sleep in parks and graveyards, they fish in streams, they earn money in a variety of ways. At last they meet a young summer session student who drives them right to Aunt Cilla's doorstep.

   But further disappoint awaits them. Aunt Cilla died several months before and her mousy daughter, Eunice, lives there now. The children discover that their mother is in a mental institution in Massachusetts but that they have a maternal grandmother, Mrs. Abigail Tillerman, who lives in Maryland. Again, the Tillermans hit the road.

They have many more adventures but finally arrive at their grandmother's. She turns out to be a bad-tempered recluse who wants no part of her grandchildren. Fortunately, Abigail allows the children to stay on a day-to-day basis and gradually she begins to mellow and show concern for their future. In time she concedes that the only major barrier to their staying is a financial one. When it is shown that through social security and revitalizing the farm, this could be overcome, she is happy to change her mind. The Tillermans have found a home at last.

Themes and Subjects
This is not only a moving story of courage and resourcefulness but also a testimony to the strength of family ties and devotion. The loving, nurturing relationship among the children is excellently presented, and Dicey, in her quiet, unassuming way, exemplifies true heroism by assuming responsibility and facing almost impossible obstacles. The importance of a real home in a child's life is stressed; and through her suspenseful narrative the author shows that exciting survival stories do not require a desert island or a remote wilderness.

Booktalk Material
An introduction to Dicey, her sister and brothers, and the situation they confront when deserted should interest readers. Specific passages are: Dicey faces the situation (pp. 13–16); James and Sammy fish and James has an accident (pp. 53–57); Sammy bargains for food (pp. 76–78); carrying bags at the shopping center (pp. 81–84); and the children meet Windy (pp. 94–100).

Additional Selections
Catherine tries to recover from guilt caused by her father's suicide in Jean Thesman's *The Last April Dancers* (Avon, 1987).

Virginia Hamilton's Newbery Medal winner *M. C. Higgins the Great* (Macmillan, 1974) is about a thirteen-year-old African American boy growing up in a loving family in Appalachia.

A migrant worker and his family settle down in a permanent home in Sue Ellen Bridgers's *Home Before Dark* (Replica, 1998).

In Paul Fleischman's *Seek* (Cricket, 2001), seventeen-year-old Rob records important sounds in his life including the voice of the father he never knew.

About the Author and Book
Authors and Artists for Young Adults. Gale. Vol. 3, 1990; vol. 30, 1999.

Bostrom, Kathleen Long. *Winning Authors: Profiles of the Newbery Medalists.* Libraries Unlimited, 2003.
Children's Books and Their Creators. Houghton, 1995.
Children's Literature Review. Gale. Vol. 13, 1987; vol. 48, 1998.
Contemporary Authors New Revision Series. Vol. 94, Gale, 2001.
Continuum Encyclopedia of Children's Literature. Continuum, 2001.
Drew, Bernard A. *100 Most Popular Young Adult Authors.* Libraries Unlimited, 1996.
Favorite Children's Authors and Illustrators. Vol. 6, Tradition Books, 2003.
Fifth Book of Junior Authors and Illustrators. Wilson, 1983.
Gallo, Donald R. *Speaking for Ourselves.* National Council of Teachers of English, 1990.
Gillespie, John T., and Corinne J. Naden. *Characters in Young Adult Literature.* Gale, 1997.
Lives and Works: Young Adult Authors. Vol. 8, Grolier, 1999.
McElmeel, Sharron L. *100 Most Popular Children's Authors.* Libraries Unlimited, 1999.
Major Authors and Illustrators for Children and Young Adults (1st ed.). Vol. 6, Gale, 1993.
Major Authors and Illustrators for Children and Young Adults (2nd ed.). Vol. 8, Gale, 2002.
Reid, Suzanne. *Presenting Cynthia Voigt.* Twayne, 1995.
St. James Guide to Young Adult Writers (2nd ed.). St. James, 1999.
Something About the Author. Gale. Vol. 33, 1983; vol. 79, 1995; vol. 116, 2000; vol. 160, 2005.
Stevens, Jen. *The Undergraduate's Companion to Children's Writers and Their Web Sites.* Libraries Unlimited, 2004.
Sutton, Roger. "A Solitary View—Talking with Cynthia Voigt," *School Library Journal,* June, 1995, pp. 28–32.
Twentieth-Century Young Adult Writers (1st ed.). St. James, 1994.
Voigt, Cynthia. "1995 Margaret A. Edwards Acceptance Speech: Thirteen Stray Thoughts about Failure," *Journal of Youth Services for Young People,* Fall, 1995, pp. 23–32.
Writers for Young Adults. Vol. 3, Scribner, 1997.
See also listing "Selected Web Sites on Children's Literature and Authors."

White, Robb. *Deathwatch.* Dell, 1972. Pap. $6.50, 0-440-91740-9 (Grades 7–12).

Introduction

Robb White (1909–90) was one of the post-World War II writers who pioneered adventure fiction for young adult readers. More than half of his over two dozen novels are set in and around the Pacific Ocean during World War II, a setting with which he was very familiar (he was born in the Philippines and served in the U.S. Navy during the war). In such now-out-of-print titles as *Up Periscope* (later filmed with his script) and *Flight Deck*, various aspects of the naval war are explored through the exploits of young heroes who overcome obstacles to accomplish daring missions. Later he experimented with more daring subjects in such novels as *Deathwatch*, which traces the outcome of a deadly cat-and-mouse game played out by a young loner and a wealthy unscrupulous businessman who is also an avid hunter. Of this novel, Keith Lawrence wrote: "[It] is the most unified and carefully plotted of all White's novels and has never been out of print since its initial publication. . . . [It] is a gripping drama and also the stuff of myth, where spirited, ingenious youth holds its own and eventually triumphs over the selfish, worldly-wise, and privileged ruthlessness of age. . . . With an exciting and significant story to tell, *Deathwatch* has attracted young readers to other of White's fiction, fiction that remains an engrossing portrait of its era."

Principal Characters
Ben, twenty-two, who acts as a desert guide
Mr. Madec, a corporation lawyer

Plot Summary
Ben, twenty-two, needs money for his last year in college so he agrees to act as a desert guide for Mr. Madec, a corporation lawyer, who wants to hunt bighorn sheep. Madec turns out to be a cunning, trigger-happy hunter. He accidentally shoots and kills an old prospector and tries to bribe Ben into not reporting the incident. Ben refuses. Madec shoots two slugs into the old man with Ben's rifle so that it will appear that the young man did the killing, then sends Ben into the desert without food or water.

So begins a cat-and-mouse game, as Madec pursues Ben with his gun, enjoying hunting human prey. Ben grows weaker, his body a raw pulp of wounds, his lips and tongue badly swollen. Just as an uncontrollable itching, the final symptom of death by dehydration, begins, Ben finds water in a small cave. He is able to kill some birds that come there to drink.

Madec, now believing Ben must be dead, begins making preparations to climb a steep butte by driving pitons into the stone wall. Ben witnesses Madec's work and that night decides on a bold plan. Using Madec's footprints to escape detection, he walks in them backward to his enemy's camp. There, close to the jeep, he buries himself completely in the sand, using a hollow slingshot as tubes for breathing.

The next morning, when Ben is sure Madec is again at work on the rock face, he emerges from the sand. He attracts Madec's attention by setting the tent on fire. Ben is able to wound Madec with a rain of buckshot from his powerful slingshot; then he takes him captive.

Ben returns to town by jeep with Madec and the body of the old prospector. But there Madec is able to fabricate such an impressive alibi that, with the help of his two crafty lawyers, few people believe Ben's side of the story. Even the slingshot, which Ben says he put in the jeep, is not found. Finally, when the slingshot is found where Madec hid it, and an investigating doctor proves that it was Madec's gun and not Ben's that killed the prospector, the case is broken. Madec is placed in custody and Ben is allowed to go free.

Themes and Subjects
Basically, a fine, edge-of-the-seat thriller, *Deathwatch* is also a study in good versus evil, with good triumphing through fair and aboveboard methods. Ben is portrayed as a young man with human faults, but also as someone who has principles that he will uphold in spite of great adversity. The author describes the desert vividly and the adaptation made by plants and animals to survive in this environment.

Booktalk Material
The significance of the title in context of the story could be used as an introduction, as well as the theme of various forms of manhunts as portrayed on television or in movies and books. Some incidents to use are: Madec finds the prospector (pp. 16–19); Madec sends Ben away (pp. 35–41); and Ben assessses his situation (pp. 44–45).

Additional Selections
April and her family are on the run trying to escape a hired hitman in Lois Duncan's *Don't Look Behind You* (Bantam, 1990).

Two Australian boys search for gold in Allan Baillie's *Secrets of Walden Rising* (Viking, 1997), a tale of adventure and murder.

Having escaped from an Australian racist cult in *Ratface* (Ticknor, 1994) by Garry Disher, three youngsters are pursued by a cult deputy.

Eighteen-year-old Tyrel faces unusual problems on his first cattle drive when rustlers attack and plan on taking no prisoners in Cotton Smith's *Dark Trail to Dodge* (Walker, 1997).

About the Author and Book
Authors and Artists for Young Adults. Vol. 29, Gale, 1997.
Children's Literature Review. Vol. 3, Gale, 1978.

Contemporary Authors New Revision Series. Vol. 1, Gale, 1981.
Junior Book of Authors. Wilson, 1951.
St. James Guide to Young Adult Writers (2nd ed.). St. James, 1999.
Something About the Author. Gale. Vol. 1, 1971; vol. 83, 1996.
Something About the Author Autobiography Series. Vol. 1, Gale, 1986.
Twentieth-Century Young Adult Writers (1st ed.). St. James, 1994.
See also listing "Selected Web Sites on Children's Literature and Authors."

6

Animal Stories

Bagnold, Enid. *National Velvet.* HarperTrophy, 1999 (1949). Pap., $5.99, 0-380-81056-5 (Grades 6–9).

Introduction

Enid Bagnold (1889–1981) spent her childhood in many different places. She was born in Kent, England, raised in Jamaica, and later went to schools in Germany, Switzerland, France, and England. She worked as a journalist before serving in a hospital and driving an ambulance with the French Army during World War I. She is not primarily a children's writer. She achieved her greatest triumphs as a playwright, with such West End/Broadway hits as *A Matter of Gravity* and *The Chalk Garden*. The latter was successfully filmed with a cast that included Deborah Kerr and Edith Evans. Her reputation in juvenile literature rests solely on one book, *National Velvet*, which was an immediate success when it was first published in the United States in 1939. It tells the story of a Sussex butcher's family of five girls and one boy, whose actions were partially inspired by the author's own children and their interest in horses. In the novel, the youngest girl, fourteen-year-old Velvet, who daydreams continually about horses, wins a piebald horse in a raffle. When a local delivery boy suggests that the horse should enter the Grand National, Velvet takes the challenge seriously. The popular 1944 film adaptation of the novel stars Elizabeth Taylor as Velvet with Mickey Rooney and Angela Lansbury in supporting roles.

Principal Characters

Velvet Brown, a young English girl
Mr. and Mrs. Brown, her parents
Her four sisters
Mi Taylor, her father's helper
Mr. Cellini, owner of a horse stable

Plot Summary

Velvet Brown lives in a small village on the English coast with her parents, four sisters, and four-year-old brother. Her father is the local butcher, and his helper is Mi Taylor. A rather fragile-looking young girl, Velvet is the opposite of her mother in physical appearance but much like her in courage and determination. Mrs. Brown is a muscular, athletic woman who once was famous as a swimmer of the English Channel. She shows her daughter much love and understanding.

Velvet has always loved horses and racing. Her sisters used to feel the same way but they have now become interested in other pursuits. The family still has one horse, but Miss Ada is now old and Velvet looks after her with tender loving care in the Browns' tradition of good horsemanship. Velvet is still so interested in horses that she enters the local horse show, but with very little hope of winning.

One day there is much commotion in town. Velvet watches a runaway piebald horse racing through the streets. She is impressed by the magnificent-looking animal and secretly dreams that she owns him. For the piebald's owner, this last escape is just another sign of the horse's rebelliousness—he will sell the horse in a lottery. A determined Velvet persuades her sisters to spend some of their hard-earned money on a lottery ticket. Velvet then dreams she is astride the magnificent piebald as they clear the stone fences and ditches of the Grand National, England's most famous race. Despite the fact that girls are not allowed to race in the Grand National, Velvet is certain she could win.

One day, Velvet delivers a meat order to Mr. Cellini, an elderly man who owns a stable of fine horses. Mr. Cellini is impressed by the young girl's love and knowledge of horses. A few days later, Velvet is saddened to learn that Mr. Cellini has died and much surprised to discover he has left her five beautiful horses. As an even greater surprise, her lottery ticket wins the piebald.

Now, with the proud, muscular piebald grazing on a high field, Velvet not only can enter horses in the local shows, but can concentrate on entering the piebald in the Grand National. Three of her sisters enter the local show, but only Velvet wins.

Mi Taylor is so impressed with Velvet's horsemanship and courage that he joins her in a secret plan to disguise her as a boy so she can ride in the Grand National. Although there are many complications—the high entry fee, the special riding habit, and the overnight lodging in London—Mi manages to overcome these difficulties. He also resolves the problem of Velvet's disguise by giving her a haircut and masquerading her as a Russian-speaking jockey.

With Mi's whispered advice in her ears—"Think of yer Ma!"—Velvet and the piebald start the race in a field of twenty horses. Mi rushes to the most treacherous jump to wait for Velvet to clear the hurdle, but the crowd is so thick that he cannot see. Before he can return to the finish line, the race is over and Velvet has won.

After the race Velvet is taken to the infirmary for an examination. The doctor discovers that she is a girl. When the news reaches the judges, Velvet is disqualified, but to Mi Taylor and her parents, she is still the winner. Velvet becomes a celebrity. Mrs. Brown remembers her own experience after the Channel swim and advises Velvet not to be swept up in the short-lived public adulation. Her mother's commonsense attitude helps Velvet to avoid the sensation-seeking crowds. Later, after some of the publicity has subsided, Velvet begins to enjoy the pleasure associated with her fame.

Themes and Subjects

Family love and personal courage are the two combined elements in this story. Many young girls will identify with Velvet and her love of horses as well as her struggle to realize her dreams. The closeness between mother and daughter is well depicted.

Booktalk Material

To stimulate interest, ask young readers "What would you do?" and then have them look for the answer in the book. An exciting read-aloud incident is Velvet's victory in the local horse show (pp. 152–57) and a humorous one is sister Edwina primping for her boyfriend (pp. 116–19).

Additional Selections

A teenage girl is fired from her job on a horse farm because she is too close to solving a mystery in Lynn Hall's *Ride a Dark Horse* (Avon, 1987).

In Robert Newton Peck's entertaining *Horse Thief* (HarperCollins, 2002), Tullis is determined to save thirteen doomed rodeo horses.

Ann Rinaldi's *A Ride into Morning: The Story of Temple Wick* (Harcourt, 1991) is the story of a woman who kept her horse in her house to save it during the Revolutionary War.

With her magic crystal, sixteen-year-old Tirza wishes for a horse for her brother in Anne McCaffrey's *If Wishes Were Horses* (NAL, 1998).

About the Author and Book

Children's Books and Their Creators. Houghton, 1995.
Contemporary Authors New Revision Series. Vol. 40, Gale, 1993.
Continuum Encyclopedia of Children's Literature. Continuum, 2001.
Fourth Book of Junior Authors and Illustrators. Wilson, 1978.

Major Authors and Illustrators for Children and Young Adults (1st ed.). Vol. 1, Gale, 1993.
Major Authors and Illustrators for Children and Young Adults (2nd ed.). Vol. 1, Gale, 2002.
St. James Guide to Children's Writers (5th ed.). St. James, 1999.
Something About the Author. Gale. Vol. 1, 1971; vol. 25, 1981.
Stevens, Jen. *The Undergraduate's Companion to Children's Writers and Their Web Sites.* Libraries Unlimited, 2004.
Twentieth-Century Children's Writers (4th ed.). St. James, 1995.
See also listing "Selected Web Sites on Children's Literature and Authors."

Burnford, Sheila. *The Incredible Journey.* Dell, 1995 (1961). Pap., $5.99, 0-440-22670-8 (Grade 6–Adult).

Introduction

Sheila Burnford (1918–84) was born in Scotland and educated in Edinburgh and in England and Germany. During World War II she served for a time in the Royal Naval Hospital's Voluntary Aid Detachment and later was an ambulance driver. In 1951, she and her husband and three daughters emigrated to Canada, where they settled in Ontario. Her love of the Canadian wilderness and of animals is apparent in her fiction. In her reminiscences, she tells of three beloved pets: an English bull terrier, named Bill, to whom she talked and read; a Siamese kitten, Simon, who bonded instantly with the dog; and, later, a Labrador retriever. From the kinship of these three animals came the inspiration for *The Incredible Journey*, an instant success when it was first published, as an adult novel, in 1961. Burnford writes so convincingly about animal habits and life in the Canadian north country that readers may feel this is a true story rather than a work of fiction. On the other hand, the work has been criticized for excessive anthropomorphism, with one critic stating, "The author ascribes just about every human characteristic except speech to her protagonists." Readers, however, seem to have ignored this feature because the story is still popular with book lovers of all ages.

Principal Characters

Jim Hunter, an English professor
Peter and Elizabeth, his children
Bodger, an aging English bull terrier
Luath, a Labrador retriever
Tao, a Siamese cat

Plot Summary
Professor Jim Hunter, his son Peter, and daughter Elizabeth, will be away in England for a year, so they leave their animals—Bodger, a bull terrier, Luath, a Labrador retriever, and Tao, a Siamese cat—with John Lockridge. Lockridge lives about 250 miles from the Hunter home in northern Ontario. The animals do not adjust to their new surroundings and after a few months they decide to go home.

Bodger has trouble keeping up on the journey. He is attacked by a bear cub and so badly wounded that the party must rest for a few days. When they reach an Ojibway encampment, the natives see the animals as a sign of good fortune and look after their needs, but the three still leave in the morning.

Soon after, Tao tries to cross a swollen stream and is carried away. She is rescued by a young girl called Reino Nurmi, who takes care of her. Three days later, Tao leaves to find her friends. She narrowly escapes death when a vicious lynx follows her but she is finally reunited with her traveling companions.

Luath is later attacked by a porcupine during a hunting expedition. With several quills embedded in his face, he can scarcely open his mouth. But they are saved by Mr. and Mrs. McKenzie, who farm land not far from the Hunter home. After Luath's wounds heal, the three resume their journey.

Meanwhile, the Hunters have returned home and are disconsolate over the loss of their pets. Then, one day, Bodger, Luath, and Tao appear on the doorstep. They are battle-scarred and near starvation, but they are home after an incredible journey.

Themes and Subjects
The author tells the story of three remarkable animals, their devotion, their courage, and their bonds of friendship.

Booktalk Material
The descriptions of the animals (pp. 5–7) are a fine introduction to the story. Excellent read-aloud incidents are: first day of the journey (pp. 24–27); the bear cub attacks (pp. 33–37); the Ojibway encampment (pp. 44–48); crossing the river (pp. 61–65); Tao's rescue (pp. 70–78); and meeting an unfriendly farmer (pp. 83–86).

Additional Selections
As spring turns to summer, a yearling buck and his twin sister travel together after the death of their mother in Jim Arnosky's *Long Spikes* (Houghton, 1992).

282 • CLASSIC TEENPLOTS

In Dhan Gopel Mukerji's Newbery Medal winner *Gay-Neck* (Dutton, 1968), a brave carrier pigeon performs dangerous missions during World War I.

Eric Knight's classic *Lassie Come Home* (Holt, 1978) is the story of how a faithful collie returns to the boy who was his first master.

The true story of a girl and her father who raise sixteen geese and help them migrate south is told in Patricia Hermes's *Fly Away Home* (Newmarket, 1996).

About the Author and Book
Children's Books and Their Creators. Houghton, 1995.
Children's Literature Review. Vol. 2, Gale, 1976.
Contemporary Authors New Revision Series. Vol. 49, Gale, 1995.
Continuum Encyclopedia of Children's Literature. Continuum, 2001.
Fourth Book of Junior Authors and Illustrators. Wilson, 1978.
Jones, Raymond E. *Characters in Children's Literature.* Gale, 1997.
St. James Guide to Children's Writers (5th ed.). St. James, 1999.
Something About the Author. Gale. Vol. 3, 1972; vol. 38, 1985.
Twentieth-Century Children's Writers (4th ed.). St. James, 1995.
See also listing "Selected Web Sites on Children's Literature and Authors."

Eckert, Allan W. *Incident at Hawk's Hill.* Little, Brown, 1995 (1971). Pap., $6.99, 0-316-20948-1 (Grades 6–9).

Introduction
Allan Eckert was born in Buffalo, New York, in 1931. Before turning to full-time writing, he worked as a postman, private detective, fireman, plastics technician, cook, trapper, draftsman, artist, and police reporter. As a nonfiction writer he gained great acclaim (including four Pulitzer Prize nominations) for his ability to merge fact and fiction in a series of popularizations of factual events. He calls this "documentary fiction." Another technique he uses frequently is "hidden dialogue," a device whereby unsubstantiated conversations are reported as if they actually happened. These dialogues are indicated by the use of quotation marks. His intense love of nature and history are evident in *Incident at Hawks Hill*, published originally for adults, is based on an actual incident in Canadian history. Six-year-old Ben, son of a pioneering family, became lost and was adopted by a female badger, which took him to her underground home and cared for him there. Although some critics have found excessive violence in the novel, this has not deterred the many readers who have been engrossed

by this story throughout the years. In 1998, the author wrote a sequel, *Return to Hawk's Hill* (Little, Brown, 1998).

Principal Characters
   Ben MacDonald, a shy six-year-old
   William and Esther, his parents
   John, Beth, and Coral, his older siblings
   George Burton, a fur trapper

Plot Summary
The MacDonalds are homesteaders about 20 miles north of Winnipeg. By 1870, their oldest child, John, is sixteen and their youngest, Ben, is six. His parents are worried about Ben, who is shy, undersized, and withdrawn. He rarely speaks. One day a new neighbor, fierce-looking George Burton, arrives with his equally fierce-looking dog Lobo. Burton asks permission to set traps on their property. Ben is terrified of Burton but, to everyone's amazement, he subdues Lobo's fierceness by imitating the animal.

Ben befriends a female badger with a battle scar, a notched right ear. One day he becomes lost wandering the prairie and crawls into a badger hole at nightfall. Later the badger tries to enter her hole, but Ben drives her off with snarls. The next day the badger returns and Ben recognizes his friend by her ear. Imitating her chattering and whining, he gains her confidence and she brings him food. Later that day, Ben sees Burton surveying the area on horseback but retreats into the hole.

As the days pass, Ben and the badger form a close relationship and she teaches him to hunt. The MacDonalds, meanwhile, are still hunting for their lost son. One day John discovers him and takes him home.

The boy's readjustment to his home is speeded by allowing the badger to enter the house as a pet. Shortly afterward, Burton again visits the farm, and when the badger attacks him, the man shoots him. MacDonald drives Burton off his property, but Ben cannot be consoled.

As he is about to bury the badger, he notices a flicker of life. There seems little chance that she will recover, but Ben and his family will do their very best.

Themes and Subjects
The amazing bond between the boy and the badger is tenderly and convincingly portrayed. The elements of family love and personal courage are additional points in the story. The author's extensive knowledge of animal life, particularly of badger lore, adds fascinating sidelights to the story, as do the details of pioneer life in the Canadian West.

Booktalk Material

Some of the author's descriptions of badgers, as given in Chapters 2 and 4, will serve as an introduction, along with a brief synopsis of the plot. Specific passages of interest are: Ben subdues Lobo (pp. 28–29); Ben is discussed by his parents (pp. 35–39); the badger digs her nest (pp. 48–52); and Ben finds the badger (pp. 69–73). With a small group, John Schoenherr's excellent illustrations also could be used, although they are murkily reproduced in the paper edition.

Additional Selections

Paul Sullivan's *Legend of the North* (Royal Fireworks, 1995) is a novel involving two narratives, the first about a young wolf and the second about an elderly Inuit.

Felix Salten's classic *Bambi: A Life in the Woods* (Pocket, 1926) is about an orphaned fawn in Austria and its growth to maturity.

A boy and a captive wolf who have both suffered at the hands of humans form a close relationship in Daniel Pennac's *Eye of the Wolf* (Candlewick, 2003).

In Jamie Bastedo's *Tracking Triple Seven* (Red Deer, 2001), teenage Benji becomes involved with biologists tracking grizzly bears in Canada.

About the Author and Book

Authors and Artists for Young Adults. Vol. 18, Gale, 1996.
Contemporary Authors New Revision Series. Vol. 45, Gale, 1995.
Continuum Encyclopedia of Children's Literature. Continuum, 2001.
Fourth Book of Junior Authors and Illustrators. Wilson, 1978.
Major Authors and Illustrators for Children and Young Adults (2nd ed.). Vol. 2, Gale, 2002.
Something About the Author. Gale. Vol. 29, 1982; vol. 91, 1997.
Something About the Author Autobiography Series. Vol. 21, Gale, 1996.
See also listing "Selected Web Sites on Children's Literature and Authors."

North, Sterling. *Rascal.* Dutton, 1984 (1963). $16.99, 0-525-18839-8 (Grade 6–Adult).

Introduction

Sterling North (1906–74) grew up on a farm close to Edgerton, Wisconsin. After graduating from the University of Chicago, he held several posts in the publishing world, including literary editor of the *Chicago Daily News,* New York's *Post,* and New York's *World Telegram and Sun.* In the field of juvenile literature, he wrote many Landmark Books for Random House and later founded and wrote for a highly respected series of biographies for Houghton Mifflin on American History called North Star Books. The series—now, sadly, out of print—included biographies of Edison, Twain, Thoreau, and Radisson. Presently, his fame rests on two novels, *So Dear to My Heart* (Dell, o.p.) and *Rascal*. The former, published in 1947, tells the story of a boy growing up at the beginning the twentieth century and his determination to raise a black sheep and enter it in the State Fair competition. *So Dear to My Heart* was filmed by Disney in 1949 and contained such popular songs as "Lavender Blue (Dilly Dilly)." *Rascal*, subtitled *A Memoir of a Better Era*, takes place in 1918, and tells how eleven-year-old Sterling found and cared for a baby raccoon. The book is largely autobiographical and is touchingly illustrated by John Schoenherr. It covers a year in the boy's life until he is forced to return the animal to the wild. This charming story has been enjoyed by generations of readers.

Principal Characters
 The author, age eleven
 His indifferent father
 Uncle Fred, Aunt Lillie, and their family
 Rascal the raccoon

Plot Summary
At age eleven, Sterling North is growing up in rural Wisconsin without a mother, with a permissive, almost indifferent father, and two sisters who visit only occasionally. His brother is in the Army fighting in France. It is a lonely life until Sterling captures a raccoon, which he names Rascal. Soon they go everywhere together, including a camping trip with Sterling's father. Sterling and Rascal even defeat rival Sammy Stillman in a pie eating contest at the fair.

When influenza strikes the area, Sterling is sent to live with his Uncle Fred, Aunt Lillie, and their family. Rascal goes too. Although the family welcomes the raccoon, it is not always easy for Sterling to keep up with him. Rascal likes bright, shiny objects and tends to steal things, like an engagement ring. He also raids the neighbors' gardens and has to be locked up. When Sammy teases him in his cage, Rascal bites him and everyone is afraid of rabies. To make matters worse, the family hires a housekeeper who is not pleased to have a raccoon underfoot.

Although he will miss him dreadfully, Sterling knows he must let Rascal go free. So one night he and Rascal take a canoe to the far end of the creek. In time, they hear the soft call of a female raccoon. Rascal hesitates, then runs to join his future mate. Sadly, Sterling paddles away from the place where they parted.

Themes and Subjects
Important themes in this novel are growth toward maturity and self-reliance. The bond between boy and animal is shown with deep feeling and affection.

Booktalk Material
Many incidents in the book are ideal for booktalks, including: Sterling and his friend Oscar Sunderland capture Rascal (pp. 18–23); Sterling has skunk trouble (pp. 29–30); Rascal eats at the table (pp. 32–34); the search for Theo's engagement ring (pp. 50–52); the pie eating contest (pp. 126–28); Rascal goes to school (pp. 138–41).

Additional Selections
   Snowy, a wolf cub that has been kept as a pet, escapes, searches for a pack, and eventually has a family of its own in Henrietta Branford's *White Wolf* (Candlewick, 1999).
   Cassie befriends an arctic wolf and must find its owners before it becomes a target for hunters or the police in *The Dog with Golden Eyes* (Milkweed, 1998) by Frances Wilbur.
   When Jim's alligator eats the neighbor's dog, he is forced to face some hard truths in Barbara Kennedy's *The Boy Who Loved Alligators* (Atheneum, 1994).
   In Charlotte Graeber's *Grey Cloud* (Macmillan, 1979), Tom and Orville become friends when they train pigeons for a big race.

About the Author and Book
Contemporary Authors New Revision Series. Vol. 84, Gale, 2000.
Major Authors and Illustrators for Children and Young Adults (2nd ed.). Vol. 6, Gale, 2002.
St. James Guide to Children's Writers (5th ed.). St. James, 1999.
St. James Guide to Young Adult Writers (2nd ed.). St. James, 1999.
Something About the Author. Gale. Vol. 1, 1971; vol. 26, 1982; vol. 45, 1986.
Third Book of Junior Authors. Wilson, 1972.
Twentieth-Century Children's Writers (4th ed.). St. James, 1995.
Twentieth-Century Young Adult Writers (1st ed.). St. James, 1994.
See also listing "Selected Web Sites on Children's Literature and Authors."

Rawls, Wilson. *Where the Red Fern Grows.* Delacorte, 1996 (1961). $16.95, 0-385-32330-1 (Grades 5–9).

Introduction
Woodrow Wilson Rawls (1913–84) was born in Scraper, Oklahoma, on a farm where he was taught primary grade subjects at home by his mother. His formal education ended in the eighth grade when the poverty caused by the Great Depression forced him to look for work. His jobs, usually as a carpenter, took him to various parts of the United States as well as Mexico, South America, Canada, and Alaska. Always an avid writer, he didn't try for publication until he was in his forties. Using his own boyhood as an inspiration, he wrote *Where the Red Fern Grows*, which was serialized in the *Saturday Evening Post* before publication in 1961 as an adult novel. It tells the moving story of a boy growing up in rural Oklahoma in the 1930s and of the mutual love and bond he shares with his two hunting dogs. The title comes from an Indian legend told in the Ozarks about a beautiful red fern—since considered sacred—that grew on the spot where a young Indian girl and boy perished during a blizzard. This novel was also the basis of a fine movie released in 1974. A more lighthearted view of the relationship between humans and animals is depicted in the author's 1976 novel, *The Summer of the Monkeys* (Dell, $5.99).

Principal Characters
Bill (Billy) Colman, ten years old
His two hunting dogs
His father and grandpa

Plot Summary
Billy Colman is ten years old when he catches "dog fever" growing up in the Ozarks. He begs his parents to buy him a pair of hound dogs, but money is scarce. So Billy sells bait, vegetables, and berries as well as pelts of small animals he has trapped. In two years, he has fifty dollars and Grandpa orders the pups from a kennel in Kentucky.

The pups cost only forty dollars, so Billy buys gifts for his family. The boy and his two dogs become inseparable. The pups show as much devotion for each other as they do for Billy. The larger and more ferocious is a male, Old Dan; Little Ann is less bold but more intelligent. With the help of one of his grandfather's hunting trucks, Billy trains the dogs to become excellent hunters. Within a few months the dogs are ready, and Billy sets out for his first coon hunt. The dogs behave splendidly.

The three share many adventures together and their hunting success is phenomenal. Billy is able to give substantial amounts of money to his mother from the sale of skins. As the fame of his dogs spreads, Billy is challenged by two of the meanest boys in the area, Rubin and Rainey Pritchard, to hunt down an elusive raccoon on their property. The dogs are successful.

Out hunting one night, the dogs tree a mountain lion, but the cat sprints and both dogs, trying to save their master, are badly cut. Old Dan dies and Billy buries him on a hillside under a tree. Little Ann refuses to eat, and within a few days she dies and is buried alongside Old Dan.

The following spring the Colmans leave the valley. By combining their savings with the money Billy won in the competition, they have enough to move to town. With an aching heart, Billy climbs the mountainside for the last time to the red oak and there he sees, as if by a miracle, that a beautiful red fern has grown between the two graves.

Themes and Subjects
This story shows the remarkable bonds of love and devotion that exist between a youngster and his dogs. Billy's transition from childhood to adolescence, and his courage, sacrifice, and engaging innocence make him appealing and believable. The wholesome family relationships and interesting use of local color add to the book's beauty and impact.

Booktalk Material
The first chapter will serve as a fine introduction (pp. 11–15) in which the narrator is reminded of his childhood. Other important passages are: Billy tries out traps (pp. 19–21); he earns fifty dollars (pp. 24–27); he collects the pups (pp. 39–41); the night in the cave (pp. 46–48); and the training period (pp. 64–66).

Additional Selections
A Native American teenager sets out to retrieve his prize-winning horse that has been stolen in Robert Laxalt's *Dust Devils* (Univ. of Nevada, 1997).

Farley Mowat's *The Dog Who Wouldn't Be* (Bantam, 1987) is the humorous story of a boy and of Mutt, a dog of character and personality.

Alan is helped to accept his father's being sent to prison through the love of a retriever in *Stormy* (Bantam, 1983) by James A. Kjelgaard.

About the Author and Book
Authors and Artists for Young Adults. Vol. 21, Gale, 1997.
Children's Books and Their Creators. Houghton, 1995.
Children's Literature Review. Vol. 81, Gale, 2002.
Contemporary Authors New Revision Series. Vol. 131, Gale, 2005.
Continuum Encyclopedia of Children's Literature. Continuum, 2001.
Drew, Bernard A. *100 More Popular Young Adult Authors.* Libraries Unlimited, 2002.
Major Authors and Illustrators for Children and Young Adults (2nd ed.). Vol. 7, Gale, 2002.
Sixth Book of Junior Authors and Illustrators. Wilson, 1989.
Something About the Author. Gale. Vol. 22, 1981; vol. 91, 1997.
See also listing "Selected Web Sites on Children's Literature and Authors."

7

Sport Stories

Brooks, Bruce. *The Moves Make the Man.* HarperCollins, 1984. $17.89, 0-06-020698-5 (Grades 7–9).

Introduction
Bruce Brooks (1950–) was born in Richmond, Virginia. His parents divorced when he was six, and he spent much of his childhood between two households. Because his mother was an alcoholic and unstable emotionally, he found living with her so difficult that he once ran away to live with his grandmother. He has said that many of his books with teenage protagonists are attempts to understand himself. He has written a series of successful young adult novels beginning with *The Moves Make the Man* in 1984. It was a Newbery Honor Book and the winner of the Boston Globe-Horn Book Award. In it, a cheeky, incoherent black student tells about his friend Bix, who is troubled after his mother's mental breakdown. It was hailed for its humor and spirited characters, and for the electric tension it portrays. These are also the characteristics of his second novel, *Midnight Hour Encores* (Harper, 1986), published in 1986. It tells of a musically talented but bossy girl traveling across the country to attend an audition and also to meet the mother who deserted her after her birth.

Principal Characters
   Jerome Foxworthy, the first black student at Chestnut Junior High
   Braxton "Bix" Rivers, a white student
   Bix's momma and stepfather
   Jerome's momma

Plot Summary

Jerome Foxworthy becomes the first black student at Chestnut Junior High in Wilmington, North Carolina. That's okay with him; his test scores make him the second-highest seventh-grader in the whole city. He also has the best basketball moves in town!

One day while watching a baseball game, Jerome sees someone else with the moves. He is Bix—Braxton Rivers the Third—and just about the best shortstop Jerome has ever seen. Sometime after that, Jerome's momma notices that he talks to himself when he is practicing basketball moves—as if he's trying to beat some mystery opponent. Jerome realizes his mystery opponent is really that natural shortstop.

Jerome and Bix meet in home economics class. They hit it off right away. One strange thing about Bix is that he wants only the truth—no faking, no fooling, no little white lies. When Jerome tries to teach Bix basketball moves, he is a natural except that he just won't learn to "fake." Jerome explains that part of being good in basketball is faking out your opponent, but Bix refuses to do this.

However, when Bix and his stepfather have a one-on-one game, Bix does fake out the older man and wins. For that, his stepfather agrees to take him to see his mother, who is in a mental hospital after attempting suicide. Jerome learns that his friend's mother attempted suicide after asking her son if he loved her. Because he will not fake the truth and because he did not love her at the time, Bix said no. After that, his mother tried to kill herself.

Jerome goes along with Bix and his stepfather to the mental hospital. But the hospital scene is a disaster. Bix's mother does not recognize him and Bix runs away.

That is the last time Jerome sees his friend. Months later, he gets a postcard from Washington, D.C. There is no message, but Jerome knows who sent it.

Jerome hasn't played ball since Bix ran away. But he doesn't think the moves are gone. In fact, maybe he'll just take Spin Light—the old lantern that he used to practice in the dark—out tonight and we'll see.

Themes and Subjects

Friendship, mental illness, obsession, sport, and humor are intertwined in this fast-paced, entertaining novel. Against a sports background that is vivid and exciting, readers are introduced to a most likable young hero and a satisfying look at family life for a black family in a southern town after the Supreme Court decision on school integration. The picture of mental deterioration is presented matter-of-factly but with compassion.

Booktalk Material

Some of the most fascinating scenes in the book depict the boys' growing friendship and Bix's obsession with the "truth"; see: Jerome and Bix in home economics class (pp. 90–91, 93–97, 99–105); Bix and the Spin Light (pp. 136–46); Jerome teaches Bix basketball (pp. 149–54, 156–62); Jerome referees the basketball game (pp. 195–202).

Additional Selections

When Noah becomes a new member of the high school basketball team, the position of the team captain, Corey, is threatened and there follows some strange accidents in Joyce Sweeney's *Players* (Winslow, 2000).

In spite of an eye injury, seventh-grader Paul Fisher shines on the soccer field and sees the truth about his family and community in *Tangerine* (Harcourt, 1997) by Edward Bloor.

In Chris Crutcher's *Running Loose* (Greenwillow, 1983), football star Louis Banks seems to have it all until he takes a stand against his coach.

Alex flirts with physical danger and trouble with the police when he joins up with Skateboarders with Attitude in Pat Flynn's *Alex Jackson: SWA* (Univ. of Queensland, 2002).

About the Author and Book

Authors and Artists for Young Adults. Gale. Vol. 8, 1992; vol. 36, 2001.
Children's Books and Their Creators. Houghton, 1995.
Children's Literature Review. Vol. 25, Gale, 1991.
Contemporary Authors. Vol. 137, Gale, 1992.
Continuum Encyclopedia of Children's Literature. Continuum, 2001.
Drew, Bernard A. *100 Most Popular Young Adult Writers.* Libraries Unlimited, 1996.
Gallo, Donald R. *Speaking for Ourselves.* National Council of Teachers of English, 1990.
Gillespie, John T., and Corinne J. Naden. *Characters in Young Adult Literature.* Gale, 1997.
Lives and Works: Young Adult Authors. Vol. 1, Grolier, 1999.
Major Authors and Illustrators for Children and Young Adults (1st ed.). Vol. 1, Gale, 1993.
Major Authors and Illustrators for Children and Young Adults (2nd ed.). Vol. 2, Gale, 2002.
Marens, Leonard S. "Song of Myself: Bruce Brooks," *School Library Journal,* Sept., 2000, pp. 50–51.
St. James Guide to Young Adult Writers (2nd ed.). St. James, 1999.
Sixth Book of Junior Authors and Illustrators. Wilson, 1989.
Something About the Author. Gale. Vol. 72, 1993; vol. 112, 2000.
Twentieth-Century Young Adult Writers (1st ed.). St. James, 1994.
Writers for Young Adults. Vol. 1, Scribner, 1997.
See also listing "Selected Web Sites on Children's Literature and Authors."

Crutcher, Chris. *Stotan!* HarperTempest, 2003 (1986). Pap. $6.99, 0-06-009492-3 (Grades 7–10).

Introduction
Chris Crutcher (1946–) has now written almost a dozen highly acclaimed sports novels and collections of short stories. He was born in Cascade, Idaho, and after graduating from Eastern Washington State University, he began working with troubled teenagers. At different times, he has been a principal and teacher in an alternative high school for dropouts, a coordinator of a child abuse protection agency, and a child and family counselor. He now lives in Spokane, Washington. All his novels explore similar themes, such as the importance of values and the struggle for justice, honesty, and tolerance. Each also uses the pursuit of a particular sport as a metaphor for the struggles and choices teenagers face on the road to physical and emotional maturity. Although sports action is an important element in each plot, the central focus is always on adolescent problems and moral development. For example, in his first novel for young readers, *Running Loose* (Greenwillow), published in 1983, Louis Banks, a senior, faces almost insurmountable odds when he rightly questions the ethics behind his football coach's order to deliberately injure the opponents' star player. *Stotan!* was Crutcher's second novel.

Principal Characters
Walker Dupree, senior and captain of the high school swim team
Lion, Jeff, and Nortie, his friends and also on the swim team
Elaine, the "den mother"
Devnee, Walker's girlfriend
Long John, Walker's Vietnam veteran brother
Max Il Song, the coach

Plot Summary
More than a love of swimming has kept Walker, Lion, Jeff, Nortie, and "den mother" Elaine together since grade school. Bonds of friendship and loyalty have forged these different personalities into almost a family. Walker Dupree, a senior, as are all the others, is captain of the swimming team. A popular, honest young man, he is concerned with winning at the Washington State swim meet, getting along with his elderly parents, coping with diminishing feelings for his girlfriend, Devnee, and caring for his drugged-out brother, Long John, a Vietnam veteran who has dropped out of life.

The other family members are Lion, or Lionel Serbousek, orphaned at fourteen and the joker of the group; Jeff Hawkins, the gorilla, a good-natured trickster and con artist; and Nortie Wheeler, the best swimmer, whose father regularly beats him up. The fifth member is Elaine, an independent thinker and wise beyond her years. Their coach is Max Il Song, a Korean American.

Max announces a Stotan week of training—five mornings, 8–12—before Christmas. Jeff finds out that Stotan is an Australian sporting term from the late 1950s; it refers to the perfect athlete who must be part stoic and part Spartan. The boys are not prepared for the backbreaking exercise this week involves. But they survive and Max gives each of them a gold ring engraved with their names and the word Stotan.

Nortie arrives late at the Christmas dance, beaten terribly by his father, who was told he is dating a black girl. With much courage, the boys face Nortie's father and move Nortie's possessions to Walker's home. Meanwhile, Walker does not have the nerve to call off his romance with Devnee and thinks he loves his old friend Elaine.

The team goes to Havre, Montana, for a meet. There Jeff collapses. The news that he has a form of terminal blood cancer is devastating to them all.

Some weeks later, Nortie is beaten almost unconscious by racist Marty O'Brian and his cohorts. Lion and Walker know he must be stopped and they visit Jeff for advice. As usual, he comes up with a plan and leaves the hospital for a few hours to help them carry it out. They push Marty's car into the river and when Marty threatens revenge, Max threatens him with real trouble if the harassment doesn't stop.

The three remaining team members score well at the meet because they know their victory is a victory for Jeff. As senior year ends, Walker realizes it has taught him a greater spirit of acceptance.

Themes and Subjects

In addition to sports and sportsmanship, this novel is about friendship, loyalty, compassion, the development of values, and the meaning of courage. The boys learn that life is not always fair and that its elements are rarely as simple as fairy tales suggest.

The novel portrays the devastating results of racial prejudice and the uncertainty of adolescent love relationships. The author also explores the effects of illness and death on teenagers.

Booktalk Material

An introduction to Elaine, the members of the swim team, and Stotan week will entice readers. Some of the important passages are: the first announcement of Stotan week (pp. 1–3); what a Stotan is (p. 27); the first encounter with Marty O'Brian (pp. 36–39); Nortie and the day-care incident (pp. 41–48); the first day of Stotan week (pp. 52–56). The three stories told during Stotan week are Jeff's (pp. 63–66); Nortie's (pp. 66–70), and Lion's (pp. 70–73).

Additional Selections

Teenage Dean is an excellent baseball player until an arm injury forces him to reevaluate his life in Randy Powell's *Dean Duffy* (Farrar, 1995).

Sonny, an excellent college basketball player, faces social and academic problems plus a vicious hazing incident when he attempts to join a fraternity in *The Squared Circle* (Scholastic, 2002) by James Bennett.

In Carl Deuker's *On the Devil's Court* (Avon, 1991), a high school basketball star believes he has sold his soul to have a perfect season.

Jimmy Doyle, a young basketball star, tries to prove to himself and his mostly African American teammates that he deserves a place on the American High School Dream Team in *Danger Zone* (Scholastic, 1996) by David Klass.

About the Authors and Book
Authors and Artists for Young Adults. Gale. Vol. 9, 1992; vol. 39, 2001.
Children's Books and Their Creators. Houghton, 1995.
Children's Literature Review. Vol. 28, Gale, 1992.
Contemporary Authors New Revision Series. Vol. 134, Gale, 2005.
Continuum Encyclopedia of Children's Literature. Continuum, 2001.
Crutcher, Chris. "The Outsiders," *School Library Journal*, Aug., 2001, pp. 5–6.
Davis, Terry. *Presenting Chris Crutcher*. Twayne, 1997.
Drew, Bernard A. *100 Most Popular Young Adult Authors*. Libraries Unlimited, 1996.
Gallo, Donald R. *Speaking for Ourselves*. National Council of Teachers of English, 1990.
Gillespie, John T., and Corinne J. Naden. *Characters in Young Adult Literature*. Gale, 1997.
Lives and Works: Young Adult Authors. Vol. 2, Grolier, 1999.
Major Authors and Illustrators for Children and Young Adults (1st ed.). Vol. 2, Gale, 1993.
Major Authors and Illustrators for Children and Young Adults (2nd ed.). Vol. 2, Gale, 2002.
St. James Guide to Young Adult Writers (2nd ed.). St. James, 1999.
Seventh Book of Junior Authors and Illustrators. Wilson, 1996.
Something About the Author. Gale. Vol. 52, 1998; vol. 99, 1999; vol. 153, 2005.
Stevens, Jen. *The Undergraduate's Companion to Children's Writers and Their Web Sites*. Libraries Unlimited, 2004.
Twentieth-Century Young Adult Writers (1st ed.). St. James, 1994.
Writers for Young Adults. Vol. 1, Scribner, 1997.
www.chriscrutcher.com (personal Web site)
See also listing "Selected Web Sites on Children's Literature and Authors."

Lipsyte, Robert. *The Contender.* HarperCollins, 1967. $16.89, 0-06-023920-4 (Grades 7–10).

Introduction
Robert Lipsyte (1938–) a long-time sports reporter and columnist for the *New York Times*, has used his firsthand knowledge of the sport of boxing to write a highly praised trilogy of interrelated novels on the subject. The first, *The Contender*, is the story of Alfred Brooks, a teenage high school dropout growing up in Harlem who finds direction in his life through boxing. The title comes from a conversation with the boy's boxing coach and promoter, who tells him, "Everybody wants to be a champion. That's not enough. You have to start by wanting to be a contender, the man coming up, the man who knows there's a good chance he'll never get to the top, the man who's willing to sweat and bleed to get up as high as his legs and his brains and his heart will take him."

In the second, *The Brave* (Harper, 1991), the focus shifts from Brooks (now Sergeant Brooks of the NYPD) to Sonny Bear, who has a white father and a Native American mother. He is a seventeen-year-old who is headed for tragedy on the streets of New York City until he finds an outlet in boxing. The last part, *The Chief* (Harper, 1995) tells how Sonny Bear becomes the sparring partner for an aging boxer, stages a comeback, and becomes involved in a dispute over legalized gambling on his reservation.

Principal Characters
Alfred Brooks, a high school dropout in Harlem
James Mosely, his best friend
Pearl Conway, Alfred's aunt
Henry Johnson, janitor at Donatelli's Gym
Sonny, Major, and Hollis, friends of James

Plot Summary
Alfred Brooks is growing up in a Harlem tenement with Aunt Pearl Conway and her three young daughters. He has a full-time job as a stock boy in a grocery store run by the Epstein brothers. His best friend, James Mosely, is also a high school dropout, but he has no job.

One Friday evening, Alfred finds James with his friends Sonny, Major, and Hollis. They taunt him about working for Jews. Alfred defends them, but the boys, eager for quick cash, decide to rob the Epstein grocery. After they leave, Alfred remembers that a silent burglar alarm has been installed. James is caught and his friends beat Alfred into unconsciousness.

Alfred recovers and Henry Johnson, the crippled janitor at Donatelli's Gym, urges him to try boxing. He goes into training and soon becomes part of the friendly group that hangs out there. After James is released from jail, Alfred searches for him and soon joins him in drinking and smoking pot. Alfred notices that James is also into heroin. Alfred has a narrow escape from the police and decides to get back into training.

In his first fight, Alfred wins in a unanimous decision. He knocks out the opponent in the second fight. But Donatelli says he lacks the killer instinct and advises him not to go professional. In Alfred's third fight, he is severely beaten.

But boxing has changed his life. He decides to complete his high school education at night. He thinks seriously of going on to a career in social work. By contrast, James's life is on the skids. His heroin habit is beginning to control his life. He again attempts a robbery of the Epstein store and jumps through a window to escape. Alfred finds him and persuades him to give himself up. He promises to dedicate himself to James's complete recovery. Alfred has his first case.

Themes and Subjects

The Contender portrays the dilemma faced by most black youngsters growing up in the ghettos—the desire to live productive lives in conflict with the negative pressures of the environment. It also shows a youngster's need for direction by understanding adults who can serve as role models and can give guidance. Virtues including loyalty in friendship, sportsmanship, and the need for self-discipline are depicted as still relevant today. Although the book gives a bleak picture of slum life, it also shows that it is possible to change those conditions.

Booktalk Material

A brief introduction to Alfred and his problems will interest readers. The story also could be introduced by relating one of several incidents: Alfred innocently causes the Epstein robbery (pp. 1–6); Alfred first goes to Donatelli's Gym (pp. 20–21); Alfred attends his first fight (pp. 61–66); and has his first fight (pp. 136–41).

Additional Selections

A high school wrestler not only fights an unbeatable foe but also wrestles with his inner problems in *Vision Quest* (East Washington Univ., 2002) by Terry Davis.

Korean American Chan Kim, a fine soccer player and all-round athlete, faces personal and athletic problems when his family moves to a small

Minnesota town in Marie G. Lee's *Necessary Roughness* (HarperCollins, 1996).

In Michael Cadnum's *Redhanded* (Viking, 2000), a teenager plans a robbery to raise money for tournament fees and to further his boxing career.

Two brothers try to assist their struggling family by boxing under the direction of an unethical promoter in Markus Zusak's *Fighting Ruben Wolfe* (Scholastic, 2002).

About the Author and Book
Authors and Artists for Young Adults. Gale. Vol. 7, 1992; vol. 45, 2002.
Children's Books and Their Creators. Houghton, 1995.
Children's Literature Review. Vol. 76, Gale, 2002.
Contemporary Authors New Revision Series. Vol. 57, Gale, 1997.
Continuum Encyclopedia of Children's Literature. Continuum, 2001.
Drew, Bernard A. *100 Most Popular Young Adult Authors.* Libraries Unlimited, 1996.
Fifth Book of Junior Authors and Illustrators. Wilson, 1983.
Gallo, Donald R. *Speaking for Ourselves.* National Council of Teachers of English, 1990.
Gillespie, John T., and Corinne J. Naden. *Characters in Young Adult Literature.* Gale, 1997.
Lives and Works: Young Adult Authors. Vol. 5, Grolier, 1999.
Major Authors and Illustrators for Children and Young Adults (1st ed.). Vol. 4, Gale, 1993.
Major Authors and Illustrators for Children and Young Adults (2nd ed.). Vol. 5, Gale, 2002.
St. James Guide to Young Adult Writers (2nd ed.). St. James, 1999.
Something About the Author. Gale. Vol. 5, 1973; vol. 68, 1992; vol. 113, 2000; vol. 161, 2006.
Twentieth-Century Young Adult Writers (1st ed.). St. James, 1994.
Writers for Young Adults. Vol. 2, Scribner, 1997.
See also listing "Selected Web Sites on Children's Literature and Authors."

Voigt, Cynthia. *The Runner.* Scholastic, 1994 (1984). Pap. $5.99, 0-590-48380-3 (Grades 8–12).

Introduction

Cynthia Voigt (1942–) introduced the Tillerman family in *Homecoming* (Atheneum, 1981; see Chapter 5, p. 270). In that book, a distraught and unbalanced Lisa Tillerman abandons her four fatherless children in a Connecticut shopping mall. The oldest, thirteen-year-old Dicey, takes charge and leads her sister and two brothers to Crisfield, a small town on the eastern shore of Maryland, where they are grudgingly allowed to stay

300 • CLASSIC TEENPLOTS

with their maternal grandmother, Abigail Tillerman, a bitter, ill-tempered recluse. Dicey later learns why Abigail has become so sour and remote. Her deceased husband, a despotic, heartless man, has driven her children from home one by one. The oldest, Dicey's mother, left to join a shiftless sailor named Frank Veriker in New England; the next, Johnny, left for college on a scholarship and never returned; and the youngest, Samuel (nicknamed Bullet), joined the Army at age eighteen and was killed in Vietnam. Although other novels by Voigt continue the story of Dicey and her family, *The Runner* is Bullet's story. It begins in September 1967, some twelve years before the events of *Homecoming*, and ends in March of the following year with Bullet joining the Army. A brief coda is dated December 1969, when Abigail learns of her son's death. This book is written for slightly older readers than the other Tillerman books.

Principal Characters
    Bullet, seventeen and a junior in high school
    His dictatorial father
    His demoralized mother
    Patrice, a fisherman
    Tamer Shipp, a new black student

Plot Summary
Bullet is seventeen and beginning his junior year because he flunked the fifth grade. Since his sister and brother left home, he is alone in his parents' farmhouse, with a dictatorial father and a mother so demoralized by her husband's behavior and her children's departure that she is practically a non-person. They lead a bleak existence.

Bullet has retreated into himself. He is a loner and emotionally wounded. His only friend is Patrice, a French fisherman for whom he works. Patrice is also a loner and understands the boy.

A new black student named Tamer Shipp joins the track team. He is nineteen, married, and trying to complete high school while working part-time jobs. When a group of whites is about to jump Tamer in the school cafeteria, Bullet tackles the leader and takes away his knife. But when the track coach asks Bullet to help Tamer improve his performance, Bullet refuses because he has been taught to believe that blacks are inferior. The coach orders Bullet off the team.

Bullet begins to learn more about Patrice, including the fact that the fisherman is part black. Bullet rethinks his racial attitudes and decides to coach Tamer.

The track team travels north for a weekend-long meet. Much to the coach's satisfaction, the team performs well and the combined talents of Bullet and Tamer help collect many precious points. At the end of the cross-country, which Bullet wins handily, he sees his mother half-hidden in the crowd, trying to remain unseen. In spite of her silence, she really cares.

On March 21, 1968, Bullet's eighteenth birthday, he joins the Army—not for patriotism or commitment to a cause, but solely to escape. As a parting gesture, he asks Patrice to hire Tamer as his replacement, and from his savings he buys the Frenchman's refurbished boat as a gift to his mother so she will have greater freedom of movement. With that, he says goodbye.

Less than two years later, his now-widowed mother answers the phone in the farmhouse and is told that her son has been killed in action in Vietnam.

Themes and Subjects
This novel contains a great deal of sports action and conveys the hypnotic therapeutic feelings that running often produces. It is also about personal integrity, an emotionally traumatized family, and the cruelty that parents can inflict on their children. In particular, it deals with one proud young man who knows only rejection and scorn and learns through painful experience the meaning of pity and compassion. The futility of war and the controversy concerning the Vietnam War are woven into the plot effectively. Bullet's moving death underlies the theme of war's tragic waste. Racial prejudice and its debilitating effects are important secondary themes. Above all, the reader will remember Bullet, a lonely young man, and his unhappy destiny.

Booktalk Material
A description of Bullet's home and school situations should interest readers, particularly those already familiar with Dicey and her family. Some important passages are: Bullet is told to cut his hair (pp. 3–5); Mr. Walker talks about war and mercenaries in history class (pp. 70–75); the incident in the school cafeteria (pp. 75–77); and Patrice talks about his war experiences (pp. 134–38).

Additional Selections
Ben, a high school senior, faces a bleak future in his hometown and decides to change things by trying out for a state wrestling title in Rich Wallace's *Wrestling Sturbridge* (Knopf, 1996).

Fleeing a family tragedy, fourteen-year-old Tyler moves to New York City and plays on a baseball league in Central Park in John H. Ritter's *Over the Wall* (Putnam, 2000).

Sports, politicking, religion, and loyalty are themes in James Bennett's *Blue Star Rapture* (Simon, 1998), about a basketball hopeful who falls for a girl in a religious cult.

Tom Coyne's *A Gentleman's Game* (Atlantic Monthly, 2001) is the story of Tommy Price, a young star golfer whose father forces him to be a caddy to learn humility.

About the Author and Book
See material under *Homecoming*, p. 270.

Wells, Rosemary. *When No One Was Looking.* Puffin, 2000 (1980).
Pap. $5.99, 0-14-130973-3 (Grades 7–10).

Introduction
Rosemary Wells (1943–) is a prolific writer and versatile contributor to many genres of children's literature. Born in New York, she entered the publishing field as an art editor and began a freelance career in 1968. As an author/illustrator, she has created a number of delightful anthropomorphic creatures for children's picture books: Noisy Nora is the middle child who craves attention in a mouse family; Stanley and Rhoda are mouse siblings who share many interesting adventures; and Max and Ruby are a toddler bunny and his sister. In the field of young adult literature, she has written a number of well-paced, exciting thrillers. In *The Man in the Woods* (Sagebrush, 2001), for example, the world of drug trafficking is introduced after young Helen discovers a man in the woods who is accused of throwing rocks at car windshields. *Through the Hidden Door* (Dial, 1987) is a gripping psychological adventure about a young boy in a posh private school who, while in trouble for informing on star athletes, discovers an archaeological ruin that indicates an ancient Lilliputian culture. *When No One Was Looking*, an Edgar Allan Poe Award runner-up, is a story about tennis, intense friendships, and murder.

Principal Characters
Kathy Bardy, fourteen and a talented tennis player
Julia, her best friend

Jody, Kathy's smart sister
Ruth Gumm, a tennis player who drowns in a swimming pool

Plot Summary
Fourteen-year-old Kathy Bardy has a talent for tennis and her parents, never well off, are scraping together every penny for her lessons. The family's entire life seems to revolve around Kathy's needs and her sister Jody—the smart one—is becoming jealous. Kathy is not sure that tennis should be her "life's work." What she really wants, she tells her best friend Julia, is to be the first woman shortstop for the Boston Red Sox.

Kathy has another problem. She has a temper on the court, which eventually gets the better of her in a match. That summer Kathy has a chance at the New England championship, but Ruth Gumm suddenly appears in town. Kathy faces her in a match and is so upset by Ruth's boorish actions that she is well on her way to losing. However, Ruth is disqualified because she didn't pay the entrance fee.

Then Ruth drowns in a swimming pool accident. Kathy enters an important tournament in Florida and although she loses in the finals, she is making a name for herself. When she gets home, she learns that police are looking into Ruth's death, seeking the person who put too much chlorine in the pool. Kathy is is among their suspects.

Kathy thinks about giving up tennis. How does she really feel about the game? Can she understand and face up to her sister's jealousy? Can she control her temper?

As Kathy takes on her first challenge in the New England championship, she learns to deal with her own shortcomings and those of others. She controls her temper in a crucial match. And she comes to realize that tennis does hold a future for her. This is what she wants to do and she believes the sacrifices are worth it.

But in gaining at last an understanding of what she is and where she stands, Kathy loses something very precious. To her great horror, she learns the truth about Ruth Gumm's death; with great sorrow, she begins to understand the mistakes that people make in the name of love and of friendship. Julia, her best friend, only wanted to help Kathy on her way to the top . . .

Themes and Subjects
This is not just a novel of sport or a young girl growing up. It deals realistically with the emphasis that today's society often places on winning and how parents often try to live out their own dreams through the lives of

their children. It shows the pressures placed on the shoulders of the young as they are urged to win, not just for themselves but for the fulfillment of others. It is an honest portrayal of a talented, likable young girl trying to do what is expected of her as she strives to overcome a crippling temper and find her own niche in life.

Booktalk Material
The various reactions and needs of different characters in this book will make excellent material for discussion: Kathy loses her temper with Ruth Gumm (pp. 32–37); Jody's reaction to Kathy's outburst (pp. 38–40); Kathy's parents discuss the importance of algebra versus tennis (pp. 77–82).

Additional Selections
In *Fearless* (Pocket, 1999) by Francine Pascal, Gaia, a seventeen-year-old who has a black belt in kung fu, discovers that she is her own worst enemy.

Stan finds something is troubling Ginny, a rising tennis star, when he attempts to help her game in Randy Powell's *The Whistling Toilets* (Farrar, 1996).

In C. S. Adler's *Winning* (Clarion, 1999), eighth-grader Vicky lacks the courage to challenge her tennis partner when she catches her cheating.

In the baseball story *Bat 6* (Scholastic, 1998) by Virginia E. Wolff, a Japanese American girl just out of an internment camp meets a bitter girl whose father died at Pearl Harbor.

About the Author and Book
Authors and Artists for Young Adults. Vol. 13, Gale, 1994.
Children's Books and Their Creators. Houghton, 1995.
Children's Literature Review. Vol. 69, Gale, 2001.
Contemporary Authors New Revision Series. Vol. 120, Gale, 2004.
Continuum Encyclopedia of Children's Literature. Continuum, 2001.
Favorite Children's Authors and Illustrators. Vol. 6, Tradition Books, 2003.
Fourth Book of Junior Authors and Illustrators. Wilson, 1978.
Major Authors and Illustrators for Children and Young Adults (1st ed.). Vol. 6, Gale, 1993.
Major Authors and Illustrators for Children and Young Adults (2nd ed.). Vol. 8, Gale, 2002.
St. James Guide to Children's Writers (5th ed.). St. James, 1999.
St. James Guide to Young Adult Writers (2nd ed.). St. James, 1999.
Something About the Author. Gale. Vol. 18, 1980; vol. 69, 1992; vol. 114, 2000; vol. 156, 2005.

Something About the Author Autobiography Series. Vol. 1, Gale, 1986.
Stevens, Jen. *The Undergraduate's Companion to Children's Writers and Their Web Sites.* Libraries Unlimited, 2004.
Twentieth-Century Children's Writers (4th ed.). St. James, 1995.
Twentieth-Century Young Adult Writers (1st ed.). St. James, 1994.
www.rosemarywells.com (personal Web site)
See also "Selected Web Sites on Children's Literature and Authors."

8

Important Nonfiction

Bell, Ruth. *Changing Bodies, Changing Lives.* Three Rivers Press, 1998. Pap. $24.95, 0-8129-2990-X (Grades 7–12).

Introduction
Subtitled *A Book for Teens on Sex and Relationships,* this expanded, third edition of the standard text that started out as *Our Bodies, Ourselves* (1976) addresses hundreds of questions relating to teenage sex, physical and emotional health, and personal relationships. In addition to a straightforward, well-organized, and informative text, the book is filled with illustrations, checklists, and resources for further help and information. Most important, it is crammed with quotes and case histories of teenagers who have faced typical situations. The author is a member of the Boston Women's Health Book Collective and has worked for many years in the field of health and sex education, specializing in work with teenagers.

Summary
The book is divided into twelve sections, each well illustrated and including comments and vignettes from teenagers. "Changing Bodies" concerns the physical changes that occur during puberty, generally starting in the early teens. The author details the specific changes that occur in both boys and girls.

"Changing Relationships" deals with changes concerning parents and family, peers and friends and discusses what to do about changing moods and how to handle opposite-sex friendships.

The third section covers aspects of sexuality, including guilt about masturbation, sexual response and orgasm, pressures among teens to engage in sexual activity, and homosexuality; while the fourth section discusses emotional changes, looking at feelings of hopelessness and powerlessness, as well as suicide among teenagers. It also talks about eating disorders such as bulimia and anorexia nervosa, which can be problems particularly for teenaged girls.

Other eating disorders and substance abuse are the topics of the fifth and sixth sections, the seventh talks about living with violence, and the eighth deals with physical health, stressing the importance of forming good health habits early in life. In sections nine and ten, the authors discuss sexually transmitted diseases, followed by safer sex and birth control. Section eleven discusses pregnancy, and in the last section, the authors recap ways in which teens can help themselves to deal with problems.

Changing Bodies, Changing Lives helps to sort out the jumble of changing emotions that can be so troubling to teenagers. It does so with straightforward talk and compassion and with clear and helpful facts that do not add to the confusion.

Themes and Subjects

This book recognizes that the teenage years can be a difficult time for boys and girls. It is a comprehensive, concise guide to surviving puberty that is both reassuring and nonjudgmental. It offers reliable information that will help teenagers make responsible choices about matters that can profoundly affect their futures.

Booktalk Material

Depending on the specific area of concern, the following sections may be of special interest: physical changes in boys' bodies (pp. 12–24); physical changes in girls' bodies (pp. 24–31); masturbation (pp. 81–83); types of eating disorders (pp. 186–94); how to deal with date violence (pp. 211–14); and methods of sex protection (pp. 286–309).

Additional Selections

Using a question-and-answer format, material on topics including abstinence, contraception, and sexually transmitted diseases are presented in Faith Brynie's *101 Questions About Sex and Sexuality* (Twenty-First Century, 2003).

In Cynthia G. Akagi's *Dear Michael: Sexuality Education for Boys Ages 11–17* (Gylantic, 1996), aspects of male puberty are explored through a series of letters from a mother to her son.

Lynda and Area Madaras have written two excellent primers on all aspects of puberty. They are: *The "What's Happening to My Body?" Book for Girls: A Growing Up Guide for Parents and Daughters* and *The "What's Happening to My Body?" Book for Boys: A Growing Up Guide for Parents and Sons* (both Newmarket, 2001).

About the Author and Book
No biographical information available.

Dahl, Roald. *Going Solo.* Puffin, 1999 (1986). Pap. $6.99, 0-14-130310-7 (Grades 7–12).

Introduction
Roald Dahl (1916–90), the celebrated English author of both juvenile and adult stories popular for their display of great imagination and wit, began his autobiography with the volume called simply *Boy* (Puffin) published in 1984. In it, he tells about his parents, who emigrated from Norway to live in the United Kingdom, and particularly about his gallant mother who was widowed when Roald was still a child. His experiences growing up are sometimes hilarious, sometimes painful, and often bizarre. He attended a fashionable English private school, Repton, and after graduating began work with the Shell Company. After a stint in Newfoundland, he is being transferred to Africa at the book's end.

Whereas *Boy* is episodic, *Going Solo* is a more cohesive, chronological narrative. It covers three years in the author's life, from age twenty-two to twenty-five, or roughly the autumn of 1938 through late 1941. The title has a double meaning because the book traces not Dahl's years of independence but also his period flying in the Royal Air Force during World War II. Most of the action takes place in Africa and the eastern Mediterranean. The book is illustrated with maps and the author's own photographs.

Principal Characters
English author Roald Dahl in his early- to mid-twenties
Major and Mrs. Griffiths, passengers aboard the *S.S. Mantola*
U.N. Savory, Dahl's cabin mate
Donald MacFarland, the snake man
Mdisho, Dahl's personal servant

Summary
In late 1938, Roald Dahl, age twenty-two, sails from London to Mombasa on the east coast of Africa to work for Shell Oil. On board he meets an amazing group of people—the Griffiths walk the deck each day in the buff; Miss Trefusis refuses to touch food and peels oranges with a knife

and fork; and U.N. Savory, his cabin mate, tries to conceal the fact that he wears a wig by sprinkling it with salt to simulate dandruff.

Dahl's job involves traveling inland from the coast and he soon discovers that he is terrified of snakes. This fear, however, leads him to alert his neighbors to the presence of a deadly green mamba. Another tussle with nature occurs when Dahl is visiting another English family and a lion makes off with the cook's wife. A shot in the air scares the animal and it drops its prey.

In September 1939, Britain declares war on Germany and Dahl is assigned to guard the only road out of Dar es Salaam (in the British territory of Tanganyika) to prevent German civilians from fleeing into neutral Portuguese East Africa. Dahl lays an ambush and, in the ensuing confrontation with the Germans, the leader of the group is killed and the civilians are turned back.

Dahl joins the Royal Air Force, receives his wings, and survives a crash in Egypt, although with a severe concussion. He leaves the hospital after five months and rejoins his squadron near Athens. Although many fellow pilots are killed, he survives the war.

Dahl's intense headaches return and he is so incapacitated that he is forced to return to Britain. After a long and dangerous passage on troop ships around the entire coast of Africa, he arrives safely in Liverpool and is reunited with his family.

Themes and Subjects
Dahl's three-year odyssey is as amazing and wondrous as any of his fictional stories. Graphic scenes of World War II in the eastern Mediterranean are unforgettable in their evocation of courage, heroism, and friendship. The acts of valor, sacrifice, and death he describes underline concepts concerning the waste and wanton destruction that war brings. In the earlier passages about Africa, the author lovingly describes the countryside and the native people he both respects and admires. In addition to these lessons in sociology, geography, and history, the reader learns to savor the personality and character of the most interesting individual in the book, Dahl himself.

Booktalk Material
After Roald Dahl is introduced to the readers, one or more of his shipmates aboard the *S.S. Mantola* might also be introduced: Major Griffiths (pp. 2–5); Miss Trefusis (pp. 8–11); and U.N. Savory (pp. 11–19). Other passages of interest are: a black mamba attacks (pp. 27–28); the cook's

wife and the lion (pp. 35–40); and the snake man and the green mamba (pp. 41–50). Two passages involving the war are: the capture of the German civilians (pp. 57–65) and the dogfight with German bombers (pp. 135–39).

Additional Selections

The author Pat Conroy describes his lifelong love of basketball and the lessons the game has taught him in his autobiographical *My Losing Season* (Doubleday, 2002).

Lord Byron's dashing and adventurous life—a century before Dahl's exciting experiences—is described in *George Gordon, Lord Byron* (Oxford, 2000) by Martin Garrett.

Janet B. Pascal describes the life of the creator of Sherlock Holmes, who was also a doctor and a spiritualist, in *Arthur Conan Doyle: Beyond Baker Street* (Oxford, 2000).

In *Alex Haley* (Chelsea, 1993), author David Shirley covers the life of the African American writer who gave us the family saga *Roots*.

About the Author and Book
Authors and Artists for Young Adults. Vol. 15, Gale, 1995.
Biography Today: Author Series. Vol. 1, Omnigraphics, 1995.
Children's Books and Their Creators. Houghton, 1995.
Contemporary Authors New Revision Series. Vol. 62, Gale, 1992.
Continuum Encyclopedia of Children's Literature. Continuum, 2001.
Favorite Children's Authors and Illustrators. Vol. 2, Tradition Books, 2003.
Jones, Raymond E. *Characters in Children's Books*. Gale, 1997.
McElmeel, Sharron L. *100 Most Popular Children's Authors*. Libraries Unlimited, 1999.
Major Authors and Illustrators for Children and Young Adults (1st ed.). Vol. 2, Gale, 1993.
Major Authors and Illustrators for Children and Young Adults (2nd ed.). Vol. 2, Gale, 2002.
St. James Guide to Young Adult Writers (2nd ed.). St. James, 1999.
Something About the Author. Gale. Vol. 1, 1971; vol. 26, 1982; vol. 65, 1991; vol. 73, 1993.
Stevens, Jen. *The Undergraduate's Companion to Children's Writers and Their Web Sites*. Libraries Unlimited, 2004.
Third Book of Junior Authors. Wilson, 1972.
Treglown, Jeremy. *Roald Dahl: A Biography*. Faber, 1994.
Twentieth-Century Young Adult Writers (1st ed.). St. James, 1994.
West, Mark I. *Roald Dahl*. Twayne, 1992.
www.roalddahlfans.com (fan club Web site)
www.roalddahl.com (personal Web site)
See also listing "Selected Web Sites on Children's Literature and Authors."

Herriot, James. *The Lord God Made Them All.* St. Martin's, 1998 (1981). $7.99, 0-312-96620-2 (Grade 9–Adult).

Introduction
James Alfred Wight (1916–95), who used the pseudonym of James Herriot, was born in England and graduated from the Veterinary College in Glasgow, Scotland. His career in veterinary medicine was interrupted by a stint in the Royal Air Force from 1943 through 1945. After the war, he returned to his practice in Yorkshire and began writing seriously in 1966. He is best known for a series of five novels, based on fact, that use lines from a well-known hymn as their titles: *All Creatures Great and Small* (St. Martin's, 1972), *All Things Bright and Beautiful* (St. Martin's, 1974), *All Things Wise and Wonderful* (St. Martin's, 1977), *The Lord God Made Them All* (St. Martin's, 1981), and *Every Living Thing* (St. Martin's, 1992). Of these works, the critic Gerald W. Morton wrote, "These stories are not just about animals and the difficulties faced by a veterinarian in the rugged north country of England. In each novel, the reader meets extremely well drawn characters like the peculiar senior partner in the veterinarian practice Siegfried, his reckless brother Tristan, and the gentle Helen (later Herriot's wife). Combining this array of characters, Herriot builds a rich texture in his novels . . . creating a tapestry of human behavior reflected by the relationships people have with the animals they rely on for both companionship and livelihood."

Principal Characters
Dr. James Herriot, a veterinarian
Humphrey Cobb, a man whose dog, Myrtle, is a constant patient
Helen and Jimmy, Herriot's wife and son

Summary
This is the fourth of the bestselling stories by James Herriot, the country veterinarian who lived at Skeldale House on the edge of the Yorkshire dales. The time is the 1950s when new advances are being realized in veterinary medicine but much else remains the same in the Yorkshire countryside, where people know hard work and the peace and solitude of the wild.

Dr. Herriot is just back from a stint in the RAF. The war has ended. One of his first calls—at 1 A.M.—comes from Humphrey Cobb, who sobs

IMPORTANT NONFICTION • 313

over the phone that his little dog is dying. Off Herriot rushes to the rescue of Myrtle, a beagle that does not seem to be in much distress, although she is panting. He soon discovers that the trouble stems from the fact that Myrtle's bed has been placed too near the stove and she is uncomfortably hot. Herriot, however, gives her a vitamin pill to make Cobb feel better.

Herriot takes a trip to Russia on a ship that exports animals to the USSR. The cargo is sheep, and on the voyage he discovers that some of these supposedly healthy animals have a cough known as husk. The animals grow sicker and he administers a new drug—cortisone—which works. It is his first experiment with the wonder drug.

Back home, life is fulfilling for Herriot, his wife Helen, and their son Jimmy, who often goes on calls with his father. Herriot has many stories to tell of his own growth as a veterinary surgeon and of the medical advances, such as the use of penicillin, that save the lives of cattle and all manner of farm animals. At first the drug is delivered to him in small tubes, not in an injectable form. When Herriot is faced with a dying cow, he realizes that penicillin might cure it and decides to attach the tubes to a hypodermic needle, which he injects into the cow's rump time after time, having no clear idea of how much is enough or too much. Would the drug be absorbed in this manner? In about three days he has his answer. The cow will live. And the doctor has learned about the wonders of penicillin.

Themes and Subjects
The Lord God Made Them All is a warm and witty collection of episodes in the life of a country veterinarian in the 1950s when the medical wonders that are much taken for granted today were new and startling developments. Any reader with a special feeling for animals will enjoy these stories of a kind and caring doctor who often has more trouble dealing with distraught owners than with sick patients. The book also gives an intimate portrait of life in the Yorkshire countryside and of the sturdy farmers and townsfolk who live there. The dedication of this veterinarian to his work and to the animals shines through in every story. For all animal lovers.

Booktalk Material
As examples of the types of episodes that make up this book, see: the doctor gets hung up on a gate (pp. 1–15); Mr. Cobb and the dying Myrtle (pp. 16–26); going to Russia (pp. 35–39); Jimmy and the wisteria (pp. 40–48); and Herriot has a close call (pp. 81–92).

Additional Selections

John McCormick's *A Friend of the Flock: Tales of a Country Veterinarian* (Crown, 1997) is a funny and sad memoir by the first vet of Choctaw County, Alabama.

Animal Patients: 50 Years in the Life of an Animal Doctor (Camino, 2001) by Edward J. Scanlon is an entertaining look at the life of a big city veterinarian, his patients, and his practice.

Allen M. Schoen's memoir (written with Pam Proctor), *Love, Miracles, and Animal Healing* (Simon, 1995) is subtitled *A Veterinarian's Journey for Physical Medicine to Spiritual Understanding.*

The story of the great naturalist noted for her groundbreaking work with chimpanzees is told in Virginia Meachum's *Jane Goodall: Protector of Chimpanzees* (Enslow, 1997).

About the Author and Book
(some of these entries are under James Alfred Wight)
Authors and Artists for Young Adults. Gale. Vol. 1, 1989; vol. 54, 2004.
Children's Literature Review. Vol. 80, Gale, 2002.
Contemporary Authors. Vol. 148, Gale, 1996.
Contemporary Authors New Revision Series. Vol. 40, Gale, 1993.
Major Authors and Illustrators for Children and Young Adults (2nd ed.). Vol. 4, Gale, 2002.
St. James Guide to Young Adult Writers (2nd ed.). St. James, 1999.
Something About the Author. Gale. Vol. 55, 1989; vol. 86, 1996; vol. 135, 2003.
Twentieth-Century Young Adult Writers (1st ed.). St. James, 1994.
See also listing "Selected Web Sites on Children's Literature and Authors."

Myers, Walter Dean. *Now Is Your Time! The African-American Struggle for Freedom.* HarperTrophy, 1990. Pap. $12.99, 0-06-446120-3 (Grades 7–12).

Introduction
Walter Dean Myers (1937–), the distinguished writer of fiction for young adults (see *Fallen Angels* on p. 204), turns to nonfiction in this account of African American life from slavery through the civil rights movements of the 1960s and 1970s to the early 1990s. In the Preface, the author states,

> The African-American experience cannot be told in one story, or even in a hundred, for it is a living experience, ever changing, ever growing, ever becoming richer. Events of the past cannot change, but they can change in our perception of them, and in our understand-

IMPORTANT NONFICTION • 315

ing of what they mean to us today. What we understand of our history is what we understand of ourselves. If it has come down to us that we are wonderful beings, blessed with all the gifts necessary to succeed, then we will naturally seek that success. If we believe that we are fully deserving of the rights to life, liberty, and the pursuit of happiness, then we will fight to retain these rights.

Interwoven with the general narrative are stories reflecting episodes in the author's own family history. The use of many quotes and beautiful illustrations adds realism to this account of struggle, despair, achievement, and, sometimes, hope.

Summary
These are true stories of the African American experience, told in twenty-three chapters. In "The Land," the author speaks of North America, the incredibly beautiful, incredibly rich land stretching between two oceans. For Europe in the 1400s, North America offered a promise of adventure. When colonies began to prosper in the New World, many people were needed to do the work. Eventually, the practice of slavery prospered and West Africa became a source of slave labor for America for some 236 years.

"To Make a Slave" details how the slave system in America was made to work. African hairstyles and religious practices were made taboo in an effort to maintain complete control over the slaves and to change the way in which blacks thought about themselves. Family structures were often ignored. Destroy the family unit and you destroy the strength of the individual.

In "Fighting Back," the author discusses resistance by captured Africans. In 1839, for instance, Africans who had been captured and taken to Cuba as the property of a pair of Spaniards broke their chains on board ship and revolted. The Spanish owners promised to sail the captives back to Africa but took them instead to New York harbor. However, local abolitionists backed the Africans, who were allowed to go free and who returned to Africa in 1842.

Many other stories are presented, including those of Nat Turner, who led a slave revolt in 1831; the Dred Scott case in the mid-1800s; John Brown's raid on Harpers Ferry, Virginia; and the civil rights work of Martin Luther King, Jr., in the 1960s.

Themes and Subjects
This book presents remarkable stories of men and women of courage who fought injustice and bigotry against overwhelming odds. It is also a simple

yet dramatic look at U.S. history through the perspective of African Americans whose lives and perceptions are forever shaped by the color of their skin.

Booktalk Material
Some of the individual stories in this book can lead to a discussion of how devastating and widespread are the ways in which slavery and injustice permeate the lives of black Americans. See: the story of Abd al-Rahman Ibrahima (pp. 11–27); the life of James Forten (pp. 53–63); and the heartbreak of Maria Perkins (pp. 74–75).

Additional Selections
From Sojourner Truth to Jesse Jackson, *Historic Speeches of African Americas* (Lyons, 2002), edited by Warren J. Halliburton, is an inspiring work of African American history.

An overview of African American history and of the contributions of African Americans to American culture is given in David Boyle's *African Americans* (Barron's, 2002).

Maurice Isserman's *Journey to Freedom* (Facts on File, 1993) describes the migration north of thousands of African Americans at the beginning of the twentieth century.

Julius Lester's *To Be a Slave* (Dial, 1968) is a powerful account drawn largely from primary documents.

About the Author and Book
See *Fallen Angels*, p. 204.

Pelzer, Dave. *A Child Called "It."* Health Communications, 1995. Pap. $9.95, 1-55874-366-9 (Grade 10–Adult).

Introduction
David J. Pelzer (1961–), who has worked as a youth counselor, a lecturer, and an advocate for child abuse victims, is primarily known as the survivor of the incredible child abuse that became the subject of a trilogy of books about his past. The first, *A Child Called "It,"* covers his childhood with his demented mother and alcoholic father from ages four to twelve in a situation that was described as one of the worst cases of child abuse on public record in California. It included starvation, beatings, and stabbings. His mother once said to him: "You are not a person but a thing to do with as I

please." Finally Pelzer's teachers risked their careers to notify the authorities of the situation and remove him to a foster home. The second volume, *The Lost Boy* (Health Communications, 1995), is subtitled *A Foster Child's Search for the Love of a Family*, and tells of his experiences, as an often defiant, rebellious youngster, in foster homes and juvenile detention centers until he found a home where he felt comfortable. He was eventually inducted into the Air Force. Subtitled *A Story of Triumph and Forgiveness*, the third volume, *A Man Called Dave* (Plume, 1999), describes how he was able to break the circle of violence and come to terms with his past. Particularly moving are the scenes where he visits his dying father and confronts his mother, who still made him feel like an outsider at the funeral. Recently, Pelzer wrote a self-help book, *Help Yourself for Teens: Real-Life Advice for Real-Life Challenges* (Plume, 2005), which offers teenagers practical solutions for overcoming their personal problems and hardships.

Principal Characters
  Dave Pelzer, the child called It
  His abusive mother
  Ronald, Stan, and Kevin, his brothers
  His father

Summary
This is a story of evil, of child abuse so dreadful it is hard to imagine. It is listed as one of the most severe cases of child abuse in the history of California. The author, Dave Pelzer, endured unbelievable treatment at the hands of his alcoholic, unstable mother. She not only denied him food or gave him scraps that an animal would not eat, but she played torturous games with him, games that very nearly ended his life. As a boy, he slept on an old cot in the cellar. His clothes were filthy. His teachers were unaware of his plight.

The book is a kind of chart of escalating abuse as his mother grows more sick in her own mind. First, she sets him apart from the rest of the family, and then the torment begins. Through episode after episode, the abuse worsens and his terror grows. He is starved, poisoned, beaten, and even stabbed. He is so isolated from everyone that his mother calls him "it." His father, instead of protecting him, gives into the boy's mother, tells his son he is sorry, and leaves the home.

Through it all, the boy learns to survive. With no one to turn to, it is only his dreams that keep him alive and able to endure the torture. He dreams of the day when someone will care for him and will love him.

Dave Pelzer survived the horror and went on to have a family of his own. This is a powerful true story of abuse and survival.

Themes and Subjects
A number of themes in the book are a good opening for a discussion of unstable families and child abuse. What was the role of the father? Why didn't the school notice the boy's plight for so long? Could he have escaped?

Booktalk Material
Dave talks about the good times before the abuse started (pp. 23–26); he is a "bad boy" (pp. 39–43); abuse with food (pp. 66–67); the stabbing (pp. 86–97); Father leaves (pp. 148–53).

Additional Selections
Jennings Michael Burch's autobiography *They Cage Animals at Night* (NAL, 1984) is the story of a boy from a broken home whose destiny is a series of shelters and foster homes.

James M. Deem's novel *The 3NBs of Julian Drew* (Houghton, 1994) is the story of fifteen-year-old Julian, who is emotionally and physically abused by his father and his demented mother.

Stephanie remembers childhood abuse when she visits a therapist because of her nervous breakdown in the novel *Acting Normal* (Harper-Collins, 1989) by Julia Hoban.

Bryan J. Grapes has edited a fine collection of documents about child abuse, covering such topics as prevalence, underlying causes, and rehabilitation of victims in the book *Child Abuse* (Greenhaven, 2001).

About the Author and Book
Contemporary Authors. Vol. 182, Gale, 2002.
See also listing "Selected Web Sites on Children's Literature and Authors."

Appendix

Selected Web Sites on Children's Literature and Authors

Print Guides

Lamb, Annette, and Nancy R. Smith. *Newbery and the Net: Thematic Technology Connections*. Vision to Action, 2000.

This innovative resource gives material for each Newbery Medal winner from 1922 through 1999 arranged in reverse chronological order. For each book, there are two or three pages of resource material including Internet sites relating to the author and to the book, plus classroom connections. Some are for pure pleasure and others explore the themes and subjects found in the book.

Stevens, Jen. *The Undergraduate's Companion to Children's Writers and Their Web Sites*. Libraries Unlimited, 2004.

About 200 American and British writers (many of them Newbery or Printz winners) are highlighted in this book. For each, there are briefly annotated lists of important Web sites (about three per author), a bibliography of biographical and critical sources (again, about three per entry), and sometimes locations where bibliographies of the author's works can be found.

Story-Huffman, Ru. *Newbery on the Net*. 2nd ed. Upstart Books, 2002.

This book outlines lesson plans for 24 Newbery winners Each plan involves an assignment, Internet resources, activities, educator materials (with important related Web sites), and lists of follow-up books.

Important Web Sites

Awards and Prizes Online; http://awardsandprizes.cbcbooks.org

The Children's Book Council maintains this fee-based site that features information on about 300 literary awards arranged under four basic divisions. Searching can be done through various access points such as award title, author and illustrator name, book title, year, age group, and keyword. The site is updated regularly and subscriptions currently are $150 a year.

Carol Hurst's Children's Literature Site; www.carolhurst.com

This site has information about children's authors and illustrators, reviews of children's books, and ideas for book-related activities.

Center for Children's Books; www.lis.uiuc.edu/~ccb/about_us.html

This is the site of the Center for Children's Books at the University of Illinois at Urbana-Champaign. Click on Collection Development to find links to many interesting sections including Book Awards in Children's Literature (which covers more than 100 key awards).

Children's Literature Awards/Prizes; www.nolanet.org/award.htm

Annotated links connect to about 20 American awards, with basic material on their origins, purposes, and criteria.

Children's Literature Book Award Information; www.tarleton.edu/~cwilterding/awards.htm

In alphabetical order, this site links to dozens of awards (mostly American) with basic information including date of foundation and basic criteria.

Children's Literature Comprehensive Database; www.childrenslit.com

This extensive online database is available to individual subscribers for about $275 a year. There are more than 1.4 million MARC records of children's and young adult books plus more than 250,000 book reviews, lists of awards and prizes, best book citations, and links to authors' and illustrators' home pages. At the time of writing, access to the author area was free. Select "Features" and then "Meet the Authors and Illustrators."

Children's Literature Web Guide; www.ucalgary.ca/~dkbrown/

This famous site from the University of Calgary in Canada was once a primary beginning source of information on children's and young adult literature. Although it still contains a wealth of information, it has not been updated for several years and therefore is valuable only for retrospective information.

Cooperative Children's Book Center; www.education.wisc.edu/ccbc

This site from the Cooperative Children's Book Center at the University of Wisconsin in Madison has links to many other children's literature sites, professional organizations, awards and prizes, and interviews with authors and illustrators.

Cynthia Leitich Smith Children's Literature Resources;
www.cynthialeitichsmith.com/

In addition to original information, this site contains about 3,000 annotated links to home pages, bibliographies, literary criticism, etc. For a substantial listing of awards, click on "State and National Awards."

Database of Award-Winning Children's Literature; www.dawcl.com/

This source covers 57 awards, giving background information, including selection criteria, and a link to each award's home page under "Explanation of Awards." Winners can be searched via such access points as setting/period, gender of protagonist, and format.

Digital Librarian; www.digital-librarian.com/

Thousands of links are arranged under about 100 topics. Clicking on "Children's Literature" gives access to hundreds of valuable sites on all facets of children's and young adult literature.

Educational Paperback Association Website; www.edupaperback.org/resources.cfm

Links are provided to an excellent selection of sites. The area dealing with children's book awards is subdivided into sections including American Library Association awards, other awards, and state and regional awards.

Fairrosa Cyber Library of Children's Literature; www.fairrosa.info

This site is subdivided into compartments, the most important being Reference Shelf and Reading Room. The former gives links to hundreds of author and illustrator home pages, general literary sources, and a separate section on articles and reviews.

Internet Public Library; www.ipl.org

Two of the most valuable areas on this site are Kidspace and Teenspace. Click on Reading Zone in these areas for an impressive amount of literature-related material including biographical information and links to other sites.

Librarians' Internet Index; http://lii.org

Maintained by librarians in California, the home page on this site contains broad subjects. After "Arts and Humanities," click on "Literature" and then "Children's Literature" for lots of links to important sites in the field.

The Michael L. Printz Award Web Page; www.ala.org/ala/yalsa/ booklistsawards/printzaward/Printz,_Michael_L__Award.htm

This Web page from the administrators of the Printz Award, the Young Adult Library Services Association of the American Library Association, gives good background material on the award including a brief biography of Printz, previous winners, and the committee's policies and procedures. The festschrift edited by Dorothy Broderick honoring Michael L. Printz, *A Printz of a Man* (YALSA, 1997), can be read and downloaded from this site.

The Newbery Medal Web Page; www.ala.org/ala/alsc/awards scholarships/literaryawds/newberymedal/newberymedal.htm

This is part of the home page of the Association for Library Service to Children, a section of the American Library Association and administrator of the Newbery Medal. In addition to general background material on the award, there are sections on criteria, committee members, procedures, and lists of past medal winners and honor books.

Resources for School Librarians; www.sldirectory.com

There are lots of great resources here, arranged in six sections. Click on "Information Access" and then "Reading Room" for plenty of material, including links to many Web sites.

Vandergrift's Children's and Young Adult Pages; www.scils.rutgers.edu/~kvander

This is probably the most understanding reference source on children's and young adult literature on the Internet. Brimming with information and links, sections include "Children's Literature Page," "Young Adult Literature Page," "The History of Children's Literature," and an "Author Site."

Additional Author Links

By typing in author's names and/or book titles at the Web sites of such standard search engines as Yahoo and Google, a fantastic amount of information can be found. As well, many publishers maintain pages (or links to pages) that provide information about their authors. Here are some samples:

HarperCollins Children's Author Pages: www.harperchildrens.com/hch/author
Houghton Mifflin: www.eduplace.com/author or www.houghtonmifflinbooks.com
Penguin Books (UK): www.penguin.co.uk
Random House Children's Books Author Pages: www.randomhouse.com/author/author_search.html
Scholastic: http://books.scholastic.com/teachers/
Simon and Schuster: www.simonsays.com

Author Index

Titles fully discussed and summarized in *Classic Teenplots* as well as those cited in the text and in "Additional Selections" are included in this index. An asterisk (*) precedes those titles for which both summaries and discussions appear.

Abelove, Joan: *Saying It Out Loud*, 108
Adler, C. S.: *Winning*, 304
Aiken, Joan: **Midnight Is a Place*, 183; *The Wolves of Willoughby Chase*, 183
Akagi, Cynthia G.: *Dear Michael: Sexuality Education for Boys Ages 11–17*, 308
Alexander, Lloyd: *The Beggar Queen*, 131, 133; *The Drackenberg Adventure*, 231; **The El Dorado Adventure*, 231; *The Illyrian Adventure*, 231; *The Jedera Adventure*, 231; *The Kestrel*, 131, 133; *The Philadelphia Adventure*, 231; **Westmark*, 131; *The Xanadu Adventure*, 231
Almond, David: *Counting Stars*, 42
Alphin, Elaine Marie: *Simon Says*, 42
Ambler, Eric: *A Coffin for Dimitrios*, 256; *Journey into Fear*, 256
Anaya, Rudolfo: *Bless Me, Ultima*, 130
Anderson, Catherine: *Always in My Heart*, 35
Anderson, Laurie Halse: *Speak*, 115
Anthony, Piers: *Split Infinity*, 149
Antle, Nancy: *Lost in the War*, 206
Apone, Claudio: *My Grandfather Jack the Ripper*, 270
Armstrong, William H.: *Sounder*, 226
Arnosky, Jim: *Long Spikes*, 281
Ashley, Bernard: *Little Soldier*, 38
Asimov, Isaac: **Foundation*, 135; *Foundation and Earth*, 135; *Foundation and Empire*, 135; *Foundation's Edge*, 135; *Prelude to Foundation*, 135; *Second Foundation*, 135
Auch, Mary Jane: *Frozen Summer*, 209
Avi: *Bright Shadow*, 134; *The Fighting Ground*, 186, 191; *The Man Who Was Poe*, 186; *Nothing But the Truth*, 234; **The True Confessions of Charlotte Doyle*, 186; **Wolf Rider*, 233

Bagnold, Enid: **National Velvet*, 277
Baillie, Allan: *Secrets of Walden Rising*, 275
Baldwin, James: *Go Tell It on the Mountain*, 71; **If Beale Street Could Talk*, 71
Barrett, William E.: *The Left Hand of God*, 75; **The Lilies of the Field*, 74
Barron, T. A.: *The Fires of Merlin*, 181
Base, Graeme: *The Discovery of Dragons*, 173
Bastedo, Jamie: *Tracking Triple Seven*, 284
Bauer, Joan: *Backwater*, 260; *Rules of the Road*, 104; *Squashed*, 122
Bawden, Nina: *Carrie's War*, 229
Bear, Craig: *Foundation and Chaos*, 135
Bell, Ruth: **Changing Bodies, Changing Lives*, 307
Belton, Sandra: *McKendree*, 196
Benford, Gregory: *Foundation's Fear*, 135
Bennett, Cherie: *Life in the Fat Lane*, 122
Bennett, Jack: *The Voyage of the Lucky Dragon*, 199
Bennett, James: *Blue Star Rapture*, 302; *The Squared Circle*, 296
Bennett, Jay: *The Dangling Witness*, 236; *Deathman, Do Not Follow Me*, 236; **The Haunted One*, 236; *The Long Black Coat*, 236
Berry, James: *Ajeemah and His Son*, 226
Berry, Liz: *China Garden*, 217
Blacker, Terence: *The Angel Factory*, 146
Blackwood, Gary L.: *Moonshine*, 194
Blair, Clifford: *The Guns of Sacred Heart*, 212
Block, Francesca Lia: *Baby Be-Bop*, 1; *Cherokee Bat and the Goat Guys*, 1; *Missing Angel Juan*, 1; **Weetzie Bat*, 1; *Witch Baby*, 1
Bloor, Edward: *Tangerine*, 293
Blume, Judy: *Forever*, 4; *Then Again, Maybe I Won't*, 4; **Tiger Eyes*, 4
Boas, Jacob: *We Are Witnesses*, 223

325

Bonner, Cindy: *Lily*, 212
Borland, Hal: *When the Legends Die*, 25
Borntrager, Mary Christner: *Rebecca*, 196
Bova, Ben: *Orion Among the Stars*, 149
Boyle, David: *African Americans*, 316
Bradley, Marion Zimmer: *Heartlight*, 167
Branford, Henrietta: *White Wolf*, 286
Brashares, Ann: *The Sisterhood of the Traveling Pants*, 65
Bridgers, Sue Ellen: *All Together Now*, 77; *Home Before Dark*, 77, 272; *Notes for Another Life*, 77
Brin, David: *Foundation's Triumph*, 135; *The Postman*, 138; *Sundiver*, 138
Brontë, Charlotte: *Jane Eyre*, 248
Brooks, Bruce: *Midnight Hour Encores*, 122, 291; *The Moves Make the Man*, 291
Brooks, Sara: *You May Plow Here*, 203
Brooks, Terry: *The Black Unicorn*, 141; *Magic Kingdom for Sale—Sold!*, 141; *The Sword of Shannara*, 141; *Wizard at Large*, 141
Brown, Irene Bennett: *The Long Road Turning*, 212
Browne, N. M.: *Warriors of Alarna*, 134
Brynie, Faith: *101 Questions About Sex and Sexuality*, 308
Buffie, Margaret: *Angels Turn Their Backs*, 3
Bunting, Eve: *Is Anybody There?*, 45; *Someone Is Hiding on Alcatraz Island*, 252; *A Sudden Silence*, 22
Burch, Jennings Michael: *They Cage Animals at Night*, 318
Burnford, Sheila: *The Incredible Journey*, 280
Butcher, A. J.: *Spy High: Mission One*, 270
Butler, Charles: *The Darkling*, 158
Butler, William: *The Butterfly Revolution*, 18

Cadnum, Michael: *Redhanded*, 299
Calvert, Patricia: *The Stone Pony*, 22
Campbell, Eric: *The Shark Callers*, 170
Cargill, Linda: *Pool Party*, 270; *The Surfer*, 158
Cart, Michael: *My Father's Scar*, 100
Carter, Alden R.: *Growing Season*, 81; *Up Country*, 81
Childress, Alice: *A Hero Ain't Nothin' but a Sandwich*, 84; *Rainbow Jordan*, 73, 84; *Those Other People*, 84
Christopher, John: *The City of Gold and Lead*, 143; *The Pool of Fire*, 143; *When the Tripods Came*, 143; *The White Mountains*, 143
Clark, Catherine: *Truth or Diary*, 62

Clark, Mary Higgins: *Weep No More My Lady*, 238; *Where Are the Children?*, 239
Clarke, Arthur C.: *Rendezvous with Rama*, 147; *3001: The Final Odyssey*, 147; *2061: Odyssey Three*, 147; *2001: A Space Odyssey*, 147; *2010: Odyssey Two*, 147
Cleaver, Bill: *Ellen Grae*, 8; *Where the Lilies Bloom*, 8
Cleaver, Vera: *Ellen Grae*, 8; *Where the Lilies Bloom*, 8
Clement-Davies, David: *Fire Bringer*, 152
Clinton, Susan: *Reading Between the Bones*, 14
Close, Jessie: *The Warping of Al*, 31
Cohen, Barbara: *Unicorns in the Rain*, 164
Cohn, Rachel: *Gingerbread*, 3
Cole, Barbara: *Alex the Great*, 87
Cole, Brock: *Celine*, 88; *The Goats*, 87, 266
Collier, Christopher: *The Bloody Country*, 190; *The Clock*, 209; *My Brother Sam Is Dead*, 189
Collier, James Lincoln: *The Bloody Country*, 190; *The Clock*, 209; *My Brother Sam Is Dead*, 189
Collins, Max Allan: *The Pearl Harbor Murders*, 258
Conford, Ellen: *Seven Days to a Brand New Me*, 173
Conly, Jane Leslie: *Crazy Lady*, 196; *Rasco and the Rats of NIMH*, 168
Conrad, Pam: *My Daniel*, 11; *Prairie Songs*, 11
Conroy, Pat: *My Losing Season*, 311
Cooney, Caroline B.: *Burning Up*, 252; *The Terrorist*, 245; *Tune in Anytime*, 32
Cormier, Robert: *After the First Death*, 241; *Beyond the Chocolate War*, 15, 18, 241; *The Chocolate War*, 15; *I Am the Cheese*, 241; *The Rag and Bone Man*, 15
Coyne, Tom: *A Gentleman's Game*, 302
Creech, Sharon: *Chasing Redbird*, 104; *Walk Two Moons*, 122
Crichton, Michael: *The Andromeda Strain*, 149; *The Great Train Robbery*, 185
Crossley-Holland, Kevin: *The Seeing Stone*, 134
Crutcher, Chris: *Running Loose*, 293–294; *Stotan!*, 294
Cussler, Clive: *Treasure*, 245

Dahl, Roald: *Boy*, 309; *Going Solo*, 309
Dain, Claudia: *A Kiss to Die For*, 217
Davis, Jenny: *Checking on the Moon*, 14
Davis, Terry: *Vision Quest*, 298
Dayton, Arwen Elys: *Resurrection*, 137

Deaver, Jeffery: *The Blue Nowhere*, 258
Deaver, Julie Reece: *First Wedding, Once Removed*, 19; *The Night I Disappeared*, 19; **Say Goodnight, Gracie*, 19
DeCure, John: *Reef Dance*, 258
Deem, James M.: *The 3NBs of Julian Drew*, 318
DeFelice, Cynthia: *The Apprenticeship of Lucas Whitaker*, 209
Delinsky, Barbara: *Three Wishes*, 248
DeMille, Nelson: *The Charm School*, 256
Dessen, Sarah: *Dreamland*, 87; *Someone Like You*, 119
Deuker, Carl: *On the Devil's Court*, 296
Dick, Philip K.: *Do Androids Dream of Electric Sheep?*, 149
Dickens, Charles: *Great Expectations*, 185; *Oliver Twist*, 185
Dickinson, Peter: *A Bone from a Dry Sea*, 14; *The Devil's Children*, 150; **Eva*, 150; *Heartease*, 150; *The Poison Oak*, 150; *The Weathermonger*, 150
Disher, Garry: *Ratface*, 275
Doig, Ivan: *English Creek*, 266
Dorris, Michael: **A Yellow Raft in Blue Water*, 22
Doyle, Arthur Conan: *The Hound of the Baskervilles*, 217
Draper, Sharon M.: *The Battle of Jericho*, 18; *Tears of a Tiger*, 80
Duane, Diane: *The Wizard's Dilemma*, 164
Du Maurier, Daphne: *Jamaica Inn*, 185; *My Cousin Rachel*, 245; **Rebecca*, 245
Duncan, Lois: *Don't Look Behind You*, 275; *I Know What You Did Last Summer*, 233; *Killing Mr. Griffin*, 248; *Locked in Time*, 233, 248; **The Twisted Window*, 248
Durrant, Lynda: *The Beaded Moccasins*, 220

Earle, Robert: *The Way Home*, 35
Easton, Kelly: *The Life History of a Star*, 104
Eckert, Allan W.: **Incident at Hawk's Hill*, 282; *Return to Hawk's Hill*, 283
Elizabeth, Van Steenwyk: *A Traitor Among Us*, 229
Erickson, K. J.: *Third Person Singular*, 258
Ernst, Kathleen: *Betrayal at Cross Creek*, 191
Even, Aaron Roy: *Bloodroot*, 77

Fast, Howard: *April Morning*, 191
Faustine, Lisa R., ed.: *Dirty Laundry: Stories About Family Secrets*, 32
Ferguson, Alane: *Overkill*, 270
Ferris, Jean: *Eight Seconds*, 65

Ferry, Charles: *A Fresh Start*, 83
Fitzhugh, Louise: **Harriet the Spy*, 26; *Nobody's Family Is Going to Change*, 26
Flake, Sharon G.: *Money Hungry*, 10
Fleischman, Paul: *Seek*, 272
Florman, Samuel C.: *The Aftermath: A Novel of Survival*, 140
Flynn, Pat: *Alex Jackson: SWA*, 293
Foley, June: *Susanna Siegelbaum Gives Up Guys*, 173
Follett, Ken: *Eye of the Needle*, 256; *The Key to Rebecca*, 256
Forsyth, Frederick: **The Day of the Jackal*, 253; *The Devil's Alternative*, 253; *The Odessa File*, 253
Fox, Paula: *The Eagle Kite*, 7; **The Moonlight Man*, 29; **One-Eyed Cat*, 192; *The Slave Dancer*, 29, 192
Francis, Dick: **Bolt*, 256; *Break In*, 256; *Whip Hand*, 256
Frank, E. R.: *Life Is Funny*, 68
Freeman, Joseph: *Job: The Story of a Holocaust Survivor*, 223
Freymann-Weyr, Garret: *My Heartbeat*, 65
Furlong, Monica: *Juniper*, 134

Gaines, Ernest J.: *The Autobiography of Miss Jane Pittman*, 203; *A Gathering of Old Men*, 203; *In My Father's House*, 73
Garden, Nancy: **Annie on My Mind*, 91; *Lark in the Morning*, 91; *Peace, O River*, 91
Garner, Alan: **The Owl Service*, 153
Garrett, Martin: *George Gordon, Lord Byron*, 311
George, Jean Craighead: *Julie of the Wolves*, 266
Gifaldi, David: *Yours Till Forever*, 263
Gilman, Dorothy: *The Amazing Mrs. Pollifax*, 241; *Mrs. Pollifax and the Golden Triangle*, 241
Goobie, Beth: *Before Wings*, 58; *Who Owns Kelly Paddik?*, 45
Gordon, Sheila: *Waiting for the Rain*, 77
Gorman, Carol: *Dork on the Run*, 28
Graeber, Charlotte: *Grey Cloud*, 286
Grapes, Bryan J.: *Child Abuse*, 318
Greene, Bette: **The Summer of My German Soldier*, 194
Guest, Judith: **Ordinary People*, 33
Gutcheon, Beth: *More Than You Know*, 248

Haddix, Margaret Peterson: *Don't You Dare*

Read This, Mrs. Dunphrey, 112; Takeoffs and Landings, 260
Haddon, Mark: The Curious Incident of the Dog in the Night-Time, 68
Hague, Michael, ed.: The Book of Dragons, 181
Hahn, Mary D.: Stepping on the Cracks, 229
Haley, Alex: Roots, 203
Hall, Lynn: Flying Changes, 10; Ride a Dark Horse, 279
Halliburton, Warren J.: Historic Speeches of African Americas, 316
Hamilton, Virginia: M. C. Higgins the Great, 156, 272; *Sweet Whispers, Brother Rush, 156
Harrah, Madge: My Brother, My Enemy, 220
Harris, Marilyn: Hatter Fox, 25
Heacox, Kim: Caribou Crossing, 59
Heinlein, Robert A.: The Star Beast, 146; *Stranger in a Strange Land, 159
Herbert, Frank: Children of Dune, 137; Dune, 137
Herman, John: Labyrinth, 155
Hermes, Patricia: Fly Away Home, 282
Herriot, James: All Creatures Great and Small, 312; All Things Bright and Beautiful, 312; All Things Wise and Wonderful, 312; Every Living Thing, 312; *The Lord God Made Them All, 312
Hersey, John: A Bell for Adano, 77
Hesse, Karen: Out of the Dust, 10; Phoenix Rising, 22; Stowaway, 188; Witness, 226
Hesser, Terry Spencer: Kissing Doorknobs, 115
Hickman, Janet: Ravine, 155
Higgins, Jack: Solo, 245
Hill, Pamela S.: Ghost Horses, 14
Hinton, S. E.: *The Outsiders, 36; Taming the Star Runner, 100
Hite, Sid: Those Darn Dithers, 3
Hoban, Julia: Acting Normal, 318
Hobb, Will: Beardance, 59
Hoffman, Alice: Green Angel, 7
Holeman, Linda: Search of the Moon King's Daughter, 185
Holland, Isabelle: Man Without a Face, 100
Holt, Victoria: The Captive, 217
Holtwijk, Ineke: Asphalt Angels, 38
Howe, James: The Watcher, 119
Hunt, Irene: No Promises in the Wind, 194

Isserman, Maurice: Journey to Freedom, 178, 316

Jackson, Dave: Danger on the Flying Trapeze, 55
Jenkins, A. M.: Breaking Boxes, 100
Johnson, Angela: Heaven, 108
Johnston, Tim: Never So Green, 45
Jones, Diana Wynne: *Castle in the Air, 162; Howl's Moving Castle, 162
Jones, Jill: Emily's Secret, 248

Karr, Kathleen: Playing with Fire, 194
Kehret, Peg: Night of Fear, 233
Kennedy, Barbara: The Boy Who Loved Alligators, 286
Kerr, M. E.: Dinky Hocker Shoots Smack!, 94; *Gentlehands, 94; Is That You, Miss Blue?, 94; Night Kites, 94; What I Really Think of You, 55
Kerrigan, Philip: Survival Game, 170
Ketchum, Liza: Blue Coyote, 93
Kherdian, David: Finding Home, 199; The Road from Home, 199
Kincaid, Jamaica: Annie John, 73
King, Laurie R.: A Darker Place, 241
King, Stephen: The Stand, 161
Kinna, Gieth: I Miss You, I Miss You!, 35
Kipling, Rudyard: Captains Courageous, 188
Kjelgaard, James A.: Stormy, 288
Klass, David: Danger Zone, 296; You Don't Know Me, 90
Klaveness, Jan O'Donnell: Ghost Island, 188
Knight, Eric: Lassie Come Home, 282
Knowles, John: A Separate Peace, 18
Koertge, Ron: *The Arizona Kid, 98; Confess-O-Rama, 176; The Man in the Moon, 98; Where the Kissing Never Stops, 98
Koller, Jackie French: The Falcon, 119; A Place to Call Home, 22; The Primrose Way, 220
Konigsburg, E. L.: *Father's Arcane Daughter, 258; From the Mixed-up Files of Mrs. Basil E. Frankweiler, 258; The View from Saturday, 258
Koontz, Dean: Fear Nothing, 161
Kress, Nancy: Beggars and Choosers, 140
Krisher, Trudy: Uncommon Faith, 209

Lasky, Kathryn: Beyond the Divide, 220; Memories of a Bookbait, 55
Lawrence, Gordon: User Friendly, 3
Laxalt, Robert: Dust Devils, 288
Layne, Steven L.: This Side of Paradise, 152

Lee, Harper: *To Kill a Mockingbird*, 129
Lee, Marie G.: *Necessary Roughness*, 299
LeGuin, Ursula K.: *The Left Hand of Darkness*, 161; *A Wizard of Earthsea*, 164
Leiber, Fritz: *The Big Time*, 137
L'Engle, Madeleine: *The Arm of the Starfish*, 101; *A House Like a Lotus*, 93; *Meet the Austins*, 101; *The Moon by Night*, 101; **A Ring of Endless Light*, 101; *A Wrinkle in Time*, 101, 158; *The Young Unicorns*, 101
Lester, Julius: *To Be a Slave*, 316
Levenkron, Steven: *The Best Little Girl in the World*, 115
Levitin, Sonia: *Escape from Egypt*, 197; **The Return*, 197
Lewis, C. S.: *The Lion, the Witch, and the Wardrobe*, 178
Lindbergh, Anne: *Three Lives to Live*, 178
Lipsyte, Robert: *The Brave*, 297; *The Chief*, 25, 297; **The Contender*, 297
Lowry, Lois: *Number the Stars*, 105; **Rabble Starkey*, 105; *A Summer to Die*, 105

Macaulay, David: *Baaa*, 178
McCaffrey, Anne: *Dragonflight*, 165; *Dragonquest*, 165; *The Dragonriders of Pern*, 165; **Dragonsong*, 165; *If Wishes Were Horses*, 279; *The White Dragon*, 165
McClain, Margaret S.: *Bellboy: A Mule Train Mystery*, 212
McCormick, John: *A Friend of the Flock: Tales of a Country Veterinarian*, 314
MacCullough, Carolyn: *Falling Through Darkness*, 80
McDaniel, Lurlene: *The Girl Death Left Behind*, 7
McDonald, Janet: *Spellbound*, 108
McDonald, Joyce: *Shadow People*, 42; *Swallowing Stones*, 68
McFadden, Cyra: *Rain or Shine*, 32
MacGregor, Rob: *Hawk Moon*, 252
McKillip, Patricia A.: *The Forgotten Beasts of Eld*, 167
McKinley, Robin: *The Hero and the Crown*, 167
McNamee, Graham: *Hate You*, 112
Madaras, Area: *The "What's Happening to My Body?" Book for Boys: A Growing Up Guide for Parents and Sons*, 308; *The "What's Happening to My Body?" Book for Girls: A Growing Up Guide for Parents and Daughters*, 308
Madaras, Lynda: *The "What's Happening to My Body?" Book for Boys: A Growing Up Guide for Parents and Sons*, 308; *The "What's Happening to My Body?" Book for Girls: A Growing Up Guide for Parents and Daughters*, 308
Mahy, Margaret: *The Changeover*, 39; *The Haunting*, 39; **Memory*, 39
Martin, Nora: *The Eagle's Shadow*, 83
Mason, Bobbie Ann: *In Country*, 206
Masterman-Smith, Virginia: *First Mate Tate*, 83
Mathis, Sharon: *Teacup Full of Roses*, 86
Mazer, Norma Fox: *After the Rain*, 43; **Silver*, 43
Mazzio, Joann: *The One Who Came Back*, 245
Meachum, Virginia: *Jane Goodall: Protector of Chimpanzees*, 314
Michaels, Melisa C.: *Far Harbor*, 143
Miklowitz, Gloria D.: *After the Bomb*, 170
Mills, Claudia: *Alex Ryan, Stop That!*, 173
Modesitt, L. E., Jr.: *The Soprano Sorceress*, 143
Morey, Walt: *Death Walk*, 170
Morrell, David: *Fireflies*, 35
Morris, Gilbert: *Journey to Freedom*, 178
Morris, Winifred: *Liar*, 48
Morrison, Toni: **Beloved*, 200; *The Bluest Eye*, 130, 200
Mosher, Richard: *Zazoo*, 97
Mowat, Farley: *The Dog Who Wouldn't Be*, 288; *Lost in the Barrens*, 266
Mowry, Jess: *Ghost Train*, 158
Mukerji, Dhan Gopel: *Gay-Neck*, 282
Myers, Anna: *Turning Burning*, 226
Myers, Bill: *The Society*, 175
Myers, Walter Dean: **Fallen Angels*, 204, 314; *Monster*, 204; **Now Is Your Time! The African-American Struggle for Freedom*, 314; *Scorpions*, 87; *The Young Landlords*, 77

Naylor, Phyllis Reynolds: *The Agony of Alice*, 28; **The Keeper*, 80, 109; *Shiloh*, 109; *Simply Alice*, 52
Neufeld, John: *Edgar Allan*, 113; *I'll Always Love You, Paul Newman*, 113; **Lisa, Bright and Dark*, 113
Nix, Garth: *Shade's Children*, 146
Nixon, Joan Lowery: *The Dark and Deadly Pool*, 235; *The Kidnapping of Christina Lattimore*, 262; *Maggie, Too*, 262; *The Other Side of Dark*, 252, 262; **The Séance*, 261
Nodelman, Perry: *Behaving Bradley*, 62
Nolan, Han: *A Face in Every Window*, 83

North, Sterling: *Rascal, 284; So Dear to My Heart, 285
Norton, Andre: House of Shadows, 263

O'Brien, Robert C.: Mrs. Frisby and the Rats of NIMH, 168; *Z for Zachariah, 168
Ormondroyd, Edward: Time at the Top, 52
Orwell, George: Nineteen Eighty Four, 140

Paldiel, Mordecai: Saving the Jews, 223
Park, Barbara: Buddies, 28; The Graduation of Jake Moon, 97
Pascal, Francine: Fearless, 304; *Hangin' Out with Cici, 171; Love and Betrayal and Hold the Mayo, 171; My First Love and Other Disasters, 171
Pascal, Janet B.: Arthur Conan Doyle: Beyond Baker Street, 311
Paterson, Katherine: Bridge to Terabithia, 207; Jacob Have I Loved, 260; *Lyddie, 207
Patneaude, David: Framed in Fire, 45
Paulsen, Gary: Alida's Song, 48; Brian's Hunt, 265; Brian's Return, 265; Brian's Winter, 265; *Hatchet, 126, 264; Mr. Tucket, 265; The River, 265
Peck, Richard: *Remembering the Good Times, 116; Secrets of the Shopping Mall, 233; A Year Down Yonder, 116
Peck, Robert Newton: *A Day No Pigs Would Die, 46; Horse Thief, 279
Pelzer, Dave: *A Child Called "It," 316; Help Yourself for Teens: Real-Life Advice for Real-Life Challenges, 317; The Lost Boy, 317; A Man Called Dave, 317
Pennac, Daniel: Eye of the Wolf, 284
Peters, Elizabeth: The Deeds of the Disturber, 241; The Mummy Case, 241
Peterson, P. J.: Liars, 236
Philbrick, Rodman: Freak the Mighty, 90
Pike, Christopher: Bury Me Deep, 264; Gimme a Kiss, 236
Platt, Randall R.: The Cornerstone, 58
Pohl, Peter: I Miss You, I Miss You!, 35
Porter, Connie Rose: Imani All Mine, 130
Portis, Charles: *True Grit, 210
Powell, Randy: Dean Duffy, 296; Run If You Dare, 112; The Whistling Toilets, 304
Pullman, Philip: Clockwork, 155; The Golden Compass, 152, 213; *The Ruby in the Smoke, 213; The Shadow in the North, 213; The Tiger in the Well, 213

Qualey, Marsha: Close to a Killer, 238; Thin Ice, 108

Ragz, M. M.: French Fries Up Your Nose, 28
Rawls, Wilson: The Summer of the Monkeys, 287; *Where the Red Fern Grows, 287
Remarque, Erich Maria: All Quiet on the Western Front, 206
Rennison, Louise: Angus, Thongs, and Full-Frontal Snogging, 62
Rinaldi, Ann: A Ride into Morning: The Story of Temple Wick, 279; The Secret of Sarah Revere, 191
Ritter, John H.: Choosing Up Sides, 55; Over the Wall, 302
Roberts, Willo Davis: Twisted Summer, 238
Rodgers, Mary: A Billion for Boris, 49; *Freaky Friday, 49
Rostowski, Margaret: The Best of Friends, 206
Rowling, J. K.: Harry Potter and the Sorcerer's Stone, 167
Ryan, Pam Muñoz: Esperanza Rising, 7
Rylant, Cynthia: *A Fine White Dust, 52; I Have Seen Castles, 196; Missing May, 53

Salisbury, Graham: Blood Red Sun, 97
Salten, Felix: Bambi: A Life in the Woods, 284
Salvatore, R. A.: The Woods out Back, 143
Sanchez, Alex: Rainbow Boys, 93
Sargent, Pamela: Alien Child, 140
Scanlon, Edward J.: Animal Patients: 50 Years in the Life of an Animal Doctor, 314
Schoen, Allen M.: Love, Miracles, and Animal Healing, 314
Scoppetone, Sandra: Happy Endings Are All Alike, 93
Scrimger, Richard: Noses Are Red, 52
Sebestyen, Ouida: *Far from Home, 120; Words by Heart, 120
Seidler, Tor: The Silent Spillbills, 97
Serraillier, Ian: The Silver Sword, 229
Shaw, Diana: Lessons in Fear, 238
Shirley, David: Alex Haley, 311
Shusterman, Neal: Downsiders, 143
Skurzynski, Gloria: The Clones, 152
Sleator, William: *House of Stairs, 175; Interstellar Pig, 174; Singularity, 174
Smith, Cotton: Dark Trail to Dodge, 275
Snyder, Midori: Hannah's Garden, 155
Sones, Sonya: Stop Pretending, 115
Speare, Elizabeth: The Bronze Bow, 218; *Calico Captive, 218; The Sign of the Beaver, 218; The Witch of Blackbird Pond, 218

Spiegelman, Art: *Maus: A Survivor's Tale II—And Here My Troubles Began*, 221; *Maus: A Survivor's Tale—My Father Bleeds History*, 221
Springer, Nancy: *Secret Star*, 11
Stevens, Marcus: *Useful Girl*, 25
Stillman, Larry: *A Match Made in Hell*, 223
Strasser, Todd: *Girl Gives Birth to Own Prom Date*, 62; *How I Changed My Life*, 90
Styron, William: *The Confessions of Nat Turner*, 203
Sullivan, Paul: *Legend of the North*, 284
Swarthout, Glendon: *Bless the Beasts and Children*, 56; *The Shootist*, 56; *They Came to Cordura*, 56; *Where the Boys Are*, 56
Sweeney, Joyce: *Players*, 293

Taha, Karen T.: *Marshmallow Muscles, Banana Brainstorms*, 52
Tanzman, Carol M.: *The Shadow Place*, 175
Taylor, Mildred D.: *Let the Circle Be Unbroken*, 223; *Roll of Thunder, Hear My Cry*, 223; *Song of the Trees*, 223
Taylor, Theodore: *The Cay*, 123; *Lord of the Kill*, 238; *Rogue Wave and Other Red-Blooded Sea Stories*, 188; *Timothy of the Cay*, 123
Thesman, Jean: *The Last April Dancers*, 272
Thomas, Rob: *Rats Saw God*, 119
Thompson, Julian: *The Grounding of Group 6*, 267; *Simon Pure*, 268; *Terry and the Pirates*, 268
Thompson, Kate: *Midnight Choice*, 175
Tolan, Stephanie: *Who's There?*, 264
Tolkein, J. R. R.: *The Hobbit*, 176; *The Lord of the Rings*, 176
Tomey, Ingrid: *The Queen of Dreamland*, 261
Townsend, Sue: *Adrian Mole and the Weapons of Mass Destruction*, 59; *The Adrian Mole Diaries*, 59; *The Growing Pains of Adrian Mole*, 59; *The Secret Diary of Adrian Mole, Aged 13¾*, 59
Truman, Margaret: *Murder in the CIA*, 240

Vail, Rachel: *Do-Over*, 90
Velde, Vivian Vande: *Dragon's Bait*, 181
Voigt, Cynthia: *Dicey's Song*, 271; *Homecoming*, 270; *The Runner*, 299; *Seventeen Against the Dealer*, 271

Vonnegut, Kurt: *Slaughterhouse Five*, 161

Walker, Alice: *The Color Purple*, 127; *Meridian*, 127; *The Third Life of Grange Copeland*, 127
Wallace, Rich: *Wrestling Sturbridge*, 301
Watkins, Yoko Kawashima: *So Far from the Bamboo Grove*, 199
Watts, Julia: *Finding H. F.*, 65
Weaver, Will: *Striking Out*, 48
Wells, H. G.: *The War of the Worlds*, 146
Wells, Rosemary: *The Man in the Woods*, 302; *Through the Hidden Door*, 302; *When No One Was Looking*, 302
Wersba, Barbara: *The Farewell Kid*, 62; *Fat: A Love Story*, 62; *Just Be Gorgeous*, 62; *Wonderful Me*, 62
Westall, Robert: *Fathom Five*, 227; *The Machine Gunners*, 227; *The Scarecrows*, 227
Westheimer, David: *Von Ryan's Express*, 256
White, Robb: *Deathwatch*, 273; *Flight Deck*, 274; *Up Periscope*, 274
Wilbur, Frances: *The Dog with Golden Eyes*, 286
Willey, Margaret: *Saving Lenny*, 112
Williams, Jean K.: *The Shakers*, 48
Williamson, Jack: *Transforming Earth*, 137
Wittlinger, Ellen: *Hard Love*, 68
Wolfert, Adrienne: *Making Tracks*, 194
Wolff, Lisa: *Gangs*, 36
Wolff, Virginia E.: *Bat 6*, 304
Woodruff, Nancy: *Someone Else's Child*, 42
Woodson, Jacqueline: *If You Come Softly*, 74; *Miracle Boys*, 104
Wrede, Patricia C.: *Magician's World*, 164
Wright, Richard: *Rite of Passage*, 38
Wyss, Thelma Hatch: *Ten Miles from Winnemucca*, 233

Yep, Laurence: *Dragon of the Lost Sea*, 181; *Mountain Light*, 199; *The Serpent's Children*, 199
Yolen, Jane: *Dragon's Blood*, 179; *Heart's Blood*, 180; *A Sending of Dragons*, 180

Zindel, Paul: *The Pigman*, 65; *Rats*, 66; *The Undertaker's Gone Bananas*, 235
Zusak, Markus: *Fighting Ruben Wolfe*, 299

Title Index

Titles fully discussed and summarized in *Classic Teenplots* as well as those cited in the text and in "Additional Selections" are included in this index. An asterisk (*) precedes those titles for which both summaries and discussions appear.

Acting Normal, 318
Adrian Mole and the Weapons of Mass Destruction, 59
**The Adrian Mole Diaries*, 59
African Americans, 316
After the Bomb, 170
**After the First Death*, 241
After the Rain, 43
The Aftermath: A Novel of Survival, 140
The Agony of Alice, 28
Ajeemah and His Son, 226
Alex Haley, 203, 311
Alex Jackson: SWA, 293
Alex Ryan, Stop That!, 173
Alex the Great, 87
Alida's Song, 48
Alien Child, 140
All Creatures Great and Small, 312
All Quiet on the Western Front, 206
All Things Bright and Beautiful, 312
All Things Wise and Wonderful, 312
All Together Now, 77
Always in My Heart, 35
The Amazing Mrs. Pollifax, 241
The Andromeda Strain, 149
The Angel Factory, 146
Angels Turn Their Backs, 3
Angus, Thongs, and Full-Frontal Snogging, 62
Animal Patients: 50 Years in the Life of an Animal Doctor, 314
Annie John, 73
**Annie on My Mind*, 91
The Apprenticeship of Lucas Whitaker, 209
April Morning, 191
**The Arizona Kid*, 98
The Arm of the Starfish, 101
Arthur Conan Doyle: Beyond Baker Street, 311
Asphalt Angels, 38

The Autobiography of Miss Jane Pittman, 203

Baaa, 178
Baby Be-Bop, 1
Backwater, 260
Bambi: A Life in the Woods, 284
Bat 6, 304
The Battle of Jericho, 18
The Beaded Moccasins, 220
Beardance, 59
Before Wings, 58
The Beggar Queen, 131, 133
Beggars and Choosers, 140
Behaving Bradley, 62
A Bell for Adano, 77
Bellboy: A Mule Train Mystery, 212
**Beloved*, 200
The Best Little Girl in the World, 115
The Best of Friends, 206
Betrayal at Cross Creek, 191
Beyond the Chocolate War, 15, 18, 241
Beyond the Divide, 220
The Big Time, 137
A Billion for Boris, 49
The Black Unicorn, 141
Bless Me, Ultima, 130
**Bless the Beasts and Children*, 56
Blood Red Sun, 97
Bloodroot, 77
The Bloody Country, 190
Blue Coyote, 93
The Blue Nowhere, 258
Blue Star Rapture, 302
The Bluest Eye, 130, 200
**Bolt*, 256
A Bone from a Dry Sea, 14
The Book of Dragons, 181
Boy, 309

333

The Boy Who Loved Alligators, 286
The Brave, 297
Break In, 256
Breaking Boxes, 100
Brian's Hunt, 265
Brian's Return, 265
Brian's Winter, 265
Bridge to Terabithia, 207
Bright Shadow, 134
The Bronze Bow, 218
Buddies, 28
Burning Up, 252
Bury Me Deep, 264
The Butterfly Revolution, 18

*Calico Captive, 218
Captains Courageous, 188
The Captive, 217
Caribou Crossing, 59
Carrie's War, 229
*Castle in the Air, 162
*The Cay, 123
Celine, 88
The Changeover, 39
*Changing Bodies, Changing Lives, 307
The Charm School, 256
Chasing Redbird, 104
Checking on the Moon, 14
Cherokee Bat and the Goat Guys, 1
The Chief, 25, 297
Child Abuse, 318
*A Child Called "It," 316
Children of Dune, 137
China Garden, 217
*The Chocolate War, 15
Choosing Up Sides, 55
The City of Gold and Lead, 143
The Clock, 209
Clockwork, 155
The Clones, 152
Close to a Killer, 238
A Coffin for Dimitrios, 256
*The Color Purple, 127
Confess-O-Rama, 176
The Confessions of Nat Turner, 203
*The Contender, 297
The Cornerstone, 58
Counting Stars, 42
Crazy Lady, 196
The Curious Incident of the Dog in the Night-Time, 68

Danger on the Flying Trapeze, 55
Danger Zone, 296

The Dangling Witness, 236
The Dark and Deadly Pool, 235
Dark Trail to Dodge, 275
A Darker Place, 241
The Darkling, 158
*A Day No Pigs Would Die, 46
*The Day of the Jackal, 253
Dean Duffy, 296
Dear Michael: Sexuality Education for Boys Ages 11–17, 308
Death Walk, 170
Deathman, Do Not Follow Me, 236
*Deathwatch, 273
The Deeds of the Disturber, 241
The Devil's Alternative, 253
The Devil's Children, 150
Dicey's Song, 271
Dinky Hocker Shoots Smack!, 94
Dirty Laundry: Stories About Family Secrets, 32
The Discovery of Dragons, 173
Do Androids Dream of Electric Sheep?, 149
Do-Over, 90
The Dog Who Wouldn't Be, 288
The Dog with Golden Eyes, 286
Donna Jo Napoli's Three Days, 126
Don't Look Behind You, 275
Don't You Dare Read This, Mrs. Dunphrey, 112
Dork on the Run, 28
Downsiders, 143
The Drackenberg Adventure, 231
Dragon of the Lost Sea, 181
Dragonflight, 165
Dragonquest, 165
The Dragonriders of Pern, 165
Dragon's Bait, 181
*Dragon's Blood, 179
*Dragonsong, 165
Dreamland, 87
Dune, 137
Dust Devils, 288

The Eagle Kite, 7
The Eagle's Shadow, 83
Edgar Allan, 113
Eight Seconds, 65
*The El Dorado Adventure, 231
Ellen Grae, 8
Emily's Secret, 248
English Creek, 266
Escape from Egypt, 197
Esperanza Rising, 7
*Eva, 150
Every Living Thing, 312
Eye of the Needle, 256

TITLE INDEX • 335

Eye of the Wolf, 284

A Face in Every Window, 83
The Falcon, 119
*Fallen Angels, 204, 314
Falling Through Darkness, 80
*Far from Home, 120
Far Harbor, 143
The Farewell Kid, 62
Fat: A Love Story, 62
*Father's Arcane Daughter, 258
Fathom Five, 227
Fear Nothing, 161
Fearless, 304
The Fighting Ground, 186, 191
Fighting Ruben Wolfe, 299
Finding H. F., 65
Finding Home, 199
*A Fine White Dust, 52
Fire Bringer, 152
Fireflies, 35
The Fires of Merlin, 181
First Mate Tate, 83
First Wedding, Once Removed, 19
Flight Deck, 274
Fly Away Home, 282
Flying Changes, 10
Forever, 4
The Forgotten Beasts of Eld, 167
*Foundation, 135
Foundation and Chaos, 135
Foundation and Earth, 135
Foundation and Empire, 135
Foundation's Edge, 135
Foundation's Fear, 135
Foundation's Triumph, 135
Framed in Fire, 45
Freak the Mighty, 90
*Freaky Friday, 49
French Fries Up Your Nose, 28
A Fresh Start, 83
A Friend of the Flock: Tales of a Country Veterinarian, 314
From the Mixed-up Files of Mrs. Basil E. Frankweiler, 258
Frozen Summer, 209

Gangs, 36
A Gathering of Old Men, 203
Gay-Neck, 282
*Gentlehands, 94
A Gentleman's Game, 302
George Gordon, Lord Byron, 311
Ghost Horses, 14

Ghost Island, 188
Ghost Train, 158
Gimme a Kiss, 236
Gingerbread, 3
The Girl Death Left Behind, 7
Girl Gives Birth to Own Prom Date, 62
Go Tell It on the Mountain, 71
*The Goats, 87, 266
*Going Solo, 309
The Golden Compass, 152, 213
The Graduation of Jake Moon, 97
Graham Salisbury's Lord of the Deep, 126
Great Expectations, 185
The Great Train Robbery, 185
Green Angel, 7
Grey Cloud, 286
*The Grounding of Group 6, 267
The Growing Pains of Adrian Mole, 59
Growing Season, 81
The Guns of Sacred Heart, 212

*Hangin' Out with Cici, 171
Hannah's Garden, 155
Happy Endings Are All Alike, 93
Hard Love, 68
*Harriet the Spy, 26
Harry Potter and the Sorcerer's Stone, 167
*Hatchet, 126, 264
Hate You, 112
Hatter Fox, 25
*The Haunted One, 236
The Haunting, 39
Hawk Moon, 252
Heartease, 150
Heartlight, 167
Heart's Blood, 180
Heaven, 108
Help Yourself for Teens: Real-Life Advice for Real-Life Challenges, 317
*A Hero Ain't Nothin' but a Sandwich, 84
The Hero and the Crown, 167
Historic Speeches of African Americas, 316
*The Hobbit, 176
Home Before Dark, 77, 272
*Homecoming, 270
Horse Thief, 279
The Hound of the Baskervilles, 217
A House Like a Lotus, 93
House of Shadows, 263
*House of Stairs, 175
How I Changed My Life, 90
Howl's Moving Castle, 162

I Am the Cheese, 241
I Have Seen Castles, 196
I Know What You Did Last Summer, 233
I Miss You, I Miss You!, 35
*If Beale Street Could Talk, 71
If Wishes Were Horses, 279
If You Come Softly, 74
I'll Always Love You, Paul Newman, 113
The Illyrian Adventure, 231
Imani All Mine, 130
In Country, 206
In My Father's House, 73
*Incident at Hawk's Hill, 282
*The Incredible Journey, 280
Interstellar Pig, 174
Is Anybody There?, 45
Is That You, Miss Blue?, 94

Jacob Have I Loved, 260
Jamaica Inn, 185
Jane Eyre, 248
Jane Goodall: Protector of Chimpanzees, 314
The Jedera Adventure, 231
Job: The Story of a Holocaust Survivor, 223
Journey into Fear, 256
Journey to Freedom (Isserman), 316
Journey to Freedom (Morris), 178
Julie of the Wolves, 266
Juniper, 134
*Just Be Gorgeous, 62

*The Keeper, 80, 109
The Kestrel, 131, 133
The Key to Rebecca, 256
The Kidnapping of Christina Lattimore, 262
Killing Mr. Griffin, 248
A Kiss to Die For, 217
Kissing Doorknobs, 115

Labyrinth, 155
Lark in the Morning, 91
Lassie Come Home, 282
The Last April Dancers, 272
The Left Hand of Darkness, 161
The Left Hand of God, 75
Legend of the North, 284
Lessons in Fear, 238
*Let the Circle Be Unbroken, 223
Liar, 48
Liars, 236
The Life History of a Star, 104
Life in the Fat Lane, 122
Life Is Funny, 68
*The Lilies of the Field, 74

Lily, 212
The Lion, the Witch, and the Wardrobe, 178
*Lisa, Bright and Dark, 113
Little Soldier, 38
Locked in Time, 233, 248
The Long Black Coat, 236
The Long Road Turning, 212
Long Spikes, 281
*The Lord God Made Them All, 312
Lord of the Kill, 238
The Lord of the Rings, 176
The Lost Boy, 317
Lost in the Barrens, 266
Lost in the War, 206
Love and Betrayal and Hold the Mayo, 171
Love, Miracles, and Animal Healing, 314
*Lyddie, 207

M. C. Higgins the Great, 156, 272
*The Machine Gunners, 227
McKendree, 196
Maggie, Too, 262
*Magic Kingdom for Sale—Sold!, 141
Magician's World, 164
Making Tracks, 194
A Man Called Dave, 317
The Man in the Moon, 98
The Man in the Woods, 302
The Man Who Was Poe, 186
Man Without a Face, 100
Marshmallow Muscles, Banana Brainstorms, 52
A Match Made in Hell, 223
Maus: A Survivor's Tale II—And Here My Troubles Began, 221
*Maus: A Survivor's Tale—My Father Bleeds History, 221
Meet the Austins, 101
Memories of a Bookbait, 55
*Memory, 39
Meridian, 127
Midnight Choice, 175
Midnight Hour Encores, 122, 291
*Midnight Is a Place, 183
Miracle Boys, 104
Missing Angel Juan, 1
Missing May, 53
Money Hungry, 10
Monster, 204
The Moon by Night, 101
*The Moonlight Man, 29
Moonshine, 194
More Than You Know, 248
Mountain Light, 199
*The Moves Make the Man, 291

TITLE INDEX • 337

Mr. Tucket, 265
Mrs. Frisby and the Rats of NIMH, 168
Mrs. Pollifax and the Golden Triangle, 241
The Mummy Case, 241
Murder in the CIA, 240
My Brother, My Enemy, 220
*My Brother Sam Is Dead, 189
My Cousin Rachel, 245
*My Daniel, 11
My Father's Scar, 100
My First Love and Other Disasters, 171
My Grandfather Jack the Ripper, 270
My Heartbeat, 65
My Losing Season, 311

*National Velvet, 277
Necessary Roughness, 299
Never So Green, 45
The Night I Disappeared, 19
Night Kites, 94
Night of Fear, 233
Nineteen Eighty Four, 140
No Promises in the Wind, 194
Nobody's Family Is Going to Change, 26
Noses Are Red, 52
*Notes for Another Life, 77
Nothing But the Truth, 234
*Now Is Your Time! The African-American Struggle for Freedom, 314
Number the Stars, 105

The Odessa File, 253
Oliver Twist, 185
On the Devil's Court, 296
*One-Eyed Cat, 192
101 Questions About Sex and Sexuality, 308
The One Who Came Back, 245
*Ordinary People, 33
Orion Among the Stars, 149
The Other Side of Dark, 252, 262
Out of the Dust, 10
*The Outsiders, 36
Over the Wall, 302
Overkill, 270
*The Owl Service, 153

Peace, O River, 91
The Pearl Harbor Murders, 258
The Philadelphia Adventure, 231
Phoenix Rising, 22
*The Pigman, 65
A Place to Call Home, 22
Players, 293
Playing with Fire, 194

The Poison Oak, 150
The Pool of Fire, 143
Pool Party, 270
*The Postman, 138
Prairie Songs, 11
Prelude to Foundation, 135
The Primrose Way, 220

The Queen of Dreamland, 261

*Rabble Starkey, 105
The Rag and Bone Man, 15
Rain or Shine, 32
Rainbow Boys, 93
Rainbow Jordan, 73, 84
*Rascal, 284
Rasco and the Rats of NIMH, 168
Ratface, 275
Rats, 66
Rats Saw God, 119
Ravine, 155
Reading Between the Bones, 14
Rebecca (Borntrager), 196
*Rebecca (du Maurier), 245
Redhanded, 299
Reef Dance, 258
*Remembering the Good Times, 116
*Rendezvous with Rama, 147
Resurrection, 137
*The Return, 197
Return to Hawk's Hill, 283
Ride a Dark Horse, 279
A Ride into Morning: The Story of Temple Wick, 279
*A Ring of Endless Light, 101
Rite of Passage, 38
The River, 265
The Road from Home, 199
Rogue Wave and Other Red-Blooded Sea Stories, 188
Roll of Thunder, Hear My Cry, 223, 224
Roots, 203, 311
*The Ruby in the Smoke, 213
Rules of the Road, 104
Run If You Dare, 112
*The Runner, 299
Running Loose, 293, 294

Saving Lenny, 112
Saving the Jews, 223
*Say Goodnight, Gracie, 19
Saying It Out Loud, 108
The Scarecrows, 227
Scorpions, 87

*The Séance, 261
Search of the Moon King's Daughter, 185
Second Foundation, 135
The Secret Diary of Adrian Mole, Aged 13¾, 59
The Secret of Sarah Revere, 191
Secret Star, 11
Secrets of the Shopping Mall, 233
Secrets of Walden Rising, 275
The Seeing Stone, 134
Seek, 272
A Sending of Dragons, 180
A Separate Peace, 18
The Serpent's Children, 199
Seven Days to a Brand New Me, 173
Seventeen Against the Dealer, 271
Shade's Children, 146
The Shadow in the North, 213
Shadow People, 42
The Shadow Place, 175
The Shakers, 48
The Shark Callers, 170
Shiloh, 109
The Shootist, 56
The Sign of the Beaver, 218
The Silent Spillbills, 97
*Silver, 43
The Silver Sword, 229
Simon Pure, 268
Simon Says, 42
Simply Alice, 52
Singularity, 174
The Sisterhood of the Traveling Pants, 65
Slaughterhouse Five, 161
The Slave Dancer, 29, 192
So Dear to My Heart, 285
So Far from the Bamboo Grove, 199
The Society, 175
Solo, 245
Someone Else's Child, 42
Someone Is Hiding on Alcatraz Island, 252
Someone Like You, 119
Song of the Trees, 223
The Soprano Sorceress, 143
Sounder, 226
Speak, 115
Spellbound, 108
Split Infinity, 149
Spy High: Mission One, 270
The Squared Circle, 296
Squashed, 122
The Stand, 161
The Star Beast, 146
Stepping on the Cracks, 229
The Stone Pony, 22

Stop Pretending, 116
Stormy, 288
*Stotan!, 294
Stowaway, 188
*Stranger in a Strange Land, 159
Striking Out, 48
A Sudden Silence, 22
*The Summer of My German Soldier, 194
The Summer of the Monkeys, 287
A Summer to Die, 105
Sundiver, 138
The Surfer, 158
Survival Game, 170
Susanna Siegelbaum Gives Up Guys, 173
Swallowing Stones, 68
*Sweet Whispers, Brother Rush, 156
The Sword of Shannara, 141

Takeoffs and Landings, 260
Taming the Star Runner, 100
Tangerine, 293
Teacup Full of Roses, 86
Tears of a Tiger, 80
Ten Miles from Winnemucca, 233
The Terrorist, 245
Terry and the Pirates, 268
Then Again, Maybe I Won't, 4
They Cage Animals at Night, 318
They Came to Cordura, 56
Thin Ice, 108
The Third Life of Grange Copeland, 127
Third Person Singular, 258
This Side of Paradise, 152
Those Darn Dithers, 3
Those Other People, 84
Three Lives to Live, 178
The 3NBs of Julian Drew, 318
3001: The Final Odyssey, 147
Three Wishes, 248
Through the Hidden Door, 302
*Tiger Eyes, 4
The Tiger in the Well, 213
Time at the Top, 52
Timothy of the Cay, 123
To Be a Slave, 316
To Kill a Mockingbird, 129
Tracking Triple Seven, 284
A Traitor Among Us, 229
Transforming Earth, 137
Treasure, 245
*The True Confessions of Charlotte Doyle, 186
*True Grit, 210
Truth or Diary, 62
Tune in Anytime, 32

TITLE INDEX • 339

Turning Burning, 226
2061: Odyssey Three, 147
Twisted Summer, 238
*The Twisted Window, 248
2001: A Space Odyssey, 147
2010: Odyssey Two, 147

Uncommon Faith, 209
The Undertaker's Gone Bananas, 235
Unicorns in the Rain, 164
*Up Country, 81
Up Periscope, 274
Useful Girl, 25
User Friendly, 3

The View from Saturday, 258
Vision Quest, 298
Von Ryan's Express, 256
The Voyage of the Lucky Dragon, 199

Waiting for the Rain, 77
Walk Two Moons, 122
The War of the Worlds, 146
The Warping of Al, 31
Warriors of Alarna, 134
The Watcher, 119
The Way Home, 35
We Are Witnesses, 223
The Weathermonger, 150
*Weep No More My Lady, 238
*Weetzie Bat, 1
*Westmark, 131
What I Really Think of You, 55
The "What's Happening to My Body?" Book for Boys: A Growing Up Guide for Parents and Sons, 308
The "What's Happening to My Body?" Book for Girls: A Growing Up Guide for Parents and Daughters, 308
*When No One Was Looking, 302
When the Legends Die, 25

*When the Tripods Came, 143
Where Are the Children?, 239
Where the Boys Are, 56
Where the Kissing Never Stops, 98
*Where the Lilies Bloom, 8
*Where the Red Fern Grows, 287
Whip Hand, 256
The Whistling Toilets, 304
The White Dragon, 165
The White Mountains, 143
White Wolf, 286
Who Owns Kelly Paddik?, 45
Who's There?, 264
Will Hobbs's Far North, 126
Winning, 304
Witch Baby, 1
The Witch of Blackbird Pond, 218
Witness, 226
Wizard at Large, 141
A Wizard of Earthsea, 164
The Wizard's Dilemma, 164
*Wolf Rider, 233
The Wolves of Willoughby Chase, 183
Wonderful Me, 62
The Woods out Back, 143
Words by Heart, 120
Wrestling Sturbridge, 301
A Wrinkle in Time, 101, 158

The Xanadu Adventure, 231

A Year Down Yonder, 116
*A Yellow Raft in Blue Water, 22
You Don't Know Me, 90
You May Plow Here, 203
The Young Landlords, 77
The Young Unicorns, 101
Yours Till Forever, 263

*Z for Zachariah, 168
Zazoo, 97

Subject Index

This listing includes only those titles fully summarized in the book. Unless otherwise noted with the label nonfiction, the subject headings refer to fictional treatments of the subject.

Actors
Clark, Mary Higgins. *Weep No More My Lady*, 238

Adolescence *see* Coming-of-Age

Adventure stories
Aiken, Joan. *Midnight Is a Place*, 183
Alexander, Lloyd. *The El Dorado Adventure*, 231
Alexander, Lloyd. *Westmark*, 131
Avi. *The True Confessions of Charlotte Doyle*, 186; *Wolf Rider*, 233
Christopher, John. *When the Tripods Came*, 143
Cormier, Robert. *After the First Death*, 241
Forsyth, Frederick. *The Day of the Jackal*, 253
Paulsen, Gary. *Hatchet*, 264
Portis, Charles. *True Grit*, 210
Pullman, Philip. *The Ruby in the Smoke*, 213
Swarthout, Glendon. *Bless the Beasts and Children*, 56
Voigt, Cynthia. *Homecoming*, 270
White, Robb. *Deathwatch*, 273

Africa
Levitin, Sonia. *The Return*, 197

Africa — Nonfiction
Dahl, Roald. *Going Solo*, 309

African Americans
Baldwin, James. *If Beale Street Could Talk*, 71
Barrett, William E. *The Lilies of the Field*, 74
Brooks, Bruce. *The Moves Make the Man*, 291
Childress, Alice. *A Hero Ain't Nothin' but a Sandwich*, 84
Hamilton, Virginia. *Sweet Whispers, Brother Rush*, 156
Lipsyte, Robert. *The Contender*, 297

Morrison, Toni. *Beloved*, 200
Myers, Walter Dean. *Fallen Angels*, 204, 314
Taylor, Mildred D. *Let the Circle Be Unbroken*, 223
Taylor, Theodore. *The Cay*, 123
Voigt, Cynthia. *The Runner*, 299
Walker, Alice. *The Color Purple*, 127

African Americans — Nonfiction
Myers, Walter Dean. *Now Is Your Time! The African-American Struggle for Freedom*, 314

Alcoholism
Carter, Alden R. *Up Country*, 81
Fox, Paula. *The Moonlight Man*, 29

Alzheimer's disease
Mahy, Margaret. *Memory*, 39

American Revolution
Collier, James Lincoln, and Christopher Collier. *My Brother Sam Is Dead*, 189

Animal stories
Bagnold, Enid. *National Velvet*, 277
Burnford, Sheila. *The Incredible Journey*, 280
Eckert, Allan W. *Incident at Hawk's Hill*, 282
North, Sterling. *Rascal*, 284
Rawls, Wilson. *Where the Red Fern Grows*, 287
Swarthout, Glendon. *Bless the Beasts and Children*, 56

Animal stories — Nonfiction
Herriot, James. *The Lord God Made Them All*, 312

Apes
Dickinson, Peter. *Eva*, 150

Appalachia
Cleaver, Vera, and Bill Cleaver. *Where the Lilies Bloom*, 8

341

Arizona
Koertge, Ron. *The Arizona Kid*, 98
Swarthout, Glendon. *Bless the Beasts and Children*, 56

Authors
Fox, Paula. *The Moonlight Man*, 29

Authors — Nonfiction
Dahl, Roald. *Going Solo*, 309

Autobiography
Dahl, Roald. *Going Solo*, 309

Badgers
Eckert, Allan W. *Incident at Hawk's Hill*, 282

Basketball
Brooks, Bruce. *The Moves Make the Man*, 291

Behavior modification
Sleator, William. *House of Stairs*, 175

Blindness
Taylor, Theodore. *The Cay*, 123

Boarding houses
Sebestyen, Ouida. *Far from Home*, 120

Boxing
Lipsyte, Robert. *The Contender*, 297

Brothers
Collier, James Lincoln, and Christopher Collier. *My Brother Sam Is Dead*, 189
Hinton, S. E. *The Outsiders*, 36

Buffalo
Swarthout, Glendon. *Bless the Beasts and Children*, 56

Bullies and bullying
Cole, Brock. *The Goats*, 87
Cormier, Robert. *The Chocolate War*, 15
Mahy, Margaret. *Memory*, 39

Camps and camping
Cole, Brock. *The Goats*, 87
Swarthout, Glendon. *Bless the Beasts and Children*, 56
Thompson, Julian. *The Grounding of Group 6*, 267

Canada
Burnford, Sheila. *The Incredible Journey*, 280
Eckert, Allan W. *Incident at Hawk's Hill*, 282
Fox, Paula. *The Moonlight Man*, 29
Paulsen, Gary. *Hatchet*, 264

Cats
Burnford, Sheila. *The Incredible Journey*, 280
Fox, Paula. *One-Eyed Cat*, 192

Child abuse
Greene, Bette. *The Summer of My German Soldier*, 194

Child abuse — Nonfiction
Pelzer, Dave. *A Child Called "It,"* 316

Civil rights — Nonfiction
Myers, Walter Dean. *Now Is Your Time! The African-American Struggle for Freedom*, 314

Colleges
Avi. *Wolf Rider*, 233

Colonial America
Collier, James Lincoln, and Christopher Collier. *My Brother Sam Is Dead*, 189
Speare, Elizabeth. *Calico Captive*, 218

Coming-of-age — Nonfiction
Bell, Ruth. *Changing Bodies, Changing Lives*, 307

Coming-of-age stories
Crutcher, Chris. *Stotan!*, 294
Lowry, Lois. *Rabble Starkey*, 105
Mazer, Norma Fox. *Silver*, 43
Peck, Robert Newton. *A Day No Pigs Would Die*, 46
Rylant, Cynthia. *A Fine White Dust*, 52
Swarthout, Glendon. *Bless the Beasts and Children*, 56
Townsend, Sue. *The Adrian Mole Diaries*, 59

Connecticut
Collier, James Lincoln, and Christopher Collier. *My Brother Sam Is Dead*, 189

Death and dying
Blume, Judy. *Tiger Eyes*, 4
Clark, Mary Higgins. *Weep No More My Lady*, 238
Cleaver, Vera, and Bill Cleaver. *Where the Lilies Bloom*, 8
Collier, James Lincoln, and Christopher Collier. *My Brother Sam Is Dead*, 189
Cormier, Robert. *After the First Death*, 241
Deaver, Julie Reece. *Say Goodnight, Gracie*, 19
Du Maurier, Daphne. *Rebecca*, 245
Duncan, Lois. *The Twisted Window*, 248
Fox, Paula. *One-Eyed Cat*, 192
Guest, Judith. *Ordinary People*, 33
Hamilton, Virginia. *Sweet Whispers, Brother Rush*, 156
Hinton, S. E. *The Outsiders*, 36

SUBJECT INDEX • 343

Konigsburg, E. L. *Father's Arcane Daughter*, 258
L'Engle, Madeleine. *A Ring of Endless Light*, 101
Mahy, Margaret. *Memory*, 39
Myers, Walter Dean. *Fallen Angels*, 204, 314
Nixon, Joan Lowery. *The Séance*, 261
Peck, Richard. *Remembering the Good Times*, 116
Peck, Robert Newton. *A Day No Pigs Would Die*, 46
Pullman, Philip. *The Ruby in the Smoke*, 213
Taylor, Theodore. *The Cay*, 123
Thompson, Julian. *The Grounding of Group 6*, 267
Voigt, Cynthia. *The Runner*, 299
Wells, Rosemary. *When No One Was Looking*, 302
Zindel, Paul. *The Pigman*, 65

De Gaulle, Charles
Forsyth, Frederick. *The Day of the Jackal*, 253

Depression (mental)
Bridgers, Sue Ellen. *Notes for Another Life*, 77
Deaver, Julie Reece. *Say Goodnight, Gracie*, 19
L'Engle, Madeleine. *A Ring of Endless Light*, 101

Dinosaurs
Conrad, Pam. *My Daniel*, 11

Divorce
Bridgers, Sue Ellen. *Notes for Another Life*, 77
Mazer, Norma Fox. *Silver*, 43

Dogs
Burnford, Sheila. *The Incredible Journey*, 280
Rawls, Wilson. *Where the Red Fern Grows*, 287

Dolphins
L'Engle, Madeleine. *A Ring of Endless Light*, 101

Dragons
McCaffrey, Anne. *Dragonsong*, 165
Yolen, Jane. *Dragon's Blood*, 179

Drug abuse
Childress, Alice. *A Hero Ain't Nothin' but a Sandwich*, 84

England
Aiken, Joan. *Midnight Is a Place*, 183
Bagnold, Enid. *National Velvet*, 277
Du Maurier, Daphne. *Rebecca*, 245
Francis, Dick. *Bolt*, 256

Townsend, Sue. *The Adrian Mole Diaries*, 59
Westall, Robert. *The Machine Gunners*, 227

England — Nonfiction
Dahl, Roald. *Going Solo*, 309
Herriot, James. *The Lord God Made Them All*, 312

Ethiopia
Levitin, Sonia. *The Return*, 197

Evangelists
Rylant, Cynthia. *A Fine White Dust*, 52

Family stories
Block, Francesca Lia. *Weetzie Bat*, 1
Blume, Judy. *Tiger Eyes*, 4
Bridgers, Sue Ellen. *Notes for Another Life*, 77
Brooks, Bruce. *The Moves Make the Man*, 291
Carter, Alden R. *Up Country*, 81
Childress, Alice. *A Hero Ain't Nothin' but a Sandwich*, 84
Cleaver, Vera, and Bill Cleaver. *Where the Lilies Bloom*, 8
Collier, James Lincoln, and Christopher Collier. *My Brother Sam Is Dead*, 189
Conrad, Pam. *My Daniel*, 11
Dorris, Michael. *A Yellow Raft in Blue Water*, 22
Fox, Paula. *One-Eyed Cat*, 192
Fox, Paula. *The Moonlight Man*, 29
Guest, Judith. *Ordinary People*, 33
Hamilton, Virginia. *Sweet Whispers, Brother Rush*, 156
Kerr, M. E. *Gentlehands*, 94
Konigsburg, E. L. *Father's Arcane Daughter*, 258
L'Engle, Madeleine. *A Ring of Endless Light*, 101
Lowry, Lois. *Rabble Starkey*, 105
Mazer, Norma Fox. *Silver*, 43
Naylor, Phyllis Reynolds. *The Keeper*, 80, 109
Peck, Robert Newton. *A Day No Pigs Would Die*, 46
Rodgers, Mary. *Freaky Friday*, 49
Sebestyen, Ouida. *Far from Home*, 120
Taylor, Mildred D. *Let the Circle Be Unbroken*, 223
Voigt, Cynthia. *Homecoming*, 270

Fantasy
Alexander, Lloyd. *Westmark*, 131
Block, Francesca Lia. *Weetzie Bat*, 1
Brooks, Terry. *Magic Kingdom for Sale—Sold!*, 141
Garner, Alan. *The Owl Service*, 153

Fantasy *(continued)*
Hamilton, Virginia. *Sweet Whispers, Brother Rush*, 156
Jones, Diana Wynne. *Castle in the Air*, 162
McCaffrey, Anne. *Dragonsong*, 165
Pascal, Francine. *Hangin' Out with Cici*, 171
Rodgers, Mary. *Freaky Friday*, 49
Spiegelman, Art. *Maus: A Survivor's Tale—My Father Bleeds History*, 221
Tolkein, J. R. R. *The Hobbit*, 176
Yolen, Jane. *Dragon's Blood*, 179

Farm life
Peck, Robert Newton. *A Day No Pigs Would Die*, 46

Father-daughter relationships
Fox, Paula. *The Moonlight Man*, 29

Father-son relationships
Cormier, Robert. *After the First Death*, 241
Naylor, Phyllis Reynolds. *The Keeper*, 80, 109
North, Sterling. *Rascal*, 284
Voigt, Cynthia. *The Runner*, 299

France
Forsyth, Frederick. *The Day of the Jackal*, 253

Friendship stories
Avi. *The True Confessions of Charlotte Doyle*, 186
Block, Francesca Lia. *Weetzie Bat*, 1
Brooks, Bruce. *The Moves Make the Man*, 291
Cole, Brock. *The Goats*, 87
Deaver, Julie Reece. *Say Goodnight, Gracie*, 19
Fitzhugh, Louise. *Harriet the Spy*, 26
Fox, Paula. *One-Eyed Cat*, 192
Greene, Bette. *The Summer of My German Soldier*, 194
Koertge, Ron. *The Arizona Kid*, 98
Lowry, Lois. *Rabble Starkey*, 105
Mazer, Norma Fox. *Silver*, 43
Neufeld, John. *Lisa, Bright and Dark*, 113
Peck, Richard. *Remembering the Good Times*, 116
Sebestyen, Ouida. *Far from Home*, 120
Sleator, William. *House of Stairs*, 175
Wells, Rosemary. *When No One Was Looking*, 302
Wersba, Barbara. *Just Be Gorgeous*, 62
Westall, Robert. *The Machine Gunners*, 227
Zindel, Paul. *The Pigman*, 65

Frontier and pioneer life
Eckert, Allan W. *Incident at Hawk's Hill*, 282
Portis, Charles. *True Grit*, 210
Speare, Elizabeth. *Calico Captive*, 218

Gangs
Hinton, S. E. *The Outsiders*, 36

Gays *see* Homosexuality

Ghosts
Hamilton, Virginia. *Sweet Whispers, Brother Rush*, 156
Morrison, Toni. *Beloved*, 200

Grandparents
Bridgers, Sue Ellen. *Notes for Another Life*, 77
Conrad, Pam. *My Daniel*, 11
Kerr, M. E. *Gentlehands*, 94
L'Engle, Madeleine. *A Ring of Endless Light*, 101

Graphic novels
Spiegelman, Art. *Maus: A Survivor's Tale—My Father Bleeds History*, 221

Great Depression
Fox, Paula. *One-Eyed Cat*, 192

Great grandparents
Sebestyen, Ouida. *Far from Home*, 120

Grief and grieving
Blume, Judy. *Tiger Eyes*, 4
Deaver, Julie Reece. *Say Goodnight, Gracie*, 19
Guest, Judith. *Ordinary People*, 33
Mahy, Margaret. *Memory*, 39
Peck, Richard. *Remembering the Good Times*, 116

Harlem
Childress, Alice. *A Hero Ain't Nothin' but a Sandwich*, 84
Lipsyte, Robert. *The Contender*, 297

Historical fiction
Aiken, Joan. *Midnight Is a Place*, 183
Avi. *The True Confessions of Charlotte Doyle*, 186
Collier, James Lincoln, and Christopher Collier. *My Brother Sam Is Dead*, 189
Fox, Paula. *One-Eyed Cat*, 192
Greene, Bette. *The Summer of My German Soldier*, 194
Morrison, Toni. *Beloved*, 200
Myers, Walter Dean. *Fallen Angels*, 204, 314
Paterson, Katherine. *Lyddie*, 207
Portis, Charles. *True Grit*, 210
Pullman, Philip. *The Ruby in the Smoke*, 213
Sebestyen, Ouida. *Far from Home*, 120

Speare, Elizabeth. *Calico Captive*, 218
Taylor, Mildred D. *Let the Circle Be Unbroken*, 223

Holocaust
Kerr, M. E. *Gentlehands*, 94
Spiegelman, Art. *Maus: A Survivor's Tale— My Father Bleeds History*, 221

Homosexuality
Block, Francesca Lia. *Weetzie Bat*, 1
Garden, Nancy. *Annie on My Mind*, 91
Koertge, Ron. *The Arizona Kid*, 98
Wersba, Barbara. *Just Be Gorgeous*, 62

Horses, Horse racing
Bagnold, Enid. *National Velvet*, 277
Francis, Dick. *Bolt*, 256
Koertge, Ron. *The Arizona Kid*, 98

Humorous stories
Brooks, Terry. *Magic Kingdom for Sale— Sold!*, 141
Fitzhugh, Louise. *Harriet the Spy*, 26
Pascal, Francine. *Hangin' Out with Cici*, 171
Portis, Charles. *True Grit*, 210
Rodgers, Mary. *Freaky Friday*, 49
Townsend, Sue. *The Adrian Mole Diaries*, 59

Hunting
White, Robb. *Deathwatch*, 273

Hurricanes
Taylor, Theodore. *The Cay*, 123

Incest
Walker, Alice. *The Color Purple*, 127

Industrial Revolution
Aiken, Joan. *Midnight Is a Place*, 183

Jails
Baldwin, James. *If Beale Street Could Talk*, 71

Jews
Levitin, Sonia. *The Return*, 197

Juvenile delinquents
Hinton, S. E. *The Outsiders*, 36

Kentucky
Morrison, Toni. *Beloved*, 200

Kidnapping
Duncan, Lois. *The Twisted Window*, 248
Konigsburg, E. L. *Father's Arcane Daughter*, 258

Lesbianism
Garden, Nancy. *Annie on My Mind*, 91

Long Island
Kerr, M. E. *Gentlehands*, 94

Los Angeles
Block, Francesca Lia. *Weetzie Bat*, 1

Love stories
Baldwin, James. *If Beale Street Could Talk*, 71
Bennett, Jay. *The Haunted One*, 236
Du Maurier, Daphne. *Rebecca*, 245
Garden, Nancy. *Annie on My Mind*, 91
Koertge, Ron. *The Arizona Kid*, 98
L'Engle, Madeleine. *A Ring of Endless Light*, 101
Pullman, Philip. *The Ruby in the Smoke*, 213
Wersba, Barbara. *Just Be Gorgeous*, 62

Machine guns
Westall, Robert. *The Machine Gunners*, 227

Maginogian (Welsh legends)
Garner, Alan. *The Owl Service*, 153

Marine science
L'Engle, Madeleine. *A Ring of Endless Light*, 101

Massachusetts
Paterson, Katherine. *Lyddie*, 207

Mental illness
Bridgers, Sue Ellen. *Notes for Another Life*, 77
Brooks, Bruce. *The Moves Make the Man*, 291
Guest, Judith. *Ordinary People*, 33
Lowry, Lois. *Rabble Starkey*, 105
Naylor, Phyllis Reynolds. *The Keeper*, 109
Neufeld, John. *Lisa, Bright and Dark*, 113
Peck, Richard. *Remembering the Good Times*, 116

Mississippi
Taylor, Mildred D. *Let the Circle Be Unbroken*, 223

Montana
Dorris, Michael. *A Yellow Raft in Blue Water*, 22

Mother-daughter relationships
Hamilton, Virginia. *Sweet Whispers, Brother Rush*, 156
Lowry, Lois. *Rabble Starkey*, 105
Pascal, Francine. *Hangin' Out with Cici*, 171
Rodgers, Mary. *Freaky Friday*, 49

Mother-son relationships
Carter, Alden R. *Up Country*, 81

Murder
Avi. *Wolf Rider*, 233

Murder *(continued)*
Blume, Judy. *Tiger Eyes*, 4
Forsyth, Frederick. *The Day of the Jackal*, 253
Pullman, Philip. *The Ruby in the Smoke*, 213
Wells, Rosemary. *When No One Was Looking*, 302

Mutiny
Avi. *The True Confessions of Charlotte Doyle*, 186

Mystery stories
Avi. *Wolf Rider*, 233
Bennett, Jay. *The Haunted One*, 236
Clark, Mary Higgins. *Weep No More My Lady*, 238
Du Maurier, Daphne. *Rebecca*, 245
Duncan, Lois. *The Twisted Window*, 248
Forsyth, Frederick. *The Day of the Jackal*, 253
Francis, Dick. *Bolt*, 256
Konigsburg, E. L. *Father's Arcane Daughter*, 258
Nixon, Joan Lowery. *The Séance*, 261
Pullman, Philip. *The Ruby in the Smoke*, 213
Thompson, Julian. *The Grounding of Group 6*, 267
Wells, Rosemary. *When No One Was Looking*, 302

Native Americans
Dorris, Michael. *A Yellow Raft in Blue Water*, 22
Speare, Elizabeth. *Calico Captive*, 218

Nazism
Kerr, M. E. *Gentlehands*, 94

Nebraska
Conrad, Pam. *My Daniel*, 11

New Mexico
Blume, Judy. *Tiger Eyes*, 4

New York (state)
Fox, Paula. *One-Eyed Cat*, 192

New York City
Fitzhugh, Louise. *Harriet the Spy*, 26
Wersba, Barbara. *Just Be Gorgeous*, 62

New Zealand
Mahy, Margaret. *Memory*, 39

North Carolina
Cleaver, Vera, and Bill Cleaver. *Where the Lilies Bloom*, 8

Nuclear war
Brin, David. *The Postman*, 138
O'Brien, Robert C. *Z for Zachariah*, 168

Nuns
Barrett, William E. *The Lilies of the Field*, 74

Oklahoma
Portis, Charles. *True Grit*, 210

Orphans
Aiken, Joan. *Midnight Is a Place*, 183

Ozark Mountains
Rawls, Wilson. *Where the Red Fern Grows*, 287

Paleontology
Conrad, Pam. *My Daniel*, 11

Pigs
Peck, Robert Newton. *A Day No Pigs Would Die*, 46

Poverty
Aiken, Joan. *Midnight Is a Place*, 183
Cleaver, Vera, and Bill Cleaver. *Where the Lilies Bloom*, 8
Levitin, Sonia. *The Return*, 197
Mazer, Norma Fox. *Silver*, 43
Paterson, Katherine. *Lyddie*, 207
Taylor, Mildred D. *Let the Circle Be Unbroken*, 223
Walker, Alice. *The Color Purple*, 127

Prairie life
Conrad, Pam. *My Daniel*, 11

Pregnancy
Baldwin, James. *If Beale Street Could Talk*, 71
Sebestyen, Ouida. *Far from Home*, 120

Pregnancy — Nonfiction
Bell, Ruth. *Changing Bodies, Changing Lives*, 307

Prisoners of war
Greene, Bette. *The Summer of My German Soldier*, 194

Psychiatry
Guest, Judith. *Ordinary People*, 33
Neufeld, John. *Lisa, Bright and Dark*, 113

Puberty — Nonfiction
Bell, Ruth. *Changing Bodies, Changing Lives*, 307

Raccoons
North, Sterling. *Rascal*, 284

Racial prejudice
Baldwin, James. *If Beale Street Could Talk*, 71
Barrett, William E. *The Lilies of the Field*, 74
Dorris, Michael. *A Yellow Raft in Blue Water*, 22
Taylor, Mildred D. *Let the Circle Be Unbroken*, 223
Taylor, Theodore. *The Cay*, 123
Walker, Alice. *The Color Purple*, 127

Religion
Barrett, William E. *The Lilies of the Field*, 74
Rylant, Cynthia. *A Fine White Dust*, 52

School stories
Brooks, Bruce. *The Moves Make the Man*, 291
Cormier, Robert. *The Chocolate War*, 15
Fitzhugh, Louise. *Harriet the Spy*, 26
Garden, Nancy. *Annie on My Mind*, 91
Neufeld, John. *Lisa, Bright and Dark*, 113
Voigt, Cynthia. *The Runner*, 299

Science fiction
Asimov, Isaac. *Foundation*, 135
Brin, David. *The Postman*, 138
Christopher, John. *When the Tripods Came*, 143
Clarke, Arthur C. *Rendezvous with Rama*, 147
Dickinson, Peter. *Eva*, 150
Heinlein, Robert A. *Stranger in a Strange Land*, 159
O'Brien, Robert C. *Z for Zachariah*, 168
Sleator, William. *House of Stairs*, 175

Sea stories
Avi. *The True Confessions of Charlotte Doyle*, 186

Seances
Nixon, Joan Lowery. *The Séance*, 261

Sex education — Nonfiction
Bell, Ruth. *Changing Bodies, Changing Lives*, 307

Sexual prejudice
Garden, Nancy. *Annie on My Mind*, 91

Shakers (religion)
Peck, Robert Newton. *A Day No Pigs Would Die*, 46

Slavery
Morrison, Toni. *Beloved*, 200

Slavery — Nonfiction
Myers, Walter Dean. *Now Is Your Time! The African-American Struggle for Freedom*, 314

Sports stories
Brooks, Bruce. *The Moves Make the Man*, 291
Crutcher, Chris. *Stotan!*, 294
Francis, Dick. *Bolt*, 256
Lipsyte, Robert. *The Contender*, 297
Voigt, Cynthia. *The Runner*, 299
Wells, Rosemary. *When No One Was Looking*, 302

Stepfathers
Childress, Alice. *A Hero Ain't Nothin' but a Sandwich*, 84

Sudan
Levitin, Sonia. *The Return*, 197

Suicide
Baldwin, James. *If Beale Street Could Talk*, 71
Bridgers, Sue Ellen. *Notes for Another Life*, 77
Peck, Richard. *Remembering the Good Times*, 116

Supernatural stories
Hamilton, Virginia. *Sweet Whispers, Brother Rush*, 156
Morrison, Toni. *Beloved*, 200

Survival stories
Brin, David. *The Postman*, 138
Burnford, Sheila. *The Incredible Journey*, 280
Cole, Brock. *The Goats*, 87
Levitin, Sonia. *The Return*, 197
O'Brien, Robert C. *Z for Zachariah*, 168
Paulsen, Gary. *Hatchet*, 264
Thompson, Julian. *The Grounding of Group 6*, 267
Voigt, Cynthia. *Homecoming*, 270
White, Robb. *Deathwatch*, 273

Swimming
Bennett, Jay. *The Haunted One*, 236

Tennis
Wells, Rosemary. *When No One Was Looking*, 302

Terrorists
Cormier, Robert. *After the First Death*, 241

Track and field
Voigt, Cynthia. *The Runner*, 299

Uncles
Koertge, Ron. *The Arizona Kid*, 98

Vermont
Paterson, Katherine. *Lyddie*, 207

Vermont *(continued)*
Peck, Robert Newton. *A Day No Pigs Would Die*, 46

Veterinarians
Herriot, James. *The Lord God Made Them All*, 312

Victorian England
Aiken, Joan. *Midnight Is a Place*, 183
Pullman, Philip. *The Ruby in the Smoke*, 213

Vietnam War
Myers, Walter Dean. *Fallen Angels*, 204
Voigt, Cynthia. *The Runner*, 299

Wales
Garner, Alan. *The Owl Service*, 153

War crimes
Kerr, M. E. *Gentlehands*, 94
Levitin, Sonia. *The Return*, 197

Washington (state)
Dorris, Michael. *A Yellow Raft in Blue Water*, 22

West Indies
Taylor, Theodore. *The Cay*, 123

Wisconsin
Carter, Alden R. *Up Country*, 81

Wizards
Jones, Diana Wynne. *Castle in the Air*, 162

World War II
Greene, Bette. *The Summer of My German Soldier*, 194
Kerr, M. E. *Gentlehands*, 94
Spiegelman, Art. *Maus: A Survivor's Tale—My Father Bleeds History*, 221
Westall, Robert. *The Machine Gunners*, 227

World War II — Nonfiction
Dahl, Roald. *Going Solo*, 309

About the Authors

JOHN T. GILLESPIE, former Dean and Instructor of Library Science, Long Island University, N.Y., has authored numerous books in the areas of library management, school libraries, and children's and young adult literature.

CORINNE J. NADEN is a freelance writer and editor based in Dobbs Ferry, N.Y. She has published more than 30 books.